So Famous and So Gay

So Famous and So Gay

The Fabulous Potency of
Truman Capote and Gertrude Stein

JEFF SOLOMON

University of Minnesota Press
Minneapolis
London

The University of Minnesota Press gratefully acknowledges the generous assistance provided for the publication of this book by the Office of the Dean, USC Dornsife College of Letters, Arts and Sciences, University of Southern California.

An earlier version of chapter 1 was published as "Young, Effeminate, and Strange: Early Photographic Portraits of Truman Capote," *Studies in Gender and Sexuality* 6, no. 3 (2005): 293–326; reprinted with permission of Taylor and Francis. An earlier version of chapter 2 was published as "Capote and the Trillings: Homophobia and Literary Culture at Mid-Century," *Twentieth-Century Literature* 54, no. 2 (2009): 129–65. An earlier version of chapter 3 was published as "Gertrude Stein, Opium Queen: Notes on an Unlikely Embrace," *Journal of Lesbian Studies* 17, no. 1 (2013): 7–24; and as "Broadly Queer and Specifically Gay: The Celebrity and Career of Gertrude Stein," in *Literary Careers in the Modern Era,* ed. Guy Davidson and Nicola Evans (Palgrave Macmillan, 2015); reprinted with permission of Palgrave Macmillan.

Published by the University of Minnesota Press
111 Third Avenue South, Suite 290
Minneapolis, MN 55401-2520
http://www.upress.umn.edu

ISBN 978-0-8166-9679-6 (hc)
ISBN 978-0-8166-9682-6 (pb)
A Cataloging-in-Publication record for this book is available from the Library of Congress.

Printed in the United States of America on acid-free paper

The University of Minnesota is an equal-opportunity educator and employer.

22 21 20 19 18 17   10 9 8 7 6 5 4 3 2 1

CONTENTS

Beneath the Mask

Get a Dog

By February 1949, Truman Capote was ready to leave the country. His first novel, *Other Voices, Other Rooms,* had been a great success of 1948, and his first book of short stories, *A Tree of Night,* was now in stores. His celebrity, which he had nursed carefully, was secure.

His personal life was not. His new boyfriend, Jack Dunphy, might have been sent by central casting as the "manly" lover of a young, effeminate gay man. Dunphy had about ten years on Capote and was a solitary man with craggy features, red hair, and a tough, working-class Irish background and manner. He also had creative authority; his first novel, *John Fury* (about a tough, working-class Irishman), had received good notices, and he had supported himself as a dancer on Broadway under Agnes de Mille. Usually, this last detail would make his masculinity suspect, but Dunphy was an unambitious dancer who refused solos; he just wanted to make a buck. Even better for Capote, Dunphy had identified as straight until recently and was fresh from a divorce from Joan McCracken, a dancer and actress known for a star turn in *Oklahoma!* Capote thus could "win" a man from an iconic American girl. In part to escape the press of celebrity, which distracted him from his writing, and in part to offer Dunphy a free trip and thus secure the relationship, Capote planned an extended stay abroad.[1]

Among those he said goodbye to was John Malcolm Brinnin. Capote and Brinnin had become friends in 1946, when both were artists in residence at Yaddo, a distinguished arts colony; Brinnin, also gay, was a poet who taught at Vassar. Later, in 1949, Brinnin would accept a position as director of the Young Men's and Young Women's Hebrew Association

Poetry Center, and in that capacity he would invite poet Dylan Thomas for his first U.S. tour, an experience that would lead to Brinnin's 1955 biography, *Dylan Thomas in America*. At the time of his meeting with Capote, Brinnin had received an advance to write a biography of Gertrude Stein, which would not be completed and published until 1959.[2]

Brinnin records in his journal that he and Capote began their visit exchanging jokes about Capote's ubiquitous appearances in the "columns of the tabloids," with Brinnin suggesting that Capote had "planted" the stories about himself for "twenty-five dollars an item." When Capote affirmed, "Of course, it's true," Brinnin posed a more serious question about Capote's growing celebrity: "But won't there come a day when that item called Truman Capote will turn into a public commodity? Won't the figure begin to take on a life of its own—separate from the person?" This question is the central point of the journal entry, which Brinnin frames by stating that he was "concerned about [Truman] in ways I'd not yet had a chance to express." Nonetheless, Capote remained confident, even defiant—"So what? *I* know who I am." Brinnin parries with an anecdote: "That's what Gertrude Stein thought. Then when she became famous, she wasn't so sure. 'I am because my little dog knows me,' she told herself, but it didn't do. 'That doesn't prove anything about me,' she said, 'it only proves something about the dog.' Truman, you don't even have a dog." After joking about Capote's lack of even a pet to keep hold of a true sense of self, Brinnin drove his friend to Dunphy's place, and Capote circled back to the great modernist: "'What you were saying about Gertrude Stein . . .' says Truman. 'Who except pedants ever knew about her until she made herself famous? It wasn't the work that did it. . . . Can you honestly say you know anyone who's read *Tender Buttons* through? The thing that made her famous was the *story* of the work and all that went *with* it. It may be a sad commentary, one you academics have trouble accepting, but people are people.'" As he was dropped off, in the pounding rain, at a tenement door, Capote offered a farewell that was also a final response to his friend's earlier concerns: "'This is it,' he says. 'Don't fret about me, just don't *forget* me.'"[3]

People Are People

I knew Truman Capote was gay before I knew he was a writer. Or before I knew who he was. Or before I knew what "gay" was. Or before I knew I was gay.

I first saw him on television, when I flipped into the movie *Murder by Death*. The movie came out in 1976, but this was later. I was seven or eight, too young to stay up past 9:00, so I must have watched it during the day. I doubt that I watched from the beginning, but even if I had, I would have been lost, as the movie depends upon knowledge that I lacked. Caricatures of Charlie Chan (and son), Hercule Poirot (and chauffeur), Miss Marple (and nurse), Sam Spade (and secretary), and Nick and Nora Charles (and terrier) come to the home of Lionel Twain, played by Truman Capote. Murder will be served with dinner, and the detective who solves it will earn one million dollars. Who gets murdered at midnight? Twain himself. Then the blind butler is killed. Then the deaf-mute cook, who was actually a *dummy.* But Twain is not dead! But he is! But the butler is not dead! But he is! And so on.[4]

My fascination was immediate and ardent. I needed to see the movie again—but how? I did not know the movie's name—or if I did, I soon forgot. I searched in the helpless, hapless way that children negotiate the big world. I could not explain what I wanted, and I could not find it in the *TV Guide*. We did not own a VCR and would not for years. All I could do was watch TV and wait. I did not see the movie again for a good twenty years—and when I did, I could not get past the first few minutes, which were bad. Not campy bad, or interesting bad, but boring bad. As Capote in the 1940s and '50s is the focus of my research, I spared myself and did not watch the movie properly until I was almost finished with this book. At a conference presentation of parts of chapter 2, I was asked how I first got interested in Capote. I said I had no idea; he had always been in my head. Later, my boyfriend reminded me of *Murder by Death,* which I must have mentioned sometime, though neither he nor I remember when. Okay then. Roll credits.

I was surprised and alarmed to learn that the movie was written by Neil Simon. My first gay aesthetic experience came from Neil Simon, the king of middlebrow stage and screen, whose reign lasted longer than the Nixon, Ford, Carter, and Reagan administrations combined? Simon's star is in eclipse now, and he never had much (if any) elite cred, but the 1970s and early '80s were spangled with his plays and the movies made from his plays and screenplays, and the awards they all won. I was also impressed by the strength of the cast of *Murder by Death*—but my seven-year-old self would not have cared. So what did I remember, and what now struck a chord?[5]

I remembered the movie's best pun, when Sidney Wang—played by

Peter Sellers, in lamentable yellowface—and son search for Twain's mansion. Imagine a cod Chinese accent:

> SIDNEY WANG: "Look at invitation. What number of house?"
> WILLIE WANG: "2 . . . 2 . . ."
> SIDNEY WANG: "Correct. 2-2 Twain."

Two-two Twain! I remembered, too, the gothic nonsense of the plot, which Simon overtly addresses through Capote/Twain's motivation for his revenge: "You've tortured us all with surprise endings that made no sense. You've introduced characters in the last five pages that were never in the book before." I especially remembered the ridiculous ending, which I am about to spoil.

The blind butler (Alec Guinness, enjoying himself in his last role before Obi-Wan Kenobi) reveals not only that he is alive (and not blind) but also that he is a succession of last-minute characters as theorized in turn by the detectives. He is Twain's attorney, then his accountant, then his daughter Eileen ("I prefer to be called Rita"), then one of the detectives, and then he pulls off a rubber mask to reveal that he is . . . Truman Capote. And then, after all the other characters have left, Capote pulls off another mask to reveal that he is . . . the deaf-mute cook. I remember the rubber masks well. So cool!

But what hit me most as a small gay boy was the gross tonnage of queerness in the film. Gay male double entendre (or, for that matter, gay innuendo, as long as the gayness is mocked) is traditional in twentieth-century American comedy, and as the gay rights movement made its way through mass culture, such entendres and innuendos gained potency. Good luck finding a "sophisticated" comedy from the late 1970s without a joke about gay men (but not gay women, who are noticeable, per usual, only in their absence). Even so, the number of gay jokes in *Murder by Death* surprises. The mock Poirot, Milo Perrier, is played by James Coco, an actor whose career was marked both by playing gay and by publicly denying his own gayness—and Perrier shares a bed with his chauffeur, Marcel, an alarmingly cute and young James Cromwell. Cromwell wears what I can call only a fishnet underall, in what must be a joke about European underwear; if *Murder by Death* has any beefcake, it is here.

The most extended gay joke comes through Sam Diamond: Peter Falk playing Sam Spade. Sam's secretary, Tess, reveals Sam's sexual history with Twain/Capote:

TESS: "Twain picked up Sam in a gay bar."
SAM: "I was working on a case! Working."
TESS: "Every night for six months?"

Diamond's exposure and denial of sex with men wends throughout the movie ("I never did nothin' to a man that I wouldn't do to a woman"), as does his repudiation of Tess:

TESS: "I'm scared, Sam. Hold me."
SAM: "Hold yourself. I'm busy."

Tess is happy to fall out of a fur-trimmed orange satin peignoir, but Sam looks away:

TESS: "Sam, why do you keep all those naked muscle-man magazines in your office?"
SAM: "Suspects. Always looking for suspects."

Tess is played by Eileen Brennan, whose remarkable portrait of failed seductive femininity could be played easily by a drag queen, as could Maggie Smith as sex-crazed heiress Dora Charleston—"Oh, Dickie!"—as could Nancy Walker as, well, Nancy Walker, who made a career out of playing "ugly," "obnoxious" women, from the dateless coed in *Best Foot Forward* (1941) to Rhoda's mother in *The Mary Tyler Moore Show* (1970–77). Here she plays the deaf-mute cook. These characters consistently fail to perform conventional femininity, either by failing to incite male desire or by being "out of category." Gay men traditionally identify with, and sometimes dress up as, such women.[6]

And so: overt gay content; a gothic spoof that mocks all manner of convention; and drag queens. From Neil Simon? Simon has a history of gay characters in his productions, but as objects rather than subjects: they never hold the point of view. Instead, they serve as litmus tests for how far a middlebrow liberal audience will tolerate gay men. We start with the worshipful best friend of an alcoholic actress in the play *The Gingerbread Lady* (1970), filmed as *Only When I Laugh* (1981) with Mr. James Coco. A more assured version of this character is married to a nervous nominee for best actress in *California Suite* (produced on Broadway in 1976, filmed in 1978 with Michael Caine and Maggie Smith, who won a real Oscar for her part). Here, the pair consummate their love, though the husband has to close his eyes ("Don't close your eyes. . . . Not tonight. Look at *me,* tonight. Let it be *me—tonight.*") Each of these men is the classic "gay best friend" character whose primary value is to offer emotional succor to a straight woman, who invariably provides the gay man his primary emotional relationship, though the gay man fails his end of the bargain in bed.[7]

As the country grew more accepting, so did Simon, and *Biloxi Blues* (produced on Broadway in 1986, filmed in 1988) contains a "gay mystery"—Who was fooling around in the latrine?—that protests the imprisonment and dishonorable discharge of gay soldiers. Here, effeminacy and homosexuality are decoupled; the fussy, girly prime suspect is not guilty, but the closeted, straight-acting moral conscience of the play is sent to Leavenworth. Despite this description, homosexuality is not a major part of the plot; once the soldier is outed, he is arrested and disappears. Both play and movie could describe but could not dramatize an admirable gay man—and that man still must be punished. All these characters were progressive for their time, at least in the mainstream, but they and their concerns were invariably subordinate. Whence came *Murder by Death,* with its prominent gay content and concerns?[8]

A partial answer may be found in the résumé of Robert Moore, who debuted as a film director with *Murder by Death.* Moore directed the original off-Broadway production of *The Boys in the Band* (1968) and played a gay paraplegic in the 1970 movie *Tell Me You Love Me, Junie Moon,* opposite Liza Minnelli. Could there be a gayer résumé circa 1976? Most of Moore's directorial résumé is intertwined with Simon—four Broadway plays and musicals, and three films—though Simon barely mentions him in his usually chatty memoirs, and then only in a professional capacity. Certainly Simon and producer Ray Stark knew Moore's history when they hired him for *Murder by Death.* At the very least, they must have wanted a camp sensibility.[9]

Secret Ending

For my young self, all the queerness swirling through *Murder by Death* was just a frame for Capote, whom I remember better than "too-too Twain" or even the face masks. I was too young to see Capote live, on talk shows, where his aggressive effeminacy and disregard for codes of conduct were highlighted against others performing their "real selves." He suffers by comparison in *Murder by Death,* where his line readings are flat and the frenetic rhythm of the farce does not suit his speech. He cannot put over

Simon's jokes, which require oomph, and he sounds vaguely peeved, even bored, throughout. His part is no help: Lionel Twain is milder than all the characters except Sidney Wang's adopted son, a wide-eyed naïf played by Richard Narita. (The joke here is that the actor playing Wang's adopted son is actually Asian—but Japanese.) Yes, Lionel Twain wields a lavender cigarette holder and sports a sparkly patterned smoking jacket with a fur-collared coat and cuffs—silver fox?—but otherwise the shtick pales.[10]

None of this matters, because Capote himself is the shtick. Plate 1, a publicity photo for the movie, captures his look but does not do his performance justice. Capote's voice and gestures alone riveted me. This riveting signaled not, of course, a mystical, essentialized call but rather a performance conditioned by culture that spoke to something I sensed but did not understand in myself. To make an expected comparison, another author and celebrity, Gore Vidal, who steadfastly insisted that gay sex was a behavior not tied to an identity, and who did not perform "gayness" as did Capote, would have made a weaker call—and a successfully closeted actor would not have made a connection at all. (Arguably, Mr. James Coco, who did make this call, was unsuccessfully closeted, or at least performed gayness too well.) But Truman Capote rocked my world.

There was simply no other man in my existence whom I could read as gay. I lived in a small town, and my parents had a small circle and a small extended family. All were insular, and these islands were in the mainstream. My only exposure to difference came through books and television—and through myself, who obviously did not fit the regime despite my best efforts. I did not know what "gay" was, but I knew it was bad, and that it was somehow associated with gendered behavior, because I had been mocked for lacking appropriate boyishness at school—but I did not associate myself with the mysterious "gay." Nor did I want to be a girl, exactly, though I did want to do "girl" things, like double Dutch. I was therefore primed to detect all signs of nonnormative male behavior, especially positive ones.

I can remember only two other examples. There was Klinger, the cross-dressing corporal in *M*A*S*H* (1972–83), who was nonetheless "one of the boys." When I excitedly asked about that (I was very young at this time, about three or four, because we were still in New York), my always already angry grandfather started to yell. So that was that. And there was Jodie Dallas on *Soap* (1977–81), the other great aesthetic frustration of my childhood, as my mother would not—would not!—let me stay up until 9:30 to watch it, and which I knew primarily through promos and other paratextual means. Like *Murder by Death*, *Soap* was a broad, silly spoof that mocked both contemporary culture and aesthetic convention. Like *M*A*S*H*, *Soap* had a man in a dress—at least in the first episode. But that character steadily de-gayed; he fell in love and had sex with women and fathered a child, and these were his storyline's concerns. He was almost as straight as Klinger, who wore women's clothes only in an attempt to be discharged from the army for insanity. These characters had limited use for me.[11]

By contrast, the ridiculous end of *Murder by Death* clarifies a girly-boy's perspective and provides a useful fantasy of revenge and control. The blind butler—cranky, structurally subservient, de-sexed, and ill used—is revealed as the mastermind who has trapped and fooled the detectives. He is *someone else,* a stranger with distinct layers of being—some masculine, some feminine—all of whom have good reasons for revenge, though these reasons all circle back to betrayal or unfairness. Here you must imagine Mr. James Coco ranting at a girlish Alec Guinness, whose fedora is tilted over one eye: "If you had your way, you would do away with all men. Would you not, Miss Twain? Men who have made you ashamed and have made you suffer because you were born with brains, talent, money—everything but that which you most desired! Beauty. It is a statement of fact, Miss Twain, that as a man you are barely passable, but as a woman, you are a dog." What girlyboy does not want to be loved and cherished *as a girlyboy*? And what is beauty? In my seven years of experience, beauty was what gave little girls what I wanted, and what I lacked: a particular kind of attention from men.

Under this succession of masks lies a deeper truth: Alec Guinness literally takes off his face to reveal Truman Capote. Capote may be unhealthily fat and his skin may be gray, but nonetheless an effeminate man has fooled and shamed the world's greatest detectives. His self-exposure has been on his own terms, and his million-dollar reward remains his own. And when the detectives go home, Capote reveals his innermost layer, whom no one else may see. He takes off his mask, tosses off his hat, shakes out his long red hair, takes a long drag on his cigarette, and blows smoke. He is Nancy Walker, who had made a career of playing the unwanted, improperly feminine woman, and he starts to laugh. His laugh is manly at first, then grows higher, and ends with hysterical cackling, which ends the movie.

No wonder I was obsessed.

Closed Circuit

That obsession closed a circuit that looped from a gay writer, through the sloppy conductor of mass culture, to a proto-gay reader. Though I would soon forget *Murder by Death,* I would remember Capote, and I would read his work once I was old enough to get myself to the mall bookstore. Capote would lead me to Tennessee Williams, and both, God help me, would corroborate and help me organize my own internal understanding of homosexuality at around eleven or twelve. These authors were neither "positive role models" nor even close to the cutting edge of the 1980s, but they had three great virtues: they were easily accessible in Yardley, Pennsylvania (we had moved); they reflected and made sense of my own melodramatic, somewhat gothic inner and outer life; and they could sustain the weight of my clumsy reading. As I was not one of those kids who took the train to Manhattan on the weekend, I was left with Williams and Capote—and I suppose Kajagoogoo.

In other words, with adolescence I gained some facility in the cultural marketplace, and I no longer had to sift network television for gay content and signifiers. Thus ends my personal reminiscence. My tone will soon stiffen, and terms like *proto-gay* and *girlyboy* will be espaliered within an inch of their lives. That hardy perennial Gertrude Stein will soon overwhelm Capote, an early bloomer who desiccates quickly. The 1970s and '80s will not be seen again. Yet one question remains: How did Capote get into a Neil Simon comedy in the first place, and thus fortify me when I was most in need?

The specifics are easy. Capote was cast not by either the writer or the director but by producer Ray Stark, "one of the most successful independent producers in postwar Hollywood."[12] Simon writes, "The only mistake Ray Stark made was casting Truman Capote. . . . He certainly didn't do it for Truman's acting ability, since it was nonexistent. Ray made no bones about wanting Truman in the picture for the same publicity value that Truman Capote attracted everywhere." Stark's reasoning is evident from the discombobulated narration at the start of the trailer: "Neil Simon's *Murder by Death*! Meanwhile, a short, sinister man who looks exactly like Truman Capote is preparing a diabolical weekend for the greatest detectives in the world." Capote has second billing, below only Simon, and he, Sellers, and Falk appear to play lead. Clearly, Capote was famous enough to draw an audience, though he was no actor—and clearly, this draw was disconnected from his status as an author.[13]

And so, what was he famous for? Not for being gay, or at least not exactly. If Stark wanted someone who could play gay for yuks, he could have chosen someone with chops; the strength of the cast speaks to his ability to attract actors. Simon struggles with Capote's appeal in an undated interview on the DVD: "I thought we could have been better served with a real actor in there, but [Capote] represented some very unique, uh, idiosyncratic character." *Idiosyncratic character*: what is that?[14]

I could also approach this question in relation to Gertrude Stein, via an especially bad comedy of this period: the 1968 hippie spoof *I Love You, Alice B. Toklas!* Surely writer Paul Mazursky knew about *The Autobiography of Alice B. Toklas,* by Gertrude Stein. Who says "I love you, Alice B. Toklas?" Gertrude Stein does. Although the title of the movie indicates a mash note, neither woman is mentioned in the body of the film. Nor is there a breath of female same-sex passion.[15]

The title must reference Toklas's recipe for marijuana brownies, as the plot turns on them, and as the *Alice B. Toklas Cookbook*—Toklas's only foothold in public consciousness apart from Stein—was notorious for its recipe "Haschigh Fudge." Why name the movie after Toklas and then never mention her? Because "I Love You, Alice B. Toklas"—a clear statement of lesbian love—also invokes all things nonsquare. This simultaneous citation and dispersion of Stein/Toklas is so remarkable that even the *New York Times* took note. In his review of the film, Vincent Canby writes: "By the end of it I was feeling a certain amount of resentment at having been had, along with Alice B. Toklas, whose name, apparently, is to become an automatic laugh, like *smog* and *girdle*." How did Stein and Toklas gain this summoning power, which, like Capote's "idiosyncratic character," both is and is not gay? How did Stein and Capote become famous in the first place, unlike so many other gay and lesbian writers who were censored or closeted, and how did they thus reach gay and proto-gay readers, such as me, who had no other access to gay and lesbian models?[16] In other words, why were Stein and Capote known and not forgotten, and what does this remembrance mean?

These questions, their answers, and their reverberations are the subject of this book.

Stein and Capote in Theory

Boring and Inherently Flawed

The academic history and writerly practice of Gertrude Stein and Truman Capote suggest that they would both find an explicit statement of terms and goals boring and inherently flawed. Both writers were as concerned with how they said as with what they said. Both gave themselves young to Flaubert and his mot juste, and both became remarkable stylists who earned and still earn raves and pans, as remarkable stylists do. In an alternate timeline where Stein and Capote read works of contemporary criticism, I suspect that they skip over the theoretical concerns of this introduction and go directly to chapter 1.

They certainly disregarded academic custom and convention in their own lives. Capote's education showed a tendency toward impatience, a preference for praxis over theory, and a desire to conflate sex and education. As a young man, he started working as a copyboy at *The New Yorker* while repeating his senior year at a different high school—not because he failed the first time but to satisfy the whim of a difficult mother. Capote then abandoned formal education and, thanks to a small allowance, was able to choose bohemia over college. Capote's interactions with English professors were conducted not in the classroom but in bed.[1]

The most important of these beds belonged to Newton Arvin, a popular professor at Smith, whom Capote met at the Yaddo art colony in 1946, when he was twenty-one. When Capote met Arvin, he had already been sleeping with a boyfriend of Arvin's, Harvard professor Howard Doughty. Though Doughty was much more conventionally attractive, Capote very quickly preferred Arvin, the better scholar. Their relations would be Capote's most substantial before he began his long partnership with Jack Dunphy. Arvin read several drafts of Capote's first published novel, *Other Voices, Other Rooms,* and Capote dedicated the novel to him. Capote ended the relationship in 1949, by which time he was a literary celebrity. His future encounters with the academy were minimal.[2]

Stein pursued her formal education much further. She matriculated at age nineteen and graduated magna cum laude from Radcliffe five years later, in May 1898. In *The Autobiography of Alice B. Toklas* (hereafter *The Autobiography*), Stein shares a remarkable exam that she wrote for a favorite professor, William James:

> Dear Professor James, she wrote at the top of her paper. I am so sorry but really I do not feel a bit like an examination paper in philosophy to-day, and left.
>
> The next day she had a postal card from William James saying, Dear Miss Stein, I understand perfectly how you feel. I often feel like that myself. And underneath it he gave her work the highest mark in the course.

Stein disregards the order of relations between herself, her professor, and the university. She disregards genre as well, forgoing the usual student rebellion for forthright cheer. Yet Stein both has and eats her cake: her refusal to honor the university over her own emotional and bodily desires is mirrored by her professor and rewarded with the highest grade.[3]

Stein's final exam became so notorious that the *New York Times* included it in her obituary, almost fifty years later. Although "The Refused Exam" charms on its own terms, its popularity as an anecdote stems from the synecdoche that reads Stein's corpus and career through her embrace by James. By these lights, Stein is always refusing to take her exam, and the brilliance of her refusal always earns an A. An unflattering variant configures Stein as a monster of confidence. She blithely transcribed whatever was in her head and was blindly acclaimed. Both understandings of Stein—the savant and the lucky fool—ignore her efforts for James, with whom she took a yearlong seminar in psychology as well as a lab. At his urging, she conducted research with a graduate student, Leon Solomons, and their research was published in the *Harvard Psychological Review*. Presumably a slacker would not have charmed so well. In truth, James was not charmed: Stein received a C for the semester that she refused to write the exam, rather than the As she earned her two other semesters with James.[4]

Stein's C did not keep her from medical school. She matriculated at Johns Hopkins in September 1897 at age twenty-three, not because she wanted to be a doctor but because, according to *The Autobiography*, James told her that a medical education was necessary for her to continue her research in psychology. Stein worked hardest at what interested her, which was original research into the function and development of the brain. Her work is quoted and referenced by her professor, Llewellys Barker, in *The Nervous System and Its Constituent Neurones*, an important work of early neuroscience.[5]

Stein was considerably less successful at her classes, which progressively bored her, and at clinical practice, which left her more concerned for her own health than that of her patients. The sexual harassment and anti-Semitism typical for that time and place did not help. Nor did her sexual and romantic relations with May Bookstaver, Stein's first girlfriend, who was already attached to another medical student, Mabel Haynes. Stein was less successful than Capote as a romantic third party and never supplanted the alpha couple. She would lick her wounds in her first three mature narratives—*Q.E.D.* (written 1903), *Fernhurst* (written 1904), and, to an extent, *Three Lives* (written 1907). Medical school itself was more easily abandoned. After five years, Stein pointedly left Johns Hopkins in 1901 without taking her degree. In *The Autobiography*, she makes her rejection acute via her thanks to a troublesome professor: "[I]f you had not kept me from taking my degree I would have, well, not taken to the practice of medicine, but at any rate to pathological psychology and you don't know how little I like pathological psychology and how all medicine bores me."[6]

This speech may be fantastic on Stein's part but makes an admirable sequel to "The Refused Exam." Again, Stein's plain speaking repudiates a hierarchy, though this time her freshness does not earn an embrace but saves her from an unwanted clinch. Whether or not the speech was given, Stein's disgust with not only Johns Hopkins but also the academic establishment as a whole may be seen in her refusal to publish in the *American Journal of Anatomy*. Here the trajectory of Stein's graduate work becomes confusing, as it may have been for Stein herself. Stein was not allowed to graduate with her class, though her application for postgraduate study had already been accepted by the Massachusetts State Hospital for the Insane. Johns Hopkins offered Stein several options for finishing her degree, and she accepted the chance to dissect and make a model of an infant brain, and to write a lengthy paper on brain development: work that she had begun for Llewellys Barker, who was now at the University of

Chicago but who agreed to supervise. The model of the baby's brain was a failure, but Barker sent Stein's paper to the *Journal of Anatomy,* presumably because he agreed that Stein had clarified the existing literature, which she called, in letters, "a hopeless mess." She hoped "to save the next man from a long preliminary work." The article would both position Stein in her field and do service through the unglamorous task of filling in gaps and reconciling competing interpretations. In contemporary terms, she would be "part of the conversation."[7]

If, that is, she were allowed to speak. At first, the journal rejected Stein's article. The Johns Hopkins professor who reviewed submissions found her work derivative and repetitive. When Barker protested that her work was both original and important, these objections were retracted. The objection and the retraction attest to aspects of academic culture that made Stein's position difficult: either her work was rejected not on its merits but because the Johns Hopkins professor objected to Stein herself; or her rejection was appropriate but overruled by Barker, whose authority could not be dismissed due to his prestige. Regardless, Stein refused to pursue the minor revisions necessary for publication, despite Barker's continued support. If Stein had been willing to jump through a few more hoops (making jumps that were well within her range) and had better tolerated her mistreatment (as did other women, other Jews, and other unfavored scientists who did gain prestige), she would have won publication as well as her degree.[8]

But Stein did not jump. More than thirty years later, she still told stories of how much she hated graduate school. Capote did not even go to college. Both authors rejected not only academia but also an academic style, if dryness, the use of jargon, and the careful positioning of one's work in terms of others' characterize such style. Though both writers wrote nonfiction throughout their career, some of it argumentative, they never did so in such a way that their style could be easily pithed from their point, or their meaning abstracted. Nor did they attempt to position their work in the context of other writers, especially if those writers were alive. Stein did align herself with the visual modernists, but there her transfer of the visual to the literary kept her nonpareil. Though she was happy to trace her own influence upon literature, she did not consider herself to be influenced by contemporary writers. How could she be, when, as she assures and reassures us in *The Autobiography,* she was a genius? Capote, too, frequently called himself a genius. At the start of his career, he resisted claims that he drew from other southern gothic writers, though such debts, especially to Carson McCullers, were obvious. Similarly, when he wrote *In Cold Blood,* in the 1960s, he claimed that he had created a new genre—the nonfiction novel—which was silly. At the end of his life, he believed that the decades spent on his unfinished opus, *Answered Prayers,* was comparable to Proust's gestation of *In Search of Lost Time.* Both Stein and Capote did not want to be "part of the conversation." They wanted others to listen.[9]

Nonetheless, the work of Stein and Capote, like the work of most authors, was influenced by their education: in form, in content, and, most importantly for our purpose here, in rebellion. Their rejection of the prescriptions of the academy were a dry run for their repudiation of the expectations of a writer's career. This book explores their refusal to renounce, revise, or repress their sexuality, which—counterintuitively— allowed them to be celebrated while so many of their similarly situated artistic peers were damned. Their work heavily features homosexual content and a queer aesthetic, and their public personae were both specifically gay and broadly queer, but they nonetheless became both mass-market celebrities and, eventually, respected and then canonical writers. They publicly profited from their homosexuality during homophobic times—which required a fabulous potency.

Fabulous and *Potency*

Fabulous, after *fable,* denotes "extraordinary, verging on the mythical," but overuse has diminished *fabulous* to "amazingly good and wonderful," and the superlative continues to descend. Frequent use of *fabulous* is associated with enthusiasm, frivolity, irony, and, less happily, with bitterness, vacuity, and the void. Such unhappiness stems from the exaggerated stance needed to find enough fabulousness to use the word often—a stance that requires the speaker to find wonder and goodness in the mundane, even if such amazement can be attained only through sustained naïveté (which wrests the perceived world into kitsch) or the rigorous application of exaggeration and irony (which wrest the perceived world into camp). *Fabulous* therefore may indicate delight and wonder, or dissatisfaction with their lack, or both: the insistence on finding delight and wonder despite their absence. All three indications may in turn be a source of further enthusiasm, frivolity, irony, and disillusion. In this way, *fabulous* subsumes its own fatigue.

But not always. I myself am embarrassed by the use of *fabulous* and am self-conscious when I say or write the word without assumed or explicit quotation marks. My embarrassment is both overt and covert. Overt: *Fabulous* is redolent of a generation and a worldview that precedes me. I am post-*fabulous* and need not resort to camp sensibility to resist oppression or to cite my sexuality. Covert: *Fabulous* is "too gay," and if I used the word, its effeminate connotations would lessen my value within the same hegemony that I supposedly resist. To me and my kind, *fabulous* is "tired," argot that suggests not only a lack of wonder but also the failure of that which aspired to wonder. But where does "tired" reside? The failure of *fabulous* grows from the conjunction of what is called "tired" and what calls it out. These make the crossbars of a sad X. Once X was fabulous, but now X cannot escape what the hegemony dictates as mundane. Now X spurs fatigue.

In both its happy and its less happy aspects, I use *fabulous* to modify *potency*. *Potency* derives from the Latin *posse,* "to be able," and conflates "having great power and influence" with the "ability to achieve erection, orgasm, and fatherhood." *Potency* rests between ability and action, and indicates the potential for sexual competence defined by the ability to penetrate women and engender children. *Potency* assumes that such potential translates to other types of strength, power, and production. The word defines male hegemony. Though *potency* and especially *potential* may be used without overt reference to masculinity, sex and gender still underwire the term. Thus, women are rarely *potent.* Instead, they are *fertile,* which is less synonymous with power.

Those populations who use and overuse *fabulous*—teen girls and the teen girlish; denizens of the fashion, decor, and beauty industries; socialites; "show people"; and, most prominently, the sexually queer—exist at an angle to masculine hegemony and potency. Either they accrue esteem and material success through activities marked as feminine, or their status as men and women is askew to the hegemonic order because of the lingering conflation of gender inversion and homosexuality. Nonetheless, the frequent employment of *fabulous* remains an existential dagger that cuts at the circumspection of these populations. Whether naive or knowing, whether kitsch or camp, *fabulous* flenses mundanity—a mundanity defined by masculine hegemony—and reveals a world spangled by wonder and delight and shot through with impermissible sex and emotion. An act of will brings revelation: one chooses to say, see, and be fabulous—and at times tired.

What happens when *fabulous* modifies *potency*? Truman Capote and Gertrude Stein.

Fabulous Potency

Capote and Stein should not have been famous. Both secured their reputations between the Wilde trials and Stonewall, when the most widely available understandings of homosexuality were inversion and perversion, and when censorship prevented the public discussion of homosexuality except in terms laced with shame, disapproval, and disgust. Yet both Capote and Stein were exclusively gay, with long-standing domestic partnerships that they made no attempt to hide. Both wrote works that directly discussed homosexuality and had a queer aesthetic. And the homosexuality of both was irreducible from their public reputations. Nonetheless, Capote and Stein were mass-market celebrities, well known even to those who had not read their books and those who did not read fiction at all. They earned scorn as well as praise, but their presence was undeniable. At a time when other gay public figures were persecuted for their sexual orientation and either remained closeted or censored, or had their careers stifled by homophobic scandal, Capote and Stein somehow profited from being gay.[10]

This "somehow" is a subject of this book, and what I mean by "fabulous potency": an extraordinary and wonderful power that is almost beyond belief; that is associated with femininity, homosexuality, irony, bitterness, vacuity, and the void; and that, like the word *fabulous* itself, now seems exhausted to some. Crudely speaking, both Capote and Stein achieved power by fucking the system with fantastic phalli until they engendered stupendous celebrity. The configuration of their phalli were unusual, to say the least, and put the form of the phallus as it is usually understood under stress. Furthermore, Capote and Stein were not masterminds who carefully engineered their public personae. Occasionally, they shrewdly situated a fulcrum that let them tilt their public personae to their advantage, as Stein did with her fable "The Refused Exam." More often, they *were* the fulcrum. Much of their "fabulous potency" was largely beyond their control, and their success, like most fantastic gifts, came at an appreciable cost. Stein's eventual mass-market triumph with *The Autobiography of Alice B. Toklas* would trigger writer's block through 1933 and '34, a grave debility for a writer as productive as Stein, and would cause her to run to her poodle for existential affirmation, as detailed in the sequel, *Everybody's Autobiography*: "I am I because my little dog knows me." And Capote would never recover from his early stardom, which progressively overshadowed his writing, transforming him from a celebrated author into pure celebrity, and then, perhaps, into freeze-dried celebrity crystals, with no liquid in sight.[11]

An Unusual Coupling and Scope

To my knowledge, Capote and Stein have not been coupled. In part, this is because they are as antithetical as they are similar—one an enfant terrible, the other an éminence grise; one a public darling, the other an avatar of the bleeding edge; one an effeminate man who lunched with the socialite wives of powerful men, the other a masculine woman who sat with the men at dinner while the wives stayed in the kitchen. But these are just details. Capote and Stein have not been coupled primarily because their great point of similarity—the unusual centrality of their homosexuality to their life, personae, and art—has not been a sufficiently apparent and attractive category of analysis.[12]

Nonetheless, Capote and Stein may serve as comprehensive test cases for the interaction of homosexuality and literature in the first half of the twentieth century. Initially, I intended to address a broader roster, but I soon found that the complications of the case required me, first, to limit my scope to Capote and Stein, and, second, to focus that scope upon their apotheosis as celebrity writers: Capote up to and including the 1948 publication of his first novel, *Other Voices, Other Rooms;* and Stein up to the 1933 publication of the memoir that finally brought her great fame, *The Autobiography of Alice B. Toklas.*

The greatest difference between Capote and Stein is gender. Their comparison allows the analysis of the complications wrought on the binary of male and female by the cultural equation of homosexuality and gender inversion, with the added complication of the different reception and visibility of male and female homosexuality in the years between the Wilde trials of 1895 and the Stonewall riots of 1969. These boundaries mark a somewhat coherent period of homophobia and homosexual censorship in mass culture, and Capote and Stein permit the scrutiny of this period in some depth.

Capote and Stein are also differentiated by popularity and reputation. Capote was an immediate and enormous success as an author as well as a celebrity, and his works have never been out of print. By contrast, though Stein became a public figure with the 1913 Armory Show, she was much better known than read until 1933. Her mass-market success as an author came after two decades of struggle. This popularity is reversed in academia, where Capote is rarely read. His legacy remains in the public domain. By contrast, any college student studying twentieth-century American literature is likely to be exposed to Stein, even in the most general survey of the period. And though there is no official score, a good case may be made that Stein is the most frequently discussed author in queer studies. She is no longer known primarily as a mass-market celebrity; she is known through her work.

I ask not only how Capote, Stein, their personae, and their art were configured by preexisting cultural understandings of sexuality, but also how Capote and Stein contributed to that construction through their cultural production and how readers constructed sexuality in their personae and work. Capote's and Stein's public personae offered important models of homosexual realization, visibility, and success; signaled the homosexual content of their work; and furnished a rubric with which to read and understand this work. For both authors, their personae serve as a dust jacket for their corpus. By the light of these personae, Capote's and Stein's early writings provide a vision of homosexuality as a fixed orientation that becomes perverse only when internal and external homophobia desiccates development and prevents a coherent, organized self. Capote and Stein offered not sentimental answers or unrealistic happy endings but rather the possibility for a deeper understanding of the social and psychological cost of homophobia and an unsentimental acknowledgment of and sympathy for this high price.

To enable a focus on the nexus between sexuality, celebrity, and text, I have chosen to discuss Capote before Stein. Capote is seen in these terms more easily than Stein, whose mass-market celebrity has receded in time. Starting with Capote helps me balance an author whose career as a mass-market celebrity and best-selling author began at age twenty-one, and an author who did not become a celebrity until age thirty-eight and did not publish a bestseller for twenty more years. Furthermore, Stein has received a vastly greater amount of critical attention than Capote, and responding to the body of Stein scholarship risks overshadowing the exploration of Capote. Discussing Capote first does run the risk of foregrounding male over female homosexuality—but is it possible for Capote to dominate Stein in a book of literary criticism? In this paragraph, chapter, and book, Stein sports more ink.[13]

Modernism and Celebrity

As writers who became known during the first half of the twentieth century, Capote and Stein are both modernist figures, and *So Famous and So Gay* is one of many interdisciplinary considerations of modernist cultural production. Two factors differentiate this study. First, the focus on homosexuality is unusual. The attempt to follow in detail the path from gay author to gay text and then, through the mechanism of cultural production, to gay reader is more so. Second, the two authors either are not conventionally considered here with respect to modernism or are considered here in unconventional ways. Capote is not often spoken of in modernist terms and is not considered fundamental in any way to the modernist movement—in part because he appears at the tail end of the movement and in part because his status of celebrity qua celebrity prevents his serious consideration.

Stein, by contrast, is fundamental to modernist study. A focus upon homosexuality, however, especially when restricted to the start of both writers' careers, leads back to an extension of the realist and naturalist project to depict characters and subjects that had not before that time been considered appropriate literary subjects, and therefore that act as agents of social criticism and incitements for change. Although this extension of realism and naturalism into modernism has been much investigated in terms of race, class, gender, and other categories and subjects, it has not earned much attention in terms of homosexuality.

A focus on homosexuality also distinguishes this book from other studies of fame and celebrity. The interaction between celebrity and modernism has been put under close scrutiny, and the stock portrait of the high-literary modernist who pooh-poohs mass culture and refuses to be marketed—who insists on the traditional privileges of the literary elite as she shreds that elite's aesthetic traditions—has been retouched, and in some cases abandoned. Stein may have been a very high modernist, but she was avid for a lowbrow embrace, which she achieved in some respects as early as 1913. As Karen Leick has shown, both Stein and her most difficult texts were well known—but, as Michael Newbury asserts, being well known does not necessarily mean that one's books are read. Although I do discuss how many of Stein's most difficult texts were bought as objets d'art rather than read as literature, I am primarily concerned with two of her most readable and popular texts, *Three Lives* and *The Autobiography of Alice B. Toklas*.[14]

The question remains, however, what differentiates celebrity from being well known. Adulation, identification, and emulation are key motifs in the study of celebrity culture, and I am interested in how Capote and Stein inspired these responses in the gay and proto-gay population. Such inspiration demands that a writer be both salable (and thus known) and somehow authentic (and thus a secure mooring for a reader's cathexis). The authenticity of a closeted gay writer was clouded in terms of homosexuality; the salability of an openly gay but unpopular writer was compromised. Capote and Stein, by contrast, allowed the fantasy of success on the broadest scale without sacrificing gay authenticity.

Such validation was unusual for its time and place, and it bypassed the usual workings of celebrity in the twentieth-century United States. Conventionally, the body of the star both restates and reinforces the dominant hegemony in terms of subject and gaze, or the body of the star becomes "a cipher for subversive, marginal fans who seek identificatory pleasures through the re-inscription and appropriation of the famous body." One admires and imitates Hemingway as a man's man; or one convinces oneself that said man ravaged Fitzgerald when both were drunk; or, as is now common, one imagines Hemingway's masculinity to be a veneer and that his authenticity resides in his frantic need to secure his facade. Both the authorized and unauthorized versions of literary celebrity offer purchase for fantasy.[15]

We must distinguish here between "celebrity," "career," and "fame." Celebrity scholarship revolves in great part around the relationship between "star" and public, with special attention to the creation and distribution of a star's light. By contrast, "career," as defined by Edward Said, is more concerned with an author's internal relationship with a corpus, with how this corpus affects the creation of a writer's work and how writerly products are situated (or not) in a career. The concepts are permeable but not interchangeable, and the difference in focus is helpful for authors such as Capote and Stein, whose celebrity extended past their literary work.[16]

More broadly speaking, "celebrity" is a form of "fame." After Leo Braudy, I believe that *fame* is "a complex word into which is loaded much that is deeply believed about the nature of the individual, the social world, and whatever exists beyond both. . . . [I]ts historical metamorphoses tell us much about how particular ages defined, promulgated, and understood what a person was or could be." Though my focus is on practice rather than theory, the function of homosexuality in Capote's and Stein's literary careers illustrates how homosexual identity might travel through culture.[17]

Broadly Queer and Specifically Gay: Definitions

Capote's and Stein's success resulted from an oscillation between what I call the "broadly queer" and the "specifically gay": between a nonsexual queerness that riveted a mass audience and specific signals of homosexuality that were easily understood by those alerted to their own sexual dissidence. I use these terms to distinguish between homosexuality and other traits, behaviors, and phenomena that are degraded or otherwise viewed and treated as counter to the dominant order. To clarify the link between the broadly queer and the specifically gay, I employ the concept of "hegemonic masculinity," which Raewyn Connell defines as "the configuration of gender practice which embodies the currently accepted answers to the problem of the legitimacy of patriarchy, which guarantees (or is taken to guarantee) the dominant position of men and the subordination of women." Connell stresses that there are multiple masculinities and that specifics of the dominant masculinity change over time.[18]

In the twentieth-century United States, male homosexuals were consistently at the bottom of the male scale, thanks to the inversion model, which views homosexuality as the adoption of behavior typical of the opposite sex. By these lights, gay men aped women, a subordinated class, and such aping left them even less valid and less valuable than women themselves. Nonetheless, male privilege still functioned for gay men, and wealth, fame, and other assets might raise their status. Lesbians both shared in the subordination of women and, thanks again to inversion, earned especially poor treatment, as they did not share in the "'fit' between hegemonic masculinity and emphasized femininity." The act of aping men might be endearing, as such masquerade strove to increase value and might heighten a woman's femininity if pitched at the right angle. But if such women extended themselves past the purlieus of cuteness and threatened male privilege—if, for instance, tomboys grew into bull dykes—they were badly punished, unless they had other assets that were sufficiently valued by the hegemonic order to excuse their perversion.[19]

Under this regime in the twentieth-century United States, especially before the women's and gay rights movements, the specifically gay was almost always broadly queer, but the broadly queer was only sometimes specifically gay. Both Capote—an effeminate, precocious southerner who made a show of his strangeness—and Stein—a large Jewish expatriate who was markedly disinterested in being conventionally attractive and who associated with avant-garde artists—were extraordinarily broadly queer in their appearance, behavior, public persona, and the form and content of their writing. This broad queerness interacted in complex ways with their specific homosexuality and with the trope of the decadent, unconventional artist—one way that queerness may be celebrated, or at least tolerated, by the dominant order.

If such flamboyance were readily available as a form of heterosexual passing, then Stein and Capote would not be so unusual. Yet Stein is the *only* canonical American lesbian writer before the 1970s who directly references homosexuality in both her public face and her work. Though the greater visibility of male homosexuality led to a greater number of publicly gay writers, Capote is nonpareil in the centrality of homosexuality to his public persona. Many pre-Stonewall writers now regarded as publicly gay, such as Tennessee Williams and James Baldwin, were closeted both in their persona and their work until after gay liberation. Male gay writers who refused the closet either found their careers forestalled or did not become mass-market celebrities.[20]

Whereas the use of "gay" for Truman Capote is unlikely to provoke impatience, some readers may be troubled by the collapse of the varieties of female same-sex experience into "lesbian," and even more so into "gay." Martha M. Umphrey's warning that "lesbian/gay historians participate in a model of history that relies on the recuperation and celebration of homosexual subjectivity and thus implicitly promotes a partial view of the history of sexuality" is well taken.[21] The portion of this book on Stein concerns the twenty-four years between 1909 and 1933, when female same-sexuality was seen through the scrims of sexology and psychoanalysis and, at least publicly, did not constitute an identity, as it often does now. My study of Stein is beholden to those who have explored the specifics of sapphic modernity—the interaction of cultures and identifications with new formulations of sexuality and gender at and after the turn of the twentieth century—as well as the configuration of the "women of the Left Bank," the literary movement created by queer women modernists whose texts embody various aspects of female same-sexuality. Although sapphic modernity and its literatures are primary sources for a recognizable modern lesbian community, they are not interchangeable.[22]

Nonetheless, I eschew *sapphist* and other more historically situated terms in favor of *gay, homosexual,* and *same-sexual* as transhistorical terms that indicate same-sex desire and object choice while acknowledging that today's lesbian and gay man are not yesterday's. Whereas *lesbian* always references female homosexuality and *gay man* always references male homosexuality, *gay* does not specify gender. The disadvantage of this schema is the risk that male homosexuality may be assumed for *gay*; the advantage is that it highlights the commonality of gay women and men. I believe in this commonality not only in the "ethnic" model of homosexuality, which holds that gays constitute a people with a distinct culture, but also in the belief that homosexual object choice, in a culture that heavily promotes heterosexuality, leads to psychological and material correspondences between gay men and women.[23]

These word choices, though hardly unprecedented, do disregard the mandate for a historically specific vocabulary for sexuality—a mandate that is not enforced for straight historical subjects. The wrangling over terms and definitions that I participate in here—de rigueur for works of queer history—is rare in works concerning heterosexuals of the past, regardless of their own multiple desires and nominations. I am indebted to work that gracefully asserts that the forms of homosexuality may differ because of historical circumstances but the fact of homosexuality does not. All that said, the primary reason that I eschew *sapphist* and other more historically situated terms is utilitarian, as the use of a common term for gay women and men helps me consider them in conjunction and as this book traces the imbrication of Capote and Stein with post-Stonewall gay identity.[24]

For we do know, as far as we *can* know, that these authors themselves were specifically gay. On the Kinsey scale that measures sexual experience, both Capote and Stein measured 6, or exclusively homosexual, for the duration of their adult lives.[25] Both extensively documented their sexual and emotional relationships with partners of the same sex, and there is no evidence that either author had any significant heterosexual interest or experience. Nor did either author pretend otherwise. I am interested in how both authors struggled to embody a specifically gay identity not only in their persons and personae but also in their texts. This struggle furnishes a specifically gay teleology that dictates not only the terms *lesbian, gay,* and *gay male* but also *proto-lesbian* and *proto-gay*. After Eve Kosofsky Sedgwick, Ken Corbett, Kathryn Bond Stockton, and others, I use these last two terms for forms of same-sex desire and identities that may progress into gay and lesbian desires and identities. This is not to say that a specifically gay identity is the only satisfactory outcome available to such subjects, but rather to say that Capote and Stein were interested in such an outcome in both their texts and their lives, and through both, they made such an outcome more available to others.[26]

The word *proto-gay* in and of itself exemplifies the tension between the notion of homosexuality as an inherent sexual orientation toward the same sex that may take a variety of forms according to historical circumstances, and the notion of homosexuality as a cultural institution. At bottom, this disagreement concerns whether sexuality is an inherent part of identity and whether homosexuality is a transhistorical phenomenon: whether we may, for instance, discuss women of different cultures and times who preferred, against considerable opposition, to experience love and sex with other women as lesbian. This is what Susan McCabe calls the paradox of queer historicism: "the transhistorical existence of historical pluralism—in other words, a history continuously riddled by multiple desires as well as nominations for sexual behaviors and experience." Proto-homosexuality attempts to reconcile this paradox. A proto-homosexual is *not* homosexual as we now understand the term—either in acts, identity, or self-knowledge—but could be and probably would be if obstacles were removed. Some preadolescents may therefore be called proto-homosexual, as may some people and characters who demonstrably experience same-sex desire, passion, and love but who cannot act upon or even name such sensations and emotions because they are forbidden or because these feelings and actions are inconceivable to them. Others have a less fixed orientation and are best served by the term *queer*.[27]

This distinction between *proto-gay* and *queer* builds upon the work of psychoanalytic practitioners and theorists such as Beverly Burch, Ken Corbett, Teresa de Lauretis, and Richard Isay, who posit the specifics of a psychosocial development into mature homosexuality. They subscribe to a model of psychosexual progression that allows for (but does not mandate) an ordered and organized sexuality without being normative, a development where "certain object relations do become privileged in individual subjectivities as a result of each contingent and singular history."[28] Though she is less focused on object relations per se and suggests that the proto-gay child may exist only retrospectively, after gay identity or desire is realized, Kathryn Bond Stockton advocates the concept of "growing sideways"—as opposed to the linear, normative "growing up"—which allows for the proto-gay adult as well as the child.[29] Homophobia enables the phenomenon of the proto-gay adult who, because of homophobia, may be chronologically mature but nonetheless not yet homosexually realized and embodied: who, in other words, has not yet "come out," whether such coming out be internal, external, or physical. I spend some time in this book discussing the difficulty, if not impossibility, of differentiating between the "truly" sexually fluid and those who experience such fluidity as part of their psychosexual development, especially under the stress and censorship of homophobia and queer suppression. Under such a regime, to be specifically gay—and realized as such—is an achievement. Both Capote and Stein in their debuts—Capote with proto-gay children in *Other Voices, Other Rooms,* and Stein with proto-gay adults in *Three Lives*—offer an achievement test.

Gay Reading and Queer Theory

So Famous and So Gay asserts that specific homosexuality was both apparent and integral not only to these writers' personal lives but also to both the public personae that won these writers celebrity and, most importantly, their art. Unsurprisingly, homophobia, censorship, and an inability to recognize homosexuality stifled public discussion of their homosexuality—especially as it related to their texts—during Stein's lifetime and during the first two decades of Capote's career. Historical particulars determine whether such subtraction is progressive or repressive. In a strongly homophobic society, literary critics who gloss over the homosexuality of an author, or the homosexual content and themes of a text, may be protective, and even progressive, insofar as this allows such authors and texts to enter the public arena. In a society more accepting of homosexuality, such glossing, especially when endemic, is equivalent to saying that homosexuality is beneath notice, or at least irrelevant. Such silence is a tacit agreement that the only "valid" sexuality—the only one that can be integral to art and thus worth literary and cultural analysis—is heterosexuality, which is assumed when no sexuality is specified.

Queer theory was instituted and developed in part to question this validity, and queer theorists' refutation of gender essentialism and insistence on the social construction of sexual acts and identities has served to deconstruct and destabilize the automatic assumption of heterosexuality. In its place, queer theory propounds a malleable sexual fluidity that underlies human consciousness and identity. Unfortunately, queer theory's mandate to destroy the assumption of heterosexual pervasiveness and to propound in its stead an unspecified queerness may itself become a universal and may lead to the same neglect of homosexual particulars that an assumed heterosexuality does. Queer theory may also act as a shield for critics' unconscious homophobia, as it allows them to avoid considering lived homosexual experience or the specific oppression of homosexuals in exchange for the flat, unwavering light of an unspecified queerness that is shared by all. In this sense, queer theory can be used to make everyone "straight."[30]

This reinstatement of orthodoxy was not intended. Consider the two founding texts of queer theory: Sedgwick's *Epistemology of the Closet* and Judith Butler's *Gender Trouble*. Both deconstruct the normal in the service of relieving minorities of gender and sexuality from oppression. Sedgwick focuses on the vital function that the homo/hetero duality serves in Western culture, and on how the many negative connotations of homosexuality neither serve the gay community nor coincide with its self-definitions; Butler proves that what seem like imitations and perversions of "natural" gender are no more constructed or performative than the "natural." Both theoretical moves are meant to counteract deep-rooted cultural homophobia, and they do so.

The normal easily bear such destabilization. And there are those whose sexualities and identities are well served by queer theory, or at least are not threatened by it. For the specifically gay, however, the argument that not only all sexual behavior but also other aspects of the self and of identity are contingent on society may be counterproductive insofar as it accords with normative institutions that tell the specifically gay that they are somehow false or, even worse, do not properly exist. For the specifically gay, queer theory may be akin to quantum physics, which increases human comprehension of the universe but which has little impact on that universe as humans experience it, an experience which is ruled by the Newtonian physics that determines the movement of particles the size of a large molecule on up. Quantum physics proves that the chair I sit on exists only as a probability of energy states; the chair may vanish, leaving me on the floor. This, however, has little application to my experience of sitting. Similarly, the insights of queer theory, though invaluable in the deconstruction and defamiliarization necessary for the estrangement and arrest of the normal, are not always useful in understanding homosexuality from the perspective at which it is lived and experienced. Gay women and men are already familiar with estrangement, as their identity tends to be not "normal" but rather hard won.

Unfortunately, queer theorists have paralleled this estrangement by preferring subjectivity over personhood as a matter of routine, and by showcasing negative affects over positive ones—negative affects that, unlike identity itself, are considered stable. Michael Snediker's observation that "in its attachment to not taking persons as such for granted, queer theory's suspicious relation to persons has itself become suspiciously routinized, if not taken for granted in its own right" is well taken, as is his point that queer theorists' affection for bad affect need not configure queer theory: "Melancholy, self-shattering, the death drive, shame: these, within queer theory, are categories to conjure with. These terms and the scholarship energized by them do not in and of themselves compromise queer theory. To argue that they do caricatures both queer theory and the theorists who have put those terms on the map. However, these terms have dominated queer-theoretical discourse, and they have often seemed immune to queer theory's own perspicacity." By the conventions of queer theory, the triumph of a coherent identity (mistake number 1) organized around homosexuality (mistake number 2) is a whited sepulcher. Such reading ignores the lived costs of incoherence.[31]

Occam's razor suggests that queer theorists have come to this high, dry pass by importing homophobia into the very mechanism by which they wish to dethrone it. Their revolution against heterosexual dominance leads to the same melancholic, shattered, death-obsessed, shame-filled state that a strongly homophobic society already presses upon gays. I do not pretend to be proof against such internalization. What gay person is? That said, queer theorists need not internalize homophobia to exhibit a mistrust of stability and preference for the covert. Sharon Marcus and James Best have shown how "symptomatic reading"—interpretations that, along psychoanalytic and Marxist lines, insist that meaning is "hidden, repressed, deep, and in need of detection and disclosure"—has become so dominant that "surface reading"—reading that attends to manifest content—has become equated with the "weak, descriptive, empirical, [and] ideologically complicit." Who wants to be that?[32]

Symptomatic reading brings us back to a theoretical preference in queer theory and queer studies for the broadly queer over the specifically gay. I am interested in how this tendency, when coupled with the valorization of subjectivity over personhood, and bad over good affect, has affected the study of Capote and Stein. As do all schools of thought, queer theory tends to showcase the figures who best suit its theses and to neglect others. Literary figures who repressed or occluded homosexuality in their life and art, such as T. S. Eliot and Henry James, or whose life and art indicated a queer sexuality that resisted compulsory heterosexuality but nonetheless was not homosexuality, such as Marianne Moore, are welcome. Those whose homosexuality was definite are either viewed in terms of "queerness" or not viewed at all. This tends to warp and suppress the study of "Kinsey 6s" such as Capote and Stein, who do not in fact seem to have had a fluid sexuality, except at the molecular level. Whereas their sexuality—like everyone's—was in certain respects fluid and contingent, an *emphasis* on that fluidity leads to misreadings of their work, and either wholesale neglect (Capote) or the neglect of fundamental aspects of it (Stein).

The warning that lesbian/gay historians should not graft their own identities upon historical subjects has become a dictum that hinders the easy recognition of historical subjects whose sexuality was in fact securely oriented around those of the same gender and whose orientation was fundamental to this identity. The warning was meant to enlarge the conversation to include the broadly sexually queer as well as the specifically gay—but now, arguably, the specifically gay is blocked at the door, as the broadly sexually queer once was. By different paths, both Capote and Stein have fallen into an abyss between the historic closeting of gay and lesbian author and texts, and the exuberant searching for "new" and "hidden" queer authors, texts, and content by gay, lesbian, and queer critics. In this way, queer theory falls prey to the binaries that the field is committed to deconstruct.[33]

I discuss in chapter 2 how Capote's blunt display of homosexuality in his person and work has made him unappealing not only to homophobic scholars but also to the queer academy, despite his prominence in queer letters. The prominence of *In Cold Blood* in Capote's corpus (a prominence enabled by scholars both in and out of the queer academy) is due in large part to the fact that the work allows critics either to ignore the homosexuality of Capote and his work or to discuss a gay subtext rather than a gay text. The dearth of work on Capote exemplifies how queer theory may unwittingly find itself in league with the historical difficulty that homosexuals have had in proving to themselves and to others that they have value.

At first, such issues seem specious in relation to Stein. Who could argue that Stein has not been considered as a lesbian, or that her work has not been interpreted in terms of its lesbian content and its lesbian author? Since the 1970s, Stein's sexuality has engendered torrents of critique. A critical genealogy of Stein would swamp this introduction, and is offered in part in chapter 5. Throughout, Stein's sexuality has been seen through a rubric that detects it in the hidden and attempts to bring it to light. This rubric has yielded bumper crops. Among these fruits are those concerning Stein's queer biography and its impact on her composition and reputation; the resurrection and reconsideration of underpublished and underread works by Stein that directly treat female same-sexuality, such as her early narratives *Q.E.D.* and *Fernhurst,* and her lyric odes to lesbian sexuality, such as *Lifting Belly*; and theoretical investigations of how Stein coded lesbianism through, say, her destabilization of patriarchal language. These last, in particular, may offer up a queer Stein rather than a lesbian Stein: a Stein configured as the Mama of Dada, as the patron saint of fluidity, when, at least in her most accessible and popular texts, *Three Lives* and *The Autobiography of Alice B. Toklas,* she is quite clear about her concern with lesbian sexuality. In chapter 5, I ask why homosexuality in Stein's *Three Lives* (1909)—not as it is "encoded" in race but as it is directly presented in the text—has not yet been sufficiently considered, despite the copious scholarship on Stein in general and *Three Lives* in particular; as if Stein's sexuality, and what she has to say about homosexuality, is not interesting or important unless it is buried in the archive, obscured by codes, or seen through the scrim of queerness; as if Stein's open, obvious, public statements about homosexuality in her most public works are beneath notice or, at the very least, tired.[34]

By contrast, I offer specifically gay readings of Capote's and Stein's debut texts. As the broadly queer does not equal the specifically gay, so a "homosexual reading" is not necessarily a "queer reading." As I employ the term, a "homosexual reading" recognizes (1) the existence of homosexuality, (2) its status as an organizing principle for homosexuals (though not for all who enjoy same-sexuality), and (3) the impact of masculine hegemony on this centrality. A homosexual reading holds that for those whose psyches are organized around homosexuality, a conscious, embodied, and positive relationship with gay desire is a valuable accomplishment, especially in a homophobic society that denies its possibility.

A homosexual reading may be further differentiated by gender. For instance, a lesbian reading is not a gay, bisexual, or transsexual reading, and is mindful of the complexity of the historical similarities and differences between the experiences of women who desire solely or primarily women and the experiences of other men and women who also differ from the sexual norm. It is preoccupied with questions of female same-sexual desire and its manifestations, and of how these manifestations are understood and received. Furthermore, a lesbian reading always keeps the strength of the historical constraints on lesbian expression and interpretation in mind, and is alert to the prevalence of historical and present-day homophobia, both internalized and externalized, both conscious and unconscious. A "lesbian reading," as I use the term, views a conscious, embodied identity based on same-sexual desire, especially before the women's and gay rights movements, as an *achievement,* though not always a necessary one or one necessarily better than other options.

Last, this book argues that gay readings—no matter how partial—can profoundly influence readers and, through them, larger social networks. This is a precept of literary study, and I would leave it unspoken if it were not for Henry Abelove's point that literature is often neglected in histories of gay liberation. The work and persons of Capote and Stein served as essential influences on gay and proto-gay men and women before and after Stonewall, and were highly significant to the gay and lesbian rights movement as a whole.[35]

Which returns me to Capote's and Stein's purported boredom with an explicit statement of terms and goals. Like a lesser society swan or visiting painter who yammers on, I look up to find Capote and Stein watching the clock. But tell me, they ask, what do you really think?

PART I
TRUMAN CAPOTE:
"Here Was This Little Creature"

Young, Effeminate, and Strange
The Debut of Truman Capote

At First Sight

We first see Joel Knox—the hero of Truman Capote's first novel, *Other Voices, Other Rooms*—from the perspective of Sam Radclif, a truck driver who offers the reader, as truck drivers do, a "real" man's view. Knox needs a ride, but Radclif hesitates.

> Radclif eyed the boy over the rim of his beer glass, not caring much for the looks of him. He had his notions of what a "real" boy should look like, and this kid somehow offended them. He was too pretty, too delicate and fair-skinned; each of his features was shaped with a sensitive accuracy, and a girlish tenderness softened his eyes, which were brown and very large. His brown hair, cut short, was streaked with pure yellow strands.

Joel's attributes are seen as inappropriately feminine rather than as a particular stripe of masculine, which corresponds with an understanding of homosexuality as a perverse femininity rather than an alternate masculinity. Radclif is offended by Joel's queerness, but he also lingers over each note: Joel is too pretty, too delicate, too fair, too sensitive, too girlish, too tender, too pure. Radclif's spoken wish to correct Knox's queerness slides into sexual attraction: "He [Radclif] took a deep swallow of beer, let forth a mighty belch, and grinned. 'Yessir, if I was your Pa I'd take down your britches and muss you up a bit.'" Radclif's fantasy of assuming a paternal role—of being a Pa who undresses Knox, disrupts his neat surface, and instructs him in properly masculine crudities—neatly encapsulates the push-and-pull between fascination with and revulsion for homosexuality for the postwar public, whose homosexual desires were screened by disgust and a will for correction even as they thrust forth.[1]

Through this trucker, Capote instructs those readers who do not identify with Knox how to take both his hero and himself. The straight-identified may be disturbed and want to "fix" the queer man, but ultimately their desire fuels his ride: as the butch Radclif is pressed by his desire into Joel's service, so the straight public read and celebrated Capote. In this chapter, I investigate how Capote used his public persona to achieve celebrity because of, rather than despite, his identity as a gay man. How did Capote conflate popular anxieties and his own queer textual and visual expression to his advantage—and how did his "fabulous potency" allow him to both eschew hegemonic masculinity and dominate a public body racked by postwar repression after the pleasures of wartime permissiveness? And how did Capote's fame help assert a subjectivity that was unintelligible as well as unspeakable—that of the specifically gay boy who properly develops into a gay man?[2]

A Fabulous Debut

Other Voices, Other Rooms was published in January 1948, within a month of Alfred Kinsey's *Sexual Behavior in the Human Male*—"the Kinsey report"—and Gore Vidal's *The City and the Pillar*. All three were *New York Times* best sellers. One of Kinsey's most noted findings was that homosexual activity was practiced by ordinary folk: homosexual activity did not, as held by contemporary psychoanalytic theory, indicate effeminacy and immaturity. Nor did same-sex desire indicate a homosexual orientation. Though these findings shocked the public, the Kinsey report was shielded to an extent by the respectability of science; by the false belief that Kinsey and his assistants, as proper scientists, did not participate in the behaviors that they studied; and by the fact that homosexuality was only part of the spectrum of male sexuality that made up Kinsey's report.[3]

Though *The City and the Pillar* (hereafter *The City*) also differentiated between effeminacy, immaturity, homosexual desire, and a homosexual orientation, Vidal, as a novelist, lacked Kinsey's protective shielding. The centrality of homosexuality to the novel and the novel's blunt and unambiguous treatment of homosexuality made it exceptionally difficult to review the book without directly mentioning homosexuality, a tendency that broke with the standards and practices of many periodicals. Yet the high reputation of Vidal's first novel, *Williwaw*, made *The City* difficult to ignore. Vidal's status as the son of a famous All-American quarterback and Olympic athlete, and his relation to a grand southern family that included a senator and several other prominent government officials and industrialists, put many editors and reviewers in a difficult position. The butch concerns of *Williwaw*—at once a war novel and a man-against-nature novel set in the Aleutian Islands, which had been marketed and reviewed in relation to Vidal's own just-completed military service—supported *The City*'s separation of homosexuality and effeminacy, which made the position of editors and reviewers even less tenable. If homosexuality could be mentioned only gingerly, then a homosexuality that could not be alluded to via immaturity and effeminacy was unmentionable.[4]

Editors and reviewers were left ill disposed toward the author, and several important newspapers, journals, and magazines—including *TIME* and the daily *New York Times*—refused to review *The City*. Those reviews that did appear ranged from poor to scathing, with a light sprinkling of occasional praise. Even though sales did benefit from the resulting controversy, so much so that ads themselves referenced the benefit to sales ("Some rave about it . . . *brilliant* . . . some are shocked . . . *disgusting* . . . but it became a bestseller"), Vidal's literary career was effectively forestalled. Vidal published one novel in 1949, two in 1950, one in 1952, and one in 1954. Reviews and sales were poor, and the *New York Times*—whose opinion carried the most clout with the most people—refused to discuss these novels at all. By contrast, Capote collaborated with public silences around and understandings of homosexuality to his professional advantage.[5]

Capote succeeded by constructing a public image that became fixed in the public eye through the widespread exposure of his author's photo from *Other Voices, Other Rooms* (hereafter, usually, *Other Voices*). In the context of Capote's two previous exposures in *LIFE* magazine, the spectacular notoriety of the novel's dust jacket is revealed as the climax of a brilliant campaign of self-representation. Capote's photographic portraits, like his description of Knox, allow their subject both to be recognized as gay and to be seen and discussed not as gay but as nonspecifically queer—as effeminate, childish, and strange. These deviations were less threatening than the bald assertion of sexual difference. Here, Capote enters into the tradition of gay and lesbian writers whose notoriety both broadcast their gay identity and disguised its particulars with a general outrageousness that played to a broad audience. Like many artists known for flamboyance, Capote purposefully stoked his fire: his notoriety was as misleading as it was self-made. For though Capote was understood as effeminate, he was not soft, delicate, or weak. Nor can a man who fashioned one of the most successful literary careers of his day be called "childish." Capote's early success speaks of an early maturity—a precociousness that, granted, reinscribes the childishness it supposedly refutes.

Capote's strangeness is more straightforward. Any successful novelist at twenty-two is by definition strange, especially if he walks a queer path to a fabulous apotheosis. If the definition of *fabulous* extends across the divide between the real and the unreal, with that extension understood both as a curious marvel and as a perversion of the natural order, then to be a gay American in the late 1940s was to be fabulous—fabulous!—and to witness one's fabulousness devoured by a public that simultaneously praised gay men as tasty and spat them out in disgust. Capote's potency came through his ability to enhance his status as a writer by manipulating this oscillation between praise and scorn, for the definitive register of meaning in his author's photos is professional: Capote is pictured as a writer of texts so spectacular that he is worthy of visual representation.

Capote in *LIFE*

The first nationally distributed photograph of Truman Capote was published on July 15, 1946, in "*LIFE* Visits Yaddo," a photo-essay by Lisa Larsen.[6] Yaddo is a prestigious artists' colony set on the estate of a Victorian Gothic mansion in upstate New York; residents are recommended by leaders in their fields, and room and board are free. Capote was not an obvious recruit. He had published his first short story, "My Side of the Matter," in 1945, when he was nineteen. That same year he published three more stories, among them "Miriam," his first critical success and the winner of an O. Henry Award.[7] Though the stories had brought Capote some attention, he had not received nearly enough notice to be accepted to the colony. He did, however, have a powerful friend in the novelist Carson McCullers. McCullers recommended Capote to Random House, which offered Capote a contract for what would become *Other Voices*. She also arranged for Capote's acceptance to Yaddo.[8]

If Capote's presence at Yaddo was noteworthy, his prominence in Larsen's photo-essay, measured by frequency of appearance, order, and size, is remarkable. *LIFE*'s readers were led to assume a greater status for Capote than he in fact had. Yaddo's residents in the summer of 1946 included composer Aaron Copland; writers McCullers, Katherine Anne Porter, and John Malcolm Brinnin; and literary critics Newton Arvin and Granville Hicks—all prominent in the art and literary worlds, and some famous without. There are nine photographs in the essay, in which Arvin, a director of the Yaddo Foundation, appears in three. Hicks, another director, appears in two—as does Capote. No one else appears more than once. The first picture, and the only full-page picture, in the essay is a portrait of Capote and Marguerite Young, best known today for her 1,198-page novel *Miss Macintosh, My Darling* (Plate 2). By size alone, Capote is the essay's largest figure. Young, by contrast, sits in an oversized bishop's chair, which shrinks her.[9]

Capote's prominence in the essay both by size and frequency of appearance does not prevent Larsen from constructing Capote as juvenile. Capote sits at the feet of Young, who herself sits cross-legged in a bishop's chair, like Alice's caterpillar on its mushroom. Capote gazes up at Young intently, mouth open. Despite the photo's caption, which states, "Guests . . . are discouraged from reading manuscripts to each other," Young seems to be reading a manuscript (his? hers?) and instructing Capote—a mother reading to her young or, in the photo's otherworldly surroundings, a sorcerer to her apprentice. The photo's construction of Capote as young is bolstered by the caption: "Marguerite Young . . . likes to sit in a bishop's chair stuffed with pillows. Her companion is 21-year-old Truman Capote, short-story writer." Young dominates syntactically; she is the subject of the photo, whereas Capote is reduced to "her companion." Note the pointed reference to Capote's age, which emphasizes his subordination to Young, whose own age is obscure. Young's name contributes a semantic confusion to the already-present confusion of an older, smaller figure placed in authority over a younger, bigger one. This topsy-turvy backdrop of text and image bolsters Capote's own exhibition of youthfulness: the disheveled formal clothes and childish bangs that combine to make Capote a dressed-up little boy. This heightening of Capote's youth through the conspicuous failure of signifiers of age and formality would recur throughout his portraits.

Capote here plays a traditional trick of upper-class schoolboys and the preppy men they become, whose too-young clothes reinforce their status as the masculine standard, so secure that they may dispense with certain signs of maturity. Capote's "youth" also permits his effeminate display. What is cute in boys may threaten in men, and *LIFE* was unlikely to picture a mature man "at home" in his negligee. But consider Capote's bangs, girlish as well as childish. Then consider Capote's left foot, which reads as dainty—girlish, effeminate—within its sock and shoe. The white sock is the brightest object in the photo and initially reads as a woman's stocking, for the height of Capote's cuff, hiked to seat level, leaves visible a length of white hose that through its extension connotes a woman's leg. The combination of white stocking and black penny loafer, common to private and parochial schoolgirl uniforms, adds a further girlish touch. The loafer itself dangles from Capote's foot, which is raised and pointed as if Capote is a dancer who chomps to practice extensions—a pose that under the time's rigorous policing of male movement would have evoked the ballerina and her iconic femininity, or the even more iconic effeminacy of the male dancer. Larsen's photo puns on the contemporary expression "light in his loafers," with its double reference to homosexuality through both effeminate walking and the ethereal steps of fairies.[10]

Effeminacy is also conveyed through the feminine particularities of the angle and extension of Capote's cigarette, and through the small silver cigarette case obscuring his crotch. If cigarettes and their cases are often employed and read as displaced phalli, then this case is small, neat, and pretty; though the case draws attention to Capote's crotch, it does not connote size and power, the usual function of the phallic substitute.

The breakdown of gender binaries is not portrayed solely through Capote in this photo. Marguerite Young, in her blunt bob, lack of makeup, and carelessly disheveled, ratty clothes, sets Capote's carefully disheveled formal dress in relief. The topsy-turviness that pervades the photo—Young as older but smaller; Capote as younger but bigger; Young as female but masculine; Capote as male but feminine; Young as authoritarian but lower-class; Capote as subservient but upper-class—extends through Yaddo's decor. Young's bishop's chair is echoed by the rest of the Victorian Gothic furnishings, the heavy complications of which, in the context of Young and Capote's interchange (though not in the rest of the photo-essay), are fantastically enchanting rather than foreboding. Capote and Young are joined by a classical female marble standing behind Capote and raised to a height where it seems to burst from his head, Athena-style. I would like to claim this idealized female figure as a commentary on the genders beneath her feet, but the photo's whimsy works against such portentousness. At the very least, the female figure is a passing goddess floating through a realm of fantasy.[11]

Capote's second appearance in the photo-essay is a small solo shot:

"In the tower room, once the secret hideaway of founder, Lady Katrina, who wrote poetry, young Author Truman Capote writes his first novel" (Plate 3). Doubly marked as young by the caption ("young," "first") and dwarfed—and thus made even younger—by the height of the room and the fussy formality of the furniture, Capote writes at a Gothic Revival desk. His expression is strained and overwhelmed, which makes him younger still. Perhaps he is overwhelmed by the femininity that shadows him: by the ghostly Lady Katrina, whom the caption links to Capote by location and profession, and by the female marble bust that watches him strain. *LIFE* pictures Capote as young, effeminate, and strange—different enough from the male status quo to be attractive, even provocative, but not dangerous or threatening and so censored or destroyed. Capote's photos, and the celebrity persona anchored by these photos, could thus push upon the poles of strict gender lines to vault him to stardom. Effeminacy, itself a product of fixed gender lines, powers a great deal of this propulsion.

Effeminate, Childish, and Strange: Definitions

Effeminacy happens when traits, tastes, and looks that are traditionally feminine occur somewhere unexpected; the initial *e* in effeminate indicates the space between appropriate and inappropriate exhibitions of the feminine. This impropriety—and this exhibition—is symptomatic of times and places where masculinity and femininity form a dialectic: where men who are not "masculine" are by definition "feminine." But these men cannot be considered feminine because of the same rigid dialectic that prevents their consideration as masculine.

Thus the *e*.

This initial *e* in *effeminate* can be traced to the Latin verb *effeminare,* which combines *femina,* the Latin for "woman," with the prefix *ex-,* which here signifies that the action of the base verb has been carried to a conclusive point. Just as the evacuated cannot be emptied further, and as the exhilarated cannot be happier, so the effeminate is as feminine as possible, though still not a woman. The prefix *ex-* can also mean "formerly," as in *exculpate* (to make formerly guilty) and *emasculate* (to make formerly male). *Emasculate* derives from *emasculare,* a synonym of *effeminare:* both mean primarily to castrate and secondly to make unmanly in less concrete terms. This synonymy correlates with the Roman conflation of masculinity with virtue, as is seen in the philological connection between *vir* (adult male) and *virtus* (moral excellence, strength, and valor), which leaves femininity to be a lack rather than a virtue unto itself. Thus, in English, after the Latin, women cannot be "effeminated" in the way that men can be emasculated, and women cannot be "emasculate" in the way that men can be effeminate. Femininity may not be cut out of the body, and when the feminine is masked, only the mask, rather than what lies beneath, may be seen. To speak of a masculine woman in a way that refers to her femaleness—in the way that *effeminate* refers to maleness—English speakers must turn to words whose direct reference to femaleness dates from the late nineteenth century, such as *butch* and *dyke*.[12]

As women cannot be effeminate, so infants cannot be infantile. When a child is scolded for being childish, the scold indicates that the child's action and attitude are inappropriate from the scolder's perspective—an impropriety that, for boys, is usually defined by a failure to adhere to a conventional code of masculinity. This hegemonic masculinity may change its specifics over time, but not its desire to prevent other masculinities from "gaining cultural definition and recognition as alternatives, confining them to ghettoes, to privacy, to unconsciousness." Boys who fail to "act their age" may thus be either inappropriately effeminate *or* immature, and "Stop acting like a girl" may not refer to specifically feminine behavior. Conversely, a homosexual boy may be effeminate not out of a desire to be girlish but out of a desire to express a masculinity that is different from straight masculinity but is still masculine rather than feminine. Hegemonic masculinity, which values only itself and that which assists its value, smushes those who fail its exam into a vague wrongness defined by lack rather than what may actually be. This collapse is heightened by the relaxed gender strictures for young children—a latitude considerably smaller for boys than for girls.[13]

Eve Kosofsky Sedgwick has investigated how the 1980 removal of homosexuality from the American Psychiatric Association's diagnostic guidelines coincides with the appearance of the diagnosis "childhood gender identity disorder," which termed boys ill if they cross-dressed or preferred "girls' pastimes," whereas girls needed to believe that they had or would grow a penis to be so tagged. As nonhegemonic masculinities, including but not limited to effeminacy, are observed, they must be beaten down and out, as they trouble gender hegemony and threaten male privilege. The scolding of women, girls, and girlish boys sustains masculine privilege through the work of projection. Birth and death, as well as childishness and femininity, are in you and not me, says Hegemonic Dad—and Sam Radclif. Grow up like me—and live forever![14]

Capote's childishness—which he disentangles from immaturity, forging an alternate adult formation—made him both attractive and infuriating to those invested in traditional male adulthood. His childishness furthermore both overtly removed him from adult sexual consideration and covertly referenced the classical man-boy dynamic that may index homosexuality. So how did this bad boy avoid being sent to his room? How did he repeat Joel Knox's trick of getting a normative culture to take him for a ride?

Capote's effeminacy and childishness were titrated to excuse the other and to cloud the homosexuality that both revealed. The straight-identified could therefore safely (which meant blindly) place their queer desire in Capote's depths. In addition, effeminacy and childishness were only two of Capote's registers of strangeness. Consider the otherworldliness that we see in the *LIFE* photos and that persists in many photos of Capote. Consider Capote's southern heritage and the American cultural schizophrenia toward what is both the "moral other and the moral center of U.S. society, both keeper of its darkest secrets and former site of a 'grand yet lost' civilization." Consider how Capote's unusual name becomes another ingredient in his strange brew. Capote, born Persons, was adopted by his Cuban stepfather, and the combination of the Spanish "Capote" with the echt–North American "Truman"—a complication now bleached by Capote's celebrity—needed explanation in 1946, when one of his earliest reviews introduced readers to "Truman Capote, the *e* being accented." Two years later, the *New York Times Book Review* still found it necessary to explain that "the final 'e' is sounded." Presumably "Truman Persons" (or "Truman Capote" with a silent *e*) would not have required explanation. The concurrent presidency of Harry Truman (1945–53) and the "true man" enclosed in "Truman" further heightened this nominal strangeness, as Capote was neither manly nor presidential by the standards of the time. The young, effeminate, and strange figure of Capote is thus crossed with a nominal hypermasculinity that caroms against the "hyperfeminized figure of the southern woman as discursive symbol for the region," which itself rebounds against the aggression—coded masculine—of Capote's effeminate display. Add the queer tropes of artistry and authorship to this semiotic incoherence, and we see the attractive overcoding that let Capote transgress without correction.[15]

Capote and Newton Arvin: A Secret Display

The oscillation between the direct exposure of Capote's gay specificity and broader queer readings can be seen in the photo-essay's secret display of his romance with literary critic and professor Newton Arvin. Capote and Arvin, by all accounts, were open about their relations at Yaddo. Even if they were closeted in front of Larsen—and Capote seems *never* to have been closeted—it seems impossible that their relations would not be referenced in her essay.[16]

On pages 112 and 113 of the photo-essay, which face each other, the photos are sandwiched between ads, as if the photos are the white portion of the French flag, bisected by the binding edge. The top photo, which stretches across both pages, features Arvin: "In a mullioned bay of what was once the boudoir of Lady Katrina and is now a study for Yaddo authors, Newton Arvin props himself up on a long window seat with a portable typewriter on his knees" (Plate 4). Barry Worth's biography of Arvin, however, tells us that Arvin was "[e]nsconced in Katrina Trask's enormous boudoir," which was not a study, but a private room. Below this photo, on page 112, there is a picture of "bed-making, here demonstrated by Author Arvin"—presumably in Lady Katrina's boudoir. Directly across from the picture of Arvin's bed-making is the picture of Capote in the Tower Room, "the secret hideaway of . . . Lady Katrina," which is directly upstairs from her boudoir. Capote sits, strained and overwhelmed, as Arvin makes the bed: this proximity, coupled with the mentions of bed-making and the close location of the rooms, would indicate Arvin and Capote's relationship to those who knew it firsthand or had heard it secondhand. Contemporary readers who were sensitive to homosexual possibility also may have inferred the relationship.[17]

Consider the same layout with Professor Arvin—a man of authority in his forties—facing a nymphet. Would *LIFE* have allowed it? The difference between the diffuse yet easily perceptible queerness of the photos—a queerness that opened a space of difference that could be utilized by viewers for a variety of purposes—and the specific yet shrouded suggestion of two men in a boudoir exemplifies how Capote's photographs fluctuate between hidden gay specificity and open queer possibilities.

Capote in *LIFE*, Again

On June 2, 1947, seven months before his novel was published, Capote made his second national photographic appearance (Plate 5) in another *LIFE* photo-essay: "Young U.S. Writers: A Refreshing Group of New-comers on the Literary Scene Is Ready to Tackle Almost Anything." Here again, the caption positions Capote as both youthful and strange: "Esoteric, New Orleans-born Truman Capote, 22, writes haunting short stories." Here, again, Capote dominates the visual field. Capote's 9¾" x 9¾" portrait, occupying almost a full page, is followed by four 4½" x 4½" photographs of novelists Jean Stafford, Thomas Heggen, Calder Willingham, and Elizabeth Fenwick. All of the photos are by Jerry Cooke except for Jean Stafford's, which was taken by Jean Speiser; both Cooke and Speiser were regular contributors to *LIFE*. Five more photographs of six more novelists follow: four 2" x 2" portraits and one 2" x 4" double portrait. The relative size imposes a rubric of relative importance on the authors. Capote is king; Stafford, Heggen, Willingham, and Fenwick are dukes; and the other six authors—one of whom is Gore Vidal—are minor nobles, if that.[18]

Both Cooke and Speiser deploy the elements and ambiance of the film-noir still, laden with high-contrast menace and overdetermined symbols, as they compose the photos of Stafford and Heggen (Plate 6), and Willingham and Fenwick (Plate 7), to reverberate with the authors' books. Stafford, author of *The Mountain Lion,* is pictured in profile with a caged mountain lion, also in profile, behind her. Heggen, who wrote "a satire on life aboard a cargo ship," is photographed in front of a naval uniform. Willingham, who wrote "a hard-boiled novel about the brutalizing effects of life in a Southern military academy," looks up with hooded eyes, face half in shadow, before a bottle of whiskey, a saber and cadet's hat, and five mysterious playing cards—all aces—hanging off a line. Fenwick, a "pretty, 27-year-old blonde" who wrote a novel of "family psychological conflict" ("family life fascinates her because she never had any of her own") quietly fumes in sweater and pearls in front of a blown-up period etching of a proper Victorian family.[19]

These photos relate the authors to, but distinguish them from, their novels' contents. Heggen does not wear the naval gear, and Stafford does not roar. Capote, by contrast, sits at a Victorian double tête-à-tête in a room cluttered with bric-a-brac, similar to Yaddo's but cheaper. What do his surroundings signify? Does their fussiness reflect Capote's too-careful, too-formal, and too-mature dress, and read as effeminate—as gay? Capote's head overlaps the picture of a still life of fruit behind him, a possible allusion to fruitiness that rhymes with the skull-bursting marble from the previous year's *LIFE*: Capote as father to Athena has become Capote as cousin to Carmen Miranda. Still, there is a marked lack of clear allusion compared to the earlier photos. Why?

The answer is found in the nexus between the caption's descriptor "esoteric" and the gay contents of *Other Voices, Other Rooms*. Cooke clearly knew his authors' work—as is evident in the mystery of the Willingham aces, which refer to the crooked gambling in his *End as a Man*. Homosexuality plays a much more prominent part than cards in the novel, which as *LIFE* coyly reports was tried for (and vindicated of) obscenity. Whether one graduates and "ends as a man" depends on whether one survives the constant "cutting of one's ass" by senior cadets or, if one is a particularly alcoholic senior, whether one is tortured by a stormy romance with a wizened sophomore with a weak heart, "that dismal, depraved, unhealthy, and all-the-rest-of-it thing—a practicing homosexual." Even after the book encountered multiple censors as its author adapted it into a play and then a screenplay, the resulting movie, released as *The Strange One*, still included appreciable gay content.[20]

Cooke evades this content in Willingham's photo by employing symbols from *End as a Man* that do not indicate homosexuality. Why not do the same for *Other Voices*? Any number of southern gothic details would have done nicely. True, the cluttered scene of Capote's photo bears a vague resemblance to Skully's Landing, the decaying mansion of his novel. Nonetheless, the setting of the photo is markedly less blunt than that of the other four, and its meaning remains esoteric.[21]

In 1941, *esoteric* meant "designed for, and understood by, the specially initiated alone; abstruse; also, belonging to the circle initiated in such teachings."[22] The photo caption's descriptor "esoteric" thus conveys Capote's otherness to those who understand its code: homosexuality as told through the fussy dandy. Stafford may be pictured with a mountain lion to indicate her book *The Mountain Lion*; but *Other Voices, Other Rooms*, whose title itself participates in a dance of indirection around homosexuality ("other" how?), cannot be indicated so easily. Cooke cannot show us a truck driver who wants to "take down [Joel's (or Capote's)] britches." Nor can Cooke show us "two grown men standing in an ugly little room kissing each other." If he wants to indicate the novel's homosexuality, all he can show is Capote himself, who holds the unspeakable within his own body. Capote is his own iconography—and his body itself is a sign of homosexuality. In the cultural lens, Capote is his own prop.[23]

Again, Gore Vidal offers a useful contrast. The final six portraits in the photo-essay are distinguished from the first five by stylistic incoherence and, especially, size. About twenty-five copies of Vidal's tiny likeness could be stuffed inside Capote's giant portrait, but comparative size is not the only sign of Vidal's lesser status (Plate 8, detail). Vidal's headshot is cropped severely from a 1947 portrait by Jerry Cooke—almost certainly commissioned for the same photo shoot—that positions Vidal in front of a giant ship that looms both above and behind. Vidal's quiff rhymes with the bow of the ship; the forward thrust of the ship parallels the forward thrust of his hair. He seems to size up the viewer, and only a close look reveals a half smile. The enormous ship expresses the power of this former maritime officer and references *Williwaw,* the war-at-sea novel that made Vidal's name as a novelist; and his expression, as well as his placement on a pier or dock—a traditional setting for a homosexual assignation—allows the viewer to read the photo as a sexual invitation. As cropped by *LIFE,* however, Vidal loses most of his potency. Only his expression remains. If Capote is his own prop—if his own body symbolizes the homosexual content of his novel—then Vidal, as pictured in *LIFE,* is just a tiny face.

The furor around *The City and the Pillar* cannot explain *LIFE*'s shrinkage of Vidal, as the novel was not published until the following year. The stylistic similarities between the Vidal photo and the Capote, Willingham, Heggen, and Fenwick photos—especially the overt picturing of a novel's content—suggests that Cooke took all five on the same assignment.[24] If so, why was Vidal demoted from the top five? Perhaps Stafford was made more prominent in the essay at the last minute because the article that accompanies the photo-essay names her and Heggen "the best of the lot" and Stafford "the only one of this group of literary psychologists who makes finished art of her material." The captions for the photos accord with this article, and Stafford's rates her as the "[m]ost brilliant of the new fiction writers." Perhaps this unexpected praise caused the editors to rethink the previous photo layout; perhaps Jean Speiser was called up at the last minute to photograph Stafford in the style of Cooke. Perhaps this explains what my eyes see in the Stafford photo as either a clumsy overliteralization or a satirical tinge: *The Mountain Lion*? The mountain lion! (Plate 6). And perhaps the March 1947 publication of Vidal's *In a Yellow Wood,* which does not feature a ship, made Cooke's photo untimely for the June 1947 essay. Perhaps the disappointing reception of this second novel decreased Vidal's stock; perhaps prickly Vidal simply aggravated the wrong person. From such tiny acts and decisions do the material bases of personae accrue.[25]

Agency and Subversion

This incorporation of the content of *Other Voices* into Capote's physical body is supported by his dominance of the photo-essay: the celebrated body invites examination. Any reader could see that Capote was the photo-essay's star, starting with its first and biggest picture, though he was the only one of the eleven featured authors who had not yet published a book. In the article that accompanies the photo-essay, critic John Chamberlain barely acknowledges Capote—which was not a slight but an appropriate gesture toward a writer of his low stature. Even Capote's publisher, Bennett Cerf at Random House, was surprised by Capote's domination of the photo-essay:

> About a week before *Other Voices* was published, my friend Richard Simon called me up and said, "How the hell do you get a full-page picture of an author in *Life* magazine before his first book comes out?" I said, "Do you think I'm going to tell you? Does Macy's tell Gimbels?" Dick said, "Come on. How did you wrangle that?" I said, "Dick, I have no intention of telling you." He hung up in a huff; and I hung up too, and cried, "For God's sake, get me a copy of *Life!*" That was the first I knew about the whole affair! Truman had managed to promote that full-page picture for himself, and how he did it, I don't know to this day.

We see here the limits of the publishing houses' ability to market books and authors as well as Capote's own potency at self-advertisement—a potency Cerf exaggerates, as it was five months, not one week, before the book was for sale, in December 1947.[26]

But what *is* this potency? Can it be proved and measured? And did Capote control it? In this particular instance, did he determine the content, form, and placement of his photos? Did Capote actively achieve his effects through careful art direction and the manipulation of people and institutions to put that art into play, or was he an unwitting cipher? With his photos, the range of possible agency slides from Larsen's and Cooke's controlling all aspects of Capote's representation to Capote's dictating his own representation. The actual agency was doubtlessly mixed, different for each shot and shoot, and compromised by editorial practice. Yet both peers and later critics credited Capote for his skills at publicity—with their backhand, as Capote's power was usually softened as "charm" and sexualized as the ability to seduce the camera, or a reporter, or his publisher, Cerf:

> Well, *that* was a day when Truman arrived at Random House! He had bangs, and nobody could believe it when this young prodigy waltzed in. He looked about eighteen.
>
> He was bright and happy and absolutely self-assured. We said we wanted to publish anything he wrote. . . . Phyllis [Mrs. Cerf] adopted Truman immediately. He was already exhibiting the charm which proved so irresistible that he soon became a society favorite.

Here Capote is trying to sell a novel of gay adolescence with explicit depictions of gay love and sex to the straight head of his desired house. Capote's introduction to Random House came not by chance but through the recommendation of McCullers and the buzz surrounding his stories, both very much supported by his deployment of a public persona as an effeminate prodigy. Capote clearly knew how to sell himself and his work—and we see how Cerf was sold.[27]

Cerf not only recognizes and names Capote's charm but attributes Capote's success to it, acknowledging both the public's and his own (through the royal "we") affection for Capote's person. Cerf deflects Capote's homosexuality through the usual triad: Capote is effeminate (he "waltzed in"), triply young (he is an "adoptable" "young prodigy"), and strange and excessive ("*That* was a day!"). It doesn't matter *what* Capote writes, because the enchanted house "wanted to publish anything he wrote"—which allows Cerf to mention the success but not the content of *Other Voices* in his memoir, although in other cases he almost always recollects the books he published in detail.

Consider how, in his memoir, Cerf follows his recollection of Capote with his memories of Mary Jane Ward, author of *The Snake Pit*, a roman à clef of mental illness. Cerf writes, "*The Snake Pit* is the story of an intelligent girl of medium circumstances whose mind suddenly snaps and she has to be committed—which is what had happened to the author." Cerf details both Ward's mental illness and her fictional representation of this illness, but he shies away from Capote's gay person and story. Insanity is bad, but homosexuality is unmentionable. Nonetheless, in a pattern that repeated in reviews of *Other Voices,* Cerf ends his disquisition on Capote with his clearest reference to homosexuality yet, as if Cerf's desire cannot be contained: "When Truman comes to the house, I am always delighted to see him, although he sometimes annoys me by throwing his arms around me and calling me 'Great White Father' and 'Big Daddy' and such. I say, 'For Pete's sake, cut that out.' But I don't mind it somehow when Truman does it." I bet not! Capote and Cerf collaborate here. Cerf may split off, contain, and safely engage with repressed fantasies by publishing Capote, just as Joel Knox gets a lift in exchange for holding Sam Radclif's desire. Thus, Capote works the room to great effect—or does the room work him? Even before he was famous, Capote did not need to be present in order for his public persona to be used as a fantastic linchpin for what postwar Americans had repudiated.[28]

Consider one of Capote's first notices, which anticipated his *LIFE* photos: "The most remarkable new talent of the year was, in the opinion of the editor, that of Truman Capote, the *e* being accented, a young man from New Orleans just past his majority. It is safe to predict that Mr. Capote will take his place among the best short-story writers of the rising generation." Here are the usual three notes of Capote's persona: his youth, his strangeness (via "most remarkable," the reference to New Orleans, and the unusual *e*), and, to my ear, his effeminacy, through the coy construction of "just past his majority." These assertions are factually true but carry other registers of meaning. Yes, Capote was young to achieve such success—but the excessive notation ("new talent," "will take his place," "rising generation," "young," and "just past his majority") registers an otherness beyond age. Capote's youth becomes an easy channel through which to both express broad queerness and repress gay specificity: an umbilical cord through which an intersubjective persona is pumped up with unspoken and possibly unconscious desire.[29]

Capote's potency came from his recognition that he was at the crux of several public discourses of queerness that referenced homosexuality indirectly. He pushed hard at that crux to excite the public even as the occluding overhang of these discourses shielded him from homophobia. Such shielding could be distasteful to those who confronted homophobia more directly. Calder Willingham opens a disapproving window on Capote in a 1948 letter: "[Capote] tries too hard to be charming . . . [and is] busy all the time at the job of getting ahead. . . . [A]lso, he uses his homosexuality in this; he uses it as comedy, and plays the role of the effeminate buffoon, thus making people laugh at him. It gets attention."

Willingham wrote this letter to Gore Vidal, whose well-documented and frequently expressed disgust for Capote suited Vidal's attempt to separate the discourses of effeminacy, immaturity, and homosexuality in his own life and work. Vidal viewed Capote's reliance on this old-school crux as collaboration with the enemy, and he unfavorably compared Capote to writers such as himself whose postwar careers were damaged by homophobia: "The only thing [about gay artists that straight critics] respect, that they put up with, is a freak like Capote, who has the mind of a Texas housewife, likes gossip, and gets all shuddery when she thinks about boys murdering people." Yet Capote and Vidal were involved in the same project of challenging the hegemonic understanding of immaturity, effeminacy, and homosexuality—one of them fighting the devaluation, the other the conflation, of these different queernesses—and it is symptomatic of the difficulty of fighting internalized as well as external homophobia that these writers expended energy attacking each other like show dogs performing tricks on talk shows rather than attack dogs chewing at "the Man."[30]

Capote's performance invokes Judith Butler's theory of gender performativity, which holds that gender must be constantly performed to appear natural, and which champions drag and other kinds of "gender performance [that] enact and reveal the performativity of gender itself in a way that destabilizes the naturalized categories of identity and desire." Capote's objective may have been less to force a wedge into the workings of the gender machine so as to reveal its nuts and bolts, and more to redirect the machine's energy to blow up his persona. Nonetheless, he offered for public consumption a man who was not limited by, but rather capitalized upon, his effeminacy and childishness. He tended to collaborate with photographers who had similar stakes in subverting straight-male hegemony: women such as Larsen, who had to struggle against expectations to make art, or men who had sex with men, such as Cecil Beaton and Carl Van Vechten. These artists had a vested interest in and sensitivities toward subversive gender coding and its appeal—a possible explanation for Larsen's focus on Capote.[31]

Capote's subversion extends past the visual: his writing violently attacks masculine hegemony, so much so that his effeminacy and infantilism can be seen as ways to both split off from and express a considerable rage. Capote's effeminacy and childishness were often experienced as aggressive, both by those who met in him person and by those who encountered only his public persona. Young, effeminate, and strange Capote might access the mass market when manly Gore Vidal was denied—and Capote used this access to promote his work, which also expressed his rage. When Vidal, referencing *In Cold Blood,* accuses Capote of getting "all shuddery when she thinks about boys murdering people," does Vidal pick up on Capote's fear or on Capote's attraction to and identification with Perry Smith and Richard Hickock, who murdered the stunningly normal Clutter family? The destruction of the social order extends through Capote's work, from the disabling of the patriarch and the confirmation of his son's homosexuality in *Other Voices* to the desecration of the upper class forty years later in *Answered Prayers,* which makes "the beautiful people" ugly. Capote's persona is a wily ambassador who smuggles these textual weapons of destruction into mass consciousness, just as the persona itself acts as a glamorous terrorist against gender security.[32]

Other Voices in Contemporary Mass Media

The postwar need for such an intersubjective persona as an indirect means to discuss and process homosexuality may be seen in critical discussions of *Other Voices, Other Rooms,* a novel better read than synopsized and best understood as a psychosexual allegory of gay adolescence. As the novel opens, thirteen-year-old Joel Knox, whose mother has recently died, is summoned to Skully's Landing, the home of Ed Sansom, Joel's father, whom Joel does not remember. In time, Joel learns that his father is bedridden and can communicate only by throwing a rubber ball; Joel was actually summoned by his stepmother's cross-dressing cousin Randolph, who had shot Sansom at the climax of a complex love tangle that centered on a boxer whom Sansom managed and whom both Randolph and Randolph's girlfriend desired. After the shooting, Randolph had the incapacitated Sansom marry Randolph's cousin, nurse manqué Amy Skully, and all three repaired to her southern gothic estate.

Joel's discovery of this family plot—as well as his introduction to puberty—takes place against the backdrop of his friendships with the butch/femme twins Idabel and Florabel, and with Zooey, the family servant who yearns to escape Skully's Landing but must care for her centenarian grandfather.[33] Joel's flirtation with tomboy Idabel climaxes in a romantic triangle with the dwarf beauty queen Miss Wisteria, who is erotically infatuated with Joel, as Idabel is with Miss Wisteria. These burgeoning sexualities overwhelm Joel, who has a nervous collapse. Joel is nursed back to health by Cousin Randolph, and the novel ends with what seems to be an erotic agreement between the two as Joel prepares to directly encounter Randolph in drag for the first time, an encounter which the novel explicitly states makes him a man: "She [Randolph] beckoned to him, shining and silver, and he knew he must go: unafraid, not hesitating, he paused only at the garden's edge where, as though he'd forgotten something, he stopped and looked back at the bloomless, descending blue, at the boy he had left behind."[34] *Other Voices* could not be discussed today without the overt mention of homosexuality. There are two explicit descriptions of homosexual acts in the novel, and many of its characters have specifically homosexual desires or manifest transgender traits, which would have been read as homosexual at a time when effeminacy was conflated with same-sex desire. Nonetheless, the novel's poetic style and the narrator's young age allowed almost all of Capote's reviews to mention homosexuality slightly, if at all, though coded references abound.[35]

TIME begins the unsigned review "Spare the Laurels" with "The author of this novel is only 23, but his literary promise has already caused a flutter in Manhattan publishing circles." The effeminate connotations of "flutter" are followed by other indirect yet unmistakable allusions to the midcentury construction of homosexuality, such as the description of "the languid and effeminate Cousin Randolph . . . who drinks sherry, calls [Knox] 'darling,' and holds his hand." *TIME* understands the text itself as gay; the novel is "immature and its theme is calculated to make the flesh crawl"—a description of the contemporary understanding of homosexuality as a morbid arrest of psychosexual development. The review must move through these euphemisms before it can actually say "homosexual": connotation becomes denotation as the review climaxes and closes with "But for all [Capote's] novel's gifted invention and imagery, the distasteful trappings of its homosexual themes overhang it like Spanish moss."[36]

The complication of public expressions of homosexuality is elaborated in the letters column of the next issue of *TIME*. In an interchange titled "Mossy Trappings," R. E. Berg protests: "You seem to advocate tolerance for the customary things discriminated against: race, color, creed, religion, etc. However, I do not believe you have ever made a reference to homosexuality (a perfectly legitimate psychological condition) without going specifically out of your way to make a vicious insinuation, caustic remark, or 'dirty dig.'" After quoting the close of *TIME*'s review, Berg himself closes: "I have seen a great deal of Spanish moss in a lot of places . . .

and I must confess that some of it is quite beautiful." Following Berg's positive revision of the moss metaphor, the editor responds: "It gives *TIME* the creeps." *TIME* thus allows not only a naming but also, through Berg, a defense of homosexuality, albeit surrounded by dismissal and disgust. *TIME*'s inconsistent representation of homosexuality is writ large in its dispassionate review of Kinsey's report, written less than a month before: "As a result of the tabulated testimony, Kinsey concludes . . . 37% [of the U.S. male population] has some homosexual experience between adolescence and old age, with the highest rate among single males 36 to 40." *TIME*, matter-of-fact with Kinsey and tortured if finally expressive with Capote, refused to review Vidal's *The City and the Pillar* altogether.[37]

These inconsistent and incoherent presentations and understandings of homosexuality are mirrored in claims that *Other Voices* itself is incoherent and obscure. There is a contrary correspondence between perceptions of the book's aesthetic merits—specifically its *realist* aesthetic merits—and the direct mention of homosexuality. If the novel is named as gay, it cannot be good. Nor can it be realist, for homosexuality indicates a novel whose content is somehow especially "artificial": inferior to the "real" and compounded by textual obscurity. The novel's obscurity, difficulty, and artificiality are chiefly situated in Joel Knox. In "Books of the *Times*," Orville Prescott relates how "[i]n the course of the summer and after some very queer experiences indeed Joel is supposed to have crossed the invisible line dividing childhood from the first manifestations of maturity. But Joel's psychological growth is not clear enough to be convincing because Joel is never a flesh-and-blood boy." Is it that Joel is never bodily realized, or is that body homosexual, which is incommensurate with the review's otherwise positive reading of the novel and which thus must be censored?[38]

All Capote's reviews struggle with the concept of a gay coming-of-age novel that follows the maturation of a specifically gay boy into specifically gay manhood—something for which there were no words at the time, and are few now. Fifty years after *Other Voices* was published, the psychoanalytic theorist Ken Corbett wrote, "There is no homosexual boyhood. That is, there is no conceptual category called 'homosexual boyhood.' . . . [W]ithin our culture, there is sufficient anxiety and resistance to the possibility of a proto-gay subjectivity that one is discouraged from even imagining (much less attempting to document) such subjectivities." *Other Voices, Other Rooms* charts and gives voice to subjectivities not yet culturally intelligible, and the media's sloppy elision of the gay content of

Other Voices was also the messy transmittal of what was repressed: that the novel is an "insurrection at the level of ontology, a critical opening up of the questions, What is real? Whose lives are real? How might reality be remade?" Gay readers who were schooled at reading the shadow of the homosexual other as it fell across mass culture could abstract the specifically gay from the broadly queer references of the reviews of *Other Voices.* The novel's demand for the recognition of what had not been previously seen as human was doubled by Capote's author's photo, which repeated in visual form the novel's assertion of an unspeakable subjectivity: the gay self.[39]

The Author Photo for *Other Voices, Other Rooms*

In the author photo for *Other Voices, Other Rooms,* Capote, photographed at his direction by his friend Howard Halma, reclines on a Victorian sofa or fainting couch, his head turned toward and staring at the viewer from a close distance that implies intimacy (Plate 9). Capote's head, on the photo's right, is balanced to the left by the seat's carved scroll, a visual parallel that cements his connection to the couch. The intimate connotations of reclining on upholstery—Does the model sleep or rise from sleep, and does the viewer observe the unguarded? Does the model entice the viewer to bed?—are traditionally feminine, so much so that a species of couch, the recamier, takes its name from David's portrait of Jeanne Recamier (1800) on the couch in question. Capote, however, in his disruptive translation of this traditional vocabulary of seduction, can best be compared to Manet's *Olympia* (Plate 10).[40]

T. J. Clark analyzes the inability of Manet's contemporary critics to discuss *Olympia* as follows: critics saw "some kind of indeterminacy in the image: a body on a bed, evidently sexed and sexual, but whose appearance was hard to make out in any steady way, and harder still to write about." Olympia disturbed because she refused the codes of representation for prostitution, thrusting an awareness of her own subjectivity upon a society whose usual view of prostitutes was flat. Olympia's subjectivity not only prevents her from being read solely as an object of desire but also forces upon the viewer an awareness of both the artificiality of her pose and the viewer's expectations of such a pose. Instead of regarding Olympia, the viewer regards his or her own desire, and how that desire is culturally shaped.[41]

Whether or not Capote and Halma were conscious of the specifics of their photograph's art-historical antecedents is unknown and, in most respects, unimportant. Halma was Capote's roommate, rather than a professional photographer, and Gerald Clarke, Capote's official biographer, notes only that the men created the photograph together. Capote—typically—had a variety of origin stories about the photograph, and often refused responsibility for either the pose or the choice of the photograph as a publicity photo. What *is* known is that Capote insisted on this photo for the dust jacket of *Other Voices* and that he provoked a strong reaction by representing himself through a pose that was strongly associated with feminine seduction. Like Olympia, the photographed Capote quotes the conventions of the odalisque even as he refutes them, provoking a desire that overflows artistic and cultural conventions and disturbs as it entices. Capote offers a mirror image of Olympia—he leans to his photograph's right, whereas she leans to her picture's left, and her tied bow is now his bow tie—but the far hand against the genitals still indicates an unexpected, discomfiting potency, and the viewer's erotic consternation is the same.

Because Capote cannot publicly present himself naked on a bed (or on a bed at all), he presents himself as a clothed nude.[42] In a trick practiced in *LIFE,* Capote decontextualizes his clothes and forces their rereading. His white long-sleeved shirt, buttoned tattersall vest, and bow tie, when combined with his informal and untraditionally masculine pose, are stripped of their usual connotations of conservative, formal, adult masculinity to shimmer with indeterminacy; their fussy propriety, like the couch's Victoriana, becomes appropriate for fantasy and play. Conformity becomes travesty, and Capote's clothes a state of undress. The photo's staginess and strangeness are referenced and focused by the glasses that Capote holds in his hand, glasses that reverberate with the staid-unto-celibate connotations of his bow tie. The librarian has taken off her glasses and revealed her beauty—and holds on to them so the remembered contrast may heighten the revelation of her face.

Capote's direct gaze—which doubles the in-your-face, "masculine" dare of publicly presenting the photo—is contradicted by the effeminacy of the glossy lips, the overtly carefully styled hair and eyebrows, and the recumbent pose. Hilton Als sees here "an assertion, a point, asserting this: I am a woman." Capote was not transgender, but he did adapt the masquerade of femininity to signal his availability for fantasy and the propriety of his objectification. Feminist theory has long exposed the prison of being the "bearer, not maker, of meaning"—but for a gay man in 1947, to be viewed in the mass media as "an American woman of style . . . something to be fucked somehow" was to bear an unusually attractive meaning. And then Capote *was* a man, if a queer man, and had some access to masculine privilege—as his gaze reminds us. Capote, like Olympia, maintains his own subjectivity even as he offers himself up for interpersonal transaction. This tension confuses his viewers and adds to his value and appeal.[43]

For Capote, like Olympia, is for sale. Capote's book wears his body as an enticement. Those who buy his novel may take his picture home. This queer prostitution is traditional. Ever since authors have sold their works—and, by association, themselves—in the marketplace, their genders have been rendered incoherent by normative codes for both men and women. Male writers, especially those, like Capote, noted for their attention to detail, have had to assert their masculinity against the "feminine" aspects of their craft. Capote's young, effeminate strangeness is a difference of degree, not kind, and his pose adheres to the law, if not the letter, of the publishing system he troubles.[44]

Broadly Queer, Specifically Gay

Sometimes Capote was read as gay, and sometimes he was not, and sometimes viewers understood that they were attracted to him, and sometimes they did not. His success at selling himself depended upon the broadly queer, those folk who may have identified with or desired Capote but who were not specifically gay. In Gerald Clarke's biography *Capote,* photographer Halma tells how he overheard two middle-aged women studying one of the photo's enlargements in a bookstore window. "I'm telling you, he's just young," said one. "And I'm telling you," replied the other, "if he isn't young, he's dangerous!" This fantastic scene was repeated so often by Capote that Clarke suspected either him or Halma of faking it. True or not, the story illustrates the elasticity of Capote's persona and his pleasure at this multiplicity. His photo's various indeterminacies allow the possibility of desire to flicker on and off for these women—a flickering that enhances desire. But for what? An underage, untraditionally manly object of their heterosexual lust? Or do the women themselves want to repeat Capote's performance—to be seductively "bad"? Or are their desires and identifications interlaced?[45]

John Malcolm Brinnin reports a different "danger" in a journal entry of January 18, 1948. Brinnin was eating breakfast in Harvard Square:

At the adjoining table, young husband in Eisenhower jacket and chinos, young wife in peasant blouse and dirndl, their infant in a high chair. They pass sections of *The New York Times* between them, now and then turning to spoon something to the baby.

"Take a look at this," says the husband, and holds up an advertisement showing the book jacket photograph of Truman supine in his calculated languor.

The wife gives it one stiff, stern glance.

"Honey," she says, "*you* stay away from *him*."

What does this studied young couple, sporting their "bohemian" flair in Harvard Square, tell us? Is the wife serious, or joking, or both? Does she view all effeminate men as dangers to her hearth, or is Capote's lure particularly strong? Does the wife read in her husband's attention an attraction that he does not know, or are his same-sexual desires a known fact? Both the middle-aged women in the bookstore and the married couple with the baby speak to Capote's wide appeal.[46]

Capote's constructed youth makes him more available for this spread of fantasy. As in the *LIFE* photos, the retaining walls of censorship and repression force the charged flood released by Capote's swing between gender poles into the discourse of age—a slippage guided by Capote's trick clothes and by the book blurb by Marguerite Young: "Rarely does one find a writer of Truman Capote's generation who shows, at the beginning of his career, those results which would seem to come only with maturity." This blurb can be reduced to Capote's precocity or, more precisely, his age's instability: the age of his generation versus the age of his career versus the age of his "results," results that correlate with the satisfaction provided by his sophisticated fiction. Capote is understood as a "boy" just as he is understood as a "woman"—to force intelligibility upon what to my eyes is not a boy, or even a teen, but a sexually provocative gay man.[47]

That said, Capote's jacket photo does literally enclose his boy hero, and readers' tendency to identify authors with their protagonists was abetted by Random House, which used the photo in print ads that read, "This Is Truman Capote," and sent huge blowups to bookstores. The *New York Times Book Review* was typical in reading the novel as autobiography: "The story of Joel Knox did not need to be told, except to get it out of the author's system." Now the "boy" might properly develop. Yet Capote's photo offers a vision of development unfit for the *Times,* for the narrated Knox never actively strikes a pose of seduction. Instead, Knox—covertly coveted by Radclif and overtly desired by Cousin Randolph, Florabel, and the dwarf Miss Wisteria—inflames desire through cluelessness.[48]

Knox sees neither the sexual desire he provokes in others nor his own sexual desire. He is properly named after Nox, the god of night, the host of darkness and sex. Throughout the novel, Knox not only resists but is sickened by sexual knowledge, which culminates in his breakdown when Cousin Randolph's and Miss Wisteria's desires overwhelm him; Knox's recognition of sexuality ends the book, as if the novel cannot contain a Knox who knows. If the novel is a claim for the humanity of gay boyhood, the photo is a picture of a nascent Knox realized by this narrative of maturity: a sexually fantastic "boy."

Capote as Seen by Gay Contemporaries

The capacity to easily read the photo's mysteries may have lessened its charm for gay men already secure in their sexual identity and worldly success. Cecil Beaton, who himself contributed to Capote's young, effeminate, and strange construction by photographing him against a garden wall festooned with roses (1948) and as a half-naked, beturbaned princeling with a long cigarette holder (1949), wrote in 1957 that "Truman Capote, then barely in his twenties, appeared on [his] dust jacket looking somewhat like a wombat and peering out from under a flaxen fringe." The musician and diarist Ned Rorem, writing in 1984, similarly mocked "the author gazing at us, doe-eyed 'neath yam-colored China-doll bangs, from a prone pose on a Victorian settee." Both note particulars of Capote's hair color that cannot be seen in black and white: extraneous knowledge is invoked to mock the photo and its subject. Similarly, Capote does not sport a china-bowl cut (though he sometimes did); is firmly in his twenties; and is neither doe-eyed nor a small marsupial, animal metaphors which both recognize and diminish the photo's "animal" sexuality. These sour retrospectives show how the photo was so closely identified with Capote that its representation stretched past its physical limits—and the descriptions' nastiness may speak to the photo's impact upon Capote's queer contemporaries. Andy Warhol offers a clear example.[49]

Warhol was only three years younger than Capote, though Capote's precocity brought him fame while Warhol was still in art school. When Warhol first saw a blowup of the *Other Voices* photo in the office of *Theater Arts* magazine, he convinced the staff to let him take it home. He then wrote Capote fan letters, sent him watercolors, stalked his building, and initiated a friendship with his mother. Warhol's obsession extended to his art: his first gallery exhibition was 1952's *15 Drawings Based on the Writings of Truman Capote,* and the first reproduction of his non-commercial art in the mass media was a 1957 photo-essay in *LIFE* of shoes painted in gold leaf, decorated with gold and silver trim, and named after celebrities: "Truman Capote" was a flower-filled slipper.[50]

Warhol's obsession affected his demeanor: a contemporary describes him as sounding "as if he had written his own part in a play by Truman Capote"—which indicates how "Capote" was shorthand for a whole school of self-dramatization. That Warhol was one of many gay men who worshiped Capote as a queer icon is proved by the art press: a 1954 review in *Art Digest* tagged Warhol as one of those "attractive and demanding young men involved in the business of being as much like Truman Capote or his heroes as possible." Warhol's greatest homage was that he too would employ homosexuality as an integral part of the persona that brought him fame. He may have traded in immaturity and effeminacy for developmental disability and asexuality as broad registers of queerness, but the purposeful stoking of notoriety through strangeness was the same.[51]

Capote in *TIME*

The media, which could barely discuss the contents of *Other Voices,* was happy to report, and so heighten (but not discuss!), the novel's visual sensation. For example, *TIME*'s negative review in January was followed by two more pieces on the photo—extraordinary coverage for a dust jacket. These pieces are in the "People" section rather than the book-review section; Capote's persona had grown past the book that displayed it. On March 15, 1948, *TIME* reported how Merle Miller, novelist and editor of *Harper's,* "took pained exception to a ripely precious publicity photograph of a pensive, reclining Capote peering up through artfully disarranged bangs. If the idea of printing that particular photograph was Capote's, Miller fumed, it was 'deplorable; if his publisher's, disgraceful.'" What, precisely, was wrong with the photo? *TIME* need not say, because its readers already knew: Capote confidently used erotic strangeness to visually tout his book. In *TIME*'s report of Miller's protest—a protest that garnered Capote yet more publicity—we see again how the tensions between fascination and disgust, and repression and advertisement, propelled Capote's persona into and then sustained its celebrity.[52]

Five weeks later, on May 3, *TIME* not only invoked but also repro-duced "the languid pose of precocious Author Truman Capote" in a rare discussion of an author's photo per se. The photo's caption disrespects both the novel, "this dank bestseller with a homosexual theme," and its use of Capote's photo as a marketing tool—"Without such shrewdly posed pictures as these, the publishing business . . . [might] be reduced to selling books on their merits"—but the photo's reproduction celebrates Capote visually even as it denigrates him literally. *TIME* reproduced the photo to report another simultaneous celebration and denigration: the author photo for *Max Shulman's Large Economy Size* (Plate 11), a col-lection of three books by Shulman. Shulman's parody was attributed to his publisher rather than the man or his photographer: "To poke fun at Random House, Doubleday and Co., Inc., dressed he-man Humorist Max Shulman in a checked weskit, also posed him sitting on his neck." Both authors are denied agency for their photos—which makes the photos' commentaries on masculinity less threatening and secures them in the normative arena of corporate play.[53]

Burly, mature "he-man" Shulman, photographed by Mina Turner, takes up Capote's pose to mock him. Shulman's awkwardness is meant to showcase the perversity of Capote's studied grace, as underscored by *TIME*'s caption, which describes Shulman as "sitting on his neck"—a term that correctly states that Shulman's neck, rather than his back, rests against the sofa but that mocks the recumbent pose through its abrupt informality. Despite Shulman's claim to appropriate masculinity, he dili-gently avoids his penis. Whereas Capote lets his far arm trail over his side to rest naturally on his genitalia, Shulman awkwardly bends his arm so as to avoid his genitals. Where Capote drapes and extends the fingers of his left hand toward his crotch, Shulman further fends off his geni-tals by balling his left hand into a defensive fist that furthers the gap be-tween performative masculinity and the penis. Shulman's manhood is further gouged by his couch. Whereas Capote is visually integrated with his furniture, Shulman's couch ascends out of the frame, dwarfing him and making him incidental. Shulman may purposefully fail at the pho-tograph's tropes, but the satire, especially placed next to Capote's mas-tery, rebounds and places his own masculinity in question. As Shulman's manly gut turns to pendulous flab, so control of the pose slips through his clenched fingers.[54]

Shulman's careful study extends to his jacket copy, a false blurb that parodies Marguerite Young's excessive statement of Capote's youth:

"Although these three books were written by Shulman at the age of eight, critics have pointed out that they show the insight and penetration of a man of nine." The detail of this satire, which was attributed to a whole publishing house, proves the depth of other writers' and publishers' consideration of Capote's success. And the joke's accessibility to the readership of a "he-man humorist," a readership not easily conflated with Capote's, tells of Capote's photo's phenomenal spread through public consciousness. Sam Radclif notes the "pure yellow strands" of Joel Knox's hair to make fun of the boy; now it's the trucker, instead of the queer boy, who needs a lift.[55]

"The Winnah!"

And so Capote got his ride. Mano a mano, he wins: his spectacular triumph marks him as an author worthy of visual representation. This champ won his title not only in spite of but also because of his differences from hegemonic masculinity. He thus brought the gender system into relief and question, through both his persona and his writing, without suffering the usual price—at least for a time. Ken Corbett cautions, "Queer theorists have had much to say about the oppression of regulatory force and the dulling consequences of normativity. But what of the strain of living outside the regular, the reliable, the customary? What does it cost to be always and already fabulous?"[56] Capote's celebrity would eventually eclipse his artistic reputation and encase him in the static persona of an alcoholic society gossip. By the time of his death, in 1984, this sad end had obscured, but does not detract from, the fabulous potency of his early portraits.

Capote, Forster, and the Trillings
Homophobia and Literary Culture at Midcentury

Strangers on a Train

In a reminiscence published in George Plimpton's oral history of Truman
Capote, Diana Trilling discusses her and her husband, Lionel's, first meeting with Capote, almost certainly in August 1946, about sixteen months
before Capote published *Other Voices, Other Rooms*. That August, Capote
was a twenty-one-year-old writer who had published several well-received
stories (among them "Miriam" and "A Tree of Night") and had just been
featured in a photo-essay on the Yaddo artists' colony in *LIFE*.[1] This
promising start could have been appreciably helped or hindered by either
of the Trillings, who were a power couple of their day. Both were prominent members of the New York Intellectuals, the cosmopolitan group of
cultural and political writers who, broadly speaking, were born poor and
Jewish, became active in the anti-Stalinist Old Left as college students in
the 1930s, and set the tone and subject of much of the intellectual discussion of the 1940s and '50s.[2] Diana Trilling had written a weekly book-
review column in *The Nation* since 1941; would later write for *The New
Yorker*, *The Atlantic*, the *Saturday Review*, and *Partisan Review*; and
would continue to publish into the 1990s. She was always best known,
however, as the wife of Lionel Trilling, literary critic, fiction writer, and
professor at Columbia University. By 1947, Lionel Trilling had published
book-length studies on Matthew Arnold and E. M. Forster, as well as several of the essays that would be collected in the influential *The Liberal
Imagination*, which established him as a public intellectual in the mold
of George Orwell and Edmund Wilson.[3]

Diana Trilling tells how Capote introduced himself in Grand Central

Station (Lionel had gone to buy tickets); Capote recognized her from a photograph in the home of his friend Leo Lerman.[4] The three sat together on the train.

> Here was this little creature, odd-looking and with his extraordinary squeaky voice, very high-pitched and very resonant: it carried the length of the car. So he sat opposite Lionel and me and proceeded to ask questions about Lionel's book on E. M. Forster. Truman wanted to know why it was that Lionel had ignored Forster's homosexuality. Now this was not only a bold question to put at the top of his shrill voice in a very crowded car in those days. I remember having very mixed feelings. One: wishing he would shut up and go away, because I was embarrassed and I thought there was going to be a lynching in the car. I was afraid people would do something. I could see that they were uncomfortable, angry at him, very angry. Truman wasn't watching or if he was he didn't let on. But the other thing was that I was extraordinarily impressed by him. . . . It was a very impressive first view.
>
> He asked Lionel the question very directly: "Why did you not treat Forster's homosexuality in the book?"
>
> "I didn't know about it."
>
> Truman said, "Well, didn't you *hear* about it?"
>
> "No," said Lionel. "I had not heard about it. I know nothing about his life."
>
> Truman said, "Well, didn't you *guess* it?"
>
> Lionel said, "Yes, as I was writing my book, it began to dawn on me that probably he *was* homosexual."
>
> "Then why didn't you write about it?"
>
> "Because it didn't seem to concern me very much. I wasn't very interested in it."
>
> Truman simply thought that was *impossible.* Lionel said that it was exactly possible.

This oral history is the fullest account of Capote's encounter with the Trillings in print. Diana Trilling's fascination with Capote, Capote's with Lionel Trilling, and Lionel Trilling's dismissal of Capote are also referenced in Diana Trilling's memoir and in two letters by Capote written shortly after his trip.[5] (Lionel Trilling continued his dismissal of Capote by leaving no record of the incident.) These various records (and lack of record) offer different perspectives on a clash among three individuals from different textual traditions who resisted the social order in different ways. First was the "man of culture," whose acclaim for his explication of liberal humanism made him the first Jew afforded tenure in the notably anti-Semitic English department of Columbia University.[6] Second was the "faithful wife," who insisted on subordinating herself to her husband yet aggressively situated her intellectual production on the masculine side of the various gendered binaries operating in the publishing world and literary culture of her time. Last was the "homosexual writer," who, from the feminine side of those binaries, successfully turned his homosexuality into a marketable good at a time when assertions of homosexuality outside of private contexts were met with censorship, derision, and oppression. All three believed that literature could and should challenge the dominant ideology, especially on behalf of the individual, yet each reached a different reckoning of how this challenge might be met and to what end. All three personally resisted social hegemony, but in three distinct registers: ethnicity, gender, and sexual orientation. And none of the three can be easily reduced to one school or philosophy, and all are known for the subtle gradations and self-conscious contradictions of their work. The mingled sympathy and antipathy of these literary players made them interesting to each other and fueled their conflict on the train.

My goal in this chapter is to use reactions to Capote's persona and work by Diana and Lionel Trilling and, to a lesser extent, by two other midcentury critics, Leslie Fiedler and Elizabeth Hardwick, as an exemplar of the relations between literary culture and homophobia at midcentury. What exactly happens when Capote forces the Trillings' attention to a blind spot of liberal humanism: the exclusion of issues of gender and sexuality from serious consideration? I will show that when Capote confronts the Trillings on the train, he attacks their identity as literary and social critics committed to the belief that literature can and should be a tool for social justice, capable of questioning both their own and their society's preconceptions, and sensitive to prejudice and minority discrimination by virtue of their heritage and, in Diana's case, her gender. The battle is waged on the Trillings' home ground—the field of rigorous close reading and the ethical responsibility of the literary critic— but the Trillings find themselves resisting rather than promoting basic principles of liberal humanism. The skirmish offers an object lesson in how homophobia was negotiated by the liberal intelligentsia: how it was performed, how it was leavened by gender, and how a false reconciliation with humanist ideology was psychologically managed.

The homophobia of the New York Intellectuals and the New Critics is received wisdom today. Some of these intellectuals and critics would come to temper their views precisely because outspoken figures like Capote forced a confrontation. By articulating how challenges to homophobia percolated though literary culture, we may see the beginnings of the cultural change spurred by individual encounters, as well as by more collective acts of protest. In addition, I wish to complicate the charges of presentism often used to defend these critics—a dismissal made specious by Capote's challenge on the train. Certainly the constraints under which earlier generations wrote should not be forgotten. Yet if Capote, in 1946, might accuse Lionel Trilling of being a poor critic because of his studied ignorance of homosexuality, we may do the same. Furthermore, if Diana Trilling and other midcentury critics chose to discuss Capote's sexuality, we may examine how.

A secondary aim of this chapter is to question the current standing of Capote in literary, gay, lesbian, and queer studies. When I offer Capote as a forerunner of the gay and lesbian rights movements, I contradict the standard reading of Capote as a careerist, an apolitical aesthete, and a celebrity qua celebrity. The politics and political impact of Capote as a best-selling, critically respected, and openly gay author who frequently wrote about homosexuality throughout his career have been neglected. Consider the only two anthologies of Capote criticism, the Waldmeirs' *The Critical Response to Truman Capote* and the *Truman Capote* volume in Harold Bloom's series Modern Critical Views, both of which consistently reference Capote's flamboyant celebrity but contain only a few speculations on his political intent and impact.[7]

Capote criticism in general favors *In Cold Blood,* the hard-boiled creative nonfiction about the murderers of a prototypical midwestern family, which was Capote's biggest seller and his last complete extended narrative. More than half of the chapters in Bloom's anthology are concerned with *In Cold Blood*; the Waldmeirs' volume is more balanced but still favors *Blood*. The biographical films *Capote* and *Infamous* share with the anthologies a preoccupation with both Capote's celebrity and *Blood*. For their dramatic tension, both films rely upon the contrast between Capote's flamboyant effeminacy and his butch narration of manly killers Perry Smith and Dick Hickock, a conflict that both films resolve through Capote's exploitation-cum-friendship-cum-romance of both the killers and Capote's assistant, the writer Harper Lee. The films therefore get to both "celebrate" Capote and portray him in the homophobic tradition that finds him a manipulative exploiter of troubled working-class straight men and their devoted women—a stereotypical assessment that in this instance is probably valid, if reductive.[8]

Yet *In Cold Blood* is atypical of Capote's work in having a homosexual subtext rather than overt gay concerns. What are commonly called Capote's "early" writings but actually constitute the majority of his completed work—the novels *Other Voices, Other Rooms* (1948), *The Grass Harp* (1951), and *Breakfast at Tiffany's* (1958), and the "early" short stories, most collected in *A Tree of Night* (1949)—frequently include overtly homosexual characters and homosexual themes. Just as director Blake Edwards removed the homosexuality and augmented the manliness of the narrator of *Breakfast at Tiffany's* in the 1961 film adaptation, so literary critics have kept Capote's homosexuality at arm's length, preferring his most "masculine" work, and acknowledging his homosexuality but seeming as disinterested in the interaction between Capote's sexuality and his work as Lionel Trilling was in Forster's.[9]

Neglect of Capote's corpus and persona extends past mainstream literary criticism into critical subgenres that might reasonably be expected to discuss and value Capote. Why have gay, lesbian, and queer scholars been reluctant to "claim" him and engage with his work? First, not only does Capote's debut antedate the homophile and gay liberation movements, placing his early career off the usual historical trajectory, but also his public persona—which progressively overshadowed his writing, transforming him in the mass media from a celebrated author into a pure celebrity—can easily be seen as the cliché against which these movements defined themselves.[10] From his debut, Capote offered the performance of shock, spectacle, and scandal that was antithetical to the homophile movement, which was preoccupied with the quest for homosexual men and women to be seen as respectable, unexceptional members of society. Conversely, gay liberationists who affiliated themselves with the counterculture might welcome certainly kinds of effeminacy but were likely to find Capote—a fixture on talk shows and a charter member of the jet set—an establishment figure to be ignored, if not repudiated. Capote's televised gender nonconformity, frequent public intoxication, and expertise at vicious gossip were understood as an embodiment of the homophobic stereotypes gay liberationists struggled to defeat.[11]

Capote's work was as unpalatable as his person to many gay and lesbian activists and scholars, especially those of the Stonewall generation. His fiction's coupling of homosexuality with effeminacy and its preoccupation with the deep psychological trauma of internalized homophobia did not mesh happily with the needs of those men and women who were fighting to delist homosexuality from the American Psychiatric Association's manual of mental disorders. Furthermore, Capote's interest in the psyches of queer and homosexual children was difficult to parse at a time when gays and lesbians were struggling to prove that homosexuality was not a result of early trauma or a stage of arrested development, when gay children made no blink on the radar of the gay and lesbian movement, and when gays and lesbians were frequently correlated with pedophiles.

Claude Summers's *Gay Fictions: Wilde to Stonewall* offers an example of the poor fit between Capote and the ideology of gay and lesbian studies. Summers's dismissal of Capote is evident in the page count alone: Capote warrants fewer than four pages, compared to twenty-five for Tennessee Williams and twenty for Gore Vidal. Nonetheless, Summers grants Capote half a chapter title—"The Early Fiction of Truman Capote and Tennessee Williams"—presumably because the historical importance of Capote to twentieth-century gays and gay fictions demands it. This inconsistency of representation here is a measure of Summers's (and the field's) discomfort with Capote.[12]

For Summers, Capote is the inferior face of the inferior school of midcentury gay representation. Summers opposes Gore Vidal's *The City and the Pillar* and the work of southerners Capote and Tennessee Williams—an opposition that I make myself in chapter 1, to different ends. Vidal offers "a significant contribution to the literature of homosexuality," because *The City* shows that "homosexuality is a normal variation of human behavior" (128, 9). Conversely, Capote and Williams, under the influence of Carson McCullers, "reveled in the extraordinariness of their exotic—even freakish—characters" and present homosexuality "less as a social problem than as a manifestation of love's essential irrationality" (130). Capote is the worst of the three southern writers, because his art is inferior (a charge Summers pronounces but does not argue) and because his vision of homosexuality is objectionable. *Other Voices, Other Rooms* lacks the "philosophical seriousness and sure vision of McCullers's work" (131) and is "muddled and sensational [whereas] Williams' gay fictions are altogether more affirmative" (25). While Capote "reduces homosexuality to the status of an affliction and makes a causal connection between homosexuality and the death wish," Williams "documents the cruelty and oppression suffered by gay people in midcentury America" and makes "strong and healthy contributions to the literature of compassion" (133, 25, 133).[13]

Summers makes this last claim while discussing Williams's "Desire and the Black Masseur," within which a masseur beats his willing client and thereby prompts the client's first orgasm. The abuse escalates until the masseur kills the client and eats his corpse. I agree with Summers that the story is "an allegory of the effects of guilt and feelings of unworthiness," but I question why Summers finds this story more "affirming" than *Other Voices,* which does not draw nearly as close a correspondence between homosexuality, pain, and death (139). Summers's primary objection to *Other Voices* seems to be that the novel offers "homosexuality [as] a negation of masculinity, not simply because it involves effeminacy and transvestitism but also, and most importantly, because it signifies passive resignation and despair" (132). After all, in "Desire," the masochism of the client is balanced by the virility of the masseur. In other words, Summers's actual objection to *Other Voices* is that the novel is too weak, childish, and "girly"—a charge that accords with Capote's persona, which is considerably more womanish than Williams's. According to Summers's active, manly, and affirming rubric—common in gay studies—Capote fails.[14]

The later generation of scholars who work within the disciplinary confines of queer studies and who hold as an overriding principle the construction of all gender and sexuality has not found Capote much more appealing. Generally speaking, queer theorists have been invested in uncovering queer aspects of the "normal" and challenging set categories such as "gay," "lesbian," and "heterosexual." Even though Capote's public performance of effeminacy puts the categories of "male" and "female" under stress, he has not inspired much queer scholarship. This is most likely due to Capote's continued popularity as a gay writer and celebrity.

Capote was one of the most famous writers in the United States throughout his long career, and his public reputation has never been eclipsed. All of his work is currently in print—a remarkable statement. His unexpected death in 1984 was followed by a media blitz that refreshed its barrage with the posthumous publication of his incomplete opus *Answered Prayers* (1987) and the positive reception of his authorized biography (1988). Both were best sellers. The biographical play *Tru* won a Tony in 1989; a televised performance won an Emmy in 1992. George Plimpton's 1997 oral history placed Capote back on the bestseller list, and in the 2000s, Random House released a spate of Capote material: his collected short stories (2004), his collected letters (2004), his abandoned early novel *Summer Crossing* (2005), and his collected essays (2007), all of which prompted retrospectives of Capote's person and work in the arts press. The movies *Capote* (2005) and *Infamous* (2006) extended such attention outside the reading public.[15] Despite Capote's low status in queer studies and gay and lesbian studies, he never lost his place as an effeminate, outrageous, dissolute gay icon of a type that predated the Stonewall era. Because Capote has never been forgotten, he cannot provide the usual thrill of discovery and revival. And because Capote was and remains so publicly gay, he is no fun to "queer."[16]

This scholarly neglect is unfortunate, as Capote's persona and writing have obvious relevance for both the political objectives of gay and lesbian studies and queer theory's interest in the creation of identity. Capote's words and actions are best seen not as arising from a coherent, established political ideology (much less a manipulative realpolitik) but rather as some of the personal stirrings from which such ideologies develop. In a letter to his partner, Richard Hunter, written on June 8, 1946, Leo Lerman offers an example of such "stirrings" a few months before Capote met the Trillings on the train:

> The other night when I was talking about homosexuality, I said—why I do not now know—how it was a sickness; how anything which deviates from the norm or the average must be or make for sickness, for the norm and the average do not condone deviations and put all who deviate outside. This outsideness—for all one's arrogance—does provide some little distortion or some anguish or some pain. This pain, this incompatibility, is part of sickness. . . . When I said this, [Capote] was furious. He said that I had a distorted view of life, that everyone condoned homosexuality, that everyone knew about it and didn't even think about it. So I saw that this creature had a very immature and idealistic approach to life. . . . When I tried to tell him that if he got into a sex scandal no one save avant-garde publications would publish him, he said that I really had the most morbid approach to life, that he couldn't believe that *[Harper's] Bazaar* would not publish him. Do you think that this is how the younger people really all think?[17]

Capote's understanding of homosexuality and its consequences differentiates him not only from the Trillings but also from Lerman, who, though he explicitly repudiates the current understanding of homo-

sexuality as mental illness, nonetheless uses psychoanalytic terms—
"sickness," "deviation"—to describe the internalized effects of discrimination and oppression. Was Capote as naive as Lerman claims, or so
willful and aggressive that he enjoyed unusual freedom? Certainly the
careers of academics such as Newton Arvin, Capote's lover at the time
of Lerman's letter, were destroyed by scandal (1960), and the fear of such
scandal helped drive others, such as F. O. Matthiessen, to suicide (1950).
Creative writers benefited from the looser constraints of bohemia, but
both their careers and the freedom to write as they chose were frequently
stunted by the threat and practice of such scandal for much of the twentieth century. Yet Capote's career never suffered in any obvious way.
In chapter 1, I argue that, on the contrary, he *benefited* from his openly
homosexual public persona and the frequent appearance of homosexual
characters and themes in his work. Furthermore, there is no record of
any homophobic violence directed toward the adult Capote. At least in
his own case, he wins his argument with Lerman. This chapter judges
whether he also wins his fight with the Trillings.

"We Had a Very Pleasant Time"

The written records of the Capote–Trilling fracas have contradictory dates.
Diana Trilling writes in her memoir, *The Beginning of the Journey* (1993),
that she met Capote in 1943 or '44 (when he was eighteen or nineteen):
close to the publication of Lionel Trilling's *E. M. Forster* (1943) but before
Capote's first major publication, the short story "Miriam," in the June
1945 *Mademoiselle.* Plimpton, however, puts Trilling's oral history in
the 1947 section of his *Capote.* The year 1946 is most likely, as Capote
writes that he "ran up to Conn. with the Trillings last Saturday" in an
August 17, 1946, letter to Mary Louise "Pidgy" Aswell, fiction editor at
Harper's Bazaar. He also mentions the train ride in a letter to Lerman the
day before, and both letters specify that this was his first meeting with
the Trillings, which accords with Barry Werth's claim that Capote es-
corted Newton Arvin to a meal with the Trillings in 1947. Diana Trilling
also seems mistaken in the Plimpton account when she claims that she
"knew [Capote's] name, of course, because I had written something
about him by this time"; I have found no reference by her to Capote before her review of *Other Voices* in the January 31, 1948, *Nation.* These
dates are important because the chronological placement of this meeting
in the trajectory of Capote's career makes the Trillings either more or

less important to him in general, and because Diana Trilling's coming or already-written review of *Other Voices* would be influential, and it would either be affected by the Trillings' encounter with Capote or itself affect Capote's reaction to the couple.[18]

In whichever year the New Haven Railroad stuttered from Grand Central Station up through Connecticut, Capote's speech and behavior constructed identity; he not only visually and audibly exhibited homosexuality but also claimed the necessary relevance of sexual orientation to the self and its products. For Capote, the elision of Forster's homosexuality was "impossible"—Forster's art could not be discussed outside the context of his sexuality. Capote interrogated Lionel Trilling on three valences of knowledge: Did he know? Had he heard? Did he guess? Certainly other critics had implied Forster's sexuality by 1946. In Diana Trilling's narrative in the Plimpton interviews, Capote correctly states that Forster "had left a homosexual novel in the British Museum, and that at his death it would be found"; this was *Maurice,* published in 1971, after Forster's death. To which "Lionel said this would be interesting but he wasn't particularly concerned about it for his book, and that was it." The conversation was over—and a silence ensued that was representative of the midcentury humanist stance toward homosexuality and gender issues.[19]

In Diana Trilling's memoir, the anecdote is much shorter and the conflict boils down: "Why, [Capote] demanded, had Lionel, in writing about Forster, not dealt with Forster's homosexuality? Lionel explained that he had not known of Forster's homosexuality when he wrote the book; the possibility had occurred to him only when he was reaching the end." Here, Diana Trilling collapses and simplifies Lionel's refusal to acknowledge Forster's orientation until browbeaten by Capote, as well as Lionel's insistence that he didn't treat Forster's sexuality in his study because he did not think it was relevant, into Lionel's belated realization. By contrast, in the face of willful disinterest from powerful authority figures, the Capote of the oral history insists that Forster's sexuality not only has marked his text but also is relevant to his literary production. Capote's comments are courageous because of his relative position of power to the Trillings within the academic and literary worlds, and because of his refutation of contemporary standards of literary criticism. Moreover, Capote demands recognition and respect for a minority not then commonly conceptualized as such, much less one deserving civil rights, or even serious attention. Such aggressive intervention was risky, for at this historical moment his demand for the discussion of Forster's sexuality was tantamount to revealing his own orientation to the Trillings and to any eavesdropper. Diana Trilling displaces this revelation onto the physical and physiological, onto the odd looks and "extraordinary squeaky voice" that, for her, reduces and dehumanizes Capote to a "little creature." Trilling thus shows her understanding of Capote's indirect (however recognizable) signification of his homosexuality. Capote's behavior is remarkable because he asserts his gay identity not only tacitly but also through the direct, public mention of homosexuality and its importance to literary analysis.[20]

Capote presumably knew the dangers of his assertion—dangers that Diana Trilling projects into her fear of a mob lynching, a fear that masks the professional risk Capote took of a literary lynching by the Trillings. Yet although Capote's direct naming of homosexuality is an aggressive assertion of homosexuality, it is still an identitarian performance rather than a direct statement of identity. Capote does not directly say that his own homosexuality causes him to find Lionel Trilling's silence "impossible," and here the difference between the connotation and the denotation of homosexuality is large. Or is it? Capote's self-consciousness about how he is perceived becomes relevant here. Perhaps Capote assumes that his look and manner offer sufficient public announcement that he is gay, as they did for Diana Trilling. If so, Lerman's letter to Richard Hunter offers evidence that Capote would assume that the passengers "condoned homosexuality, that everyone knew about it and didn't even think about it." Certainly Capote's letter to Pidgy Aswell lacks an overt politics: "I ran up to Conn. with the Trillings last Saturday (how this came about is very amusing; Leo [Lerman] had shown me some photographs of them, and while I was buying my train ticket who should be standing in line behind me but etc. . . . [S]o I introduced myself, wasn't that bold? and we had a very pleasant time) and liked them ever so much." Capote is less sunny in the previous day's letter to Lerman: "I introduced myself, and I am glad I did, for [the Trillings] were very sweet, and we had a pleasant ride on the train together. I liked them enormously—but, because of various things, I'm afraid I was in rather a jittery state, and made a bad impression." Contrast this fear of a bad impression with Diana Trilling's fear of a lynching, or her more modest claim in her memoir that "the mere sound of Capote's voice roused the passengers in our railroad car and as he went on to speak of Forster's homosexuality, one could feel the air thickening with hostility." As she tells and writes it, the Trillings' encounter with Capote stretches from the tense to the terrible. If this were the case, Capote would have shared his concern with Lerman and Aswell, with whom he often shared career troubles and personal disasters.[21]

Did Capote's "amusing time" with the Trillings indeed make the other passengers "uncomfortable, angry at him, very angry"? Perhaps when Diana Trilling writes that "Truman wasn't watching or if he was he didn't let on," she is accurate; perhaps he did not find the conversation extraordinary. But for the Trillings, Capote's very existence as an assured gay man was violent, and his casual conversation was aggression of an extreme and unusual kind. He asserted a formulation of homosexuality that they could not incorporate into their liberal imaginations—demonstrating precisely the failure of the liberal imagination that Lionel Trilling exposes in *E. M. Forster*.[22]

The Limits of the Liberal Imagination

Lionel Trilling's baldly stated lack of concern for and interest in Forster's homosexuality is of a piece with Wimsatt and Beardsley's manifestos against the intentional and affective fallacies, which delineated the New Critics' demand that criticism be restricted to the text. Such demands were shaped by the value of impersonality in art found in T. S. Eliot's "Tradition and the Individual Talent" and "Hamlet and His Problems," which hold that artistic success depends not on self-examination but on the ability to produce a concrete expression of emotion. As the text itself contains what is needed for its interpretation, Wimsatt and Beardsley find an author's intent and a reader's subjective experience immaterial to literary criticism.[23]

The Trillings were not New Critics but shared their tone of high seriousness and practice of rigorous close reading, and they were very much part of the paradigm shift that led to Wimsatt and Beardsley's manifestos. The New York Intellectuals wanted to democratize literary criticism, and shunning the intentional and affective fallacies released the critic from the need to be justified by ethnic, religious, or racial background. This move accorded with the New York Intellectuals' past as collegiate Trotskyites who believed in an international proletariat and the brotherhood of humanity. This move also had the additional benefit of helping Lionel Trilling and others win tenure at schools that previously had rarely, if ever, granted it to Jews. Although the political engagement that the New York Intellectuals inherited from the Old Left led them to historicize texts for political purposes, such historicization skirted personal biography in general and sexual orientation in particular, and on the New Haven Railroad of 1946, Trilling's dismissal of Forster's homosexuality would seem to need no defense against a young, effeminate stranger. Yet Trilling's dismissal is difficult to defend in the context of *Maurice* and in relation to his own attack upon the limits of the liberal imagination.

Consider how Trilling drops Capote's proffer of *Maurice*. By 1946, Forster had published five novels: *Where Angels Fear to Tread* (1905), *The Longest Journey* (1907), *A Room with a View* (1908), *Howards End* (1910), and *A Passage to India* (1924). Another novel would have been relevant to Trilling, whose *E. M. Forster* was composed of an introduction, a chapter on Forster's intellectual and artistic development, a chapter on the short stories, and a chapter on each novel. Trilling might choose not to write about an unpublished novel (or to discuss the matter with Capote), but it is unlikely that it did not "concern [him] very much." Yet neither Diana nor Lionel Trilling acknowledged, much less commented upon, *Maurice,* either within the longer anecdote or in its frame. Instead, *Maurice* closed the conversation—and disappeared entirely from the memoir's shorter version.[24]

Lionel Trilling's second edition of *E. M. Forster* and its preface (1964) continue to avoid *Maurice* and Forster's sexuality; Trilling writes that he has become friends with Forster but feels that "the reader, and Mr. Forster's art, and criticism itself, are best served by early and impersonal opinions." Trilling's book was reissued in 1971, two years after the Stonewall Riots, probably in the hope of catching some sales following the 1971 publication of *Maurice*. Hence, 1971 was a big year for Forster in both mass and literary culture—but Trilling, though he was still writing, did not comment on the author's and the novel's homosexual focus either in a new introduction or anywhere else. As Diana Trilling writes, "That was it." The novel, like Capote's comments, cannot be incorporated into either Trilling's liberal imagination.[25]

Lionel Trilling introduces his collected essays, *The Liberal Imagination,* by noting his "abiding interest in the ideas of what we loosely call liberalism, especially in the relation of those ideas to literature." He notes that "the conscious and the unconscious life of liberalism are not always in accord" and demands the recollection of liberalism's "first essential imagination of variousness and possibility, which implies the awareness of complexity and difficulty." In *E. M. Forster,* Trilling offers a path to such recollection: a sense of "moral realism, which is not the awareness of morality itself but of the contradictions, paradoxes and dangers of living the moral life."[26] Through Forster, Trilling diagnoses the liberal unconscious:

> [A]ll [Forster's] novels are politically and morally tendentious and always in the liberal direction. Yet he is deeply at odds with the liberal mind, and while liberal readers can go a long way with Forster, they can seldom go all the way. They can understand him when he attacks the manners and morals of the British middle class, when he speaks out for spontaneity of feeling, for the virtues of sexual fulfillment, for the values of intelligence. . . . But sooner or later they begin to make reservations. . . . [T]hey feel that he is challenging *them* as well as what they dislike. And they are right. For all his long commitment to the doctrines of liberalism, Forster is at war with the liberal imagination.
>
> Surely if liberalism has a single desperate weakness, it is an inadequacy of imagination: liberalism is always being surprised.[27]

The Trillings are certainly surprised by Capote, who hangs Lionel by his own critique. Diana tells us that Lionel's comprehension of Forster "began to dawn on" him, had "occurred to" him, as he wrote his critical study. How? Why? If Lionel Trilling restricted himself to a close reading, then homosexual erotics and thematics must be embedded within the text itself for such a dawn to rise. Furthermore, Forster's treatment of homosexuality in *Maurice,* and his refusal to publish, would seem relevant to "the contradictions, paradoxes and dangers of living the moral life." Moreover, Forster's homosexuality would seem to have aided him in achieving the critical perspective on liberalism that Trilling admires— and Trilling admits that "[b]iography intrudes itself into literary judgment and keeps it from being 'pure.' . . . [A]lthough we call extraneous the facts that thrust themselves upon us, they inevitably enter into our judgment." Trilling mentions this in the context of gaps in Forster's novel writing; that these gaps were filled in part by writing *Maurice* as well as the homoerotic stories posthumously published in *The Life to Come* goes unmentioned.[28]

Maurice aside, homosexual erotics and themes are easily extracted from Forster's work. Trilling, a keen reader of class, proves blind to them— or chooses to overlook them. Consider the most conventional of the novels, *A Room with a View,* within which Lucy and George, a man and woman (unlike *Maurice*) of the same race and ethnicity (unlike *Where*

Angels Fear to Tread and *A Passage to India*) and the same class (unlike all the other novels), remain within accepted gender roles and bounds (unlike all the others) as they overcome a variety of obstacles on their way to a happy and presumably fruitful heterosexual marriage (unlike all but *Howards End*). On a country outing, Lucy Honeychurch finds herself in a field of flowers:

> From her feet the ground sloped sharply into view, and violets ran in rivulets and streams and cataracts, irrigating the hillside with blue, eddying around the tree stems, collecting into pools in the hollows, covering the grass with spots of azure foam. . . . For a moment [George] contemplated her, as one who had fallen out of heaven. He saw radiant joy in her face, he saw the flowers beat against her dress in blue waves. The bushes above them closed. He stepped quickly forward and kissed her.[29]

Charlotte Bartlett, Lucy's maiden aunt, removes Lucy not only from the kiss but also from Florence and into the arms of Cecil Vyse. Cecil and Lucy share the next kiss, which does not parallel the first: "She gave such a business-like lift to her veil. As he approached her he found time to wish that he could recoil. As he touched her, his gold pince-nez became dislodged and was flattened between them." The actual parallel to the "pools of violets" comes when George, Lucy's brother, and the parson bathe in a pool, the Sacred Grove. This is the only scene within which Englishmen exhibit physicality, much less naked abandon; as Eric Haralson writes, "[M]asculine bodies and desires notably romp."[30] Plotwise, there is little reason for this romp's length and breadth. Though the scene does eventually offer a naked George up to Lucy, the action is mano a mano a mano, with greens on the side:

> [I]t reminded one of swimming in a salad. Three gentlemen rotated in the pool breast high, after the fashion of the nymphs in Götterdammerung. . . . Then all the forces of youth burst out. [George] smiled, flung himself at them, splashed them, ducked them, kicked them, muddied them, and drove them out of the pool. . . . They ran to get dry, they bathed to get cool, they played at being Indians in the willow-herbs, they bathed to get clean. . . . [T]he two young men were delirious. Away they twinkled into the trees, Freddy with a clerical waistcoat under his arm, George with a wide-awake hat on his dripping hair.[31]

The scene is remarkable in the context of the otherwise proper action of the novel—and the parallel of the vegetation and the water imagery is unmistakable. The pool of violets has become the Sacred Grove.

Trilling's knowledge of the unpublished *Maurice* shows how easily he might recognize such displacement, and Leslie Fiedler's groundbreaking 1948 analysis of homoerotics in "Come Back to the Raft Ag'in, Huck Honey!"—in the *Partisan Review,* no less—shows that homosexual readings were being made and published.[32] Yet Trilling demonstrates little attention to Forster's detailed sensuality. Trilling does not note the water imagery of the first kiss, and ignores the Sacred Grove except to say that "George has been swimming with Freddy and Mr. Beebe in the pool, and the pool in the sun and wind 'had been a call to the blood and the relaxed will' and had dispelled his bleak neurotic despair." From a critic aware of Forster's sexuality, a critic who holds that, in *Room with a View,* "as always in Forster, sexuality and right political feeling have a point of contact," a critic who, summarizing the main theme of *Room,* quotes Forster in that "Love is of the body—not the body, but of the body"—such poor reading is remarkable.[33]

Nonetheless, Lionel Trilling was invaluable to the investiture of Forster's reputation and brought his work to a larger public, among them lesbians and gays. Furthermore, Trilling's study defends Forster against previous homophobic reviewers, such as F. R. Leavis, who tagged the author as "bent" and "spinsterly." Such mixed messages let us parallel Trilling to Lucy's Aunt Charlotte. When Lucy at last achieves her happy ending, she realizes that her aunt, at first an obstacle to the marriage, engineered a later meeting that confirmed it. Trilling writes: "For when the heroine at last fulfills her destiny, deserts Miss Bartlett and marries the man she has unconsciously loved . . . she comes to perceive that in some yet more hidden way Miss Bartlett had really desired the union." Yet, like Charlotte, Trilling performs the role of matchmaker at considerable cost. Even as Trilling raised Forster's critical profile, he did substantive damage to Forster's capacity, at least as transmitted by literary critics, to communicate specifics of a homosexual politics and subjectivity. Robert K. Martin and George Piggford hold that Trilling's work, in its refusal to comment directly on homosexuality and its consistent abstraction of a broad liberal utopianism, is "responsible for a number of well-meaning generalizations that dangerously obscure the very precision of Forster's observations and the sophisticated political analysis that underlies them and that totally efface any nuanced treatment of sexuality." The path to Forster for an individual gay or lesbian reader was occluded.[34]

Nonetheless, for those gay men and women who were primed by their own mental deftness and revolutionary consciousness (and, in Capote's case, an intimate relationship with literary critic Newton Arvin), Trilling's critique could easily be extended to liberatory ends. Capote and Trilling, and Lucy and Charlotte, are liberal humanists, though Trilling and Charlotte are unwilling to directly argue on behalf of sexuality; note how Trilling leaves the body out of his critique of a limited liberalism that "drifts towards a denial of the emotions and the imagination." It is not his critical strategy and ethics but his homophobia—either his own or his fear of his readers'—that leaves him silent in his study and on the train. It is this reticence where there could so easily be speech that fascinates Capote. This complex silence contrasts with the relative volubility of Elizabeth Hardwick and Diana Trilling, whose response to Capote is shaped by the construction of the "feminine" within the midcentury intelligentsia.[35]

A Dainty Blow

Capote's first novel, *Other Voices, Other Rooms,* was a succès de scandale, in no small part because of Capote's author photo, as is discussed in chapter 1. Most reviews of *Other Voices* reference the photo as much as the text; the reviews of the text itself are positive, with significant reservations. By contrast, *Partisan Review,* the mouthpiece of the New York Intellectuals, trashes *Other Voices* in a March 15, 1948, review by novelist and critic Elizabeth Hardwick. Hardwick was a frequent contributor to the *Partisan Review* and helped found its intellectual heir, the *New York Review of Books.* To a large extent, Hardwick's clouded recognition of the novel's homosexuality *is* her critical apparatus, though she mentions it by name only in her opening statement, when she claims that *Other Voices* "rings a tinkling funeral bell for some of our recent Southern fiction. Here at last is the parody whose appearance was inevitable; amidst sherry and gloom, withering homosexuals, and dainty sadistic young women, many of the devices that have served young Southern writers well have been literally done to death." Where Lionel Trilling is silent, Hardwick is abusive. Furthermore, her reduction of sexuality to a device, a fictional trope, is profoundly antihumanist and moves past the New Critics toward a radical formalism.[36] Hardwick's other writing reveals her to be a humanist in relation to heterosexuality—which leaves homophobia, rather than metaphysics, as the fundament of her argument. Note how Hardwick reduces homosexuality to an example of local color parallel to "dainty sadistic young women," and how these women are given terminal and therefore dominant status among the novel's characteristics but do not actually appear in *Other Voices*. Miss Amy and Florabel might be called "dainty," but neither is sadistic, and one is middle-aged and the other preadolescent. If *dainty* is stretched to mean "small," the dwarf Miss Wisteria qualifies, but she too is not sadistic. Instead, the dainty sadist is Hardwick, whose style is executed with satire and cruelty, and armored by the delicate deployment of vocabulary and tone.

Hardwick's "dainty" yet canny blow forecloses charges of willful ignorance and censorship. She signals sophistication; she is not averse to discussing homosexuality in the novel but considers it only as important as sherry. Yet consider her own use of the phrase "rings a tinkling funeral bell," with its arch construction and indirect reference to fairies, in its self-consciousness closer to the writing of Ronald Firbank than Capote. If homosexuality is so unworthy of consideration, why does Hardwick use camp for homophobic ends? She indicates enough familiarity and ease with homosexual dialect to discredit it—a doubly reversed discourse that perverts Firbank. Hardwick's slight mention of homosexuality and use of camp dialect is just that: a slight, as serious consideration would require a politics that allowed for the apprehension of homosexuality as a serious subject.

Such consideration did not come quickly for Hardwick. Fifteen years later, while reviewing Christopher Isherwood's *A Single Man* for the *New York Review of Books,* she wrote, "[The hero] has a fairly modest anal disposition, respectable enough, with a finicky, faggoty interest in the looks of things," thus displaying not only the particulars of her homophobia but also her inability to consider homosexuality as an important yet not determining factor within a subject: an explicit focus of Isherwood's novel, recognized as such by many critics of the time. Hardwick's exploration of homosexuality continues in her own best-regarded novel, *Sleepless Nights,* which sports a gay character whose "anal disposition" is more pronounced: his "unyielding need to brush his perfect teeth after dinner . . . did much to inhibit his sex life." The novel's lesbian fares worse: "[G]rinding away in rage for her Ph.D., she became or decided she was a lesbian. In a frightened, angry plunge, she fell into a desperate affair with a handsome older woman from England. And what did she find there? Happiness, consolation? No, she found, with her ineluctable ill-luck, a nightmare of betrayals, lies, deceits, shocks, infidelities, dismissals." This is the sole example of female same-sex desire that I have found in Hardwick's corpus, of which Joan Didion has noted that "the mysterious and somnambulistic 'difference' of being a woman has been, over 35 years, Elizabeth Hardwick's great subject, the topic to which she has returned incessantly." Such mysteries do not include sexual orientation, as female same-sex desire in Hardwick's world is a product of rage and productive of nightmares. Hardwick offers a case study of a writer who defines herself as a social liberal but whose past degradation of homosexuality is neither addressed nor rethought in print.[37]

Although I do not pretend to understand fully Hardwick's distaste for homosexuality in general and *Other Voices* in particular, I believe that it stems in part from the gendered mechanisms responsible for the publication and reproduction of Capote's fiction. For from the broad generic sward upon which Capote pitches his specific fictional tent, to his places of publication, to the superstructure of the career that supports this publication, Capote almost invariably lands on the feminine side of a gendered binary. Until *In Cold Blood*, Capote's career, as well as his persona and art, was almost entirely effeminate—and thus, in the cultural context of the late 1940s, supremely queer. When it comes to self-promotion, Capote was a career girl nonpareil.

Girls' School

In 1955, Leslie Fiedler identified two schools of fiction:

> one associated with *Harper's Bazaar,* the other with *Partisan Review.*
> I pick *Harper's Bazaar* to stand for a whole group which includes
> *Mademoiselle* and *Vogue.* . . . *Harper's Bazaar* is, of course, not pri-
> marily a literary magazine at all, but an elegant fashion magazine for
> women, read not only by those who can afford the goods it advertises
> but by many who cannot and who participate in its world of values,
> picking it up on the table of a beauty-parlor waiting room. Finding
> a story by, say, Truman Capote tucked away between the picture of
> a determinedly unbeautiful model and an ad for a brassiere, most of
> the readers of *Harper's Bazaar,* one assumes, must simply skip the
> meaningless pages; and knowing this, the editors know that they can
> print anything they please.

Fiedler's binary is strengthened by his clever use of *Harper's Bazaar*—a distaff spin-off of the securely "male" *Harper's*—as the standard-bearer of feminine discourse.[38]

Fiedler's protean sensibility and deadpan satire make him hard to parse. His view of the material considerations of publishing in mid-century women's magazines is accurate in denotation if not connotation: the material experience of reading Capote's stories as first published was marked by women's advertising. Nonetheless, Fiedler's use of Capote as an emblematic author of a degraded "female" fiction, in essence filler be-tween ads, reveals Capote's power and effeminacy in literary culture, and how this culture was gendered and valued by an influential critic who placed himself on the *Partisan* side of the line. Thus, Capote confided his encounter with the Trillings to Leo Lerman and Pidgy Aswell, whose association with *Harper's Bazaar* secured them on the "female" side of Fiedler's bifurcated literary world.[39]

Fiedler makes "art" the province of *Partisan* writers, positions their writing as masculine, and gives it value. As Diana Trilling sniffed, "There was nothing light-mindedly fashionable about reading the *Nation*. It was an obligation of intelligence." Fiedler parallels Capote with rich women whose glamour seduces the poor to share in capitalist ideology through vicarious commodity fetishism. He dismisses and dirties both, fulfilling the demand of masculine hegemony that other holders of power (here, women with money and men who do not toe the sexual line) be put down. Fiedler, a Jewish egghead with a groundbreaking study of homo-erotics to his androgynous name, bolsters his masculine bona fides by showing how rich women and homosexual men are not interested in art but decoration, thereby fortifying the palace of art against the feminine intruder—or, more precisely, making these "feminine" contributions superficial, additions to interior decoration instead of structural sound-ness. Any evidence of intellectual sophistication in *Harper's Bazaar,* whether it be a "determinedly unbeautiful model" or Capote's fiction, is either a complicated form of advertising or "meaningless." Those who are not (straight) men do not read or compose art, but instead participate in

> a new sort of sensibility, defined by a taste for haute couture, classical ballet, baroque opera, the rites and vestments of Catholicism—and above all for a type of literature at once elegantly delicate and bit-terly grotesque. This new kind of sensibility, although (or perhaps because) it is quite frankly a homosexual one, appeals profoundly to

certain rich American women with cultural aspirations, and is therefore sponsored in their salons and published decoratively in magazines that cater to their tastes.

The direct mention of male homosexuality crowns a litany of disgust and
damns an entire aesthetic with the red robes of Baron Corvo. Against such
fiction, Fiedler positions *Partisan Review* writers such as Saul Bellow who
are "'political' in the European sense of the word. . . . Not only do they
have Marx in their blood . . . but also Freud . . . as well as contemporary
sociology, anthropology, and philosophy in general." In other words, these
are serious, important (straight) men who write about serious, important
things: (straight) men's things.[40]

Fiedler takes a middle position between Lionel Trilling and Elizabeth
Hardwick; he neither consigns homosexuality to silence nor dismisses
it with clever abuse but rather offers a considered (if homophobic) opinion. Furthermore, he complicates his binary: *Partisan Review* has published "wickedly witty" Mary McCarthy, and Tennessee Williams and
Paul Bowles, who retain a "sensibility, shriller or icier, but not fundamen-
tally different from that which informs the fiction of the ladies' magazines." But in general, Fiedler's lines of gender, sexuality, and value draw
Hardwick and Diana Trilling into a cross-gendered position—and reveal
the stakes in their response to homosexuality (as linked to effeminacy) in
general and to Capote in particular.[41] The pressure upon these women to
distance themselves from and degrade Capote must have been considerable. Consider Fiedler's perception of Capote as a girlish Satan, "almost a
caricature of the type: the 'queen' as American author, possessing a kind
of beauty, both in person and as an artist, which belongs to childhood
and early adolescence, and which withers before it can ripen." Hardwick
and her intellectual sisters exhibit the tendency of the subordinated to
raise their own standing by attacking each other instead of making common cause to change the parameters of dominance.[42]

Yet without Diana Trilling's close attention, the record would be bare.
We see Capote–versus–Lionel Trilling primarily through her eyes, and
though we may seek to correct her astigmatism, only her memory, relation, and understanding keep us from near-complete conjecture. Diana
Trilling speaks only in her narrative frame, not on the train, where she
acts the demure "little woman." It is likely that her own subject position
and self-representation gave her common (if subterranean) cause with
Capote at a time when homosexuality was very closely associated with

femininity. This would explain her fascination with Capote's attempt to discuss the unmentionable—and with her husband's silence at Capote's charge that he had insufficiently attended to sexuality, then inseparably intermingled with gender. By this train of argument, Capote says what Diana Trilling can neither say nor consciously desire saying. Thus her fascination and reportage.

A Double Response

Diana Trilling acknowledges ambivalence as she begins her review of *Other Voices* in *The Nation*: "It is seldom that I have so double a response to a book. . . . [N]ot since the early work of Eudora Welty has there been an example of such striking literary virtuosity. . . . On the other hand, I find myself deeply antipathetic to the whole artistic-moral purpose of Mr. Capote's novel. In Mr. Capote's case, as with so many of our gifted contemporary artists, I would freely trade eighty percent of his technical skill for twenty percent more value in the uses to which it is put" (230). We see here an aesthetic that requires art to have moral purpose and value.[43]

Trilling's politics, though complex and bivalent, were consistent and overt throughout her reviewing career (1942–49). Her collected reviews emphasize that fiction both represents and acts upon culture—"literature is no mere decoration of life but an index of the health or sickness of society" (208)—and that this index, as it catalogs, must have social utility: "Probably there has never been a time when so many people wrote so 'well' as now but to such meager purpose" (224). Yet Trilling rejects unrefined recipes for social change. She dislikes "the use of the novel as a crude vehicle for argument or as an educational display-piece" (199), decries "the chief trend in our progressive literary culture . . . this mechanical notion that the individual finds himself by losing himself in some larger social manifestation" (183 [ellipses mine]), and observes that "a large part of the anemia of our current fiction must surely be due to the soft political idealism which is its major inspiration" (133). What does she prefer? "[A]n analysis of political forces without political analyses" (104). This parallels Lionel Trilling's belief that crude systemization inevitably leads to unfortunate simplification.[44]

Diana Trilling's consistent demand—stronger than her husband's—that literature have and inspire humanist values and therefore actively promote political good ties her to existential humanism and distinguishes her from other New York Intellectuals, "cultural radicals" who never found an ideology to replace the certainty of the Old Left's faith in Marxism and held what Irving Howe calls "a radicalism without immediate political ends but pointed towards criticism of a meretricious culture." Diana shares their aggression but, instead of arguing her position, simply pronounces each week in "Fiction in Review." Lionel, by contrast, argues at length—but without Diana's certain tone, perhaps because his view of his work's importance and attendant responsibility is stronger. Diana Trilling's marks of subordination—her gender, her status as the wife of a more respected critic, and her job as a writer of book reviews whose length does not allow sustained analysis—thus harden into a defensive shield. Why attack Diana and her witty reviews when one may go after Lionel at length? She therefore gained authority and influence from her column without much dissent.[45]

Diana Trilling details her internal and external challenges as a woman writer in her autobiography, where she writes that she was offered a named column after writing a few unsigned reviews at *The Nation*: "Now that I was to sign what I wrote, the question arose of what name I should choose, my maiden name or my name as Lionel's wife. Socially I was always known by my married name. We consulted our friends at *Partisan Review*. They were united in the advice that I write under my maiden name; they feared that I was going to be an embarrassment to Lionel. But Lionel was adamant that I write as his wife." The *Partisan* friends corroborate Diana Trilling's own internalization of the lesser value of women's writing—a judgment Trilling often extends in her own reviews of women writers. Trilling's self-subordination extends even to her autobiography's title—*The Beginning of the Journey*, which alludes to her husband's novel *The Middle of the Journey*—and its subtitle, *The Marriage of Lionel and Diana Trilling*. She reflects: "The question most often asked of me by interviewers is: How did it feel to be Lionel's wife? How, they mean, did it feel to be a critic in my own right but married to a better and more famous critic than I? My honest if unfashionable answer is that it felt fine. . . . I never had any doubt in my mind but that, of the two of us, he was the more important writer." Diana Trilling's investment in this judgment ensures that she would be threatened and repulsed (if also fascinated) by the homosexuality that was understood as a perversion of gender norms and development not only in the mass media of the 1940s but also in the midcentury psychoanalytic establishment that corroborated this narrow view of gender and sexuality. Such revulsion was heightened by Capote's aggressive and successful presentation of an effeminate, hypersexualized public persona and the extraordinary success of *Other Voices,* a novel that was written in a feminine idiom and overtly references homosexuality.[46]

Nonetheless, Trilling is more tolerant than many of her peers. She does not exhibit a problem with homosexuality and gay and lesbian authors as such, and Isherwood's *Prater Violet* receives her best review of the decade; it is "the most completely realized new novel I have read in a long time but it is also a charming novel which yet reverberates with important meaning." *Prater Violet* fulfills her requirement that this meaning not be simplistic; the novel "is a book without a political moral yet a profound moral-political statement. It is gay, witty, and sophisticated but it is wholly responsible." Trilling affords her praise in part because "it is a book written in the author's own person but is without ego" (137); the queerness of the narrating "Christopher" is incidental to a novel that focuses on a leftist Jewish German refugee who fulfills Trilling's definition of a proper hero much better than the narrator—or Joel Knox.[47]

Trilling's review of *Other Voices,* and her struggle with her homophobic subject position and with the public silence that swathed homosexuality in the late 1940s, underscores the political importance of Capote's words on the train. Compelled by her politics to support humanist values and reject any blanket ideology, Trilling achieves greater depth in discussing homosexuality in Capote's work than any other contemporary critic—but her inability to recognize homosexual identity as a positive achievement manipulates this great humanist into the crudest type of demonization. For as Capote is Satan to Leslie Fiedler, so Joel Knox, to Diana Trilling, is Hitler. She interprets the novel's thesis thus:

> Despite its fantastic paraphernalia, *Other Voices, Other Rooms* does manage to convey a serious content. At the end of the book young Joel turns to the homosexual love offered him by Randolph and we realize that in his slow piling up of nightmare denial, Mr. Capote has been attempting to re-create the mental background to sexual inversion. What his book is saying is that a boy becomes a homosexual when the circumstances of his life deny him other more normal gratifications of his need for affection. (231)

There could be no clearer statement of the midcentury view of homosexuality as an unfortunate detour of psychological development. Instead of seeing Joel's nightmarish experiences as products of both external and internalized homophobia, she sees them as *productive of* homosexuality.

After adopting her husband's strategy of silence and disinterest—"Well, I am not equipped to argue whether or not this is a sound explanation of the source of homosexuality. Nor does the question interest me here"— Trilling repeats the transference we saw on the train, when she projected her own anger and fear onto the unlikely supposition that there would be a lynching (231–32). Note her rhetoric and the extent of her displacement as she states that the cause of homosexuality is immaterial to the propriety of prejudice against homosexuals:

> Much more arresting is the implication of Mr. Capote's book that, having been given an explanation of the *cause* of Joel's homosexuality, we have been given all the ground we need for a proper attitude *toward* it and toward Joel as a member of society. For what other meaning can we possibly draw from this portrait of a passive victim of his early circumstances than that we must always think of him in this light, that even when Joel will be thirty or forty we will still have to judge him only as the passive victim of his early circumstances. But in exactly the same sense in which Joel is formed by the accident of his youthful experience, we have all of us, heterosexuals no less than homosexuals, been formed by our early experience. Is no member of society, then, to be held accountable for himself, not even a Hitler? (232 [italics Trilling's])

How does Trilling get from the Joel at the book's close to Joel at thirty or forty? Via his author, famously in his early twenties. Trilling abandons the New Critics' script, holds Capote accountable for writing *Other Voices,* and gives notice that neither now nor in the future should he expect to be forgiven for being gay because he has written about his childhood. The grown-up Joel, by virtue of his homosexuality, is analogous to the Hitler who, for Diana Trilling, a politically active antifascist Jew, is the nadir.

After pronouncing homosexuality's cause and treatment, Trilling draws an existentialist moral and rails against "an adult world of passive acceptance in which we are rendered incapable of thinking anybody responsible for anything." Here Trilling clarifies that homosexuality *is* a choice, and a bad one. Her reading of *Other Voices* as an origin tale of homosexuality allows her to criticize the novel's "blanket indorsement of the deterministic principle. . . . With startling regularity our most talented young novelists present us with child heroes who are never permitted to grow up into an adulthood which will submit them to the test of *conduct*" (232 [ellipses mine, italics Trilling's]). The Test of Conduct: Capote should put his characters into a position where they may actively *choose* heterosexuality and be praised or condemned for their success or failure.

Still, Diana Trilling is alone among contemporary reviewers in, however distantly, approaching the incestuous abuse that undergirds *Other Voices*. It is possible that Trilling, in her condemnation of thirty- or forty-year-old Joel/Capote, actually addresses Cousin Randolph, who forces his ward, young Joel, himself in search of a father, to act as Randolph's "old man." Rather than continue along these or any other lines, Trilling retreats by granting that "the problem" is "complex" and that she does not "mean to close out all social or personal causality"; she asks only "for some degree of mediation between the extremes of causality and freedom" (232). But what *is* her suggestion for Joel? How *should* he resist the "slow piling up of nightmare detail" (231) and happily embrace genital heterosexuality? Trilling's critical conscientiousness, coupled with the impossibility of a happy heterosexual embrace by Capote's proto-gay and -lesbian characters, frustrates her into invoking Hitler.

If, as Lionel Trilling writes, "the conscious and unconscious life of liberalism are not always in accord," then Diana Trilling at least recognizes "mixed feelings" in her anecdote, a "double . . . response" in her review, instead of merely acting out as Hardwick does. Yet though Trilling tries to understand her reaction, she does so by looking at the person who caused it, rather than at herself or her society. I read Trilling's reaction as follows: "This book, like its author, fascinates yet disgusts me." But instead of then asking "Why am I disgusted?," she asks, "What did the book, and its author, *do* to disgust me?" Her inability to ask the first question not only limits her criticism but may also fragment her memory of the New Haven Railroad, as seen in the temporal confusions discussed at this chapter's start.[48]

Diana Trilling closes her review by solving the dilemma of how to both retain her humanist values and condemn homosexuality: "[W]ere we to ask of fiction, as we once did, that it base its claim to accomplishment on its moral stature, most of the writing we celebrate today would fall into its proper place as no more than a feat of literary athletics" (233). The provocations of *Other Voices* have been properly placed as senseless grandstanding and thus dismissed. Diana Trilling's anecdote and review, combined with her husband's refusal to treat Forster's homosexuality, exemplify how homosexuality was discounted within progressive movements at midcentury; and Capote's actions on the train suggest how asserting gay and lesbian identity might offer redress.

Capote's relations with literary culture forecast a change in the relation among literary culture, homophobia, and homosexuality that eventually contributed to the ascendance of the identitarian critical politics that have dominated literary criticism for the past two decades. In this respect, Capote wins his argument with the Trillings. By reading the various representations of this meeting and its three characters through different scrims of reportage, we are able to observe the postures, attitudes, and psychologies with which our three characters wage war over the terrain of literature and literary worth in the borderlands where sexuality, humanism, and self-representation abut; and to watch as the battle threatens the assumptions on which liberal humanists and their supporters have based their moral worth. We see how major players in the New York intelligentsia that arbitrated literary worth (who makes it and who does not) and "appropriate" criticism (what "counts" and what goes unsaid) are unsettled in their status quo when a volatile iconoclast like Capote refuses certain silences and strategically performs his queer persona in order, if not to crash the train of literary culture, at least to ride its iron horse. Such showmanship served not only as a support for Capote's career but also as one of the many acts of self-affirmation and articulation that, as the twentieth century progressed, would eventually force a greater freedom of expression and interpretation for homosexuals in literary as well as popular culture.

PART II
GERTRUDE STEIN:
A Further Order of Strange

Gertrude Stein, Opium Queen

Notes on a Mistaken Embrace

An Impossible Success

The Autobiography of Alice B. Toklas (hereafter *The Autobiography*) was published in 1933, an unpromising year for a biography of a lesbian partnership: a year that saw the height of the worldwide Great Depression, the ascendance of the Nazis in Europe, and the consolidation (broadly speaking) of the restriction of personal freedom that followed the 1920s. Nonetheless, the memoir and its author quickly became not only an international bestseller but also a focus of broad cultural interest.[1]

The Autobiography was initially printed in a run of 5,400 by Harcourt Brace & Company, the first of Stein's publishers with enough money to invest substantially in advertising and publicity. The official publication date was in September 1933, though reports of the specific day vary, perhaps because the first edition was available before the official publication date, as is common. What matters is that the first edition sold out before its official publication. In part, this was due to *The Atlantic Monthly*, which published more than half of the memoir in its May, June, July, and August issues. Since 1919, Stein had waged a strenuous and unsuccessful campaign to be published in *The Atlantic,* which during her youth was a strong contender for the most prestigious journal in the country and had great influence on intellectual culture, especially in literature. Though *The Atlantic* had waned a bit by 1933, the journal remained associated with the cultural elite, especially that of New England, and its contributors, by definition, deserved respect and attention.[2]

In July, *The Autobiography* was also a main selection of the Literary Guild, a popular book-of-the-month club that published editions of new books for subscribers. The editorial board, headed by Carl Van Doren, a public intellectual of his day, promised to guide consumers:

> You no longer need to buy books haphazardly. You no longer need to go without the best books of the year because you have no sound criterion for determining what the best books are. The Literary Guild has changed all this. As a member, you receive a good new book by a contemporary writer every month, that has the stamp of approval placed upon it by six of the most competent writers and judges of literature in America. . . . The Guild does not ask you to gamble— to pay for something you do not get. It does not ask you to pay for failures or literary "duds." You are assured of receiving through the mail—without waste of time or effort on your part—the best books that could be found.[3]

The Literary Guild was a mass-market venture that made money through its own prestige, which had to be sufficient to reassure middlebrow consumers that selections were both "classy" and respectable. The guild's business model forbade it from recommending any, or at least too many, works that would shock mainstream America in form or content. Such book-of-the-month clubs aimed for the low end of the middlebrow, for those who desired "culture" but required guidance. These readers did not see that such guidance, especially when visually signaled by the special editions printed by the clubs, also signaled that they were in this sense clueless. That both *The Atlantic* and the Literary Guild—one at the high end of middlebrow, and one at the low—published *The Autobiography* early proves their confidence in its mainstream appeal. This confidence was rewarded not only by sales but also by reviews of the memoir, which were excellent, by far the best of Stein's career.

The Autobiography's success was reflected and heightened by the September 11 issue of *TIME* magazine, which featured Stein on the cover. A second printing of 2,000 would be struck in 1933, as would a British edition with Bodley Head; and a third printing of 2,500 copies would be struck in 1934, as was a French edition with Gallimard. All the while, Stein stayed fixed in the public eye. In February 1934, her and Virgil Thomson's opera, *Four Saints in Three Acts,* opened on Broadway to both success and acclaim. Stein herself went on the road for a well-received lecture tour of the United States in 1934 and 1935, with an audience that extended past the usual suspects to embrace the general public. As sales kept exceeding expectations, *The Autobiography*'s fourth printing, of 1,500 copies, was struck in 1935, as well as an edition through the Week-End Library, a British book-of-the-month club. In short, Gertrude Stein and her work, for years an embodiment of the avant-garde, if not the lunatic fringe, were accepted, popular, and, if not conventional, then at least applauded by those who were.[4]

Surprisingly, this middle-class acceptability and mass-market fame were associated with a blatant manifestation of lesbian erotics and love. *The Autobiography of Alice B. Toklas* links Stein and Toklas in its title, offers photographs of the women at home, relates decades of their domestic life, and clarifies the women's sexual connection. True, Stein neither names their homosexuality nor shows the women in bed together, but such naming and showing are also absent from concurrent memoirs of straight couples. *The Autobiography* contains the usual markers of a memoir of extended intimacy and love: both the sense that life before the women met was a preamble, and casual asides that, in a memoir of a heterosexual couple, would be understood as signs of a marital contract, if perhaps not a legal one. Consider the following, usually cited in relation to Stein's cocky flourish of her genius, but which is even more aggressive in her flaunting of her relationship with Toklas. The "I," as throughout, is Stein writing as Toklas:

> Before I decided to write this book my twenty-five years with Gertrude Stein, I had often said that I would write, The wives of geniuses I have sat with. I have sat with so many. I have sat with wives who were not wives, of geniuses who were real geniuses. I have sat with real wives of geniuses who were not real geniuses. I have sat with wives of geniuses, of near geniuses, of would be geniuses, in short I have sat very often and very long with many wives and wives of many geniuses.[5]

"Toklas" parallels herself at length and in detail with other wives. If Toklas is a wife, then Stein is a husband and Stein and Toklas are coupled—and their coupling is parallel to the legal bond of other husbands and wives. *Quod erat demonstrandum*: Stein is not closeted, and *The Autobiography* is not a closeted text. Nevertheless, many readers put themselves in the dark, or if they could see, pretended not to. Such blindness does not change the fact that *The Autobiography* put a lesbian relationship in plain sight and thus protested a culture that did not acknowledge such relations.

The Autobiography completes Gertrude Stein's ascension as the only lesbian writer before the women's movement who (1) enjoyed mass-market success, (2) earned a canonic perch, (3) wrote works with gay and lesbian content and a queer aesthetic, and (4) was easily identifiable throughout her career as lesbian by those primed by subcultural knowledge or their own sexual dissent. How did Stein achieve such singularity? Why was Stein acceptable to the mass market at all, when she openly sported so many attributes that inspired hatred and fear? Stein was unmarried when marriage was expected, financially independent when women properly depended on men, obviously Jewish when anti-Semitism was expected, expatriate when "abroad" was suspect, and androgynous, if not masculine, as she flouted hegemonic standards of beauty with her large and aggressively uncorseted frame. Independently, these attributes might have elicited disgust and censure. For many, they did. Why, then, was Stein so popular?

The answer resides in how Stein's celebrity persona walked the line between what I call the "broadly queer" and the "specifically gay." As I discussed in the Introduction, I use these terms to distinguish between homosexuality and other traits, behaviors, and phenomena that are understood as inferior to or inappropriate for the dominant order. In the twentieth-century United States, the specifically gay was almost always broadly queer, but the broadly queer was only sometimes specifically gay. In her personal life, Stein was specifically gay: all evidence suggests that her erotic life was entirely oriented toward women. Her specific homosexuality interacted in complex ways with her broad queerness—as well as with the trope of the decadent, unconventional artist—to put both hegemonic censure and Stein's own image under pressure, and eventually to allow her public celebration. It is too simple, however, to view Stein's flamboyance as a "disguise" for her homosexuality, for if such flamboyance were readily available as a form of heterosexual passing, then Stein would not be so singular.

My inquiry here concerns not identity but rather how the same-sex desire evident in Stein's public persona and work was both clearly broadcast and effectively obscured by a balancing act whose climax is the success of *The Autobiography of Alice B. Toklas*. I focus neither on *The Autobiography* itself nor on the specifics of how Stein and the biography sold themselves in the marketplace, but on the celebrity persona that not only fueled but also permitted the memoir's success. In this chapter, I establish the public parameters of Stein's broad queerness, and in the next, I consider her growth as a respectable commodity. First, however, we must put the memoir's commercial success in the context of a remarkably ill-selling career.[6]

A Late Debut

In addition to "How?," the memoir's success begs the question "Why now?" For decades, Stein was forced to subsidize her publication or to fund it outright. After she failed to place her first two novels, *Q.E.D.* and *Fernhurst,* with any publisher in 1903 and 1904, she paid for the publication of the third, *Three Lives,* in 1909, with a vanity press. For an edition of 1,000 copies, Grafton charged Stein $660, roughly $15,000 as I write in 2015. *Three Lives* received some respectable reviews but sold poorly.[7]

Then came the Armory Show. Stein first became a public figure in conjunction with this 1913 three-city exhibition, officially called the International Exhibition of Modern Art, that introduced modern art to the United States and established Stein as a writer who adapted modernist techniques to prose. Alas, Stein's notoriety did not increase her sales. The following year, in 1914, Stein published her second major work, *Tender Buttons.* Her new fame helped her receive a small advance and thirty-seven notices—mostly poor—upon publication. This was almost twice as many reviews as her debut received, even though *Three Lives* was fiction and *Tender Buttons* poetry. Nonetheless, the thousand copies of *Tender Buttons* sold slowly and poorly. The poetry was not reprinted for decades, was not published in paperback until a pirate edition was printed in 1958, and despite Stein's fame never sold better than *Three Lives,* which remained Stein's best seller until the publication of her memoir.[8]

Stein's other works did considerably worse. Between *Three Lives* and *Tender Buttons,* Stein put out 300 stitched pamphlets of *Portrait of Mabel Dodge at the Villa Curonia* (1912), which were offered as gifts. After *Tender Buttons* came the stapled *Have they attacked Mary. He giggled* (1917), which was issued in a tiny edition of 200 by *Vanity Fair* as amends for unintentionally dropping lines from the title poem in the magazine. In 1922 Stein paid for the printing of her collection *Geography and Plays* by the obscure but respectable Four Seas Press in an edition of 2,500 copies, her biggest yet. *Geography and Plays* has an introduction by Sherwood Anderson, then a hot young author, and Stein hoped that the collection would make her as much read as she was known. Nonetheless, *Geography and Plays* sold so poorly that it took eighteen years for all the printed sheets to be bound. To this day, those seeking Stein's early work in collectible editions are faced with an abundance of *Geography and Plays*.[9]

Stein's sales diminished even further with her magnum opus, *The Making of Americans* (1925), which no established publisher would accept, though Stein drew upon all her connections and urged her friends to draw on theirs. Finally, Robert McAlmon arranged for the printing of 500 copies, which sold miserably and then stayed out of print for forty-one years. In 1926, *A Description of Literature* came out in an edition of 200 copies, and there were similarly tiny editions of *Composition as Explanation* (1926), *A Book Concluding with As a Wife Has a Cow* (1926), *A Village, Are You Ready Yet Not Yet: A Play in Four Acts* (1928), *Useful Knowledge* (1928), and *Dix Portraits* (1930). After decades of frustration, Stein, in 1930, at the age of fifty-six, sold part of her art collection to found her own press, Plain Editions. She and Toklas could now publish Stein's work themselves, and *Lucy Church Amiably* and *How to Write* were printed in 1931. Stein and Toklas could not place them in stores, however. That same year, even the Library of Congress refused to purchase any more of Stein's books. Her fame remained constant—and constantly split from her sales.[10]

Stein's eventual solution to the divorce between her fame and her readership was to simplify her style and to make her celebrity persona the subject of her text. *The Autobiography* offers Stein at the peak of her control over her career; she carefully edits its history, both overtly, through what she includes and discusses, and covertly, through elision and focus. Stein's career thus becomes coherent. Stein happily fulfills Edward Said's prescription for a literary career: "The career permits one to see a sequence of intelligible development, not simply of accumulation.... [T]ime is transvalued into a sequence of personal achievements connected by a dynamic of their own." Her career comes into focus not *despite* the nonlinear structure and the narrative posture of writing in the voice of Toklas, but *because* this structure and occluded voice embody Stein's nonlinear, occluded corpus and celebrity. Stein's work had been viewed on a spectrum that ranged from incomprehensible nonsense to esoteric wisdom; an autobiography, which was told out of order from the perspective of someone else but was nonetheless easy and fun to read, shifted this body of work from forbidding to friendly. This now-intelligible history then climaxed outside the pages of *The Autobiography* with what Stein called "La Gloire": the public validation of success and the enormous personal celebrity that followed. After twenty-two years of hard labor, a mass-market author made her debut.[11]

In this chapter, I offer three "case studies" that mark Stein's rising celebrity and illustrate how her broad queerness allowed for public acceptance of her as her persona grew. First I consider two of Stein's mass-market debuts: the birth of Stein's celebrity persona in the *New York Press* (1910); and the first parody of Stein in a national magazine, in the *Saturday Evening Post* (1913). I then consider how aspects of this persona led to an eventual understanding of Stein as a phantasmic "bad girl" that drew promiscuously and without historical specificity from the cabinet of female fatality. Stein might be understood as an opium-addicted temptress luring men to her salon, or she might be the equally fatal vamp of 1910s silent film. These messy, mistaken embraces made the bed for Stein's public coupling with Toklas and served to cover their same-sex desire. Throughout, I show the process by which the pressure of Stein's broadly queer attributes overwhelmed the public, which chose to marvel instead of persecute. At the same time, Stein's broad queerness prompted an audience primed for such reception to see how she embodied same-sexual erotics and identity. Thus, Stein became an important touchstone for pre-Stonewall lesbians: a visually identifiable lesbian who was celebrated in the mass media and whose celebration could lead lesbians and proto-lesbians who were not part of a queer community to her work, and possibly to a more defined lesbian identity.[12]

"A Zolaesque American": Stein's First Celebrity Profile

Stein's celebrity persona proper dates from February 13, 1910, when the unattributed "A Zolaesque American" appeared in the *New York Press*, a daily newspaper with an interest in café society. Whereas reviews of *Three Lives* focused on the text, the *Press* profiled Stein as a Paris "character" and art collector. The lead for the second section of the paper is a feature about animal portraiture; page 5 offers theater trivia above the fold, and below the fold are jokes, cartoons, and "A Zolaesque American." Stein was considerably less newsworthy than dog models. The unimportance of the item and its offhand manner offer a more transparent window than a studied portrait might on the cultural discourses that fed Stein's persona.[13]

There is almost nothing about Zola or his writing in the article. What, then, does its title mean? In 1910, the name Zola rang four chimes:

(1) Jewish, (2) naturalist, (3) French, and (4) iconoclastic. Zola was and remains best known for *Les Rougon-Macquart,* a series of twenty novels that follow a French family through the Second Empire. In 1910, however, Zola was best known as the author of "J'accuse!" (1898), an open letter that charged his government with anti-Semitism in the wrongful conviction of army captain Alfred Dreyfus for espionage. Zola was convicted for libel, dismissed from the Legion of Honor, and forced into exile to avoid jail. Dreyfus and Zola were fully exonerated only in 1906. Though Zola himself was not Jewish and though Stein's own identification as a Jew was inconsistent, the title of "A Zolaesque American" served a double (though inexplicit) notice to readers of Stein's Jewishness via both Zola's Jewish-flavored recent fame and Stein's own Jewish name.[14]

The question "What is a 'Jewish name'?" is complex, as some Jews do not have them, as some do who are not Jewish, and as Jewishness may be defined by religion, culture, and/or heredity. Public perception, especially when occluded by anti-Semitism, has little patience for such niceties. To the great American ear, "Stein" sounded Jewish. "Gertrude Stein" was a run-of-the-mill Jewess at a time when Jews were often viewed as atypical, inferior Americans. This perception was particularly strong at the turn of the twentieth century, which saw enormous waves of Jewish immigration and a corresponding rise of anti-Semitism.[15]

Both the French and American publics linked Jews with broad sexual queerness and specific homosexuality. Marcel Proust in *In Search of Lost Time* and, after him, Eve Kosofsky Sedgwick in *Epistemology of the Closet* use the Dreyfus Affair to illustrate the overlap of Judaism and homosexuality in France. Note that the most effective evidence against Dreyfus was the willful misunderstanding of a "secret dossier" of love-and-sex letters between a German diplomat and an Italian military attaché who could not exonerate Dreyfus for fear of exposure. Siobhan Somerville has observed the subtle reciprocities of nonwhite and nonstraight orders within modernism: "[B]oth sympathetic and hostile accounts of homosexuality were steeped in assumptions that had driven previous scientific studies of race." As Daniel Boyarin notes, "While there are no simple equations between Jewish and queer identities, Jewishness and queerness yet utilize and are bound up with one another in particularly resonant ways."[16]

Americans needed neither theory nor the Dreyfus Affair to conflate Jews with broad sexual queerness and specific homosexuality. Consider the 1924 understanding of Leopold and Loeb, "two boys whose Jewishness 'naturally' predisposed them to homosexuality, a 'crime against nature' that incited them to further crimes against humanity." Jewish cultural studies has shown the traditional association of Jews with improprieties of sex and gender: Jewish men were often understood as insufficiently masculine, Jewish women as inappropriately feminine, and both as variously over- and undersexed. The Jewess shared in the orientalist tropes pictured by Ingres and Gérôme, and we shall see how the odalisque contributes to Stein's configuration as an opium queen. Such swarthy conflation was routine in the United States at a time when the distinction between Turks and Arabs was routinely erased. And, like all women in the fantastic harem created by the Christian West, the Jewess was sexually excessive.[17]

As were the French, from an American vantage point. Naturalists in general and Zola in particular were known for relatively sexually explicit, pessimistic fiction that exposed and deplored the material affronts of poverty and traced how such nurture determined character and fate. The American public was not particularly interested in the definition of French naturalism but was invested in national stereotypes and read the naturalists' breakage of taboos as an example of "naughty" French sexuality. Anglo-Americans have a long tradition of viewing France as a site of comparative sexual freedom, as seen in synonyms for tongue-kissing *(French kiss)* and condoms *(French letters).* In literature, painting, and fashion, *French* has been a byword for the new and unconventional— usually with a frisson of sexual impropriety—since at least the seventeenth century. Thus *avant-garde* and *au courant,* common English terms of French origin that have long been naturalized but still enjoy French pronunciation, as "special Frenchness" is essential to their meaning. In short, Frenchness in general and French naturalism in particular were markers of a broad, sexualized queerness for the au courant readers of the *New York Press.*

Such impropriety suits the last pitch of Zola's chord: iconoclasm. Stein, like Zola, resists convention: A "woman of strong personality, independence of thought, and the utter disdain of conventionalities . . . she possesses a small fortune, and she is not controlled by nor does she fear the criticism of others." Like Zola, she bears a movement's standard: "The little coterie of old friends who have long been associated with Miss Stein eagerly awaited this first production." The article clarifies that Stein is intrinsically special: "[E]ven in the doll stage the authoress gave evidence of an unusual mind." Stein is broadly queer from birth, the baby born with the caul. Such babies are often celebrated, for "iconoclasm" when properly couched has mass-market appeal. Zola truly did challenge traditional beliefs, customs, and values. Yet "J'accuse!" rejuvenated Zola's sales within and without France, as he recovered his reputation as a socially progressive rebel. In this sense, "J'accuse!" was not iconoclasm but good publicity.[18]

Similarly, Stein was not so iconoclastic—at least according to the *Press*—that she could not be comfortably placed as just another madcap. What made Stein newsworthy was the extent to which she fit the tradition of Parisian outrageousness that extended from Oscar Wilde to Natalie Barney and Djuna Barnes. Portraits of such figures, when denatured of their homosexuality, were easily absorbed in the broadly queer population that fascinated the readers of the *Press*. If Stein's "iconoclasm" had *truly* overturned traditional beliefs, customs, and values, then it would not have been reported. And Stein's lesbianism did go unmentioned, though the unnamed writer, who knew Stein well enough to write about her as a public figure before anyone else, almost certainly knew that she and Toklas lived openly as a couple.

By contrast, Stein's broad queerness is immediately established. The article begins by complicating her citizenship: "Paris has launched another authoress into the limitless field of literature. Miss Gertrude Stein, whose book, 'Three Lives,' has just been published, is an American, born in Pennsylvania, but whose early life was spent principally in California." Even in the United States, Stein's identity is unstable. The *Press* details her American pedigree but specifies that she was "launched" by Paris, which, in concert with the article's title, dovetails with her Jewishness and her iconoclasm. The article rings changes on these themes until the six paragraphs end with their sole literary criticism: "In her writing Miss Stein leans toward materialism. Many incidents in *[Three Lives]* . . . are Zolaesque in plainness of treatments, and one wonders if the reserved American taste will rebel." The nexus of Zola, Stein, Jewish, French, and naturalist is made explicit, and the article concludes.[19]

Throughout, Stein is portrayed as a consumer, producer, and judge of broad queerness, "one of the first to discover great merit in that revolutionary and eccentric painter, Henri Matisse." For Stein is a visual iconoclast herself. Though there is no illustration, her clothes are carefully described: "For a street costume she wears always a brown corduroy suit, a short coat, and small, inconspicuous hat. When the telltale signs of wear and tear appear Miss Stein simply orders a duplicate to be made. . . .

[S]he walks the streets of Paris in brown sandals regardless of the many impertinent glances that she is forced to encounter." Stein's iconoclasm extends to her body: "The homely axiom 'laugh and grow fat' certainly applies to Miss Stein. . . . [H]er avoirdupois is of the 'spreading kind.' The corset, that modern invention for the suppression of unruly flesh, is an unknown article in the simple wardrobe of Miss Stein." All Stein's visual attributes refute traditional femininity, and she must withstand "impertinent glances." She eschews conventionally female dress yet maintains her "male" costume with a dandy's precision. This simultaneous attention to visuality and repudiation of the dominant gendered visual hierarchy meshes with the modernist project of Matisse. The *Press* extends Stein's visual perversion to her body, which does not fulfill contemporary standards of proper femininity and is not subject to the corset. Instead, her flesh goes untamed.[20]

This picture offers signifiers of specific same-sexuality to those who can see them, those who are not looking for conventional feminine representation but who *do* want, in the words of just one sentence, a "homely," "laughing" "character" with "avoirdupois" of the "spreading kind." Those seeking not only female masculinity but also a *happy* female masculinity need look no further. To contemporaries primed by their own dissident desires to carefully scan cultural ephemera for signs of nonnormative female sexual desire and expression, this description tells, well before Stein's look became a standard visual shorthand of lesbian identity.[21]

Stein and the Armory Show:
Word Portraits and "La grand fête américaine"

The link between Stein and the visual modernists was soon strengthened by further coverage in the popular press. For an elite few, Stein became a creator as well as a collector of modern art in 1912, when "Henri Matisse" and "Pablo Picasso" were printed in Alfred Stieglitz's *Camera Work*. Stein called these essays "portraits," as she aimed to replicate her subjects' pictorial styles in prose. She begins the first like so:

> One was quite certain that for a long part of his being one being living he had been trying to be certain that he was wrong in doing what he was doing and then when he could not come to be certain that he had been wrong in doing what he had been doing, when he had completely convinced himself that he would not come to be certain that

he had been wrong in doing what he had been doing he was really
certain then that he was a great one and he certainly was a great one.

If readers are at all typical, their speed will crash at that quote from "Henri
Matisse." The words are simple, but the syntax is novel, which forces engagement—as viewers of Matisse were also forced to engage, especially before his visual idiom became familiar. Stein dramatizes Matisse's struggle
to create a new pictorial language as she revives the cliché of the groundbreaking but insecure artist and reflects it in her own struggle.[22]

"Henri Matisse" lets us see how different readers might work out Stein's
broad queerness and specific homosexuality on a textual level. The broad
public was likely to avert its eyes from such writing. Readers unwilling to
make an effort take away only that Stein's work is difficult and mysterious. These readers hold Stein in whatever regard they hold the esoteric,
and—at least via the passage—they associate her with queer sexuality only
so far as they find such queerness esoteric. Those who *do* read "Henri
Matisse" may understand the passage simply as cleverness or parody,
yet the quotation is extraordinarily specific about the internal process
of gaining confidence in a new way of being and doing that at first seems
"wrong." Stein does not specify what *kind* of new "being" and "doing" is
under discussion. Certainly, her depiction of Matisse gaining confidence
in his style easily translates to her own growth in confidence with her
own style. Those who are sexually queer and those who are familiar with
Stein's biography and persona may further understand this passage as a
meditation on *sexual* style: the solidification of sexual desires and activities that the beholder must convince him- or herself are not "wrong" but
rather proof that one is "a great one." This interpretation validates those
who have similarly struggled not only to achieve a sexual identity based
on their desires but also to find pride in that certainty; and the fact that
Stein often referred to herself as "a great one" makes the passage autobiography to those readers who know the reference.

Stein wrote a third word portrait in 1912, *Portrait of Mabel Dodge at the
Villa Curonia* (hereafter, usually, *Portrait*), a textually cubist rendering of
the home of art patron Mabel Dodge, who paid for publication. Despite a
tiny print run of 300 copies, all intended as gifts, *Portrait* was fundamental to Stein's fame because of its close association to the Armory Show.
Before the show, young, unorthodox artists had almost no opportunity
to show their work in the United States. From February 17 to March 15,
1913, 1,250 artworks by more than three hundred avant-garde artists were

shown in New York City's Sixty-Ninth Regiment Armory. The show amazed an American public whose artistic exposure had been restricted to more realist representations, and the Armory Show received more attention in the press than any event in the world of art and literature since the Wilde trials. Twenty-five years later, the painter Walt Kuhn, executive secretary of the exhibition, described how the show had done much more than increase the profile and acceptance of contemporary art: "The exhibition affected every phase of American life—the apparel of men and women, the stage, automobiles, airplanes, furniture, interior decorations, beauty parlors, plumbing, hardware—everything from the modernistic designs of gas pumps and added color of beach umbrellas and bathing suits, down to the merchandise of the dime store." This impact lent some of its force to Stein's authorial persona.[23]

An important fulcrum for this transfer of force was "Speculations; or, Post Impressionism in Prose," an article by Mabel Dodge that closed a special issue of the high-end periodical *Arts and Decoration*. This special issue served as a quasi-official program for the Armory Show and offered an "explanatory statement" by its sponsor, the Association of American Painters and Sculptors. *Arts and Decoration* was roughly comparable to today's *Architecture Today:* a periodical read by the trade, yes, but aimed primarily at a moneyed audience that conflated art with decoration and wished to substantiate its rarified taste and intellect by reading the magazine. Dodge's article is set at the end of the issue, in counterpoint to the frontispiece, which is a paean to the future written by van Gogh in archaic prose and typeset with a large dropped initial. In contrast to this faux-medieval frontispiece, the start of Dodge's article wraps around a photograph of Brancusi's *Mademoiselle Pogany,* associating Stein with both the sculpted head and its modernist aesthetic. This sculpture, unreferenced by the article, offers the largest departure from traditional aesthetics of all the art illustrated in the issue, including work by Matisse, Cézanne, and van Gogh. "Speculations" is therefore presented not only as parallel to van Gogh in importance, because of its placement, but also as parallel with the show's most progressive art. "Speculations" is also the only one of the ten essays in the issue that is not directly concerned with visual art and visual artists—an oddity explained by Dodge's treatment of Stein as a visual artist who works in the medium of words.[24]

Dodge's fortune and social position gave her words weight among the journalists and members of the cultural elite who were obliged to consider seriously the climactic article of the show's de facto program.

Dodge's profile of Stein repeats three primary claims—really, pronounce-ments. First: Stein is a genius, and anyone who disagrees is wrong. Sec-ond: Stein's art is the essence of the "new," and whosoever disagrees is an idiot or at least one in "the sad plight which the dogmatist defines as being a condition of spiritual non-receptivity." Third: Stein's art is paral-lel to the visual modernists'. These repetitive foci are leavened with de-tails of Stein's working habits and descriptions of the aesthetic aims and methods of the artists at hand. In an impressive bit of logrolling, the ar-ticle is sprinkled with quotes from *Portrait,* which Dodge offers as proof of her claims. In short, Dodge's article firmly established Stein's associa-tion with modern art, an association that greatly inflated Stein's public persona through the powerful bellows of the Armory Show.[25]

"Speculations; or, Post Impressionism in Prose" was essential to the establishment of Stein's status as *the* American literary analogue of the French modernists, but its distribution was limited. To see how Stein and her work were publicly understood at the start of her national repu-tation, consider their first extended treatment in a national magazine: "La grand fête américaine," in the March 22, 1913, issue of the *Saturday Evening Post,* which came out the week after the show closed in New York, as it began touring. The *Post* was then the most successful and in-fluential magazine in the country, offering middlebrow and middle-class Americans entertainment, information, and politics each week. This au-dience was well aware of the show.[26]

"La grand fête américaine" was written by Samuel G. Blythe, a promi-nent humorist. Blythe presents Stein and her writing as so famous that no name is necessary; he liberally quotes her but never identifies her. Blythe also presents Stein and her writing as so extraordinary that no parody is necessary: her quotations are left unaltered, unmocked, and unmisinterpreted. Blythe assumed that readers needed no help to find Stein ridiculous and extraordinarily queer.[27]

Stein's persona in "La grand fête américaine" rings the same chimes as "A Zolaesque American," though in a different chord. Jewishness is muted; naturalism is superseded by modernism; and Frenchness, expa-triation, and iconoclasm take the lead. Stein provides the finale of a "great American party" that has seen French chorus girls in Native American drag and long yellow wigs perform tableaux of "that life in America with which the French are so familiar," including the "*Invasion des Comanches,* a most terrifying onslaught of Indian warrioresses dressed in the latest Parisian styles" (10–11). The article both mocks the French and makes a case for their queer vision: "Who wouldn't prefer to be tomahawked by a Comanche who wears a pink silk dress and gold slippers and has a dimple in her chin to eating ham and eggs?" (11).

The fete progresses through various travesties, including a tribute to American aviation complete with wind-up planes, and a *tableau vivante* of "Oncle Sam" with a monocle, black beard, and thirty-three "daughters" dressed in the stars and stripes. Throughout, mistranslations of both French and American culture and artifacts make them more sexual and fun. The dull sonnet "À l'Américaine" becomes ridiculous: "La Fayette, suivant la jeune soldatesque, / Deploya l'étamine à l'azur étoile; / Et, du soleil ardent, brusquement dévoilé" becomes "And Lafayette, who was some kid, believe me, / Ripped the upholstery out of the azure sky / And told the burning sun where to get off" (11). The fete seems chaotic but is precisely programmed, with scheduled poetry readings, a musical interlude, and dance-hall skits. The party's chaos truly goes out of bounds only with a reading from Stein's *Portrait,* which closes the show:

> By two o'clock the whole place was a whirl of laughing, shouting, pirouetting girls and boys, singing, dancing, throwing confetti, sailing their rubber pigs in the air, scattering flowers about.... Then there came a sensation. A tall, pale, serious young man rose.... As an American he desired to read a few extracts from the greatest work of the century—a work destined to go down the ages as imperishable prose. He alluded to a work he held in his hand, a small pamphlet with a gaudy cover of flowered paper, and straightaway he began to read. (11 [ellipses mine])

Blythe directly quotes eight substantial passages from *Portrait* and shows us how Stein's work frightens, angers, and estranges the partiers. Blythe never names Stein but does name *Portrait of Mabel Dodge at the Villa Curonia*. Did he assume that his audience would know Stein by her style and connect both works with Stein, or was he making an inside joke?

The answer is, both. To an extent, Blythe's audience was self-selected. Those readers most interested in France and the avant-garde were those most likely to read his parody and to have heard of Stein. And though modernist writers had very few contemporary readers, this did not mean that they were not becoming well known: as Karen Leick writes, "[I]t would have been difficult for any literate American to remain unaware of modernists like Joyce and Stein in the 1920s, since their publications in little magazines were discussed so frequently in daily newspapers and popular magazines."[28] Whether or not readers were familiar with Stein, they would have understood that even in the context of *la grande fête*'s celebration of the foreign, Stein is a further order of strange: "Those who were listening pinched themselves to find whether they were not asleep. They glanced round apprehensively to see whether their minds were working" (11). The listeners protest; they are confused ("'What is it?' cried the merrymakers. 'What is it?'") and angry ("'Hey stop it! Stop it!' yelled a big American. 'Either you're crazy or I am'" [11, 32]).

Portrait threatens not only sanity but also the traditional gender and sexuality of the party. Seeming transgressions such as the raid of the pink Comanches are, at bottom, ornamental flourishes meant to prime the standard sexual pump. Only "the tall, serious, pale young man" is differentiated; his paleness reverberates with his refusal of the heterosexual bacchanalia and his impromptu eruption of Stein's words. This differentiation suits her text: "'So much breathing has not the same place when there is that much beginning. So much breathing,' he declaimed, 'has not the same place when the ending is lessening. So much breathing has the same place and there must not be so much suggestion. There can be there the habit that there is if there is no need of resting. The absence is not alternative'" (11). The connotations of the particulars of rhythmic breathing and their delineation in relation to states of mind are undeniably sexual, but they cannot be parsed in terms of conventional frolic, and cannot be subsumed into *la grande fête*.

The "dazed listeners" attempt to place and categorize the reading, guessing that *Portrait* is "cubist," "futurist," and "rhythmist" (11, 32). The pale young man repeats only "It is the word." This reference to the sacred is accented by the young man's treatment of *Portrait* as a holy text: he "lifted the little paper-covered book to his lips and kissed it reverently." Even after he is hauled from the stage, the young man clasps "his little paper-covered book to his heart and his eyes were rolling in a fine frenzy." (32) This parody of artistic devotion reaches back to aestheticism. Indeed, "La grand fête" may be read as an updated version of the parodies that circulated in the United States during Wilde's national tour in 1882, when Blythe was fourteen. Blythe was twenty-seven when the Wilde trials began, and as Wilde's tour and trial were among the few news stories on the arts with as much buzz as the Armory Show, Blythe was sensible to reference parodies of aestheticism as he mocked modernism.

Though Blythe's narrator dismisses *Portrait* as a bore, his copious quoting of Stein—without comment—materially validates the pale young man's wonder and insistence that the text may not be stifled. "La grande fête" both places Stein in the realm of the broadly, traditionally queer and perceives in her and her work a hard, indigestibly foreign center beneath the sweet froth of noisy, amusing inconsequence. She alone has the power to estrange.

Stein and Her Work as Objets d'Art

Whereas *Portrait,* via "Speculations" and "La grande fête," linked Stein to the Armory Show and modernism, the 1914 publication of *Tender Buttons* extended the link to a chain. *Tender Buttons* applies the technique of *Portrait* to a series of portraits of objects, foods, and rooms, but reviews were less interested in specific critique than in the modernist movement as a whole and in Stein as its figurehead. For instance, the *Chicago Daily Tribune* did not discuss the work of this "literary cubist" but merely quoted her as the "high priestess" of modernism, devoting just three paragraphs of review to forty-nine paragraphs of quotation from *Tender Buttons.* We see here and in other reviews a repetition of Blythe's refusal to comment in "La grand fête": neither analysis nor parody may supersede the work itself.[29]

Stein's association with modernism made her useful to those who wanted to damn the movement, as critics who could only fulminate about visual modernism might substantiate their distaste via Stein. For instance, the Armory Show received its least sympathetic reviews in Boston, and Stein fared no better:

> Boston has seen some of the paintings of Matisse and Picasso, the sculptures of Brancusi, which created such a stir of amazement and contempt last spring. It has heard too, perhaps, of the new symphonies, wild sounds produced on new and unmusical instruments, which originated lately in Italy. Boston has not tried to understand them, nor to admit that here is anything to understand, not even in the point of view of the perpetrators. So, in a way perhaps, these books which show the contemporary anarchy of art in the form of literature may serve as examples and explanations of the thing which has upset Paris and roused New York to a cynical interest.

In other words, Boston disliked *Tender Buttons* as much as the rest of the "new art," but Boston did appreciate that Stein trafficked in words, for this fact let Boston expound on its disgust.[30]

Some bad reviews were extraordinary. Consider the full text of "Officer, She's Writing Again": "Miss Gertrude Stein, who is at the head of the Cubists and Futurists in Paris, has produced *Tender Buttons* recently. The volume, according to one description, is a 'sort of trilogy' on: 'Objects,' 'Foods' and 'Rooms.' After reading excerpts from it a person feels like going out and pulling the Dime Bank Building over himself." The brevity of the review and the severity of its judgment make it absurd, and the hostility behind the absurdity gives it weight. Such nastiness is typical for reviews of Stein in the 1910s; critics seemed to experience Stein and her work as a personal attack. Bad publicity is nonetheless publicity, and such striking badness helps explain how Stein could be both so well known and so little read.[31]

Even those modernists who resented Stein's ascension acknowledged how well she had caught the public eye. Among the modernists who found her unworthy was the poet and editor Alfred Kreymborg. His "Gertrude Stein—Hoax and Hoaxtress" attempted to prove that Stein was a pretender to the modernist throne but concluded with realpolitik:

> Whether you wrinkle your brow and curl your tongue for a long, ponderous defense of her work, or whether you scowl and shoot your tongue for a venomous attack, or whether you merely lean back your velvet easy chair and open your mouth for a good roaring laugh, Miss Stein will have benefited you. She will have given you a new sensation. And sensations are so rare, particularly in these days of warfare, that you don't want to deny yourself the opportunity of one. You can always go back to sleep again.

In other words, "I, Kreymborg, know who deserves the modernist crown— and Gertrude Stein does not. Yet I cannot deny her crude power even as I deplore it."[32]

The backwash from all this celebrity flowed upstream to *Three Lives,* which was reviewed in a modernist light by periodicals that initially ignored its publication. For instance, the *Philadelphia Public Ledger* warned that "the blur which this futurist in writing at first creates cannot be cleared until we are willing to bring the thought and intelligence to its interpretation which we needed when examining [Duchamp's] *The Nude Descending the Stairs.*" We see here a logic whereby the mass public required a visual analogue to interpret the writing. Compare this to the *Boston Evening Transcript* review quoted earlier, which uses the writing as an analogue to interpret visual art. Though the two reviews travel the bridge between Stein's literature and visual modernism from different abutments, they walk the same path. Such visual rubrics were frequently used to understand and judge Stein's person as well as her writing, as we saw in "A Zolaesque American."[33]

The link between Stein, her work, and the visual modernists is obvious and was intended by the author herself. A more rarified version of the association was the phenomenon of Stein's books themselves as objets d'art. Just as Stein's persona, rather than her work, was the focus of the mass public, so the material form of her work—which frequently incorporated drawings, lithographs, photographs, and other visual material—frequently superseded its content in elite and highbrow culture.

At first, in "Henri Matisse" and "Pablo Picasso," Stein was interested in reproducing visual spectacle through the content of her text. With *Portrait of Mabel Dodge at the Villa Curonia,* this interest takes a material form. The 300 copies of *Portrait* were bound in wallpaper in thirty-five different patterns, each a facsimile of a multicolored eighteenth-century floral Florentine design.

How do we read this wallpaper? The Florentine design rhymes with the Florentine Villa Curonia. The designs, though hardly modern, rhyme with modern still lifes in their abstraction. Most importantly for my purpose here, the covers were made of an unusual material and were visually remarkable. The rarity of the limited edition and the difficulty of a text that lacked traditional mimesis all made *Portrait* easier to regard and exhibit than to read. Note how Blythe insists on the physicality of the book in "La grande fête américaine": "a small pamphlet with a gaudy cover of flowered paper" (11); "[t]he pale young man lifted the little paper-covered book to his heart and kissed it reverently" (32); "he was clasping his little paper-covered book to his heart" (32); "I took the book, a slim pamphlet of eleven printed pages" (32). Even though readers of the *Saturday Evening Post* might not understand the text, they could understand that it was, as well as caused, a spectacle.[34]

Even when the material surface was not remarkable, the physicality and provenance of Stein's work triggered an unusual amount of comment. The first edition of *Tender Buttons* has yellow covers, which, though not standard, was not rare and would not have provoked much comment for an artist whose persona did not prime her reader to think in visual terms. A harsh review carefully noted the material surface of this "slim little book bound in bright canary covers" and its production by Claire Marie, a "publisher of books for people with exotic tastes," before attacking its content. The following month, Robert E. Rogers began his review in the *Boston Evening Transcript* with the volume's press and material surface: "There is in New York a new publishing company called simply the 'Claire Marie,' which issues occasionally slender books bound in pale blues and greens, oranges and light lemons. The titles are, for instance, *Sonnets from the Patagonian: The Street of Little Hotels, Saloon Sonnets and Sunday Flutings, Sacral Dimples* and *A Piety of Fans.* These seem mad, but there is one that seems madder. It is *Tender Buttons* by Gertrude Stein." The very surfaces of these books, their "mad" titles and unusual colors, made them suspect. Rogers proceeds to inform us that Claire Marie, presumably in its own words, wanted to publish "books for people who are tired of bestsellers and of the commonplace, who are eager for the sincerely exotic, the tomorrow of literature . . . [by authors] who have no wish to teach or to tear down, who are concerned only with the beauty of life." Rogers informs readers of this aesthetic credo only to disagree with it, as he believes *Tender Buttons,* despite its innocuous "light lemon" cover, exemplifies "anarchy in art." In other words, *Tender Buttons* may *look* like an objet d'art, and its publisher may *claim* that its products are *art pour l'art,* but this volume of poetry poses great danger to aesthetics as we know them.[35]

Claire Marie's reputation as a publisher of "mad" books worried Mabel Dodge, who offered Stein a marketing analysis in a letter of March 29, 1914:

> [A friend thinks that Claire Marie] is absolutely third rate, & in
> bad odor here, being called for the most part "decadent" and
> Broadwayish and that sort of thing. . . . I think it would be a pity
> to publish with [Claire Marie] *if* it will emphasize the idea in the
> opinion of the public, that there is something degenerate & effete &
> decadent about the whole of the cubist movement which they *all* con-
> nect you with, because, hang it all, as long as they don't understand a
> thing they think all sorts of things. My feeling in this is quite strong.

The horror of Broadway: if Stein published with Claire Marie, she would decrease not only her own value but also the value of all the cubists. Given that the mass public supported Broadway, Dodge's "public" clearly references the elite—those who both supported modern art and considered Broadway beneath their notice. Stein expands on Dodge's "public" in *The Autobiography*: "Mabel Dodge immediately conceived the idea that Gertrude Stein should be invited from one country house to another and do portraits and then end up doing portraits of american millionaires which would be a very exciting and lucrative career. Gertrude Stein laughed." Let me elaborate on Dodge's point. Say that Stein is a couturier, one of a number of dressmakers interested in the hobble skirt. Claire Marie is willing to produce Stein's designs under its label, but Claire Marie is a house whose clients are not of the highest caliber. Broadway—"degenerate & effete & and decadent" Broadway—patronizes Claire Marie, and that patronage ensures that Dodge's rich but otherwise respectable "public" will never view Stein in particular, and the hobble skirt in general, as chic again. Dodge's public follows fashion without *understanding* fashion, and so no matter how exquisite Stein's dresses may be, the air of Broadway will taint them. Such subtleties of moneyed discrimination are more usual for fashion and other visual arts than for fiction—and suit Dodge's view of Stein as a "society painter."[36]

Stein nonetheless published with Claire Marie, almost certainly because the publisher, the poet Donald Evans, offered Stein an opportunity to see her work in print without subsidizing it. He even offered Stein royalties: "10% on the first 500 copies sold and 15% on all after that." For the next two decades, however, Stein would largely adhere to Dodge's rule, though not for her reasons, and published only with presses on the bleeding edge, as only these would publish her. Intentionally or not, Stein kept her cachet high and her audience exclusive via presses that, though they may have been "degenerate & effete & decadent" were certainly not "Broadwayish."[37]

Broadway aside, Stein's publishers would not only continue but augment Claire Marie's visual interest. They consistently rarified her product through deluxe editions. These were often more visually striking and always more expensive and rare than the standard editions, even when the latter were already visually notable, and were published in an extremely small run. For instance, although all 102 copies of the first edition of *A Book Concluding with As a Wife Has a Cow: A Love Story* (1926) had lithographs by Juan Gris, only the 10 copies of the deluxe edition were signed by the author and artist and printed on *Japon ancien* vellum. Vellum is the high-quality parchment made of calfskin used in medieval manuscripts; Japanese vellum is a thick, smooth, glossy, durable paper suitable for engravings, produced from plant fibers of an unusually great length; and *Japon ancien* vellum is paper treated with hydrochloric acid to resemble Japanese vellum. Despite these two degrees of separation from actual vellum, *Japon ancien* is a very fine paper that appreciably changes the material experience of reading and viewing Stein and Gris. Their autographs, however, serve only as material traces of the writer and artist; they impart value only through scarcity and through the belief that the authority of Stein and Gris transfers to those who hold a relic of their bodies as well as their minds. Such cachet was available to those who had no interest in actually *reading* Stein. Consider the 5 copies of *The Making of Americans* (1925) that were printed on Japanese vellum and lettered in gold on the cover. Whether these 5 copies were read was incidental and even inimical to their value, as the heavy handling necessary for reading almost a thousand difficult pages would decrease the value of this investment.[38]

The variegation of Stein's deluxe editions was taken to its largest extreme with the 1930 *Dix Portraits*. These ten portraits, like Stein's earlier "Henri Matisse" and "Pablo Picasso," seek to embody the work and person of ten different creative artists in words. Who would buy *Dix Portraits*? An audience with a sincere interest in difficult experimental contemporary literature (never large) and an audience that wanted to display its wealth and taste (somewhat larger). Why would this second group buy one of the 400 unsigned, unillustrated copies of the first trade edition of *Dix Portraits,* available for fifty francs, when they could spend and get so much more? Note the similarity between the description of the varieties of *Dix Portraits* that follows and the ad copy of a luxury catalog that assures its readers that its high-quality products are indeed exclusive. Potential consumers who received the latter had to be a part of the tiny subculture of rich people interested not only in avant-garde art but also in *avant*-avant-garde art, as Stein had trouble publishing even in small literary magazines. The exclusivity of the audience for this ad copy, knowledgeable enough to appreciate these editions and rich enough to afford them, is breathtaking:

> The first edition of *Dix Portraits* has ten tissue-guarded illustration plates by a stunning array of the greatest lights of the avant-garde: the great modernist Pablo Picasso, the Russian émigré artist Pavlik Tchelitchev, the Dutch painter Kristians Tonny, the Neo-Romantic artist and designer Christian "Bébé" Berard, and as a special treat, two composers working in a new medium: the eccentric rebel Erik Satie and the promising young American Virgil Thomson. All cop-

ies of the first edition are signed by Stein as well as her translators, Thomson and the poet Georges Hugnet, who together render her word portraits from English into French in this bilingual first edition. Three different varieties of the first edition are available: 65 on *vélin d'Arches* paper (125 francs), 25 on the more expensive *Hollande van Gelder* paper (300 francs), and the 10 most expensive on *Imperial Japon* vellum, with part of the text copied out in Stein's own hand (500 francs).

Possible revenue for the one hundred copies of the three deluxe editions was 20,625 francs, versus 20,000 francs for the four hundred copies of the trade edition. Advantage deluxe.[39]

Stein's deluxe editions are best understood as artists' books, created for a limited, exclusive audience rather than the public. Many of her works before *The Autobiography* may be understood not as unsuccessful works by a writer but as artists' books in a limited edition that were produced for an extremely select audience and were not expected to be read by even them. As a creator of spectacle and as a conveyer of cachet in both her person and work, Stein was a success.

Stein in the Land of Futile Piffledom: Don Marquis and *Hermione*

For many, the success and spectacle were empty. We have seen how Stein's ability to index modernity and the avant-garde made her a figure of fun for those who viewed them as ridiculous. For some, Stein was more specifically associated with the misuse and misunderstanding of modernity. Alfred Kreymborg was not the only modernist to view her spectacle as empty. We see this in the work of Don Marquis.

Marquis, a popular humorist and newspaper columnist of the 1910s and '20s, is best known for *Archy and Mehitabel* (1916–1935), which chronicles a cockroach in unrequited love with a cat. During his courtship, Archy writes free verse, some of which draws on Stein. Marquis also included Stein by name in several parodies in the *New York Evening Sun* that were collected as *Hermione and Her Little Group of Serious Thinkers* (1916).[40] Hermione is a proper young lady who becomes infatuated with the "little groups" of Greenwich Village: "the land of Futile Piffledom; / a salon weird where congregate Freak, Nut and Bug and Psychic Bum." Stein is an idol for Hermione's salon:

We've taken up Gertrude Stein—our little
Group of serious thinkers you know—
and she's wonderful; simply WONDERFUL

She Suggests the Inexpressible, you know.
Of course, she is a Pioneer. And with all
Pioneers—don't you think?—the Reach is greater
than the Grasp.

Not that you can tell what she means

But in the New Art one doesn't have to mean
things, does one? One strikes the chords, and the
chords vibrate.

Aren't Vibrations just too perfectly lovely for
Anything?

The Hermione poems are variations on a joke. Hermione juxtaposes serious matter (the Bhagavad Gita, Nietzsche, vers libre) with feminine
diction of the day ("Aren't Vibrations just too perfectly lovely for / anything?") and juvenile repetition and capitalization ("and she's wonderful;
simply WONDERFUL"). The titles alone serve as meditations on false
sophistication: "Hermione on Fashions and War"; "Will the Best People
Receive the Superman Socially?"; "How Suffering Purifies One!"; "Prison
Reform and Poise."[41]

Marquis differentiates his types of ridicule. Sometimes, Hermione
misunderstands "valid" art; sometimes, she is taken in by hucksters.
Stein is special. Hermione *does* understand Stein's poems, for they have
no meaning except as a marker for the worthless avant-garde. In this way,
"Stein" is comparable to a brand name that gives value to an ill-designed,
ill-constructed handbag. Marquis expresses this succinctly in "Gertrude
Is Stein, Stein Gertrude: That Is All Ye Know on Earth, and All Ye Need
to Know," which Marquis offers to a "Puzzled Reader" who asks, "Who is
Gertrude Stein?"

Who is Meredith? And Hardy? Who is Conrad? Who is James?
All we know of Gertrude—really—is that she is Gertrude Stein!
'Tis enough for us we have her—(she, the subtle Theban Sphinx:
All the spheres swoon in silence when she stutters out her thinks!)[42]

Alison Tischler, discussing a slightly different version of this poem, observes that "Marquis has placed his poem and Steinian language in an aesthetic loop; the similarity of his response to the reader's query and Stein's own writing style is underlined by [its] title." Tischler makes the excellent point that such parodies taught a mass public the aims and means of Stein's language. The poem's intended purpose, however, is to mock Stein. Hermione and friends respond to Puzzled Reader's "Who is Gertrude Stein?" with parallel questions about authors at the height of respectability in 1914. This move implies that all five authors are brand names whose meaning is inherent in their status and not their work. Lines 2 through 4 reiterate the title's claim that Stein is Stein, which is sufficient to prove her worth: the success of her persona does not require her work to be understood. The closing couplet reiterates: "Let us search not, seek not, ask not, why the blessing has been sent— / Little Groups, we have our Gertrude: worship her, and be content!" In other words: adore and shut up.[43]

Marquis views the cult of Stein as harmless foolishness, like Hermione herself. Others, such as the writer and editor Michael Gold, viewed this cult more gravely. Marquis and Gold offered visions of Stein at different bad ends of decadence: decadence as naive, superficial, and ineffectual, and decadence as perverse, destructive, and insane. Sherwood Anderson and Richard Wright offered two examples of the impact of these visions upon Stein, and the struggle necessary to detach her from them.

Gertrude Stein, Opium Queen

My next observation is hard to credit. Nonetheless, I will show that from the 1910s until the 1930s, many pictured Gertrude Stein lounging on a divan that drew from fin de siècle clichés as well as tropes of silent films. Sometimes she was intoxicated, and sometimes she hallucinated. Sometimes she smoked opium, and sometimes hash. We see cognates of this fantasy in "A Zolaesque American," when Stein is situated in Bohemian Paris, and in "La grand fête américaine," where Blythe configures Stein's disciple as a "pale young man" whose "eyes were rolling in a fine frenzy." Just as Stein's followers were portrayed as decadent, so was Stein herself.[44]

Now, although Stein did many things in her long, eventful life, she never lolled on a chaise longue, batting heavy eyelids as she turned from her silver-gilt syringe to lure her victim to his doom. Nor, as a secret sister of Theda Bara, did she leach men of virility and independence until all that was left was a hollowed-out shell. Stein, a practiced hostess, did hold court at parties, and she certainly had a memorable and sexual presence. Yet she seems never to have offered a traditional display of heterosexual accessibility in the service of seduction. She preferred to appreciate the feminine display of others. As for herself, she displayed female masculinity.

Nonetheless, Stein did share one important attribute with the opium queen and the vamp: ethnicity. The orientalist valences of Judaism rhyme well with the Asian accoutrement of the opium den, as well as the public personae of vamps of the silent screen. The marketing of Theda Bara is instructive here. Bara was born Theodosia Goodman of a Jewish, Polish-born father and a Swiss mother, probably in 1890. She came to prominence in the 1915 film *A Fool There Was,* inspired by Kipling's poem "The Vampire." As the vampire, Bara drags an upstanding married industrialist into decadence, alcoholism, and the grave. The vamp recollects the fin de siècle not only in her textual origin but also in the salons that she hosts and the debauchery that she provokes, and in exotic accoutrements. The film is still remembered today by the oft-parodied "Kiss me, you fool!": a corruption of the "Kiss me, my fool!" with which the vamp taunts her prey.[45]

The success of the film was beholden to the sculpture of Bara's celebrity persona by Fox public relations. Bara was promoted as the daughter of a French artist and his Egyptian concubine—or was she the Egyptian-born daughter of a French actress and an Italian sculptor? In any event, she was raised in the shadow of the Sphinx. Publicity shots of *The Serpent of the Nile* surrounded her with skeletons, crystal balls, and other orientalist tat, and Bara was encouraged to discuss the occult in public. Need I mention that she was photographed upon divans? (See Plate 12.) When Bara's *Cleopatra* was released, in 1917, her name was revealed as an anagram of "Arab Death," and in interviews she claimed to be the reincarnation of a daughter of the high priest of the pharaohs. Her filmography reveals that any orientalist temptress—Salome, Mata Hari, La Esmeralda—might be projected upon Bara's "Jewish" features, her large nose and large dark eyes. Bara would make thirty-eight films over the next four years, until Fox dropped her contract and effectively ended her career—but not before intensive publicity had helped her to a prominent seat in the cultural imaginary's decadent salon.[46]

Interestingly, Fox simultaneously promoted Bara's exoticism and revealed that her persona was false. At her first press conference, Fox explained that Bara was accustomed to the torrid heat of Arabia, which was why the room was overheated and why, despite the swelter, she was swathed in layers of velvets, veils, and tiger skins as she sprawled on her chaise. Biographer Eve Golden relates how, after the press conference, "Young Louella Parsons—not yet a famous Hollywood gossip columnist—witnessed the Arabian star ripping her veils and coat off, staggering to the window, throwing it open, and gasping in perfect Mid-American, 'Give me air!'" This witnessing was as scripted as Bara's lounging and lines: Fox intended a two-tiered publicity campaign wherein some would believe Bara to be Arabian and some would appreciate being "in the know." The combination left Bara both provocative and unthreatening to a public that could toggle between being excited by Bara's "heritage" and being reassured that it was just play. Overall, the public seems to have enjoyed and believed both that Bara grew up in a spacious tent pitched by the pyramids *and* that she was a nice Jewish girl from Cincinnati. We see this in protests by Irish groups over Bara's assumption of the title role in the 1919 film *Kathleen Mavourneen,* adopted from the traditional ballad of the same name. Bara's plasticity did not extend to the face of innocent Kathleen, and the public could not excuse the impropriety of a "Jewess" playing her. After riots that resulted in thousands of dollars' damage to projection equipment and death threats that promised worse, Fox pulled the film.[47]

Other vamps, including Pola Negri and Alla Nazimova, also had their sexuality heightened through emphasis upon their eastern European or Middle Eastern origin, which was often false. Nita Naldi was born Mary Dooley. Olga Petrova was born Muriel Harding. Marin Sais was Mae Smith. Stein did not need to change her name in order to grease her entry into this harem, for the public drew this conclusion from available evidence. Stein was a Jewish, unmarried, financially independent woman who lived in France and collected art, socialized with the most avant-garde artists, and was herself an experimental writer. After *Portrait of Mabel Dodge at the Villa Curonia* (1912), the Armory Show (1913), and *Tender Buttons* (1914), Stein's broad queerness was so pronounced in the American imagination that she was freely associated with behaviors and attributes that were not her own but were nonetheless present in stereotypes of inappropriate female behavior. Putting Stein on the opium couch and in the orientalist harem made her safer and more comprehensible, both more appealing and easier to dismiss.[48]

The reminiscences of Sherwood Anderson and Richard Wright, who recalled their own misconceptions of Stein as an opium queen, exemplify this mistaken embrace. Anderson and Wright offer evidence that Stein's broad queerness was so strongly fixed in the public imagination that it could travel freely along nonnormative chains of association. This was the freedom that, when coupled with Stein's newfound respectability, successfully cloaked the exhibition of lesbian identity and erotics in *The Autobiography*. Sherwood Anderson illustrates how this took place in his 1922 essay "The Work of Gertrude Stein": "I had myself heard stories of a long dark room with a languid woman lying on a couch, smoking cigarettes, sipping absinthes perhaps and looking out upon the world with tired, disdainful eyes. Now and then she rolled her head slowly to one side and uttered a few words, taken down by a secretary who approached the couch with trembling eagerness to catch the falling pearls." The metaphor of falling pearls implies that Stein is so rich that she may strew gems, and so indolent that her only effort is to slowly roll her head. Stein has "tired, disdainful eyes" not from work but from the fatigue that plagues those who exhaust all pleasure. Her sexual appeal is not explicit but is nonetheless inherent in the trope of "a languid woman reclining on a couch." Kiss me, my Fool![49]

Anderson wrote within seven years of Theda Bara's lying languid on a divan in *A Fool There Was*, smoking with disdain as she rebooted the clichés of the fin de siècle. Note the fantasy of Stein "sipping absinthes perhaps." And what kind of cigarette is Stein smoking? What makes an opium den besides women smoking on upholstered sofas? Eastern stage dressing, here supplied by Jewish Stein. Anderson's conflation of opium and absinthe is sensible, as absinthe, opium, and hashish had the advantage of being both widely known in the United States and definitely foreign through their association with, respectively, France, China, and the Middle East and India. The drugs were tags for the dangerous, the foreign, and the unnatural in the American imagination—as well as for their "deadly appeal." The image of Stein seductively smoking on her divan offered the added advantage of challenging neither the dominance of heterosexuality nor the idea that female sexual appeal was for the benefit of men.[50]

Yet Anderson's description also makes plain how Stein's persona referenced her homosexuality, both generally, through louche bohemia, and specifically, through her partner. We may detect Toklas in the secretary who approaches Stein with "trembling eagerness," though the actual Toklas was not prone to trembling. Those who did not recognize Toklas did know that single women working in the arts were sexually suspect. Furthermore, the American public believed Paris to be the natural habitat of the lesbian. Until Radclyffe Hall's *The Well of Loneliness* (1928)—which itself positions Paris as a decadent lesbian haven—most available depictions of female same-sexuality were in French literature. This meshed nicely with the sexual freedom that Americans associated with France.[51]

When Anderson and, later, Wright received reports of Gertrude Stein, opium queen, they were nascent writers who had only one foot in bohemian circles; they bespeak Stein's reputation outside the bounds of elite culture. Anderson knows his misunderstanding is at large: "As there is in America an impression of Miss Stein's personality, not at all true and rather foolishly romantic, I would like first of all to brush that aside." He notes the appeal and extent of this "foolishly romantic" persona, which he happily displaces: "You will perhaps understand some of my own surprise and delight when, after having been fed up on such tales and rather Tom Sawyerishly hoping they might be true, I was taken to her to find instead of this languid impossibility a woman of striking vigor, a subtle and powerful mind, a discrimination in the arts such as I have found in no other American born man or woman, and a charmingly brilliant conversationalist." Elsewhere, Anderson assures America that Stein possessed good midwestern characteristics and values. She was vigorous in body and powerful in mind, with an unusual capacity for telling good from bad. Anderson goes so far as to characterize Stein as a folksy grandmother: "She is an American woman of the old sort, one who cares for the handmade goodies and who scorns the factory-made food, and in her own great kitchen she is making something with her materials, something sweet to the tongue and fragrant to the nostrils." Stein is off the couch and in the kitchen.[52]

The similarity of Anderson's account to Richard Wright's is remarkable—especially as the men were of different races, were born thirty-two years apart, and wrote their recollections almost twenty-five years apart. Anderson wrote in 1922, remembering his conception of Stein before he met her, in 1921; Wright wrote in 1946, probably remembering 1934. Anderson was a lifelong midwesterner best known for the short stories in *Winesburg, Ohio,* which exposed the loneliness and desperation of small-town America; Wright was a southerner who wrote two important works of African American literature: *Native Son* and *Black Boy.* Though both men were politically liberal and wrote in the American modernist tradition, they were never part of the same artistic circle, except for their common friendship with Stein.[53]

Throughout his career, Wright was Stein's fan, and after they met he tried to correct her public persona and increase her readership. Like Anderson, Wright offers an anecdote for those misled by vampy Stein. He could not reconcile his admiration for *Three Lives* with her degenerate reputation: "But in the midst of my delight, I was jolted. A left-wing literary critic whose judgment I had been led to respect, condemned Miss Stein in a sharply-worded newspaper article, implying that she spent her days reclining upon a silken couch in Paris smoking hashish, that she was a hopeless prey to hallucinations, and that her tortured verbalisms were throttling the revolution. I was disturbed. Had I duped myself into worshiping decadence?"[54] Although I cannot confirm which "prominent left-wing critic" caused Wright to doubt his appreciation of Stein, Wright almost certainly refers to "Gertrude Stein: A Literary Idiot," a caustic review written by Michael Gold, the editor in chief of the *New Masses,* which served as an unofficial voice of the Communist Party USA and its fellow travelers. (When Wright first read Stein, he was strongly committed to the party.) Even if Wright does not refer to "A Literary Idiot," what he does reference is written along the same party lines. Gold accused Stein of hallucinating on a couch when she should have been worrying about the plight of the worker and coming to his aid. Stein's writing was symptomatic of the decadence of wealth: "[T]o Gertrude Stein and to the other artists like her, art exists in the vacuum of a private income. In order to pursue the kind of art, in order to be the kind of artist Gertrude Stein is, it is necessary to live in that kind of society which will permit one to have a private income from wealthy parents or sound investments." Gold told his readers how they should respond: "They see in the work of Gertrude Stein extreme symptoms of the decay of capitalist culture. They view her work as the complete attempt to annihilate all relations between the artist and the society in which he lives."[55] Wright is so ashamed that he designs a test to prove Stein's leftist bona fides:

> Believing in direct action, I contrived a method to gauge the degree to which Miss Stein's prose was tainted with the spirit of counter-revolution. I gathered a group of semi-literate Negro stockyard workers . . . into a Black Belt basement and read *Melanctha* aloud to them. They understood every word. Enthralled, they slapped their thighs, howled, laughed, stomped, and interrupted me constantly to comment upon the characters.
>
> My fondness for Stein never distressed me after that.

Out of context, Wright's story of "Melanctha" and the stockyard workers may read as parody. But the depth of Wright's commitment to both Stein and the Communist Party proves his sincerity.[56]

To an extent, the disagreement between Gold and Wright is false. Wright discusses Stein's *Three Lives,* which exposes the plight of women oppressed by race, gender, ethnicity, and sexual orientation, whereas Gold discusses her experimental word portrait "Matisse"—and perhaps has her deluxe art books in mind, which suit his thesis well. Nonetheless, the class analysis of "A Literary Idiot" shines further light on how the fantasy of the opium queen enrobes Stein's specific homosexuality within broad queerness, just as the Communist Party (and the Old Left in general) held homosexuality to be yet another symptom of how the rich "seek new sensations, new adventures constantly in order to give themselves feelings." The association between homosexuality, decadence, and the upper classes—the last already positioned as effeminate in America because of their apparent estrangement from "manly" work—had been cemented by the Wilde trials. The starry ranks of the Parisian lesbian demimonde strengthened the link between moneyed bohemian decadence and female same-sexuality for Americans. Gold's portrait of Stein thus both indicates and critiques her homosexuality.[57]

Gold's 1934 attack on Stein demonstrates that the understanding of Gertrude Stein as a fin de siècle decadent held strong even after she published *The Autobiography of Alice B. Toklas* and graced the cover of *TIME* magazine in 1933, saw the successful Broadway run of *Four Saints in Three Acts* in 1934, and crisscrossed the country for a well-received lecture tour in 1934 and 1935. Although Stein could shape some aspects of her literary career, neither *The Autobiography* nor any direct evidence provided by her presence on the lecture stage was able to do away with a celebrity persona that the public was unwilling to relinquish. Gold's, Wright's, and Anderson's perceptions of Stein testify to the power of her broadly queer attributes to fascinate the public even as they collaborated with the historic invisibility of lesbians to allow *The Autobiography* to avoid homophobic censure despite its extended depiction of lesbians in a sustained and loving domestic embrace. Thus, audiences primed by their own same-sexual erotics and identity were able to recognize and benefit from Stein's specifically lesbian memoir and persona, even as her broad queerness allowed a sustained, if mistaken, commercial kiss.[58]

Gertrude Stein in *Life* and *TIME*
A Respectable Commodity

The Thrill Is Gone

To read and, even more, to buy a book by Gertrude Stein in the 1910s and '20s *meant* something. Her readers supported with time and perhaps money an aesthetic that was proudly and self-consciously avant-garde, and often derided at large. Whether readers were moved by interest or curiosity, by fuel for cultural capital, or by fodder for ridicule, readers did not experience Stein's work in a vacuum but enjoyed the benefit of reading work that was very much à la mode. They enjoyed the extra ice cream, if you will, of the active exploration of subversive art.

Readers of *The Autobiography of Alice B. Toklas* could still enjoy this ice cream, but without the risk of being complicit, however privately and passively, in a subversive activity. To extend the metaphor, Stein's ice cream now contained neither fat nor lactose and was a safer foodstuff but also less tasty. By 1933, the modernist art of the Armory Show had become a valuable commodity, and Stein herself a long-established figure. There was no risk of identifying with artists and writers whose work or person threatened the established order, as Picasso, Hemingway, and friends had joined it. Pictorial modernism had been configured into much the shape it holds today, and it steadily accrued worth in both the academy and the market. *The Autobiography* would be less cheerful if more of those profiled had died hungry and unknown.[1]

This safety extended to form as well as content. No, the five parts of the book are not in chronological order, but the parts themselves are. Yes, Stein wrote her autobiography from the perspective of Toklas, but this voice is consistent and friendly, and its syntax is easy to follow. And yes, the conflation of Stein and Toklas in the point of view and in their domestic life embodies same-sex relations; but the broad queerness of Stein's reputation, as well as her age, served to cover this exposure, except for those who wished to peel back the blanket.

The aging into respectability of Stein's persona, and the simplification into popularity of her work, is a convention of Stein studies, and I subscribe to it. In the crudest version of this narrative, *The Autobiography* and its success made a clean break from Stein's previous work and audience. This chapter augments this narrative in three ways. First, I consider Stein's various publications in the mass media before *The Autobiography,* and how they associate with broad queerness and specific homosexuality and how they do not. The strength of Stein's persona, as well as the critical investment in her queerness, has made it difficult to see ways that her work was *not* queer but instead easily digested by hundreds of thousands of readers as early as 1917. At the same time, her work and her person asserted same-sexuality, an assertion that ranged through the spectrum from hidden to bold. Second, I consider how Stein's staying power on the public scene caused her and her work to become that common paradox, the "shocking" figure of the avant-garde whom time and familiarity have made respectable. This respectability hollowed out some of Stein's broad queerness and offered her more freedom to denote and connote same-sexuality without triggering homophobia or censorship. Third, I examine Stein's much-described and -portrayed physical form, and how her visual portraits show what cannot be told, through her astonishing 1933 cover story in *TIME* magazine: a beachhead for the representation of female same-sexuality in the public eye.[2]

Stein in *Life*, 1917: "Relief Work in France"

On December 27, 1917, *Life* published a short poem by Gertrude Stein, "Relief Work in France." Two years later, on September 19, *Life* published another, "A League." *Life* is not *LIFE,* the photojournalism magazine founded by Henry Luce that ran from 1938 to 1972. Instead, *Life* (1883–1930) was an influential humor magazine popular in middle- and upper-class homes. A contemporary analogue in form is the "Talk of the Town" section of *The New Yorker*: a collection of short anecdotes, both visual and written, some signed and some not. (In 1925, before its first issue, *The New Yorker* would raid the staff of *Life*.) *Life* also included theater and cinema reviews and drawings and cartoons, including many iconic images of the Gibson girl. Though editor John Ames Mitchell founded *Life* as an American version of the British *Punch,* the magazine soon became known for attacks on indecency, Prohibition, "politics as usual," and William Randolph Hearst. The magazine's targets frequently sued, and these court cases raised *Life*'s profile as an advocate for the public interest, which helped shift its reputation from indecent to upstanding.[3]

Life offered Stein her biggest and most respectable outlet to date. "Relief Work in France" and "A League" were Stein's most widely published works for the first twenty years of her career; few of her readers read anything else by Stein that was not included in a parody or review. And "few" understates, as the combined print run of Stein's three most popular works of the 1910s and '20s—*Three Lives, Tender Buttons,* and *Geography and Plays*—was 4,500 manuscript sheets, many of which were not sold or even bound for decades. By comparison, *Life* had 150,000 readers in 1916. They did not seek out Stein but read her in the magazine. Thus, "Relief Work in France" and "A League" had a readership greater by a factor of 83 than her first three major books combined. Yet the poems make a poor showing in Stein studies. Each is included in one anthology: "A League" in *Useful Knowledge,* edited by Stein herself, and "Relief Work in France," in *Reflections on the Atom Bomb.* The only substantive critical analysis of either poem that I have found is by Margaret Dickey, who does not consider the poems' status as Stein's most circulated work before 1933. Why is their mass audience—extraordinary for Stein—not in and of itself worthy of comment?[4]

This is not necessarily a useful question. Stein wrote a lot, and much has received little consideration. But note that the *Life* poems, especially the first, propose an alternate career trajectory for Stein, one where her notoriety would not shape the presentation of her work and where the work itself would not be queer in form or content. The lack of any contemporary scandal further contributes to their poor showing. Stein herself takes notice of "Relief Work in France" in *The Autobiography,* where she explains that its acceptance was due to a clever letter to the editor: "Gertrude Stein suddenly one day wrote a letter to Masson who was the editor of Life and said to him that the real Gertrude Stein was . . . funnier in every way than the imitations, not to say much more interesting, and why did they not print the original. To her astonishment she received a very nice letter from Mr. Masson saying that he would be glad to do so. And they did." Stein refers to three limp parodies, all titled "Cubist Poems—after Gertrude Stein," that *Life* published in summer 1917. The letter sheds light on her consciousness of her public persona, her limited control over it, and her desire to be more widely read. (The story also suggests that the editor of *Life* was a good sport.) As *Life* did not publish Stein's letter, and as the three parodies were published half a year before "Relief Work in France"—a long time for a weekly magazine—the only editorial positioning of Stein in the latter publication is a parenthesis after the poem's title: "Miss Gertrude Stein sends us this contribution from Paris, and it has been set in the style of type in which Miss Stein's verses usually appear.—Editor of Life." The editor establishes Stein as a credible war reporter, as she sends the poem from Paris, and the careful delineation of her usual font of small capitals communicates (1) that she has a body of work that (2) is worthy of special type. Stein registers as special, but her specialness is not accompanied, as usual, with either ridicule or deification.[5]

The poem opens five windows upon its subject in five irregular stanzas. Here are the first two, as indented in *Life*:

THE ADVANCE
IN COMING TO A VILLAGE WE ASK THEM CAN THEY
COME TO SEE US. WE MEAN NEAR ENOUGH TO TALK;
AND THEN WE ASK THEM HOW DO WE GO THERE.
THIS IS NOT FANCIFUL.

MONDAY AND TUESDAY
IN THE MEANTIME WHAT CAN WE DO ABOUT WISHES?
WISH THE SAME.
AGREED FOR A MINOR.
AND FOR MY NIECE. WHAT ARE YOU DOING FOR MY NIECE?
BABY CLOTHES.
AND MILK.
MALTED MILK.

The poem offers a lucid mimesis of relief work. The first stanza suggests the complex transactions necessary to approach strangers in wartime, and the second offers the overlapping voices and thoughts of the aid workers and villagers during the two days between requests for aid and their fulfillment. Only "AGREED FOR A MINOR" is hard to unlock. Other verses are less transparent, but the practice of aid may be discerned.

In the context of this issue of *Life,* "Relief Work in France" is neither difficult nor avant-garde. (See Plate 13.) The lead article, "-Less Days in Germany," unsigned like much of the work in *Life,* sets the subject of war and the tone of wordplay and resembles "Relief Work" as a series of fragmented stanzas on the war. In some respects, "-Less Days" is *less* traditional than Stein's poem, with more nonce words and less traditional syntax. Instead, a series of words, often with more than one meaning, are made parallel by the addition of the suffix *-less* and are organized into seven lines of comparable length, headed by, but with only occasional relation to, the seven days of the week.

MONDAY. Tasteless, friendless, virtueless, beerless, jestless, wasteless, thankless, provisionless.

TUESDAY. Victoryless, butterless, shoeless, heartless, soupless, matchless, cigarless, peaceless, dietless.

WEDNESDAY. Bankless, hapless, faithless, fishless, flourless, regardless, pipeless, warmthless, rationless.

THURSDAY. Kulturless, fortuneless, consciousless, breakfastless, supperless, joyless, pitiless.

FRIDAY. Comfortless, powerless, truthless, meatless, respiteless, slumberless, eggless, eatless, drinkless.

SATURDAY. Helpless, financeless, cheerless, virtueless, colorless, breadless, banquetless, lawless, masticationless.

SUNDAY. Gottless, honorless, neverless, restless, hopeless, cruelless, endless, nutrimentless, lifeless.

Once its rule is understood, "-Less Days" is easily parsed, whereas "Relief Work" remains unstable and ambiguous, and thus more challenging in form. "-Less Days" is more politically challenging, however, as German words such as *Gott* and *Kultur,* as well as *beer,* then inaccurately believed to be the quintessential German drink, suggest that the poem reflects the perspective of German troops. Though the Germans are "honorless" and "lawless," they are also "helpless," "hopeless," "nutrimentless," and finally "lifeless." The poem extends some sympathy to the enemy, which is surprising, as *Life,* like most U.S. magazines by 1917, dehumanized Germans as a matter of course.[6]

The rest of the December 27, 1917, issue of *Life* sports an abundance of medium, genre, and attitude. Pages 1075 and 1076 are typical. "Relief Work in France" follows "Wanted: Safe-Keeping for Bonds," an earnest plea for a "special, country-wide provision for safe-keeping of [liberty] bonds for small investors." After "Relief Work in France" comes the unsigned "Locating the Germans," a parody of anti-ethnic hysteria so precisely calibrated that it is impossible to state what is being satirized except ethnicity itself. Even Stein's special type does not draw attention to itself; the drawings on pages 1076 and 1077, as in the rest of *Life*, are as numerous and varied as the written contributions, both in form and in content. "Relief Work in France" is kitty-corner from a one-panel cartoony visual joke wherein a suitor drops his candy as "She" reveals the pointed Prussian helmet her soldier boyfriend has sent her, conflating the suitor's fear of a killer fiancé with his own shame at not fighting in the war. This cartoon is itself kitty-corner, across the binding edge of the facing page, from the thirty-first installment of E. Forster Lincoln's absurdist serial *The Willowbys' Ward,* which is anchored by the conflict between the absurd goings-on and the naturalist, almost photographic combination of drawing and wash (see Plate 13). As "Locating the Germans" reminds us as it mocks both vigilance and lassitude, "It is astonishing what new arts one has to practice in wartimes." Seen in this context, Stein's poem is not broadly queer but entirely appropriate for *Life.*[7]

Stein in *Life*, 1919: "A League"

Stein's next poem in *Life* reflects upon the League of Nations. The league was proposed in January 1919 and established on June 28 at the Treaty of Versailles, and "A League" was published on September 18. The editor frames Stein less sympathetically than in 1917: "Miss Gertrude Stein is one of the pioneers of Free Verse. We gladly publish her poem as a fit accompaniment to President Wilson's elucidation of the League of Nations— EDITOR OF LIFE." "Wilson's elucidation of the League of Nations" references the president's difficulty (and later failure) in persuading Congress to ratify the entry of the United States into the league; the editors position "A League" as an unwitting satire upon Wilson and thereby mock "Free Verse," a term that had been coined only four years before. In context, the introduction suits the poem, as the difficulty of "A League" does not suit *Life* as well as "Relief Work in France" does.[8]

"A League" reads as follows:

> Why don't you visit your brother with a girl he doesn't know?
> And in the midst of emigration we have wishes to bestow.
> We gather that the West is wet and fully ready to flow.

And we father that the East is wet and very ready to say so.
We gather that we wonder, and we gather that it is in respect to all of
    us that we think.
Let us stray.
Do you want a baby? A round one or a pink one?

The poem personifies, sexualizes, and urges on the creation of the League
of Nations in intimate lesbian terms. Whereas "Relief Work in France"
represents same-sexuality only to those who read Stein and Toklas's biography into the poem, "A League" requires no such outside knowledge,
though Stein's queer public persona, as ever, offers cues.

The first line of "A League" calls for social, probably romantic, mixing outside one's circle, possibly the introduction of a potential fiancée
to one's family. This possibility is heightened by the line's syntax: the repeated negative, the question with the rising inflection, which indicates
a Yiddish accent. The line's accent and content suggest the voice of an
interfering Jewish mother—soon revealed to be plural: a league of yentas—
here uncharacteristically asking for relations outside the tribe. This call
for exogamy is transposed to an international key by the title "A League"
and by the next line's "wishes" (presumably "good wishes"), bestowed by
the first-person plural narrator "in the midst of emigration." Note that
"best wishes" was the polite congratulation to a new bride for much of
the twentieth century, and "congratulations" implied that a bride had actively promoted engagement rather than passively waited to be chosen,
as was appropriate. Note too that "emigration" is an accurate metaphor
for a woman in a patriarchal society who leaves her father's house for her
husband's.

The encomium continues with an embodied, female same-sexualization
of West and East, both of which are "wet." The narrators "gather," or com-
pile information from various sources, that the West is "fully ready to
flow"—they intuit or learn not only the Western woman's arousal but
also her *anticipation* of arousal. The narrators also "father" that the East
is not only "ready" and "wet" but also vocal about her readiness for an international sexualized congress. Stein sometimes references her heritage
as "oriental," or Eastern, which may explain how the narrators "father"
(somehow inseminate, are genetically related to) the East's availability
for mixing—a knowledge that the narrators are "very ready to say."

Biography aside, Stein's call for a community of nations introduces
its climax with "Let us stray," a profane, sexualized rewrite of "Let us pray,"

and extends this climax with a proffer of reproduction: "Do you want a baby?" This question is queered by the end of the climactic line: "A round one or a pink one?" These two choices—round or pink, a particular shape or a particular color—are not in the same order of things and, as such, put categorization itself in doubt. In the context of a poem that promotes promiscuous national blending, this disordering disrupts the poem's two scales of ordering—sexuality and ethnicity—to fertilize unusual fruit. "A League" is therefore intimately lesbian in content, if not obviously and invariably so. To most readers of *Life,* Stein was an occasional political poet whose queerness was textual rather than sexual, and not extreme. The poem manages to state its lesbian terms in the public ear without being publicly censored or understood. Its textual queerness offers a trail of bread crumbs that, if properly followed, leads to a lesbian door.

Stein in *Vanity Fair* and at War

Stein's other mass-market outlet during the 1910s and '20s was *Vanity Fair,* which published the poems "Have they attacked Mary. He giggled" (June 1917), "The Great American Army" (June 1918), and "A Deserter," "The Meaning of the Bird," "J. R.," and "J. R. II" (all March 1919), as well as the short story "Miss Furr and Miss Skeene" (July 1923). *Vanity Fair* had less than half the circulation of *Life* in the 1910s, and its readers were the cultural elite and those who wished to be. These wishers might use *Vanity Fair* as an instruction manual to "society." The magazine was very much the vision of editor Frank Crowninshield, who himself embodied the stereotype of the elegant, charming gay man whose interests may be graphed by a Venn diagram of the intersection between aesthetics and wealth: "My interest in society—at times so pronounced that the word 'snob' comes a little to mind—derives from the fact that I like an immense number of things which society, money, and position bring in their train: paintings, tapestries, rare books, smart dresses, dances, gardens, country houses, correct cuisine, and pretty women."[9]

The editor's introduction to Stein's four poems in the March 1919 issue exemplifies how her status as a pillar of the avant-garde gave her, as pillars do, a certain stability and authority: she might be depended upon to shore up *Vanity Fair*'s high-culture credentials as a judge of who was "in" and who was "out": "[J]ust as surely did Miss Stein introduce a new artform. Whether or not you like her art form—or lack of it, rather, whether or not you understand the cryptic meaning of her verses, there she is, and there is her influence, and there are her changes, and there will they remain. Vanity Fair has published poems by Miss Stein before; poems that have, to be sure, been often greatly misunderstood. But these are some which have just reached us from her in Paris." And of course *Vanity Fair* would publish them, for *Vanity Fair,* unlike those who misunderstood, was not an idiot. "Readers, be assured: comprehension is not needed for appreciation, for 'There she is.'" In chapter 3, we saw how Stein's work was presented without commentary or parody by those secure that no one could ridicule Stein more than her work itself could; now, her work itself, without explanation, secures her status, whether readers understand her or not.[10]

For *Vanity Fair* and, to an extent, at large, Stein's capacity to be respectable *because* of her broad queerness was greased by her role as an ambulance driver in World War I, a keynote of her legend. Patriotism was complicated for Stein by her identification with France, where she spent most of her postcollegiate life. The American Fund for French Wounded let her serve both masters. Stein and Toklas did not drive the wounded but delivered supplies to French hospitals until the armistice. Was Stein's war experience "considered so unusual that she was able to publish war poetry in such popular magazines as *Life* and *Vanity Fair* at a time when she was having great difficulty in placing her work in avant-garde journals"? Did her service make her work more salable?[11]

Stein's ambulance driving is stressed in her biographies and autobiographies and still contributes to her mystique. The volunteer work is heroic, and some details are funny, such as Stein's dislike of reverse gear, her poor sense of direction, and her cars Auntie and Godiva. The two women's close relations with American GIs are interesting and engaging; inspire Stein's lovely, warm prose piece *Brewsie and Willy*; and, along with the driving, are the focus of *Wars I Have Seen*. Nonetheless, there is little evidence that Stein's volunteer work was well known *during* the war. *Vanity Fair* makes much of it, but *Life*—which, unlike *Vanity Fair,* was a mass-market magazine—does not mention Stein's service, though "Relief Work in France" narrates one of her and Toklas's trips. Nor is it certain that Stein's volunteer work, if commonly known, would have been considered broadly queer.[12]

Wars that involve a significant percentage of a population usually strain the preexisting gendered division of labor. Although men who did not support the war effort in WWI were mocked as unmanly, women who supported the effort were not necessarily seen as unfeminine. The

American Fund for French Wounded was run by Mrs. Isabel Winthrop, who was wearing "a pink dress with pearls and a garden party hat" when she met Stein and Toklas. Stein's bumbles at the wheel were appropriately feminine and further normalized her war work. Many other volunteers of the American Fund for French Wounded ran greater risks and did greater good.[13]

Nonetheless, in its June 1918 issue, *Vanity Fair* makes Stein's service nonpareil: "Gertrude Stein, the first and most representative of the so-called cubists in prose, has, since the outbreak of the war, been living in France and working in war relief as an ambulance driver. Few American women have taken a more active part in the conflict than she. During the past few weeks, the continued arrival of our troops in France has inspired her to compose this poem." As if that were not enough, both the introduction and poem, "The Great American Army," are dwarfed by a lithograph by Lucien Jonas, "one of the ablest of the French official war painters," which looms above (see Plate 14). In the image, titled *Courage, mes braves! J'arrive!*, American soldiers come to the aid of France under the aegis of the Statue of Liberty, who returns to her birthplace with a fierce, grave expression.[14] Liberty regards the viewer directly but is modeled less substantially than the three doughboys, who look to the left, presumably encouraging *La France*. Jonas presents the French vision of Liberty, a vision that France gave to the Americans, who supervises the return of liberty to France through American means. The transaction is straightforward: only a forced reading could make this queer. The introduction and lithograph cue us for a blunt patriotic anthem, which "The Great American Army" is not, from the start:

I found an acorn to-day.
Green
In the center.
No, on the end.
And what is the name of the bridge?
This is what we say.
"The Great American Army,"—
This is what we say.

The poem ends triumphantly—"We have hope: / Certainly— / And Success!"—but the average reader of *Vanity Fair*, despite an investment in seeming well read, would have been challenged to do much more with this poem than recognize an oblique association between American troops and new life.[15]

This challenge explains why *Vanity Fair* goes to such lengths to position Stein as a war heroine. Her, and to an extent the magazine's, association with the rich, the avant-garde, and decadence must be reconciled with the patriotic mood of the times. Ads in the June 1918 issue, as throughout the war, attempt to square luxury goods with the war effort. Some are blunt: "Buy a Liberty Bond with your discarded Jewels!" Some strive clunkily for subtlety, as on this issue's second page, where two stylish women chat as they knit above this tagline: "Hosiery—each the best of its kind,—home knit for our soldiers and Onyx Hosiery, for those whose needs demand the essential combination of Style, Quality and sound Value."[16]

Vanity Fair knits a careful line. Its usual mocking, self-conscious sophistication naturally holds itself aloof from the mainstream and must be carefully basted to an emotion that by its definition suits the masses. Consider "How to Live in War Time: Hints for Patriotic Women Based on Information from the Latest Ladies Magazines," on the page that faces "The Great American Army." Stephen Leacock offers sample menus for "Plain Luncheons for Four," such as Tuesday's "Potage Croute au Pot, Beef War Steak with War Mushrooms, Fresh War Asparagus au Beurre, Peach Méringue à la Guerre, War Coffee." These should be enjoyed while wearing "a simple war gown suitable for eating a war lunch." This satire and others like it appear cheek by jowl with articles they satirize in *Vanity Fair*, such as "High Lights of Wartime Simplicity: The Perfect Accessory Is the Keynote of the Perfect Costume," which suggests without irony, "No more must one wait to be a dowager to possess the most formidable weapon known to woman—the lorgnette." By mocking others' lip service toward the war effort, *Vanity Fair* shields its own lip service from criticism *and* situates itself above the common. This fulfills *Vanity Fair*'s (and high society's) larger task of placing itself above respectability while being respectable. By both establishing Stein's impeccable patriotic credentials and showcasing her difficult, if apparently patriotic, poetry, *Vanity Fair* reconciles its own sophistication and patriotism.[17]

As for Stein herself, the undeniable bravery of her war effort, especially as showcased by *Vanity Fair*, augmented the cultural heft, and thus respectability, that comes to those who endure in the public eye. By the 1933 publication of *The Autobiography*, Stein had been a public figure for twenty-four years, and familiarity had dulled her queerness. Stein's "respectable queerness" thus provided both a closet and a platform for aspects of her work and persona that were specifically lesbian.

Stein on *TIME*

The September 11, 1933, cover of *TIME* magazine confirmed Stein's ascension to mass celebrity (see Plate 15). The magazine, published the same month as *The Autobiography,* offered a widely available image of Stein to Americans who may not have been interested in writing, art, or Stein but nonetheless read *TIME,* one of the most popular magazines of its day. Even those who did not read *TIME* would be likely to see the cover of Stein at the newsstand, then a site of considerable commerce and cultural importance. Stein was now part of the visual vocabulary of those who did not read.[18]

TIME was the first weekly newsmagazine in the United States, founded in 1923 by Briton Hadden and Henry Luce, then both twenty-four. Hadden and Luce had edited competing publications at Hotchkiss, one of the great American prep schools, and were respectively chairman and managing editor of the *Yale Daily News.* Hadden's desire for a fresh, fun publication coupled with Luce's more traditional approach to news reporting led to heavy coverage of popular culture and the entertainment industry as well as more traditional subjects. Even when covering government, crime, international affairs, and economics, *TIME* tried to tell the news through individual people—for instance, by reducing complex politics to single politicians and making those politicians celebrities. This methodology was exemplified by the standard cover of *TIME:* a portrait of a single person, surmounted by the title and, after 1927, surrounded by a red border. These covers led to the "Man of the Year" issues, which *TIME* publicized so relentlessly that the yearly selection became newsworthy in itself. The promise of imparting intimate knowledge of the most important man on the planet placed these issues among the year's best-selling issues of any magazine.

Stein's cover is best approached in the context of other portraits of her, and in relation to other covers of *TIME.* In "Stein's Way," his cover story on Stein, James Agee notes the unusual number of Stein portraits: "If posterity understands present-day art, it is likely that the future will have a pretty good idea of what Stein looked like. Picasso has painted her, Picabia has drawn her, Jo Davidson has done a joss-like statue of her." Neither Davidson's 1922 statue nor the Picasso or Picabia paintings is pictured; Agee assumes that his readers know them or other, similar portraits of Stein. Agee also notes that Stein is understood at least in part through visual means: "We picture her as the great pyramidal Buddha of Jo Davidson's statue of her, eternally and placidly ruminating the gradual developments of the processes of being, registering the vibrations of a psychological country like some august seismograph whose charts we haven't the training to read." Agee reinforces the fabulous potency of Stein's public persona and its unusual connection with visuality.[19]

How did *TIME* respond to this tradition of Stein portraiture? The editors did not commission a new work. Instead, they cropped a 1931 photograph of Stein at home in Bilignin, France, taken by her friend gay fashion photographer George Platt Lynes (see Plate 16). In the Lynes photo, Stein does not engage her audience in the usual roundelay of gaze and desire; her eyes neither seek nor avoid her viewer. The proximity of her body accentuates the distance of her gaze. For Stein looks out in the distance; we cannot see what holds her gaze, as her focus extends past the boundary of the photo. What we do see is a spacious landscape. The close focus on Stein and the wide depth of field leave the landscape less defined than Stein; even a causal viewer may make a formal observation about the photograph's focus. Stein is thus more "real" than her setting, a material woman in Arcadia. Her expression is pensive and self-contained, implying that even if she looks at other people, her attention is not fixed upon them. Her eyes are in shadow, further obscuring her expression. She appears to offer her full attention to whatever or whomever she considers, "eternally and placidly ruminating the gradual developments of the processes of being."[20]

In the context of the 1930s, and especially in the context of *TIME*, by far the most notable aspects of the photo are Stein's hair and clothes, which are extraordinarily masculine. Stein's haircut is shorter than the conventional female crop; in profile, her hair resembles Caesar's on a Roman coin, as noted by Ernest Hemingway: Stein "got to look like a Roman emperor and that was fine if you liked your women to look like Roman emperors." Stein wears a masculine vest over a striped blouse, and the brooch that fastens her collar does not soften her outfit but registers as a medal or necklace. Her attire is plain, "natural," and does not draw attention to itself—all aspects of traditional masculinity that have been part of Stein's public persona since its birth, in 1910.[21]

Moroccan Interlude

Is this drag? For most of the twentieth century, male drag worn by female celebrities was understood to put the wearer's femininity into sharper relief and thereby to increase her heterosexual appeal. Stein was unusual in that her portraits could *not* be easily read in terms of heterosexual appeal. A useful comparison may be made between the 1931 Lynes photo and two still photos from the 1930 film *Morocco,* directed by Josef von Sternberg, which prominently feature male drag. Consider the difference between Marlene Dietrich's tuxedo in Plate 17 and Stein's vest. Under the studied studio glamour of Dietrich's makeup and hair, and on top of a conventionally beautiful female body, the tuxedo's masculinity is in quotation marks. In other words, the tuxedo is "masculine" and draws attention to itself, unlike Stein's vest. Stein did not sport a costume but wore masculine clothes.[22]

Morocco, Dietrich's film debut in the United States, was a popular and well-received movie that reveals how male drag might be profitably presented within popular culture. The movie earned 2 million dollars at the box office (equivalent to more than 150 million today) and nominations for Best Actress, Best Director, Best Art Direction, and Best Cinematography. When world-weary nightclub singer Amy Jolly—a pun on *amie jolie,* "beautiful lover"—makes her debut on the "best-paying stage in Africa" before an orchestra pit packed with the French Foreign Legion, she struts out wearing a top hat and tails. The legionnaires, nonplussed, growl and shout. Jolly lights herself a cigarette in an assertive, masculine manner, and stands smoking until applause rises. Then she hitches up her trouser leg, sits on a railing, and starts to sing. When men attempt to fondle her, she glares them down; the legionnaires roar. She takes a flower from a high-ranking woman in the audience—"May I have this?"—and, when the song is over, kisses her on the lips. The woman simpers and hides her face. The crowd howls.

Dietrich's overall presentation in *Morocco,* both in the movie's marketing and in the movie itself, is that of a conventional temptress. This may be seen in Plate 18, an advertisement in *Photoplay* that shows her provocatively reclining on a chaise longue as, in an inset photo, the male lead, Gary Cooper, stares entranced. Here, Dietrich is presented as Stein was imagined by Anderson and Wright: as a femme fatale in a fantastic fin de siècle. Dietrich has the "tired, disdainful eyes" that Anderson imagined for Stein, and she is "reclining upon a silken couch," as Wright

Plate 1. Truman Capote as Lionel Twain in *Murder by Death,* directed by
Robert Moore (Columbia Pictures, 1976). Publicity photo.

Plate 2. Marguerite Young reads to Truman Capote at Yaddo. Photograph by Lisa Larsen. *LIFE,* July 15, 1946, 110. The LIFE Picture Collection/ Getty Images.

Plate 3. Truman Capote in the Tower Room at Yaddo. Photograph by Lisa Larsen. *LIFE,* July 15, 1946, 113. The LIFE Picture Collection/ Getty Images.

IN A MULLIONED BAY of what was once the boudoir of Lady Katrina, and is now a study for Yaddo authors, Newton Arvin props himself up on long

window seat with a portable typewriter on his knees. Arvin is a director of Yaddo, a professor of English literature at Smith and a biographer of Hawthorne.

BED-MAKING, here demonstrated by Author Arvin, is sometimes done by Yaddo guests because servant problem has cut original staff of 20 down to 5.

IN THE TOWER ROOM, once the secret hideaway of founder, Lady Katrina, who wrote poetry, young Author Truman Capote writes his first novel.

STROLLING GUESTS like authors Jerre Mangione and Granville Hicks are discouraged from dropping in on other guests in studios before 4:30 p.m.

YADDO'S FOUNDERS are buried on estate's highest hill. Katrina's carved ledger stone is in center, flanked by two smaller stones for her husbands.

Plate 4. Pages 112 and 113 of *LIFE,* July 15, 1946. Photographs by Lisa Larsen. Top: Newton Arvin in boudoir. Center left: Bed-making demonstrated by Arvin. Center right: Truman Capote in Tower Room. Lower left: Granville Hicks and Jerry Mangione. Lower right: Gravestones of Lady Katrina and her two husbands. The LIFE Picture Collection/Getty Images.

YOUNG U.S. WRITERS

A REFRESHING GROUP OF NEWCOMERS ON THE LITERARY SCENE IS READY TO TACKLE ALMOST ANYTHING

Just as soon as the end of war promised an end to paper rationing, U.S. book publishers started shopping around for new talent. They found, ready and waiting with manuscript in hand, a brand-new batch of writers who had grown up during the depression. Some had also fought through World War II. All of them seemed more studious, more sober and less pessimistic than "the lost generation" which followed World War I.

These young writers of the 1940s, of whom LIFE presents on these pages a representative selection,

are bringing a new freshness to the American literary scene. One of them, 30-year-old Robert Lowell, has just won the Pulitzer Prize for poetry (LIFE, May 19). A young team wrote the novel, *Mrs. Mike*, the March Literary Guild selection. Other young writers have produced four best-sellers and a half-dozen major and minor critical successes. As a group these new writers, many of whom are in their early 20s, do not suffer in comparison with the early fiction produced by the writers of the 1920s and 1930s. They are busily tackling, in every con-

ceivable style and manner of fiction, almost every subject under the American sun—schooldays, family life, county fairs, mountain lions, Freudian symbolism, roadside drive-ins, Pacific cargo boats, Northwest mounties, Southern poor whites, lack of communication between human beings, and kleptomania.

On pages 81 and 82 LIFE's John Chamberlain, who, as New York *Times*'s and *Harper's* famous critic, watched the last literary generation grow up, gives his estimate of these new young writers.

CONTINUED ON NEXT PAGE

Plate 5. Truman Capote at tête-à-tête. Photograph by Jerry Cooke. *LIFE,* June 2, 1947, 75. Photograph was published at 9¾ x 9¾ inches. The LIFE Picture Collection/Getty Images.

JEAN STAFFORD

Most brilliant of the new fiction writers is Jean Stafford, 31, wife of Pulitzer Prize-winning poet Robert Lowell. In *Boston Adventure* she wrote about Boston bluebloods with such insight that critics promptly compared her to Proust. Her latest, *The Mountain Lion*, which tells in Freudian terms of a Colorado childhood and adolescence, is even better.

THOMAS HEGGEN

This 28-year-old ex-Navy lieutenant wrote *Mister Roberts* (LIFE, Oct. 7, 1946), a satire on life aboard a cargo ship, which was both a best-seller and a critical success. His University of Minnesota classmate, Max Shulman, who wrote *The Zebra Derby* (LIFE, Feb. 4, 1946) and *Barefoot Boy with Cheek*, is helping Heggen turn *Mister Roberts* into a play.

CONTINUED ON PAGE 78

Plate 6. Portraits of Jean Stafford and Thomas Heggen. Photograph of Stafford by Jean Speiser; photograph of Heggen by Jerry Cooke. *LIFE,* June 2, 1947, 76. Photographs were published at 4½ x 4½ inches. The LIFE Picture Collection/Getty Images.

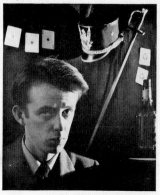

CALDER WILLINGHAM

The 24-year-old author of *End As a Man*, a hard-boiled novel about the brutalizing effects of life in a Southern military academy, is one of the few young writers devoted to realism. His book was attacked this spring by John S. Sumner's Society for the Suppression of Vice, which said *End As a Man* was obscene. It was later cleared in the courts.

"See, Mom? A baby's life isn't all sunshine!"

BABY: Such a face, Mom! Folks'll think you don't *enjoy* being me—having a life that's all "sun and fun"!

MOM: All "sun and fun," eh? Did *I* say that? All "squirms and wriggles" is more like it! I'd forgotten babies work and play so hard. Ooh, my skin's uncomfortable!

BABY: Bless my booties, Mom, that's what *my* skin feels like *all* the time! Now maybe you'll be sympathetic when I tell you I need Johnson's Baby Oil and Johnson's Baby Powder!

MOM: So that's what you've been fussing for, sweetie! But do you need *both*?

BABY: Gracious, yes, Mommie. After my bath, just you smooth me all over with pure, gentle Johnson's Baby Oil. And use it every time you change me, too, to help prevent what my doctor calls "urine irritation."

As for Johnson's Baby Powder—haven't you noticed the chafes and prickles I get these hot summer days? Plenty of cool sprinkles with Powder will help fix that!

MOM: Honey, I've been a behind-the-times mama. But watch me catch up!

BABY: Swell, Mom! Don't let me rush you, but how about a little jaunt out for Johnson's *right* now!

Johnson's Baby Oil
Johnson's Baby Powder

Johnson & Johnson

ELIZABETH FENWICK

This pretty, 27-year-old blonde wrote *The Long Wing*, a first novel dealing with family psychological conflicts. Her polished prose has been compared to that of the distinguished Anglo-Irish novelist, Elizabeth Bowen. Miss Fenwick, who had a peripatetic U.S. childhood, says that family life fascinates her because she never had any of her own.

CONTINUED ON PAGE 81

78

Plate 7. Portraits of Calder Willingham and Elizabeth Fenwick. Photographs by Jerry Cooke. *LIFE*, June 2, 1947, 78. Photographs were published at 4½ x 4½ inches. The LIFE Picture Collection/Getty Images.

PEGGY BENNETT, 22, who lives in Appalachicola, Fla., won critical praise for her first novel, *The Varmints*, which is about Florida poor whites.

GORE VIDAL, 21, writes poetry and Hemingwayesque fiction (*Williwaw*, *In a Yellow Wood*). He was in the Aleutians, now lives in Guatemala.

Young U.S. Writers CONTINUED

cations between human beings . . . the failure of men and women to ever fuse completely with one another."

The obscure emotion, the tenuous reaction, the fluctuating play of inner feeling—these are raw material of Jean Stafford, Elizabeth Fenwick, Gore Vidal, Truman Capote. Jean Stafford is the only one of this group of literary psychologists who makes finished art of her material; *The Mountain Lion* is an extremely able story of what happens to the younger children of a mother who is overburdened with a sense of guilt. If the symbolism of *The Mountain Lion* is obscure, the evocation of childhood moods is not. Truman Capote is also tantalizingly obscure in his symbolism, but he can create a mood of hallucination, as his short story, *Miriam*, proves. Elizabeth Fenwick tries to unravel the inner drama of what happens when a matriarch, an old maid, a disappointed man and an adolescent girl all try to live under one roof; the theme is beyond her present powers, but she gives it a courageous and heart-warming try.

Peggy Goodin's *Clementine*, which won the 1945 Avery Hopwood Award, is Tarkingtoniana—but Booth Tarkington is an underrated writer at the moment, which means there is something to be said for Peggy's story of a feminine Penrod Schofield. *Mrs. Mike*, by Benedict and Nancy Freedman, is a sentimentalized treatment of courage. Courage is also the theme of *Mama Maria's* by Ann Chidester, a realist who is interested in emotions under stress.

What a reading of the new novelists adds up to is significant: the '30s, with their literary emphasis on economics, the psychology of class struggle and class war, have gone to join the hoopla and the wonderful nonsense of the '20s in the mothball-laden prop room of history. What is to succeed the '30s in the '40s and '50s is still in the making; it will probably run to symbolism and the use of imagery and a continued revolt against naturalism and realism. But the boys and girls are experimenting; they are the growing points of new traditions. Not one of the novelists pictured in LIFE this week has yet written a book to be set beside *Main Street*, *My Antonia*, *The Great Gatsby*, *The Sun Also Rises* or *The Forty-second Parallel*. But before *Main Street* Sinclair Lewis wrote *Free Air*; before *My Antonia* Willa Cather wrote *Alexander's Bridge*; before *The Great Gatsby* Fitzgerald wrote *The Beautiful and Damned*; before *The Sun Also Rises* Hemingway wrote *Torrents of Spring*; before *The Forty-second Parallel* Dos Passos wrote *Streets of Night*.

NANCY AND BENEDICT FREEDMAN hit the Literary Guild jackpot last March with their first novel, *Mrs. Mike*, a story of a stouthearted Irish girl who lives in the Canadian Northwest. *Mrs. Mike* has sold 750,000 copies. Nancy, 26, and her husband Benedict, 27, turn out radio gags for Red Skelton.

Plate 8. Page 82 of *LIFE*, June 2, 1947, features portraits of Gore Vidal and other authors. Photograph of Vidal by Jerry Cooke. Photographs on the page were published at 2 x 2 inches and 2 x 4 inches. The LIFE Picture Collection/Getty Images.

Plate 9. Portrait of Truman Capote taken by his roommate, Howard Halma. This was the author photograph for *Other Voices, Other Rooms* (New York: Random House, 1948).

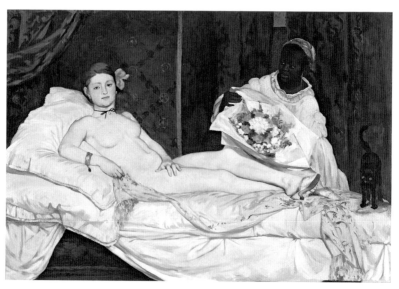

Plate 10. Edouard Manet, *Olympia,* 1865. Musée d'Orsay, Paris.

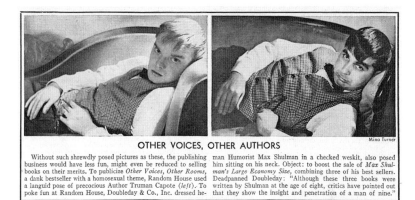

Mina Turner

OTHER VOICES, OTHER AUTHORS

Without such shrewdly posed pictures as these, the publishing business would have less fun, might even be reduced to selling books on their merits. To publicize *Other Voices, Other Rooms*, a dank bestseller with a homosexual theme, Random House used a languid pose of precocious Author Truman Capote (*left*). To poke fun at Random House, Doubleday & Co., Inc. dressed he-man Humorist Max Shulman in a checked weskit, also posed him sitting on his neck. Object: to boost the sale of *Max Shulman's Large Economy Size*, combining three of his best sellers. Deadpanned Doubleday: "Although these three books were written by Shulman at the age of eight, critics have pointed out that they show the insight and penetration of a man of nine."

Plate 11. Portrait of Truman Capote, by Howard Halma, next to a parody portrait of Max Shulman, by Mina Turner. *TIME,* May 3, 1948.

Plate 12. Theda Bara in *Cleopatra*, directed by J. Gordon Edwards (Fox Film Corporation, 1917). Publicity photo.

Relief Work in France

(Miss Gertrude Stein sends us this contribution from Paris, and it has been set in the style of type in which Miss Stein's verses usually appear.—EDITOR OF LIFE.)

THE ADVANCE

IN COMING TO A VILLAGE WE ASK THEM CAN THEY COME TO SEE US. WE MEAN NEAR ENOUGH TO TALK; AND THEN WE ASK THEM HOW DO WE GO THERE. THIS IS NOT FANCIFUL.

MONDAY AND TUESDAY

IN THE MEANTIME WHAT CAN WE DO ABOUT WISHES? WISH THE SAME.
AGREED FOR A MINOR.
AND FOR MY NIECE. WHAT ARE YOU DOING FOR MY NIECE?
BABY CLOTHES.
AND MILK.
MALTED MILK.

THE RIGHT SPIRIT

THE RIGHT SPIRIT. THERE ARE DIFFICULTIES, AND THEY MUST BE MET IN THE RIGHT SPIRIT.
THIS IS AN ILLUSTRATION OF THE DIFFICULTIES WE HAVE IN MANY WAYS.
THEN WE GO ON.

VICTORY

QUEEN VICTORIA AND QUEEN VICTORIA.
THEY MADE YOU JUMP.
AND I SAID THE MOTHER; YOU SAID THE MOTHER.
I DID NOT REMEMBER THE MOTHER WAS IN PARIS, BUT YOU DID.

AGAIN

WHEN THE CAMELLIAS ARE FINISHED THE ROSES BEGIN.
ARE THE FRENCH PEOPLE HEALTHY?
I THINK THEM HEALTHY.
AND AS TO THEIR INSTITUTIONS?
AS TO THEIR INSTITUTIONS, THERE IS NO DOUBT THAT THEY LIKE A PARK.
AND FORESTS?
IN THE SENSE IN WHICH YOU MEAN, YES.
THAT IS A QUESTION I MEANT TO ASK.
IT IS ANSWERED.

Gertrude Stein.

Locating the Germans

IT is astonishing what new arts one has to practice in wartimes. There is, for example, the art of segregation. Where shall the process of segregating the Germans stop?

It is obviously impossible to intern all of them. Probably the majority of those in this country are good citizens. But the rub comes to determine this. To keep them away from ammunition factories and other critical spots is well. But the air carries secrets, and there are numerous ways to convey information. The whole problem is complicated by the fact that it is not always possible to tell whether a man is a German or not. Some of those who have done us the most harm have not been Germans.

But, at any rate, as fast as they are located they ought to be compelled to wear a license tag with a number, just as motor cars do. These numbers ought to be visible at thirty feet, and lighted up at night.

If you are the unhappy possessor of a cold-storage plant and an ammunition factory, and you see a German with his tag on approaching it, you can take his number. The next morning, in case the plant is destroyed, you can apply to the State Department for the German's address. Later on in the day you can call on him personally and expostulate with him for his rude conduct.

Then the laugh will be on him, for no German likes to be expostulated with. He regards it as bad form.

A HAPPY NEW YEAR?

On the Front Walk

"BETTER wait a little, mister. Mother is having a fight with father."

"But I'm in a hurry."

"Well, in five minutes more there won't be much china left. I guess it will be safe for you to enter the house then."

She: PARDON ME A MOMENT WHILE I OPEN THIS PACKAGE FROM WALTER

Plate 13. Pages 1076 and 1077 of *Life,* December 27, 1917. Note Gertrude Stein's poem "Relief Work in France" on page 1076.

THE WILLOWBYS' WARD. 31

MOLLY AND MRS. WILLOWBY RETURN IN TIME TO RESCUE THE PROFESSOR FROM A WILY BOOK AGENT

The God Idea Still Limited

THE Hohenzollern idea that "I Am God" has had a host of imitators in that sort of literature which may be designated under the general name of "Uplift." When an author in this literary field is out of material he can always fall back on that idea. "I am Monarch of all I survey" is a short step to usurping the prerogatives of the Almighty. The value of this idea does, however, depend upon its exclusiveness, for it is evident that if everybody practiced it it would necessarily fail. Its own weight would carry it down. The Kaiser is a good illustration. So long as he wanted to be known as God in Germany he was on safe ground. In his own family circle they didn't mind. On the contrary, they were rather proud of having a personal God ruling over them, one that was on the spot. But when the Kaiser tried to expand the idea and extend it to the rest of the world he got into endless trouble. Even in being Gott a man must practice humility.

TO have and to hold—One's tongue.

Diagnosed

STARTING with a wonderful burst of oratory, the great evangelist had, after two hours' steady preaching, become rather hoarse.

A little boy's mother in the congregation whispered to her son, "Isn't it wonderful? What do you think of him?"

"He needs a new needle," returned the boy sleepily.

TO FILL A VACANCY

"Courage, mes braves!
J'arrive!"

*A lithograph by Lucien Jonas,
one of the ablest of the French
official war painters*

The Great American Army
By GERTRUDE STEIN

I FOUND an acorn to-day.
Green
In the center.
No, on the end.
And what is the name of the bridge?
This is what we say.
"The Great American Army,"—
This is what we say.

I write to loan.
We do work so well.
And what must we do?

In the world.
What do you call them?

Plates.
And where do you use them?
In guns.
The French pronounce it Guns.
So do the English.
What do the boys say?
"Can we?"

In the middle.
Or in the middle.
The Great American Army.
Nestles in the middle.
We have hope;
Certainly—
And Success!

*G*ERTRUDE STEIN, *the first
and most representative of the
so-called cubists in prose, has, since
the outbreak of the war, been living
in France and working in war relief
as an ambulance driver. Few American women have taken a more active
part in the conflict than she. During the past few weeks, the continued
arrival of our troops in France has
inspired her to compose this poem.*

Plate 14. Page 31 of *Vanity Fair,* June 13, 1918. Stein's poem "The Great American Army" appears beneath a reproduction of *"Courage, mes braves! J'arrive!,"* by Lucien Jonas.

Plate 15. Cover of *TIME,* September 11, 1933, with a cropped photograph of Gertrude Stein, by George Platt Lynes.

Plate 16. Portrait of Gertrude Stein, by George Platt Lynes, taken at her home in Bilignin, France, in 1931. George Platt Lynes (American, 1907–1955); Gertrude Stein, 1931; toned gelatin silver print; sheet 198 x 248 mm (7¹³⁄₁₆ x 9¾ inches). The Baltimore Museum of Art: The Cone Collection, Gift of Adelyn D. Breeskin, BMA 1985.3.

Plate 17. Marlene Dietrich as Amy Jolly in *Morocco,* directed by Josef von Sternberg (Paramount, 1930). Publicity photo.

Plate 18. Advertisement for *Morocco,* featuring Marlene Dietrich as Amy Jolly, in *Photoplay,* January 1931, 4.

"MOROCCO"
with

Reckless soldier of fortune, Gary Cooper, Adolphe Menjou, sophisticate, man of the world. A flaming cafe beauty, Marlene Dietrich...mysterious, alluring, dangerous as the Sahara. "Morocco," the turbulent story of these three.

**GARY   MARLENE   ADOLPHE
COOPER ° DIETRICH ° MENJOU**

Directed by
JOSEF VON STERNBERG
*Adapted by Jules Furthman. From the play
"Amy Jolly" by Benno Vigny.*

In "Morocco" Paramount presents the continental star, Marlene Dietrich, whose ravishing beauty and exotic personality will electrify all who come under her spell. A not-to-be-missed Paramount Picture, "best show in town."

Paramount *Pictures*

PARAMOUNT PUBLIX CORPORATION, ADOLPH ZUKOR, PRES., PARAMOUNT BLDG., NEW YORK

Plate 19. Cover of *TIME*, March 2, 1925: Amy Lowell.

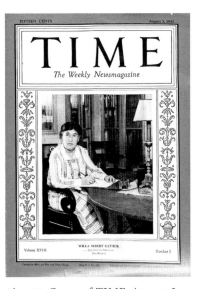

Plate 20. Cover of *TIME*, August 3, 1931: Willa Cather.

Plate 21. Cover of *TIME*, January 28, 1935: Kathleen Thompson Norris.

Plate 22. Cover of *TIME*, April 12, 1937: Virginia Woolf.

Plate 23. Cover of *TIME*, January 28, 1946: Craig Rice.

Plate 24. Cover of *TIME*, December 8, 1947: Rebecca West.

Plate 25. Cover of *TIME*, April 14, 1961: Jean Kerr.

Plate 26. Cover of *TIME*, June 18, 1965: Phyllis McGinley.

fantasized. Dietrich reclines in what looks very much like an opium den, from the chinoiserie urn backed by exotic plumes to the fabrics in Asian, Turkish, and Middle Eastern motifs. The film's North African setting, with its strong association with hashish—a national concern in the 1930s, when the United States began to regulate cannabis—further associates Jolly with a decadent salon.[23]

Both within and without the confines of *Morocco*, Dietrich's masculine dress, stance, walk, and kiss do not threaten but entice. Her departure from gender norms provokes rather than refutes traditional appetites. Dietrich attracted both the minority who read same-sexual erotics in her performance, and the majority who saw a particularly *fatale* appeal to men. Furthermore, Dietrich's same-sex kiss is in the context of a nightclub act and is removed from the viewer by a greater level of artifice and fantasy than the rest of *Morocco*. Even the "real" part of the film was at a far remove from its viewers, whose lived experience was likely to be distant from the film's stylized romance between a down-on-her-luck nightclub singer and a French legionnaire.

Even within the nightclub act, the same-sex kiss is carefully couched in a heterosexual exchange. Before Jolly kisses her fan, she takes a flower from her; after the kiss, Jolly gives the flower to the legionnaire played by Gary Cooper. Although I have not been able to substantiate the legend that Dietrich suggested both the kiss and the means for sneaking it past the censors, the fact remains that the kiss *did* evade censorship, almost certainly by being presented as part of a heterosexual flirtation. The kiss was thus made nonthreatening even to those officials responsible for policing appropriate sexuality. Of course, giving a flower to a man was itself provocative in relation to gender roles, though perhaps less so when accompanied by drag, which makes it more easily understood as a joke, and therefore unthreatening. Overall, Dietrich's performance of masculinity—her male drag and her homosexual kiss—was made acceptable by the carte blanche of the femme fatale.[24]

Stein on *TIME,* in the Fullness of Time

By contrast, Stein's masculine presentation on the *TIME* cover, as in almost all of her portraits, does not pay obeisance to straight-male desire. This was unusual, as male drag that could not be read in the service of heterosexual provocation usually did not enter the public sphere. True, Stein was neither acting in motion pictures nor vetted by censorship boards, but she *was* vetted by *TIME* and other media outlets. Stein was able to publicly present herself—and, in forums where she had little agency, to be presented—outside the standard female continuum for two reasons. First, her sexual appeal was so unconventional that it was not easily seen. This was always true, but Stein's advancing age removed her even further from the conventional sexual marketplace—and what cannot be seen or at least sensed cannot threaten. Second, Stein's public persona was that of a woman already outside of normal categories, so much so that she was not judged by the usual sartorial rules.

Stein's body as well as her clothes did not suit a femme fatale. The shape of Stein's body extended past the conventional limits of the female body as it was usually seen in the media—and Stein's form was not shielded or disguised, as one might expect of a bodily display that would not be considered conventionally attractive. When the editors of *TIME* cropped the 1931 George Platt Lynes photo for their September 11, 1933, cover, they made Stein look larger than she did in the original photo, as seen in Plates 15 and 16. The cover photo accentuates Stein's size; her body fully fills the left half of the picture frame, sloping out past the median line toward the bottom.

In "Stein's Way," James Agee sustains this focus on Stein's size. He begins with a grand metonymy: "Like a huge squat mountain on a distant border of the literary kingdom, obscured not only by the cloudy procession of more Aprilly authors but by the self-induced fog that hangs around her close-cropped top, she has loomed from afar over the hinterland of letters, a sphinxlike, monolithic mass. Twenty years she has squatted there; eyes accustomed to the landscape are beginning to recognize something portentous in her massive outline." The "mountain" is figurative and references Stein's literary influence, but there is some slippage into a physical description of Stein's "massive outline" and "close-cropped top." Stein is not only described but also dramatized as a mountain, complete with atmospheric effects. Her bulk is made fantastic and used to symbolize her place in the literary world.[25]

Such an unvarnished representation of a celebrated woman's size is remarkable for both the cover and content of *TIME*. Nonetheless, the Lynes photo is more conventional in some respects than most images of Stein, which is presumably a reason why the editors chose that photo for the cover. In most images of Stein, she meets or comes close to meeting the viewer's gaze, often with a challenging, interrogatory, or otherwise "masculine" expression. On the cover of *TIME*, however, Stein does not challenge or otherwise interact with the viewer. She is shown in full profile, which removes her gaze even further. Full profile heightens the impression of psychological distance, which runs counter to *TIME*'s promise of intimacy with the most important man of the week. Yet Stein is not brought closer to readers. Why not?[26]

Because Stein's eccentricity—her distance from the norm—is what brought her wide notice. Agee writes in "Stein's Way," "At one long-deferred bound she has moved from the legendary borders of literature into the very market-place, to face in person a large audience of men-in-the-street." Note here how Agee turns "man in the street"—a phrase that is not particularly male by convention but references both genders—into "men-in-the-street," a phrase that leaves Stein facing a crowd of staring men. Note, too, how Agee equates Stein with a legendary, "fabulous" animal "bounding" from distant surroundings to a domestic zoo. Was Stein in fact a fabulous beast to be stared at by ordinary men?[27]

In *TIME*, yes. For who held the cover of *TIME*? White men over fifty from the eastern establishment that included Hadden and Luce. The only women shown on the first hundred covers are Eleanora Duse (July 30, 1923) and Mrs. Herbert (Lou) Hoover (April 21, 1924). For a broader perspective, consider *TIME*'s first fifty-four years of publication, 1923 to 1977. Toward the end of these years, second-wave feminism had an appreciable impact on the portrayal of women in the mainstream media. Yet in these fifty-four years, only 350 of 3,336 covers, or 10.5 percent, were emblazoned by women. Only four women held the cover more than four times: Queen Elizabeth II, Eleanor Roosevelt, Pat Nixon, and Betty Ford, all of whom attained prominence at least in part through their fathers or husbands.[28]

How often did women earn the cover through their writing, and what kind of writers did *TIME* profile? Writers are pictured on 90 of the first 3,336 covers: 2.7 percent. Eight of the 90 are women: 8.9 percent of the writers, comprising 0.24 percent of the total number of covers. Of the writers, 37 are novelists, and 4 are women: Willa Cather, Kathleen Thompson Norris, Virginia Woolf, and Craig Rice (Georgiana Ann Randolph Craig). Eleven writers are poets, of whom 2 are women: the modernist Amy Lowell and Phyllis McGinley, who wrote light verse on married life in suburbia and won the Pulitzer Prize for Poetry in 1961. Fifteen of the writers are playwrights, of whom 1 is a woman: Jean Kerr, who is best known today for the essay collection *Please Don't Eat the Daisies*, adapted into a 1960 film vehicle for Doris Day. The 20 remaining writers earned the cover for nonfiction. Of these, 2 were women: Rebecca West, a modernist best known then and today for *Black Lamb and Grey Falcon,* a gargantuan analysis of Yugoslavia, and Gertrude Stein, who earned the cover for *The Autobiography of Alice B. Toklas.*[29]

At first glance, this selection seems arbitrary. There are only 3 un-arguably canonical writers—Cather, Woolf, and Stein—and 2 from the midlist—Lowell and West. The rest are largely unknown today. Kathleen Thompson Norris, for instance, won the cover for the publication of her fiftieth romance novel, *Woman in Love.* TIME claimed that she was the best-paid working woman in the United States, at $300,000 a year. When Jean Kerr won the cover, her play *Mary, Mary* had just broken the record for the longest-running nonmusical play on Broadway, at 1,500 performances. There seems to have been no precipitating event behind Phyllis McGinley's cover besides her lunch at the White House with Lyndon Johnson, but *TIME* made her a figurehead of conservative opposition to Betty Friedan's *The Feminine Mystique:* "The strength of Phyllis McGinley's appeal can best be measured by the fact that today, almost by inadvertence, she finds herself the sturdiest exponent of the glory of housewifery standing alone against a rising chorus of voices summoning women away from the hearth." *TIME* exercised some lati-tude for many of its cover stories on the arts; editors could commission and then hold them for a slow news week. This latitude gave the editors particular discretion in their choices, which makes Stein's cover all the more remarkable.[30]

Of these 9 cover portraits, only Stein's lacks a traditionally respect-able feminine representation.[31] Here I am tempted to join in the tradition of claiming that Stein supersedes analysis and to simply direct my reader to her portrait. Which of these covers is different from the others? Con-sider the women writers in order of appearance: Amy Lowell (March 2, 1925, Plate 19), Willa Cather (August 3, 1931, Plate 20), Gertrude Stein (September 11, 1933, Plate 15), Kathleen Thompson Norris (January 28, 1935, Plate 21), Virginia Woolf (April 12, 1937, Plate 22), Craig Rice (Janu-ary 28, 1946, Plate 23), Rebecca West (December 8, 1945, Plate 24), Jean Kerr (April 14, 1961, Plate 25), and Phyllis McGinley (June 18 1965, Plate 26). Though Lowell, Cather, and Woolf all had extensive homoerotic ex-perience, and though possibly Lowell and probably Cather identified as lesbian, their visual representations on the *TIME* covers are unexception-ally feminine, as these authors' images usually were, at least in the public domain. Lowell and Cather sit with their long hair pinned up, Lowell reading in her rocking chair, Cather writing in a print housedress in a domestic setting. Woolf, in a tailored suit with a foulard bow, is poised to lecture. West may wear Athena's helmet, but she also drinks tea. Mystery writer Rice may sport a male pen name, but her eyebrows are plucked and shaped, and her mouth is a bright red bow. The clothes and hair of Kerr and McGinley suit women in moneyed suburbs in the early 1960s, and both of their cover stories clarify that they are friends and neighbors in Larchmont, Connecticut. The sole exception is Norris, who is portrayed as "southern mountaineer white trash" in an amateur theatrical by the Palo Alto Community Players.[32]

Norris's cover is an elaborate joke on her readers and their expectation that she would look like her romantic heroines. Nonetheless, *TIME* assures us that Norris fulfills her domestic duties: she is "a dynamo of energy that can leap from typewriter to cooking pot to evening dress and back again, a wife, a mother, a chatelaine, all in one highly individual bundle." Norris's photograph may be striking in terms of class—especially before the cover story reveals the joke—but Granny Diogenes of Appalachia is a traditional gal.[33]

Stein falls off the bell curve drawn by these women, and her hair, body, and clothes all astonish by the standards of *TIME*. Casual viewers need not read the article to be struck by this photograph, or for it to register as homoerotic in a culture that equated homosexuality with one's assuming characteristics of the opposite gender. Unsurprisingly, Agee pays particular attention to Stein's looks. He refers to "Mountain Stein" throughout, but he also brings his description down to earth: "Never a beauty, she is now massive, middle-aged, 59, would strongly resemble a fat Jewish hausfrau were it not for her close-cropped head."[34]

Agee meant this and other, similar comments to be unkind. He did not interview Stein for the cover story. Instead, "Stein's Way" is very much an analysis of Stein's public persona and its then-recent aggrandizement. But Agee contributes to as well as reports on the history of disparaging Stein. Does he have a stake in degrading her, or does he toe *TIME*'s line? Agee is best known today for *Let Us Now Praise Famous Men,* his nonfiction collaboration with Walter Evans, and the unfinished novel *A Death in the Family,* but in 1933 Agee was a frequent contributor to *Fortune,* which was part of Time Inc. He was very much a working journalist, and he knew and performed the house style of wry sarcasm from a world-weary perch. Yet even for *TIME,* such comments are strong.[35]

James Agee Comes to the Mountain

Agee's history puts him at an interesting angle to Stein. Both were talented, ambitious writers from comfortable homes who went to Harvard/ Radcliffe and eventually settled in bohemia, Stein in Paris and Agee in Greenwich Village. Both had unconventional desires in relation to sex, love, and aesthetic form and content, and both struggled to reconcile these with both their own moral sense and social expectations. Agee, however, followed a more conventional path, and maintained fruitful relationships (notwithstanding the usual agonies) with three great institutions: the Catholic Church, the fourth estate, and Hollywood.

Though his sexual attraction to and for women is beyond question, Agee was sufficiently moved by homosexual desire throughout his life to write letters about his concerns to his friends and priest. The clearest record of gay love in Agee's life is found in his correspondence with Dwight Macdonald. Agee was a promising underachiever at Phillips Exeter Academy, and the prep school reached out to alumnus Macdonald, then a college undergraduate, and asked him to write Agee. Agee, for his part, was interested in a short story Macdonald had written for the *Phillips Exeter Monthly* on male "romantic friendships," a school tradition. Agee then wrote Macdonald about his intense love for his best friend. After Agee tried to embody this love through sex, the best friend would see Agee only at meals—a rejection that haunted Agee for years. Agee's same-sex love and desire persisted, and eventually he did achieve a kind of sexual union with a close male friend by successfully engineering sexual liaisons between his two wives and his great friend Walter Evans, once with Agee present.[36]

Nonetheless, Agee never broke with convention to the extent that Stein did, either in his personal life or in his writing. Although Stein always wanted to publish in the mainstream and was certain that she belonged there, she was not about to change her style—until *The Autobiography*. By contrast, Agee often managed to be both innovative and appropriate for a commercial forum. For instance, his movie reviews for *The Nation* are known for their unusual and arguably unprecedented moral seriousness—which was of course appropriate for the high moral seriousness of *The Nation,* as would be Diana Trilling's book reviews. Agee's film reviews for *TIME*, by contrast, breeze by.[37]

Agee's own public persona is bivalent. Some view him in the romantic tradition, as a talented writer who squandered his gifts through alcohol, smoking, a complex social and sexual life, and a sustained frittering away of his talent on journalism and screenplays; others claim that his best work, including *Let Us Now Praise Famous Men* and his film criticism, came out of his work as a journalist, which offered him structure as well as funds. In 1933, however, Agee was far from the mass-market renown that then rained down on Stein, renown that his article would further engorge. The generosity of his later writings on Stein, including a defense of her difficult novel *Ida* for *TIME* in 1941, complicates the hostility of "Stein's Way." Were the phrase "fat Jewish hausfrau" and the like motivated by misogyny, homophobia, anti-Semitism, or jealousy (or dictated editorially), or do they simply fulfill the tradition of larding Stein with insult? Note that Agee is careful not to overtly call Stein masculine, much less lesbian, and thus overstep the bounds of acceptable broad queerness.[38]

Casual viewers who read the cover story would find a discussion of the broadly queer aspects of Stein's persona that almost mandate an unusual visual display. All the aspects of Stein's public persona since birth are present: her French residence and Jewishness, her association with visual modernism, her bulk and its unfeminine presentation. Agee notes Stein's ethnicity and expatriate status early in the article: "Gertrude Stein hates to be called an expatriate, in spite of the fact that she has lived most of her adult life in France and seems to be settled there. Born in Allegheny, Pa. (then a suburb of Pittsburgh) 'of a very respectable middle class family' of German Jews, she was taken abroad at an early age." Even before the article starts, an epigraph in the form of a limerick associates Stein with two other Jews who were widely viewed as incomprehensible though brilliant: physicist Albert Einstein and the sculptor Jacob Epstein, here incorrectly called "Ed" instead of "Ep":

> I don't like the family Stein
> There is Gert, there is Ed, there is Ein;
> Gert's poems are bunk,
> Ed's statues are punk,
> And nobody understands Ein.

Agee clarifies Stein's relation with the art world later in the article, but he spends considerably more time on how she had been perceived as nonsensical:

Who & What is Gertrude Stein? "Widely ridiculed and seldom enjoyed," she is one of the least-read and most-publicized writers of the day. Her incomprehensible sentences, in which an infuriating glimmer of shrewd sense or subacid humor is sometimes discernible, have generated the spark for many a journalistic wisecrack; except to the adventurous few who have been hardy enough to read her in the original (and to some of those) she has the reputation of a pure nonsense writer. To the man-in-the-street, she is the synonym for what Critic Max Eastman calls "the cult of unintelligibility." In man-in-the-street lingo, "Gert's poems are bunk."

Agee positions Stein's reputation against her new, "perfectly comprehensible, eminently readable memoir." Agee also positions Stein's respectability against her broad queerness and illustrates how this respectability results from Stein's durability in the avant-garde: "By the time-honored process of getting older, Gertrude Stein, though she remains as mysterious as ever, has made herself a background place in the literary panorama." The new, mass-market Stein does not erase her history but deposits a new stratum that both obscures and is shaped by her previous persona.[39]

Most importantly for our purpose, "Stein's Way" illustrates how Stein's broad queerness supports signs of her specific homosexuality. Agee is not subtle. The title itself—"Stein's Way"—puns on *Swann's Way,* the first volume in *Remembrance of Things Past* (as it was then called), by Marcel Proust, first translated into English in 1922, and published in the United States in 1925. *Swann's Way,* like *The Autobiography,* is a masked autobiography that both disguises and presents the author's homosexuality. Lesbians abound. Furthermore, Proust and his work shared with Stein's persona and work the nexus of extremely high culture, Frenchness, Jewish identity, the fin de siècle, and the fact of being more talked about than read.[40]

Agee also references Stein and Toklas's love. He specifies the length and strength of their relation: "No fancy figment but a real live companion-secretary, Alice B. Toklas is a Californian (her father was a Pole) who has lived with Gertrude Stein for the last 26 years. Authoress Stein says she often urged Companion Toklas to write her autobiography, finally decided to do it for her." Agee, paraphrasing from *The Autobiography,* relates how, when Toklas met Stein, "a bell rang." This cliché denotes a visceral response to stimulus, as suits its probable origin in the dogs of behavioral psychologist Ivan Pavlov, who in a famous experiment offered food with a ring until bells alone could make the dogs slaver. What rings the bell for Toklas? Her recognition that Stein was "a genius"—a recognition that progressed to domesticity, as Agee notes: "When Miss Toklas, unattached spinster with artistic leanings, met Gertrude Stein in Paris (1907) she immediately recognized a genius. . . . They set up house together, at No. 27 Rue de Fleurus, have been together ever since." The other lesbian signifiers in the quotation, such as "unattached spinster" and the sense of "genius" as something that was fabulous and extraordinary, offer ample opportunity for Toklas's visceral response to be read as attraction.[41]

Agee's quotation was, or was at least close to, the most positive and visible indication of a lesbian couple in 1933 that a lesbian or gay adolescent was likely to see in the mainstream media. Agee closes the article with a three-part hint: the observation that Stein "hardly mentions" love, the mention of an unnamed adolescent torment, and the reference to unmentionable privacies. Though room is left for other interpretations, a more explicit mention of female homosexuality in a noncriminal context is difficult to imagine in a cover story of *TIME* in the first half of the twentieth century: "It *[The Autobiography]* is a strangely impersonal book. Her only reference to her interior life is the admission that when she was 17, 'the last few years had been lonesome ones and had been passed in an agony of adolescence.' If curious readers wonder why she passes over these matters so lightly, they may answer themselves by reflecting that no doubt Gertrude Stein, like everyone else, has autobiographical passages which she does not choose to run." Lonely and unhappy teen years have never been rare, so they do not call for this showcased silence. What, I wonder, could be the cause of Stein's "impersonality"? What are these unmentionable "passages"? Do they resemble the following, written by Agee to Macdonald, concerning Agee's prep-school romance? "Of late, too, I had been wonderfully happy simply looking at him—chiefly at his head or hands. . . . [W]e had a roughhouse, and in that physical contact I thought I had found the complete fulfillment of the ideal friendship I'd built up. It rather distressed me, however. I was quite sure he didn't feel this at all; and I felt the only thing I could do was to tell him." Stein knows; Agee knows; an appreciable portion of the public knows. QED: Stein's specific homosexuality fuels the broad queerness that makes her fascinating to the public, and this same broad queerness allows an unusually frank display of female homosexuality. Yes, Agee and *TIME* censor Stein's sexuality and insult her; but this greases their broadcast of her sexuality and celebrates her person as it, too, serves as a cue for Stein's sexuality. Thus, Stein set the mold for many women of how a masculine lesbian looks and lives.[42]

Three Lesbian Lives

A Map of Same-Sex Passion

I Do Not Even Understand the Title

Once *The Autobiography of Alice B. Toklas* made Stein a best-selling author as well as a mass-market celebrity, readers returned to *Three Lives*. More precisely, they turned to it for the first time.[1]

When Stein paid to print 1,000 copies of *Three Lives* in 1909, her contract called for five hundred manuscript sheets to be bound immediately, and the rest on demand. There was no demand. Six years later, the rest remained unbound, and the John Lane Company bought three hundred; these were published as the first British edition. Sales dribbled. *Three Lives* was not reprinted in the United States until 1927, in a small edition of an unknown number by the boutique publisher Albert & Charles Boni. After the success of *The Autobiography*, however, the Modern Library, soon to become Random House, quickly reprinted *Three Lives*. Very quickly: *The Autobiography* was published in September 1933, and 5,000 copies of *Three Lives* in October.[2]

Bennett Cerf, the publisher of Random House, met Stein on her American tour in 1934, which he supported, as Stein was now one of his authors. Cerf was enchanted with Stein, as he would later be with Capote. At Stein's going-away party, he promised to publish a new book of hers each year, sight unseen, if she wrote another biography for Random House. And he made good on his promise: *Lectures in America* was published in 1935, *The Geographical History of America* in 1936, and *Everybody's Autobiography* in 1937. Cerf did not pretend to understand these works. The publisher's note on the dust jacket for *The Geographical History of America* reads as follows:

This space is usually reserved for a brief description of a book's contents. In this case, however, I must admit frankly that I do not know what Miss Stein is talking about. I do not even understand the title.

I admire Miss Stein tremendously, and I like to publish her books, although most of the time I do not know what she is driving at. That, Miss Stein tells me, is because I am dumb.

I note that one of my partners and I are characters in this latest work of Miss Stein's. Both of us wish that we knew what she was saying about us. Both of us hope, too, that her faithful followers will make more of this book than we are able to!

Perhaps Cerf saw these books as advertisements for another bestseller in Stein's future, though she would not give Random House another until 1955, when 15,000 copies of the first paperback edition of *The Autobiography* was published under the Vintage imprint. Perhaps Cerf thought that Stein's prestige would reflect well on his house. From a material perspective, what matters is that even difficult works by Stein were now printed by a major publisher and could be easily found or ordered. In fact, their difficulty was used as advertising, at least for Cerf and Random House, if not for the book itself. In short: success![3]

In relation to the masses, however, Stein's readership would remain restricted to *The Autobiography* and *Three Lives*. Some of this prominence is due to the Modern Library. "The Modern Library of the World's Best Books" attempted to establish a canon of twentieth-century English-language fiction, which Random House promoted as a public-service-cum–marketing strategy. The Modern Library became a major player in the election of twentieth-century "classics," comparable only to the Library of America. The Modern Library edition of *Three Lives* sold so well that the first paperback edition, in 1958, had a print run of 10,000. The novel has stayed in print and sold consistently ever since.

These sales came with instructions: Stein's new mass celebrity not only brought her a reading public but also instructed that public how to read her. Readers understood that *Three Lives* was the product of a broadly queer—and, for many, a specifically gay—woman, which for some inspired and for most affected their reading. Almost twenty-five years after its first publication, *Three Lives* finally came out in public as the debut of a lesbian author—and I will show that this first book is concerned with the coalescence of gay identity. Nonetheless, critics have not, by and large, read *Three Lives* in this light. Most readings do not even heed the title, *Three Lives,* which asserts that the three lives are in conjunction, but focus intently on just one. This chapter aims to read *Three Lives* as a series of proto-lesbian portraits and to explore why this most obvious reading of the text has not been publicly conducted, thanks to the persistence of the apparitional lesbian.

Do Lesbians Exist?

A, and perhaps *the,* primary goal of lesbian rights movements for much of the twentieth century was the positive assertion of female same-sexual desire, both now and in the past: positive as in "certain," and positive as in "good." Male homosexuality was hypervisible between the Wilde trials and Stonewall, but female homosexuality and its products were often denied. The female same-sex desire that did enter public consciousness through media, history, or literature was misread, misunderstood, or at the least misnamed. When recognition was forced, the acknowledged desire was acknowledged as bad, and was soon censored in memory, if not in fact. Lesbians and proto-lesbians thus escaped some of the punishment earned by queer men, but at a cost. Many had to configure and understand (or *not* configure and *not* understand) their desire in ignorance and isolation. Those privy to subcultural or localized examples of same-sex desire and identity were likely to find these examples at least in part destructive. Those fortunate enough to find positive examples also knew that such examples were unknown and unspeakable at large.

More than twenty years ago, Terry Castle dubbed the phenomenon of unseen and unacknowledged female homosexuality "the apparitional lesbian" and criticized literary scholars for hosting her without setting a place for her at the table. Castle demanded readings that (1) recognize the existence of lesbians in literature written before our current formulation of the "lesbian"; (2) do not equate the lack of heterosexual desire with pathology or asexuality; (3) do not assume that women who desire women are stand-ins for men who desire men; and (4) do not view lesbian identity and desire as incidental but understand them as significant and perhaps vital to good reading. Though Castle did not apply the concept of the apparitional lesbian to identity or sexual repression, those who deny internal evidence and refuse to read their own same-sexual emotional and sexual desires may host the apparitional lesbian in their own individual consciousnesses. "Lesbian readings" for both people and literature became more common as the women's and gay rights movements percolated through culture; many scholars who did not agree with Castle's precepts nonetheless enlarged the discussion of female same-sexual passion.[4]

Why, then, has *Three Lives*—popular, canonical, and suffused with lesbian content and themes—not been read in Castle's "lesbian terms"? And what would such a reading be?

Gertrude Stein Comes of Age in Fear, Striving to Be Free

In 1895, Gertrude Stein was a twenty-one-year-old sophomore at Radcliffe College interested in philosophy and psychology who had begun to write fiction. By all accounts, Stein had not yet had sexual encounters, though she was exposed to the constant pressure—acute in Jewish families—for women her age to be married. The year 1895 also brought the Oscar Wilde trial, which changed the public discourse of homosexuality. At a time of life when proto-lesbians were likely to gain same-sexual experience, Stein was swamped with proof of its danger.

Wilde had been a mass-market celebrity in the United States since 1882, when Richard D'Oyly Carte, the Gilbert and Sullivan impresario, booked Wilde on tour. Carte hoped for symbiotic marketing with the tour of the comic opera *Patience,* which satirized aestheticism in general and, as he grew more famous, Wilde in particular—and which would further cement the association between homosexuality and fine art, decadence, and wealth. Wilde ran three separate rounds through the United States and Canada, usually with 20 or more stops per month, usually with 2 lectures per stop—140 lectures in 260 days, a singular success. His fame soaked the nation as Wilde was promoted in the local press of his many destinations.

Wilde's fame was bolstered by *The Picture of Dorian Gray,* which was serialized in 1890 and published in 1891 in both England and the United States, and by the London runs of *Lady Windermere's Fan* (1892), *A Woman of No Importance* (1893), *An Ideal Husband* (1895), and *The Importance of Being Earnest* (1895). Each earned more critical praise and public applause. When Wilde sued his lover's father for libel, he earned even more media attention: he had moved from "entertainment" to "news." When Wilde lost, he was prosecuted for public indecency. *The Importance of Being Earnest* sold out throughout both trials, which lasted from April 3 to May 25, 1895, and kept Wilde in the news. If Wilde had won either lawsuit, the two suits might now be seen as a brilliant publicity stunt that rhymed with his topsy-turvy plays.[5]

The entire affair must have impressed upon young Stein (and everyone else who read newspapers) that even private displays of homosexuality, once publicly known, had the power to sentence even rich, powerful celebrities to years of hard labor breaking rocks. Though public reactions to male and to female homosexuality cannot be conflated, Stein still had ample reason to fear her own same-sex desire. Fifty years later, in *Wars I Have Seen,* Stein wrote of her realization that she was not "free" but that her homosexuality, as well as her Jewishness, put her at risk:

> There is no doubt that every one really wants to be free, at least to feel free, they may like to give orders or even to take them, but they like to feel free, oh yes they do like to feel free, and so Oscar Wilde and the Ballad of Reading Gaol was the first thing that made me realize that it could happen, being in prison.
>
> And then the next thing was the Dreyfus affair, that is anti-semitism.

Wilde wrote "The Ballad of Reading Gaol" after his release from jail, and the poem explicitly links the narrator, a prisoner who seems to be Wilde, with a prisoner about to be hanged for murder: "For each man kills the thing he loves, / Yet each man does not die." This conflation of homosexuality, imprisonment, murder, and state-sanctioned execution frightened Stein, who wrote in her journals that she was "very afraid" when she read "The Ballad of Reading Gaol" in college. Stein's fears from the trial and its aftermath may explain why she did not engage in the appreciable culture of female same-sex passion at Radcliffe that was typical for women's colleges of the time.[6]

Stein did not come of lesbian age until 1900, when, as a twenty-six-year-old in her third year in medical school, she became involved with May Bookstaver, who was already involved with (and supported by) Mabel Haynes, a classmate of Stein's. Unhappy with both her school and her lover, Stein decamped to Europe, where the affair finally ended in 1902. After some wandering, Stein collated her thoughts and feelings on the affair in 1903, when she wrote *Q.E.D.,* a close transcript of her sexual and identitarian awakening in the context of the triangle. Stein broke free, but her cognate, Adele, does not; at the end of the novel she remains attached. Thus the title, *Q.E.D., quod erat demonstrandum,* which announces the close of a mathematical proof of a claim, in this case, the stability of a three-sided polygon.

In 1904, Stein remixed the affair in the novella *Fernhurst,* which enlarges the love triangle into a square and grafts it to a scandal at Bryn Mawr that touched on Stein's social circle. In some ways, *Fernhurst* is closer to Stein's experience than *Q.E.D.,* as Stein includes excerpts from her and Bookstaver's letters. The established couple still comprises two women, the president of a women's college and a professor, but the interloper is now a man, Philip Redfern, who comes to teach at Fernhurst College with his wife, Nancy. Stein splits herself (and Adele, from *Q.E.D.*) between Philip and Nancy; Stein gives Philip her own aggression and Nancy her moral rumination. If there is a hero, it is Nancy. In real life, the male lecturer ran off with the female professor and married her in Paris, but in *Fernhurst,* the professor and the college president stay together. Stein changes her model to give the lesbians a happy ending, although, and possibly because, their sexual bond is less explicit than in *Q.E.D.* and *Three Lives.* Stein/Adele/the Redferns still "lose," yet female same-sexuality is no longer equated with miserable deadlock; the president and the professor are left content.[7]

Fernhurst was followed a year later by *Three Lives,* written in 1905 and '06, which comprises three thematically linked but otherwise distinct "lives" of three women. Anna, Lena, and Melanctha are two immigrant German servants and an African American wanderer who all live in the small city of Bridgepoint, a thinly disguised Baltimore. Each "life" follows its heroine from childhood to death, and each features prominent same-sex passion. Lesbian romance, love, and sex in *Three Lives* are clearly and repeatedly told and shown. Stein's own affair is cited by "Melanctha," within which the love triangle is not a triangle, exactly: the female couple, Melanctha and Jane, have broken up before Melanctha begins her romance with Jeff Campbell. Nonetheless, Jane creates difficulties. May Bookstaver / Melanctha is now the protagonist, whereas the hesitations of Stein/Adele/Rose are now borne by Jeff. Stein directly references May through the subtitle of "Melanctha": "Each One as She May." The word *may* retained its electric charge: Ulla Dydo has discovered that Toklas was so disturbed by Stein's use of the word *may* in *Stanzas in Meditation* (written in 1932) that she insisted Stein change it. At least for Toklas, *may* still referenced Bookstaver even three decades after the affair.[8]

Clearly, Stein's development as a proto- and then realized lesbian informed her development as a writer, as would her education, which left her well versed in the scientific method of looking at brains and behavior, and well read in contemporary psychological theory. Her original title for *Three Lives* was *Three Histories,* which she changed at her publisher's suggestion.[9] Both titles suggest an affinity with the literature of the case study, which in Stein's time was often referred to as a "case history," or "history," or "life." *Three Lives* was written the same year as Freud's *Three Essays on the Theory of Sexuality,* and the books came out of the same moment in the study of sexuality. In addition to psychological study, Freud and Stein shared a common Jewish German heritage, a preoccupation with sexuality, and sufficient will and force to impose their vision on an unreceptive public. I read Stein along with Freud to illustrate the context within which Stein understood human consciousness and desire as much as to investigate their interconnection or "truth."[10]

Unlike Freud's, Stein's own experience as a homosexual allowed her a subjective understanding of lesbian psychosexual development. The composition of *Three Lives* and the concomitant working through of the Bookstaver affair may be seen as part of that development, as Stein established her relationship with Alice Toklas the next year. *Three Lives* delineates three proto-lesbians who, unlike Stein, remained in Bridgepoint/ Baltimore and who, also unlike Stein, never lost their *proto-* prefix; they are the unhappy alternatives to the life Stein built with her partner. This relationship, and its eventual portrayal in another roman à clef, *The Autobiography of Alice B. Toklas,* may be seen as a further iteration of her lesbian development. In this way, *The Autobiography* is a kind of sequel to *Three Lives,* just as its sales completed the fame Stein achieved decades before and crowned her "debut."

One Hundred Years Later: The Critical Edition

I hold in my hands the 2006 Norton Critical Edition of *Three Lives.* Norton is an unusual publisher; the firm has not been absorbed by a conglomerate but is wholly owned by its employees. In part, Norton maintains its market share through its authority over the canon and canonical interpretation via anthologies and critical editions. Critical editions signal academic popularity, because for them to be feasible, the books must not only be frequently required textbooks but also be taught in a way that warrants criticism and other supporting materials.[11]

In its critical edition, Norton publishes *Three Lives* in concert with *Q.E.D.,* yet lesbian romance, love, and sex do not concern the critical edition. Norton materially links two literary incarnations of Stein's affair with Bookstaver—as is noted by editor Marianne DeKoven in her introduction, and in footnotes throughout—yet only one of the twenty-two articles and excerpts provides more than a glance at lesbian issues. Even that one article—"African Masks and Passing in Stein and Larsen," by Corinne Blackmer—is concerned primarily with race. The twenty-one other articles do not broach these questions: How do *Q.E.D.* and *Three Lives* portray same-sex desire? How do desire, emotion, and identity interrelate? What are the gradations between same-sex friendship, physical loving, and emotional partnership in a society that validated only the first and demonized the others? The articles never consider the inverse relationship between how closely Stein sticks to the facts of her and Bookstaver's relationship and how many readers, and how much critical credibility, her fiction gains. Nor do they consider how both external and internalized homophobia shape the above. Never mind the sophisticated discussion required for consideration of these issues in the unstable terms necessary for a time when "lesbian" as an identitarian category, though hardly nascent, was nonetheless understood differently than it is today. Even basic biographical information about Stein and Bookstaver and the two texts is offered no more than a quick gloss in these articles, with the exception of the introduction, Blackmer's article, and a brief excerpt from Linda Wagner-Martin's biography. Why elide the connecting tissue when *Q.E.D.*'s role as a precursor for *Three Lives* is the reason for linking the texts? Why is the material acknowledgment of the underpinning of both texts in lesbian desire not paralleled by critical assessment?[12]

The answer lies neither in editorial choices nor in policy but in a critical dearth. Broadly speaking, literary critics have read three "lesbian registers" in Stein's oeuvre: (1) the direct reference of same-sexuality through naturalistic representation and lyric erotica; (2) the encoding of lesbianism into style, race, and class; and (3) the impact of Stein's subject position, which includes her sexuality, upon her writing. Archival work in the first register has led to the publication of openly lesbian work that Stein either could not or would not publish in her lifetime, such as *Lifting Belly* or the unexpurgated *Q.E.D.* Stein's reputation for obscurity is at odds with the bluntness of such work.[13]

That said, Stein's work often *is* obscure. This obscurity may be interpreted as camouflage for smuggling lesbian content into the public arena— camouflage that resolves into crystalline focus when viewed through the decoder ring of lesbian sexuality. As Shari Benstock writes, "Stein's language renders meaning if one is familiar with its essentially lesbian code. . . . Once the code is broken, meaning spills out." By this rubric, Stein's obscurity is her means, not her object, as Catharine Stimpson notes when she finds that Stein consistently "takes certain lesbian or quasi-lesbian experiences and progressively disguises and encodes them in a series of books," an act that "distances the representation of homosexuality from its enactment in life." Critics in this second, "encoding" register pay attention to linguistic cryptography, as in the titular pun of *Tender Buttons,* and to the translation of lesbianism into other aspects of identity, such as race, nationality, and class.[14]

The third lesbian register traces neither Stein's direct nor her disguised relation of same-sex passion through her writing but rather how her writing and consciousness assert her subject position despite hegemonic strictures upon language and thought. Some critics who work in this register are explicitly concerned with Stein's sexuality. More frequently, Stein's sexuality is only part—and not necessarily an important part—of her standing as a Jewish, intellectual, expatriate woman: "Stein simultaneously concealed and encoded in her literary work feelings about herself as a woman, about women's helplessness, and particularly about lesbianism. . . . Stein's rebellion was channeled from content to linguistic structure itself, [which is] much easier to ignore or misconstrue, but its attack, particularly in literature, penetrates far deeper, to the very structures which determine, within a particular culture, what can be thought." Here, the second and third registers are beautifully marbled, but by this rubric Stein's embodied sexuality is easily configured as less interesting, less sophisticated, and less revolutionary than her transgressive textuality. None of these registers are essential or even integral to much Stein criticism, which is, if not dismissive, then largely disinterested in Stein's direct denotation of the lesbian in both her writing and her public persona.[15]

Historically, critics may have been oblivious to lesbian content that now seems obvious, or silent about lesbian content because of disgust or hostility. Sympathetic critics may have tried to protect Stein from homophobia by shrouding the sexual contents of her work and life, or by alluding to it only in code. Only those critics secure in both their professional lives and their public heterosexuality could discuss it without concern for their professional standing. More recent critics may find lesbian issues worthy of recognition but less compelling than other aspects of Stein's work. Many writers are unconcerned with Stein's sexuality or, if concerned, are uncomfortable with a lesbian label. Such unconcern and discomfort may or may not collude with conscious and unconscious, and internalized and externalized, homophobia. Writers interested in Stein as a lesbian may censor themselves because of practical considerations. Queer theorists may find the category of "lesbian" reductive or inaccurate, or may believe that the connections between Stein's own sexuality and the sexual content of her work need to be explored on a broader canvas. Last, the generic conventions of academic writing—in particular, the positioning of the critic as a brilliant detective who uncovers hidden truth and limns delicate distinctions—discourage such "basic" work.

That said, Terry Castle is hardly the sole lighthouse on the lesbian shore. Her invocation of the apparitional lesbian is coterminous with Karla Jay and Joanne Glasgow's observation that there was no previous collection of lesbian scholarship—"no convenient place to send students to, no volume which contained an overview of recent trends, methodologies, theories, and new research on lesbian writers." Jay and Glasgow thus offer the critical collection within which Shari Benstock insists upon the importance of sapphic modernism. Benstock demands that overt as well as covert modernist treatments of female same-sex passion be acknowledged, and that postmodern celebrations of gay women writers pay proper attention to sex. The works of Gertrude Stein were not "spurred by purely intellectual concerns . . . [but] were responses to Sapphic impulses that she first concealed and later celebrated."[16]

Unfortunately, Benstock never extends her analysis to *Three Lives*. Most criticism on *Three Lives* is concerned with "Melanctha," and that in terms of modernism or of race. A restricted reading of "Melanctha" so dominates the critical discussion that criticism of the other two "lives" has languished altogether, and the *direct* representation of female samesexuality in "Melanctha" and "The Good Anna" barely receives lip service. This invariably warps the understanding of *Three Lives*, which was conceived and published as a unified work in three parts, as was *Q.E.D.*

Surely we can both appreciate the brilliance of much critical work on Stein and deplore its neglect of the lesbian content of *Three Lives* that I will argue is the primary raison d'être of the work and provides the best way to read the work as a coherent novel. All this appreciation does not lessen the damage of this century of silence and the implicit message that it has given to readers of Stein. My own goal here is to offer a lesbian-centered reading. I offer a critical history not only to offer a broader context for the discussion of *Three Lives* but also to embody how persistently the meat of the text was dismissed in favor of the skin. If I had my way, every time that someone read or heard about the importance of *Three Lives* to the modernist movement, or about its queer textuality, she or he would also hear or read about the lesbian *content* of the text.

Ghost Map: A Naturalist's Guide to the Apparitional Lesbian

Three Lives is a palimpsest, three overlaid portraits of proto-lesbians in a small southern city at the turn of the twentieth century. In "The Good Anna," "Melanctha," and "The Gentle Lena," Stein offers case studies of three working-class women whose same-sex orientation is neither consciously realized nor sexually embodied, to their detriment. *Three Lives* is a map of same-sex passion: three paths that do *not* lead to lesbian sex, much less lesbian identity, though the paths are so firmly rooted in same-sex desire that there is nowhere else for them to go.

All three heroines offer ample evidence of both same-sex desire and the internalized homophobia that saps the will to fulfill that desire, and all embody the apparitional lesbian. Stein offers three degrees of ghostliness: Lena, the most spectral, who cannot solidify herself enough to affect the material world; Anna, who can materialize only as a sexless spinster; and Melanctha, the most sexually substantial but ultimately still apparitional lesbian. All three sit near the bottom of the economic, racial, and ethnic pecking order, where opportunities for self-expression, personal freedom, and privacy are circumscribed. These constraints are so strong that Anna and Lena neither have sexual relations with other women nor consciously experience sexual pleasure or desire. Their epithets prevent them from removing the prefix *proto-* from *lesbian*: they are too much the "good" Anna and the "gentle" Lena.

Anna, the first heroine, channels her erotics into an idealized romance with another woman and dies a virgin. Her strong ego allows her to experience and act upon her lesbian desire while denying its sexual aspect. If psychological stability is the ability to effectively act in the world coupled with the ability to repress disturbing aspects of the self, then Anna is the most psychologically stable of the three heroines. This stability costs Anna a conscious or embodied sexuality and demands the rigorous and inhumane enforcement of sexual propriety in others as well as herself. Lena, by contrast, can barely retain a coherent ego, much less either conceptualize or act upon her desires. Her sexuality can be understood only in relation to her fragmentation, for her only experience of desire, will, and pleasure comes in a same-sexual context, whereas active heterosexuality effectively kills her.

Melanctha is the most psychosexually evolved of the three heroines. She struggles to understand and express herself sexually, and to understand how her society prevents her from achieving this understanding and this expression. Melanctha is conventionally understood as bisexual or sexually fluid, though her same-sex experience has earned much less attention than her heterosexual encounters. I offer a different reading of Melanctha, as a proto-lesbian whose partial success at self-realization means that her story cannot be told transparently. Stein had tried and failed to publish two previous novels with frank depictions of lesbian sexuality and identity; both, like "Melanctha," fictionalized versions of Stein's own first lesbian affair. Each successive version included more heterosexuality, and we should not be surprised that the heterosexual relationship in "Melanctha" has eaten the lion's share of the attention paid to *Three Lives,* to the detriment of the book as a whole.

Once the heterosexual relationship in "Melanctha" is dethroned, a naturalist text comes into relief. We see a realistic rendering of three women whose primary emotional and sexual tendencies are demonstrably same-sexual, but who are prevented by historical circumstances from realizing their desires in mind and body. Stein's depiction of characters' psychological states through a repetitive, nonlinear style—not yet a modernist commonplace—rightly designates the text a modernist landmark. Nonetheless, *Three Lives,* like Stein's first two novels, also should be viewed as "a notable piece of realism"—the title of one of its first reviews. Early reviews link the book to the work of Dreiser, Crane, Norris, and other American naturalists whose generation protested the taboos against sexuality and violence and the glorification of bourgeois individualism present in the work of the realist writers dominant in Stein's youth, such as Howells and the young James.[17]

The reviewers made an easy call. Novels such as Crane's *Maggie: A Girl of the Streets* and Dreiser's *Sister Carrie* expanded the ability of sympathetic characters to sexually express themselves outside of marriage and withheld happy endings and conventionally moral conclusions. Many naturalist works skirted the edge of respectability, and the novels of French naturalists of a generation before—such as Balzac, Flaubert, and Zola—were frequently banned in the United States, where they were synonymous with "dirty books." Many particularly risky naturalist works had to be self-published, such as *Maggie,* or were dropped by the publisher upon their first publication and did not sell, such as *Sister Carrie*. Still, few of the American naturalists pushed the boundaries of what could be represented as far as did Stein, whose characters are on the fringe of society not only by virtue of ethnicity, poverty, and immigrant status but also because of race and, especially, sexuality.[18]

Servants of Love: Stein and Flaubert

In the first "life," Stein creates a proto-lesbian character who has one great romance—"too sacred and too grievous ever to be told"—with another woman but denies herself direct sexual expression for the sake of power, respect, and security (30). In hegemonic terms, Anna deserves her adjective: she is "good." She knows her place as a poor, female, immigrant servant in Baltimore at the turn of the twentieth century and almost never acts or lets herself think inappropriately. Instead, Anna wages war against others who fail to meet her own high standards. In a brilliant (if unconscious) move against her subordinate position, Anna pursues her role with such extraordinary vigor that she accrues worldly power, finds considerable outlets for her aggression, and manages a same-sex romance. She does this by forsaking self-consciousness and sexual expression as well as retaining a servant's sensibility even after she acquires property and runs a business in her own right.[19]

For clarity, I will use the terms *sjuzet* and *fabula* in my discussion of the structure of the "lives," as their denotation is relatively fixed, unlike, say, *diegesis*. For our purposes, the sjuzet is the chronological order of the narrative, and the fabula is the chronological order of *what* is narrated. In this book, Capote comes first in the sjuzet, and Stein in the fabula. We need these terms because none of the three "lives" has a linear narrative, so all have two beginnings, one textual, the other chronological: one in the sjuzet, one in the fabula.[20]

For instance, "The Good Anna" has three parts. The first part is a nonlinear portrait of Anna at the time in her life when her "goodness" is most fully realized: when she is Miss Matilda's housekeeper, bargaining hard with shopkeepers; badgering her employer, underservants, and pets; and probably estranged from her romantic partner, who is conspicuously absent. The second part, "The Life of the Good Anna," marks Anna's first appearance in the fabula and tells the chronological story of her working life, from her entry into service at seventeen through her emigration from Germany and her employment by three masters: Miss Mary, Dr. Shonjen, and Anna's favorite, Miss Mathilda. Stein also relates Anna's personal life: her romance with the midwife Mrs. Lehntman, her friendship with the housewife Mrs. Drehten, and her encounters with the Lehntmans, the Drehtens, and the family of her brother, the Federners. The final part, "The Death of the Good Anna," takes up Anna's life after Miss Mathilda moves to Europe, leaving Anna her house and its furnishings. Anna opens a boardinghouse but abandons her financial shrewdness, charging too little and working too much, until she dies from overwork.

Transferred from Normandy to Baltimore, updated from the start to the end of the nineteenth century, and constructed around lesbian desire, "The Good Anna" retells Flaubert's "Un coeur simple," usually translated as "A Simple Heart." "Un coeur simple" is the first part of Flaubert's last complete work, *Trois contes*, published to great praise and middling sales in 1877. *Trois contes* was still influential in the Paris where Stein wrote *Three Lives* in 1905 and '06; Stein planned a translation but instead wrote a loose adaptation.[21]

Both "Un coeur simple" and "The Good Anna" are the first of three connected stories and are based in part on each author's past servant: Flaubert's nurse, Caroline "Julie" Herbert, and Stein's Baltimore servant, Lena Lebender. Though some critics have found Stein's citation of "Un coeur simple" and the tripartite structure of *Trois contes* to be nothing more than good form for an author writing in 1905, the parallels extend past form to content. Both are biographies of devoted housekeepers that concentrate on their working lives. Both heroines are remarkably free of conventional eros yet lead lives of vibrant passion and love, which complicates their adjectives of "simple" and "good." The unusual configuration of this passionate love as well as the difference between Flaubert's and Stein's styles have disguised these similarities for many readers.[22]

Before the action of "Un coeur simple," Flaubert fixes Félicité in a normative sexual matrix: "[L]ike other girls, she had once fallen in love" (5). Yet teen Félicité fiercely resists consummation, and after her fiancé deserts her to marry an older woman who can excuse him from military service, Félicité lacks desire along traditional lines. Years later, while traveling, her guide references the woman for whom Félicité was dumped:

> In the town center of Toucques, for instance, as they were passing alongside a house with nasturtiums growing around the windows, he said, with a shrug of his shoulders, "There's a Madame Lehoussais lives there and, rather than take a young man . . ." Félicité did not hear the

rest, for the horses had broken into a trot and the donkey had run on ahead. They turned down a track, a gate swung open, two young farm-hands appeared and they all dismounted by the manure-heap right outside the front door of the farmhouse. (11 [ellipsis Flaubert])

Félicité, who knows that her fiancé left her for an older woman named Lehoussais, fails to ask for the rest of the anecdote, which is cradled in precise material specifics that underline its murkiness. Didn't Mme. Lehoussais *take* the young man from Félicité, and from the army? What does *rather* signify? The reader knows that Félicité's fiancé and Lehoussais *took* each other in marriage *rather* than have the fiancé join the military, but this reading is not syntactically possible with the anecdote, which is no clearer in French. Neither Félicité nor any other character, including the narrator, references either Lehoussais or the fiancé again. Flaubert, famous for his precision, aims for the reader to have a private and thus more powerful revelation: Félicité is so little interested in her previous romance that she is less aware of it than her reader.[23]

Félicité's only other conventional romance is with a Polish soldier who "even said he would like to marry her, but they had a serious argu-ment when she came back one morning from the angelus to find him en-sconced in her kitchen, calmly helping himself to a salad which she had prepared for lunch" (28). This is the whole of Félicité's Polish romance, subordinate to a larger paragraph about her kindness to the Polish regi-ment and to cholera victims, itself part of a detailed list of her attach-ments, most of which fill a full paragraph and some of which occupy pages. Félicité's sole heterosexual romance as an adult woman is decidedly minor—and decidedly subordinate to her work. Yet Félicité does not seem to have abandoned heterosexuality per se. Instead, her same-sex relations are part of a broader queerness that never coalesces around genital sexu-ality of any kind. This *coeur* is hardly *simple*.

Félicité's cathexis skips from her fiancé to her mistress's children, her nephew, her mistress, the Polish regiment, a dying old man with a tumor who lives in a pigsty, her pet, and the Holy Ghost, ranging across class, gender, species, and beyond. Even though some critics have interpreted "Un coeur simple" as "the intimate history of a love that never found an object," Flaubert explicitly conceived of this plurality of objects as ends in themselves, rather than failed way stations.[24] In a much-cited letter, Flaubert wrote that "Un coeur simple" is "quite simply the tale of the obscure life of a poor country girl. . . . One after the other she loves a man, her mistress's children, a nephew, an old man she nurses, then her parrot; when the parrot dies she has it stuffed, and when she is on her deathbed she takes the parrot for the Holy Ghost. It is in no way ironic (though you might suppose it to be so) but on the contrary very serious and sad."[25] Félicité's idealization and devotion are not conventionally romantic, and any specifically sexual desire is undetectable. Nonetheless, the intensity of Félicité's feeling, which wells up around keepsakes of the beloved that she sensually worships, gives her passions a palpable though inchoate sexuality. Here Félicité watches her young charge Virginie at her First Communion:

> Even from a distance, she could recognize her beloved little Virginie by the delicate line of her neck. . . . Félicité leant further forwards so that she could see her and, with that singular imagination that is born of true love, she felt she was herself Virginie, assuming her expression, wearing her dress and with her heart beating inside her breast. As Virginie opened her mouth, Félicité closed her eyes and almost fainted.
>
> The next morning, bright and early, Félicité went to the sacristy and asked to be given communion. She received it with due reverence but did not experience that same rapture. (16)

Communion has no kick without Virginie. Félicité's idealization and identification with the little girl exemplify the projection of an internal object upon another person—a projection often understood as romantic love.[26] Even after Virginie's death, her relics transport Félicité:

> [Félicité and her employer] found a little chestnut-colored hat made of long-piled plush, but it had been completely destroyed by the moths. Félicité asked if she might have it as a keepsake. The two women looked at each other and their eyes filled with tears. Madame Aubain opened her arms and Félicité threw herself into them. Mistress and servant embraced each other, uniting their grief in a kiss that made them equal. . . . Félicité could not have been more grateful if she had been offered a priceless gift and from then on she doted on her mistress with dog-like fidelity and the reverence that might be accorded a saint. (27)

Madame Aubain's kiss lets Félicité transfer her internal object to her employer, as is seen by the extremity of her adoration and devotion, identical to her feelings for Virginie during Communion.

Félicité keeps the hat, along with mementos of other passions, until death. Toward the end of her life, the fluidity of the objects of her affection becomes extreme:

> When she went to church, she would sit gazing at the picture of the Holy Spirit and it struck her that it looked rather like her parrot. . . . In her mind, the one became associated with the other, the parrot becoming sanctified by connections with the Holy Spirit and the Holy Spirit in turn acquiring added life and meaning. . . . She developed the idolatrous habit of kneeling in front of the parrot to say her prayers. Sometimes the sun would catch the parrot's glass eyes as it came through the little window, causing an emanation of radiant light that sent her into ecstasies. (35–37 [ellipses mine])

The transformed corpse of Loulou the parrot has received much critical attention, and Stein's cavalier treatment of a parrot in "The Good Anna" has been read as a repudiation of Flaubert. Anna receives the parrot as a peacemaking gift from the daughter of Miss Mary, and Anna "liked the parrot very well," but not as much as her other, much-loved pets (19). The parrot remains nameless and almost entirely undescribed and undramatized, until Anna gives it away: "She had really never loved the parrot and now she hardly thought to ask for him" (44). I see this "disrespect" for Loulou as Stein's signal that her adaptation of Flaubert is complex. Those looking for a "parroting," one-to-one correspondence will be disappointed.

A Great Romance

Anna's desires are more definitely oriented than Félicité's. Anna is fond of her male employer, Dr. Shonjen; of her male tenants when she runs a boardinghouse; and of her dogs of both sexes, but the face of her desire is firmly turned toward other women, and her internal object is projected only once in strength, on Mrs. Lehntman. Though the extent of the women's sexual relations is not precisely delineated (as it is not in most fiction), Stein's explicit depiction of sex between women elsewhere in *Three Lives* makes overt sexual relations between Anna and Lehntman unlikely.

That said, there is no question that Mrs. Lehntman is Anna's great love:

The widow Mrs. Lehntman was the romance in Anna's life. (19)

Remember, Mrs. Lehntman was the romance in Anna's life. (22)

Her affair with Mrs. Lehntman was too sacred and too grievous ever to be told. (30)

Neither the good Anna nor the careless Mrs. Lehntman would give each other up excepting for the gravest cause. (33)

But what could our poor Anna do? Remember Mrs. Lehntman was the only romance Anna ever knew. (34)

And then, too, Mrs. Lehntman was the only romance Anna ever knew. (35)

Though many treatments of "The Good Anna" mention this "romance," they do not acknowledge how hard the reader is beaten about the head with it. Nor, to my knowledge, is there a nuanced assessment of Anna that takes her sexual orientation into account.[27]

That said, romance is more than a mixture of sexual desire, idealization, and loss of ego. Romance is also a literary genre—and Stein, who spent years reading through the canon, knew well the genre's admixture of saint's lives, quest narratives, battle accounts, and hymns to pure love. Romance as a genre does not contain much romantic love as we now know it. The 1911 *Encyclopedia Britannica,* a strong contender for the single greatest edition of any English-language encyclopedia, and certainly the most definitive general compilation of public knowledge at the start of the twentieth century, describes romance in this way: "the absence of a central plot, and the prolongation rather than the evolution of the story; the intermixture of the supernatural; the presence and indeed prominence of love-affairs; the juxtaposition of tragic and almost farcical incident; the variety of adventure arranged rather in the fashion of a panorama than otherwise." These characteristics serve the "purity" of love in the romance, which contrasts with the sexuality of the farce and which retires "the classical assumption that love is an inferior motive, and that women, though they 'may be good sometimes' are scarcely fit for the position of principal personages."[28]

This definition suits all six parts of *Trois contes* and *Three Lives.* Certainly the stories of Félicité and Anna are episodic, juggle the tragic and the comic, and include the supernatural (Anna with a fortune-teller, Félicité with the holy parrot). Per the *Britannica,* Anna and Félicité are romantic heroines, and their tales extend heroism to new subjects. Both women are chaste, and both are faithful to love objects that are usually considered inferior. For instance, Félicité's love for her parrot is usually regarded either as a sign of insanity or as a way for her to process her epilepsy rather than a way to experience passion under extraordinary constraints.

Stein uses the generic conventions of romance to portray an idealized love without sexual expression—a strategy used by twentieth-century gays and lesbians in life as well as art to avoid both internal and external homophobia. This strategy has been successful both for Anna and her readers, who have commented on the similar generic conventions of *Trois contes* and *Three Lives* but not on how the genre interacts with sexuality.[29] Yet Stein's map of same-sex passion exhibits considerable articulation. Anna and Lehntman's romance is the story's most prominent through line. The romance keeps Anna from leaving town with her first employer: "Perhaps if Mrs. Lehntman had not been in Bridgepoint, Anna would have tried to live in this new house" (22). The two great crises of the story are conflicts between Anna and Lehntman, both sparked by a strange male. First, Mrs. Lehntman adopts an illegitimate baby boy, which is consistent with her impulsive kindness; but Anna finds this one act indefensible. Second, Lehntman has a murky relationship with a doctor who performs abortions. Anna cannot forgive a nonspecified "it"—"it was just as bad as it could be" (41)—and Anna and Lehntman never recover: "Now, slowly, Anna began to make it up with Mrs. Lehntman. They could never be as they had been before. Mrs. Lehntman could never be the romance in the good Anna's life, but they could be friends again" (45). Whatever Lehntman did with the doctor, it destroyed Anna's love.

This love is not replaced. Anna's other associations cannot compare, whether they be with her other close friend, Mrs. Drehten—"There was no fever in this friendship, it was just the interchange of two hard working, worrying women" (29)—or with her favorite employer, Miss Mathilda, who "was not a romance in the good Anna's life, but Anna gave her so much strong affection that it almost filled her life as full" (41). Here Stein clarifies that Anna and Lehntman's bond extends past "normal" friendship and "strong affection" to a "fever" that "filled her life." Sounds like passion to me. Why, then, is this "maiden german mind" with her "angular, thin, spinster body" so emphatically pure—or, from a perspective that values sexual expression, so thwarted? (24). More crudely, why don't Anna and Lehntman do it?

Why Don't They Do It?

This question is broached inside the text. Anna's sister-in-law, Mrs. Federner, entertains the possibility:

> The Federners [Anna's brother's family] had never seemed to feel
> it wrong in Anna, her devotion to this friend and her care of her
> and her children. Mrs. Lehntman and Anna and her feelings were
> all somehow too big for their attack. But Mrs. Federner had the
> mind and tongue that blacken things. Not really to blacken black,
> of course, but just to roughen and to rub on a little smut. She could
> somehow make even the face of the Almighty seem pimply and a
> little coarse. (32)

Anna and Lehntman's relationship is too "big"—too intense? too sacred? too outside the norm?—for the open discussion of its sexuality, which is nonetheless apparent. Mrs. Federner is degraded as perverse for her perception, which the narrative cannot bear to directly state; only the narrative's disgust at her perception may be related. This is a standard defense for a homosexual in denial: she who *sees* and even more so, *names* the desire is made perverse, rather than the desire itself, which after all "is not there." Federner "did not mean to interfere," but perception alone is enough. Whether the accusation of "the mind and tongue that blacken things" is a transcription of Anna's thoughts as the point of view takes her perspective, or the narrator's ironic statement, or both, Anna/the narrator sees Federner's observation as "rub[bing] on a little smut," as in corrupting an ideal with dirt; as "black," as in dirty, and, if Stein uses a racist calculus, as insufficiently "white"; as "pimply," a swelling of untoward fluid, an embarrassing, adolescent bodily expression; and as "a little coarse," as in unfortunately crude and insufficiently refined.

Sex with Mrs. Lehntman is not inconceivable, exactly, but it is *not to be thought of.* Note that "Lehntman" is a near homophone for "Lenten," something meager enough for Lent, the period before Easter that Anna as a faithful Catholic would observe in prayer and self-denial. Anna's romance is thus both her great passion and a Lenten denial. The physicality of the relationship is appropriately meager for a consciousness that crucifies the possibility of lesbian sex. There is no lesbian Easter for Anna— and her insistence on propriety tells us why.

Anna controls even her dogs' sexuality: her "high ideals for canine chastity and discipline" lead her to punish the dogs' "periods of evil thinking [which] came very regularly. . . . At such times Anna would be very busy and scold hard" (8). For Anna, sexual impropriety trumps lying: "'Peter was the father of those pups,' the good Anna explained to Miss Mathilda, 'and they look just like him too . . . but Miss Mathilda, I would never let those people know that Peter was so bad'" (8). Note that the slang meaning of "Peter" as "penis" was well established by the date of the composition of *Three Lives*. Anna is equally controlling of the servants who work under her, and her attempts to quash the romance of Sallie and the butcher boy are dramatized in part 1.[30]

Anna's investment in propriety extends to aesthetics: she knows "so well the kind of ugliness appropriate to each rank in life" and buys presents "having the right air for a member of the upper class" for her bosses, and gifts with the appropriate "awkward ugliness" for her servant friends—all at the same cost (25–26). Anna's standards and rules infect the narrative itself, where "girls" are always called by their first name, and where married women, even romantic friends, are invariably called "Mrs."; we never learn Mrs. Lehntman's first name, and Anna presumably never uses it. No matter how old or successful Anna becomes, she still identifies as a proper servant girl. "No argument could bring her to sit an evening in the empty parlour, although the smell of paint when they were fixing up the kitchen made her very sick, and tired as she always was, she never would sit down during the long talks she held with Miss Mathilda. A girl was a girl and should always act like a girl" (15). Even when she owns a boardinghouse, she is never "Miss Anna," much less "Miss Federner," and she always does a servant girl's work. Throughout, Stein details how Anna's insistence on servile perfection weakens and then kills her: "She worked away her appetite, her health and strength, and always for the sake of those who begged her not to work so hard. To her thinking, in her stubborn, faithful, german soul, this was the right way for a girl to do" (21).

Master and Servant

Though Anna's work ethic kills her, to view her as a victim would be incorrect, for she dies in her own service. Anna profits from her fidelity to hegemony in direct proportion to how she suffers, for within the constraints of "goodness" she is master. Here Anna differs from Félicité, who also has reservoirs of strength when defending chastity and innocence. Félicité may resist her fiancé's advances, and she may save her charges from a rampaging bull, but she does not share Anna's joy in the fight. By contrast, "The Good Anna" begins with Anna's pleasure in aggression: "The tradesmen of Bridgepoint learned to dread the sound of 'Miss Mathilda,' for with that name the good Anna always conquered" (7). Compare this to Félicité: "[The farmers] would both come bearing chickens or cheeses which they hoped they might persuade her to buy. But Félicité was more than a match for their banter and they always respected her for this" (8). "Dread" versus "respect," "conquered" versus "more than a match": these differences of affect transcend questions of translation. Anna's station is the armor that allows her to conquer, and conquering fills her with fierce joy.

Anna manipulates her servility to allow herself this joy. Though Anna subjects herself to propriety—to her role in hegemony as she understands it—she is not abject in the temporal realm, for she serves only those she can dominate: "Anna found her place with large, abundant women, for such were always lazy, careless or all helpless, and so the burden of their lives could fall on Anna, and give her just content. Anna's superiors must always be these large helpless women, or be men, for none others could give themselves to be made so comfortable and free" (16). The same hegemonic masculinity that makes Anna inferior to men also keeps male masters from correcting her as long as she stays in her appropriate place. Men may tell Anna what her duties are but not *how* to do them. Therefore, Anna "loved to work for men, for they could eat so much and with such joy. And when they were warm and full, they were content, and let her do whatever she thought best" (24).

Women are more difficult employers, for they are entitled to enter the feminine sphere and thus to interfere, which Anna finds intolerable. She works only for "large helpless women" who allow Anna complete control in her domain. Consider Anna's relations with Miss Mary's children: "She naturally preferred the boy, for boys always love better to be done for . . . while in the little girl she had to meet the feminine, the subtle opposition, showing so early always in a young girl's nature" (16). This little girl issues the only direct order that Anna disobeys (19). Anna leaves Dr. Shonjen's service when he gets married, and she leaves Miss Mary when she moves in with her daughter, now grown. When Anna runs a boardinghouse, women are not allowed.

Anna thus redeploys a social position that is stacked against her. She uses her female, servile, immigrant status to attain dominance while hewing to the standards of her subordinate position, a move that requires a highly developed consciousness of the "firm old world sense of what was the right way for a girl to do" (15). When shielded by her servitude and empowered and assured by goodness, Anna is a joyful knight: "But truly she loved it best when she could scold" (24). As she controls herself, so she fights to reproduce her strictures in others.

Stein offers a detailed recital of Anna's pains in teaching a series of underservants and other women to be "proper." Anna's understanding of goodness also allows her to nag and harass her employers, as long as she stays with bounds. She scolds Dr. Shonjen, "whom she could guide and constantly rebuke to his own good" (24), and she scolds Miss Mathilda for not dressing as she should and for buying too many objets d'art (14). Though such scolding is inspired by affection, Anna also scolds out of duty: "Not that [Mrs. Lehntman's daughter] was pleasant in the good Anna's sight, but it must never be that a young girl growing up should have no one to make her learn to do things right" (25). Anna's love of scolding reveals that, like many soldiers, she prefers fighting for her cause to living in secure territory. If Anna really loved hegemonic propriety, she would work for women who by virtue of their status might boss Anna as they wished. Instead, Anna chooses mistresses whose soft confusion is overwhelmed by Anna's hard certainty. Anna's lower status makes the contest a fair fight, and the relationships are both stable and exciting.

. . . Then Comes Baby in the Baby Carriage

Anna's preference for being a soldier extends to her erotic life. Thus, her great romance is with the uncontrolled and feckless Lehntman, with "her happy way of giving a pleasant well diffused attention" (27). Anna may have the dominant personality, but she does not dominate Lehntman: "Anna *wanted* Mrs. Lehntman very much and Mrs. Lehntman *needed* Anna" (35 [italics mine]). Anna's hard certainty of right and wrong and her desire to enforce this certainty find no purchase with Lehntman, who "could not really take in harsh ideas [and] was too well diffused to catch the feel of any sharp firm edge" (28). In her last appearance, Lehntman remains "as diffuse as always in her attention" (45). She runs her house with "slackness and neglect" and does "not trouble much with [her daughter], but gave her always all she wanted that she had, and let the girl do as she liked"—leaving Anna to pick up the slack and to recognize that such "neglect" was "not from indifference or dislike on the part of Mrs. Lehntman, it was just her usual way" (24–25).

Lehntman is Anna's opposite not only in the "softness" of her diffuse personality but also in her relationship to being a "good girl." As a midwife, Lehntman makes her living from female sexuality and its products. She gains economic independence and supports two children through her skill with birth, that extremity of intimate physical mess. Later, Lehntman enlists Anna's help and money for buying and running a home for pregnant unmarried women: "Mrs. Lehntman in her work loved best to deliver young girls who were in trouble" (20). Both the material specifics and the gender politics of her job calibrate her as a love object for the repressed, proper Anna. Only Lehntman's involvement with the abortionist—the "evil and mysterious man who had been the cause of all her trouble"—pushes Lehntman so far from propriety that Anna cannot forgive her (45). While the romance lasts, however, loving Lehntman allows Anna to love the sexual and social "badness" that she has repressed in herself. As Anna probably could not permit herself to love a woman who herself was promiscuous, a woman who makes her living from other women's sexual expression is ideal.

Anna feels a physical as well as a psychic attraction to Lehntman, who earns the longest, most concentrated physical description in Anna's life. Lehntman is a "good looking woman. She had a plump well rounded body, clear olive skin, bright dark eyes and crisp black curling hair" (19). She is "pleasant, magnetic, efficient and good. She was very attractive, very generous and very amiable" (19). She "entirely subdued [Anna] by her magnetic, sympathetic charm" (20). Stein specifies the same-sex nature of Mrs. Lehntman's power of attraction—"A certain magnetic brilliancy in person and in manner made Mrs. Lehntman a woman other women loved" (33)—and clarifies the extent of Anna's desire—"Anna wanted Mrs. Lehntman very much" (35). Anna's romance with the beautiful bad girl Lehntman, and, to a lesser extent Anna's preference for large, indolent mistresses, is reminiscent of the iconography of twentieth-century butch culture: commanding, rigorously controlled women paired with femmes whom they might "serve and protect." Though Anna and Lehntman do not make a classic butch/femme couple, the paradigm remains an effective ground, as does Stein's own relationship with Toklas.[31]

Stein and Toklas sported respective butch and femme looks, and their gendered division of labor permeates *The Autobiography of Alice B. Toklas.* Stein eats, and Toklas cooks; Stein writes, and Toklas types; Stein supports Toklas financially, and both consider Toklas the "wife." In a famous passage, "Toklas" notes, "I had often said that I would write, The wives of geniuses that I have sat with." Note, however, that Toklas's extensive caretaking of Stein references the parent/child dynamic, as do many intimate configurations. Both Stein and Toklas used "Baby" as a private nickname for each other—a habit that may have derived from Stein's childhood nickname "Baby"—and the butch/femme and parent/child dynamics interpenetrate and oscillate. Similarly, though Anna's relationship with Lehntman primarily indexes the butch/femme binary, Anna's relationships with her employers, especially the Misses Mathilda and Mary, more clearly reference the love between a hardworking mother and a willful child or baby. At the same time, Mathilda and Mary support and house Anna. In this way, Anna is the baby or, more precisely, the good daughter.[32]

In *Three Lives*, Baby the dog is the "child" of Anna and Lehntman's chaste romance. In her first appearance in the "life," Lehntman is linked with "the new puppy, the pride of Anna's heart, a present from her friend the widow, Mrs. Lehntman" (17). Baby is the most sexually "decent" of Anna's dogs: "Innocent blind old Baby was the only one who preserved the dignity becoming in a dog" (8). Stein's next reference to Baby clarifies Anna's love: "[B]est of all animals she loved the dog and best of all dogs, little Baby, the first gift from her friend, the widow Mrs. Lehntman" (19). The first mention of Anna and Lehntman's special relationship follows, set off in a one-sentence paragraph: "The widow Mrs. Lehntman was the romance in Anna's life" (19).

As Anna and Lehntman's relationship weakens, so their child sickens and dies: "[Baby] got weak and fat and breathless. . . . Baby did not die with a real sickness. She just got older and more blind and coughed and then more quiet, and then slowly one summer's day she died" (47). A similar desuetude permeates the women's final relations, as seen in Lehntman's final mention in both fabula and sjuzet: "Mrs. Lehntman she saw very rarely. . . . They did their best, both these women, to be friends, but they were never able to touch one another nearly. There were too many things between them that they could not speak of, things that had never been explained nor yet forgiven" (50–51). So ends a great romance.

"The Good Anna" and the Hard Bargain

In the light of her commitment to propriety and her historical context, Anna's inability to conceptualize her sexuality, much less actively express it, does not surprise. "The Good Anna" is both a blatant description of a lesbian romance and a thorough dramatization of the repression that thwarts the romance from arising to either self-consciousness or sexual fruition. "Romance is the ideal in one's life and it is very lonely living with it lost"—in part because the idealization serves to block out the larger absence of an unrealized sexuality (35). To be more blunt, Stein would need bullet points.

Which, as always with the apparitional lesbian, is easy to say but hard to prove. Here are three last points to consider. First, there is a conspicuous lack of evidence of heterosexual romance, passion, or intimate relations of any kind for Anna, no analogue to Félicité's fiancé or even her Polish soldier. Second, Stein's two previous narratives, *Q.E.D.* and *Fernhurst*, showcase lesbian relations, and *Q.E.D.* especially establishes the difficulty of the path to lesbian self-consciousness and sexual realization through a heroine who needs other lesbians to tell her, "[Y]ou are queer and interesting even if you don't know it and you like queer and interesting people even if you think you don't." When Adele is chided for her separation of "affectionate comradeship" and "physical passion," and for her "puritanic horror" of the latter, she decides that she "could undertake to be an efficient pupil if it were possible to find an efficient teacher." Anna will not receive such critique.[33]

Last, the antipathy bordering on revulsion that Anna provokes in literary critics may signal their knowing or unknowing comprehension of her same-sex orientation and their conscious or unconscious homophobia. At the least, such distaste indicates a lack of appreciation for the difficulties of Anna's psychosexual situation. Anna is undeniably a bossy prude. She is also steadfast, loyal, and so charitable that she bankrupts herself. Her charity extends to those who disobey her prescriptions. How many prudes underwrite homes for unwed mothers? Blame the hegemony for defining "good," not Anna for fulfilling it. Stein's nuanced portrayal makes the critical distaste suspect.

For instance, James Mellow's description of Anna as "domineering" seems reasonable, and no less sympathetic than his description of Félicité as "bovine," but the fervor of Carl Wood's distaste for Anna indicates something unsaid: "[T]he middle-aged, sharp-tongued, immigrant housekeeper with whom we are confronted at the beginning of the story is clearly a petty and incorrigible domestic tyrant." Though Stein shows and tells us how Anna works herself to death, Wood holds that "her life could be called arduous and troubled only from her own point of view."

Even kind critics find Anna somehow "wrong." When Richard Bridgman calls her "[a] conscience-ridden german catholic housekeeper who drives herself and those under her remorselessly, at the cost of recurrent headaches," he agrees that she is as hard on herself as she is on others but elides her constant charity. Marianne DeKoven speaks for the majority when she writes, "[T]he 'good' in 'The Good Anna' is highly ironic." Even critics who define themselves as feminists sensitive to lesbian issues lack compassion for Anna and her hard bargain. Instead, discussion of lesbian sexuality in *Three Lives* has focused on "Melanctha," and then only in terms of its racial translation.[34]

Melanctha and the Mainstream

If Anna invests her self-image in her stock as a proper servant and strikes the hard bargain of epistemological certainty, psychological security, and narrow but deep worldly power at the cost of an embodied sexuality, then Melanctha is Anna's opposite, a woman who fights social constraints and sexual normativity at the cost of powerlessness, instability, and depression. Melanctha is a mixed-race flaneuse who "wanders" through lovers and jobs at the cost of perpetual restlessness and a steady swing between mania and misery. Her dogged, unsuccessful search—for what?—brings on depression so great that she wishes for death: "[A] woman whom [Melanctha] knew had killed herself because she was so blue. Melanctha said, sometimes, she thought this was the best thing for her herself to do" (54). Melanctha's "life" traces her erotic, romantic, and familial relationships from her sexual awakening through her four primary attachments—Jane, Jeff, Jem, and Rose—until her death from tuberculosis, probably in her thirties. She never sustains a close relationship, either with family or with lovers. Her only consistency is a state of flux.

With "Melanctha," we enter into the mainstream of criticism of *Three Lives,* which is in essence criticism of "Melanctha" removed from the other two lives. This focus is understandable. "Melanctha" is (1) the most experimental "life" in terms of style; (2) the most unusual "life" in terms of its heroine, a psychologically sophisticated African American woman; (3) the most biographically notable "life" in terms of subject, as it transmutes the affair between Stein and Bookstaver into the relationship between Jeff and Melanctha; (4) the most exciting "life," with considerably more sex, drugs, violence, and death than the rest; and (5) the longest "life," as well as the last written. These merits leave "Melanctha" well suited for interpretive strategies that are valuable in their own right but allow the easy circumlocution of homosexuality.

A fully comprehensive critical history of this circumlocution would swamp this book and repeat instead of illuminate the subordination of sexuality. My goal here is to materialize the apparitional lesbian. This is largely a history of absence and glancing reference, and it exemplifies the effect of homophobia on critical reading and the increments by which it has been beaten back. To showcase this absence, I provide this discussion before my reading of "Melanctha," which requires me to reference characters and events that I have not yet explored. Those unfamiliar with "Melanctha" may wish to read the next section later.

A Peculiar History

Three Lives was published on July 30, 1909, by Grafton, a vanity press. Vanity presses earlier in the century were not as redolent of publication for self-gratification as they are now; Grafton was respectable, but its charter did not allow for much editorial discretion. A representative sampling of its catalog might include *The Threefold Path to Peace,* a metaphysical, somewhat theosophical exploration by Xena, who followed her name with a Greek delta, and *The Tories of Chippeny Hill, Connecticut: A Brief Account of the Loyalists of Bristol, Plymouth, and Harwinton, Who Founded St. Matthew's Church in East Plymouth in 1791.* Even so, the president of Grafton, Frederick H. Hitchcock, warned Stein that she had "written a very peculiar book and it will be a hard thing to make people take it seriously."[35]

Early reviews prove Hitchcock right about peculiarity and wrong about serious consideration. There were five reviews of *Three Lives* in 1909 and thirteen in 1910—and then none till the 1913 Armory Show sparked interest in Stein as a figure and an artist. The first three reviews—brief and unsigned, in the Sunday, December 12, 1909, *Washington [D.C.] Herald* and the following Sunday's *Boston Globe* and *Kansas City Star*—serve as a template for the book's reception before the Armory Show. All three reviews mark the text as strange: *Three Lives* is a "peculiar exposition" with an "originality of . . . narrative form" by "a literary artist of such originality," a "new and original artist in the field of fiction" whose "style is somewhat unusual" and who uses a "most eccentric and difficult form." The noteworthy merits and demerits of this strangeness differ, however.

The *Herald* observed that Stein eschews a "statement of ultimate and fixed condition" and offers instead "a detailed showing of the repeated thoughts in the brain by which such conditions are arrived at." Stein's choice of heroines is unfortunate: though "such repetition does occur, even in cultivated and brilliant minds . . . it is a question if the mind-working of such persons as Miss Stein has chosen could be made interesting by any process whatsoever." Stein should not have chosen "minds of low caliber and meager cultivation, the three lives depicted being those of three servant women, one of whom is a mulatto."[36]

The *Boston Globe*, like the *Washington Herald*, proved capable of seeing through Stein's style to focus upon her subject: "It is only when one has read the book slowly—not as a story, but as a serious picture of life—that one grasps the author's conception of her humble character[s], their thought and their tragedies." Here, peculiarity issues from style, not subject: *Three Lives* is "difficult" and "somewhat unusual," and "sometimes . . . becomes prosy." Stein did best in Kansas City, where *Three Lives* was called "[a] fiction which no one who reads it can ever forget, but a book for a strictly limited audience. . . . As a character study one can speak of it only in superlatives." The *Star* intimated that the book's style *is* its subject: "In this remarkable book one watches humanity groping in the mists of existence. . . . As these humble human lives are groping in bewilderment so does the story telling itself." This makes *Three Lives* "a very masterpiece of realism, for the reader never escapes from the atmosphere of those lives, so subtly is the incantation wrought in these seeming simple pages." The review also compliments Stein's ability to cross classes: "The indwelling spirit of it all is a sweet enlightened sympathy, an unsleeping sense of humor, and an expansive carefulness in detail."

Some reviews were more detailed, but none substantially differed in focus, tone, or content, and none read the text as specifically gay, either overtly or covertly. A lesbian conclusion may be reached only by appreciating how Stein in some reviews was placed as "other" by race, class, and gender, and then by extrapolating from these patches of queerness a broader quilt of difference: an iffy journey of common cause. Note that "peculiarity" is not equivalent to the "strangeness" seen in reviews of *Other Voices, Other Rooms* in chapter 1. Consider the denotation and connotation of *peculiar* as opposed to those of *young, effeminate, strange,* and *esoteric,* the code words for Capote's sexual dissidence. The 1911 *Encyclopedia Britannica* defines *peculiar* as "a word now generally used in the sense of that which solely or exclusively belongs to, or is particularly characteristic, of an individual; hence strange, odd, queer." This single "queer" is the sole touchstone of sexual oddness in the penumbra around *peculiarity*, which is bereft of the subcultures referenced by *esoteric* and *effeminate*. The first suggests a secret known only to initiates, and the second, a gender variance similar to other such variances. *Peculiar*, by contrast, is individual. Similarly, *original, unusual, odd*, and *eccentric* conveyed the singular in 1910 and do so today. There is no community here, no sense of a human trait that any reviewer has previously seen, read, or heard.[37]

Reviews of *Three Lives* after the Armory Show were written because of Stein's association with the visual modernists, and they view her work as an example of modernism rather than an extension of naturalism. They were more likely to focus on "Melanctha" than on the other two "lives" and were more interested in style than content; for several of the reviews, the style of "Melanctha" *is* the content of *Three Lives*. Some of the first appreciations of the content qua content of "Melanctha" came from writers of the Harlem Renaissance, who focused on race much more than sexuality, though many of these writers were queer. In a 1927 letter, Carl Van Vechten reported that Nella Larsen found "Melanctha" "the best Negro story she has ever read." Larsen herself wrote Stein the following year to wonder "just why you and not some one of us should so accurately have caught the spirit of this race of mine." She enclosed her unpublished novel *Quicksand*. Stein and Van Vechten could be valuable allies for Larsen, and her praise may have been motivated by a desire to please them. Nonetheless, the influence of "Melanctha" on Larsen's novels speaks to her sincerity.[38]

In another letter, Van Vechten reported even higher praise from James Weldon Johnson. Van Vechten quoted Johnson: "'I think "Melanctha" is marvelous. What surprises me is that in it Gertrude Stein is the first (I believe I'm right) white writer to write a story of love between a Negro man and woman and deal with them as normal members of the human family. Her style, which on the surface seems so naive—some might say childish, is really consummate artistry.'" Johnson wrote to Van Vechten in 1933, when Johnson was a well-established writer who held the chair of creative literature at Fisk University and had just won the Du Bois Prize for Negro Literature. Johnson, who had served as the operating officer of the NAACP, presumably would not have falsely praised Stein.[39]

Note that Stein is commended for two different things here. Larsen appreciates the authenticity of Stein's portrait of "the spirit of this race of mine"—of how Stein captures a specific and perhaps "essential" blackness—and Johnson appreciates how Stein does *not* write about black people differently than she does white. Others in the Harlem Renaissance agreed with Johnson but deplored this equality. Claude McKay objected that "Melanctha" offers nothing striking and important about Negro life: "Melanctha, the mulattress, might have been a Jewess. And the mulatto Jeff Campbell—he is not typical of mulattoes I have known anywhere. He reminds me more of a type of white lover described by a colored woman."[40] McKay did not believe that Stein had captured essential, or at least "typical," blackness. In this, he agreed with Stein's brother Leo, who offered the unusual perspective of a straight man who was aware of Stein's sexuality and familiar with *Q.E.D.*:

> I read the first novel. . . . [I]t was the original material of Melanctha and had nothing to do with Negroes—the writing was impossible. . . . [A] very intelligent Negro writer . . . said to me once that Gertrude was the only white person who had given real Negro psychology. I laughed and said, of course, the book was really not about Negroes and had only Negro local color, and as the psychology of whites and Negroes of the same cultural grade is essentially the same, the extra psychology will give Negro psychology, provided he understands that cultural group.

Leo speaks out of both sides of his mouth. "Melanctha" is "really not about Negroes and had only Negro local color" at the same time that "the psychology of whites and Negroes of the same cultural grade is essentially the same." Which is it? Leo cannot explain, because he does not mention, much less discuss, either the lesbian erotics and conflicts of *Q.E.D.* or how those erotics and conflicts inform "Melanctha." Note how he discusses the different races of the characters in *Q.E.D.* and *Melanctha* but not the different genders. Note, too, how he discusses the "impossible" style of *Q.E.D.* but not the content. Leo was writing to a close friend of both Steins; there was no need for discretion. He has the dubious distinction of being the first critic of "Melanctha" to use a critical discussion of race and style to displace a discussion of the lesbian sexuality that he knew is there.[41]

Leo's letter was private; the public discussion of Gertrude's sexuality grew with the publication of lesbian particulars in her biographies and of *Q.E.D.* For instance, in the 1951 *New Yorker* review of *Things as They Are* (the censored version of *Q.E.D.*, finally published in a tiny print run of 516 in 1950 with the most overt lesbian passages removed), Edmund Wilson observed that "the vagueness that began to blur [Stein's writing] from about 1910 on and the masking by unexplained metaphors that later made it seem opaque, though partly the result of an effort to emulate modern painting, were partly also due to a need imposed by the problem of writing about relationships between women of a kind that the standards of that era would not have allowed her to describe more explicitly."[42] Wilson here makes the "coding" argument that figures in so much Stein criticism, and notes the correspondence between the obscuring of sexual identity and desire and the modernist refusal of conventional visual representation. Wilson's public discussion of Stein's sexuality is the first in wide circulation for a general audience and is authorized in part by his security as a straight man who could discuss homosexuality without putting himself in question, either in public or in private. Wilson's diaries reveal a critic who neither demonized homosexuality nor saw it swamping other aspects of an author or her writing, but who was comfortable and familiar with various sexualities in both people and books. Compare Wilson's quiet assertion with Agee's hysterical winking in *TIME*. The difference cannot be explained by any relaxation of homophobia from the 1930s to the 1950s.

Wilson was an outlier; most lesbian-inflected critique would need to wait until John Malcolm Brinnin's 1958 biography of Stein and, especially, the further revelations of biographers Richard Bridgman (1970) and James Mellow (1974). None discuss the lesbian content of *Three Lives*. Bridgman's poor use of sexuality as an interpretative model is typical and may be productively paired with his incision in terms of race. His objections to Stein's racism are pointed: "Stein's treatment of the Negro is both condescending and false. The principals of the story are not black at all, but only new, revised [racist] versions of the characters Gertrude Stein had described in *Things as They Are*." Bridgman agrees with previous critics that Stein does not differentiate between her treatment of blacks and whites in "essential" blackness: Stein's characters are not "black at all." For Bridgman, the portrait is not only inauthentic but also condescending and false, and therefore deeply racist. Bridgman goes to considerable effort to specify his objections but makes no mention of lesbian sexuality in "Melanctha," apart from a brief mention of Jane and Melanctha's "sexual overtones." When he examines the link between *Q.E.D.* and "Melanctha," he carefully denatures the sexual translation: "Provided names, the forces are Jeff Campbell, a Negro physician who while attending a sick woman, falls in love with the woman's daughter Melanctha. Their earlier names were [*Q.E.D.*'s] Adele and Helen." Historically, this equation of same- and different-sex passion is progressive. Still, the lesbian content remains largely apparitional. With Bridgman, we see ectoplasm, but knocks on the table by "forces" are not conversation.[43]

Bridgman is right that in 1961, and even more so now, "Melanctha" disturbs in terms of race. Like Anna and Lena, Melanctha is drawn in the context of her heritage, and when her "life" is read out of context, the narrator's racism is certainly offensive. Part of this offense is integral to the racial and ethnic hegemony of turn-of-the-century Baltimore, as in "The Gentle Lena": "These hard working, earth-rough german cousins were to these american born children, ugly and dirty, and as far below them as were italian or negro workmen, and they could not see how their mother could ever bear to touch them, and then all the women dressed so funny, and were worked all rough and different" (153). This observation is filtered through the consciousness of the "american born children" and observes a hierarchy without subscribing to it. Such passages in "Melanctha" cannot be explained away by point of view: "[The paler Melanctha] tended Rose, and she was patient, submissive, soothing, and untiring, while the sullen, childish, cowardly black Rosie grumbled and fussed and howled and made herself to be an abomination and like a simple beast" (53). This is easily reduced to a good, submissive, paler woman versus a bad, infantile, animalistic darker woman. My argument is not whether such comments are racist: they are, just as in other respects the text is racially progressive. Instead, I am concerned with whether race represents something other than itself.[44]

One reason why critics have been preoccupied with such masquerade is that literary criticism in terms of race was, for decades, more available than criticism in terms of homosexuality. Certainly when Bridgman wrote in 1961, there was less language available for a critic who wanted to discuss the lesbian content of *Three Lives*, and less of an audience willing to read it. Professionally, such criticism had little value, and what value it had was likely to be negative. Even since gay liberation, the talk has remained superficial. Consider Catharine Stimpson's 1977 "The Mind, the Body, and Gertrude Stein," which documents the direct quotation of *Q.E.D.* in "Melanctha." This article is much cited because it allowed so much that came afterward. Yet Stimpson restricts her inquiry to coding: how the lesbian passion of *Q.E.D.* is made straight in "Melanctha," and how "problematic passion among whites is transferred to blacks, as if they might embody that which the dominant culture feared." This observation would become influential, and the substitution of lesbian passion with black passion in relation to their similar hegemonic abjection would become a dominant trope.[45]

Stimpson shies away from anything but the lesbian origins of the text; she elides the *overt* sex and love between Melanctha and Jane and backpedals at the article's end: "[O]ne must wonder if future scholars will not ask about us, 'Why were they so interested in sexuality? What did the fascination with sexuality itself encode, disguise, and hide?'" This po-faced apologia set the tone for the next decade. Throughout the 1980s, feminist critics, like nonfeminist critics, looked past the overt lesbianism of the text. At best, they acknowledged Jane and Melanctha's relationship briefly and moved on.[46]

Consider Sonia Saldívar-Hull, who took to task feminist critics who champion Stein even as they "forget that real people, races, and classes are affected by the stereotypes [Stein] never challenges." Saldívar-Hull exemplifies how the move in third-wave feminism toward recognizing the different experiences of women often did not extend to lesbians and lesbian issues, which receive two and a half sentences in eight pages of her analysis on *Three Lives*. In her own disregard of the lesbian content of a fundamental work in the gay canon, Saldívar-Hull risks the same type of "willful insensitivity" of which she accuses others. Are we competing, then, to see who is more ill used? I hope not. As I insist that attention be paid to the lesbian content of the text, so Saldívar-Hull insists that readers pay attention to Stein's dramatization and narration of race and class. As I insist that my experience as a gay man gives me a valuable, even necessary, perspective on the text, so Saldívar-Hull overtly links her critical insight with her perspective as a woman of color from a working-class background who confronts a critical establishment that she finds blind to her concerns. We both insist on a surface as well as a depth hermeneutic.[47]

By the 1990s, Stimpson, Benstock, Castle, Jay, and many others had made it more difficult to leave female same-sexuality out of the critical conversation around Gertrude Stein. (They did not, however, make it uncommon.) In relation to "Melanctha," Corrine Blackmer best addresses Benstock's call for attention to "sapphist modernism." Blackmer is one of very few critics to read Jane as Jeff's equal, and her use of the term "lover" for Jane and Melanctha's relationship—a basic show of respect offered by no other critic treated here—is a striking moment of visibility. For Blackmer, Melanctha cannot sustain this or any romantic relationship, because (1) she cannot imagine a nontutelary relationship with a woman as "adult" and (2) she cannot have a structurally inferior position of power in a relationship, which dooms her relations with men.[48]

Blackmer's primary concern, however, is neither Melanctha and Jane's relationship nor Melanctha's sexuality. Instead, Blackmer aims to build upon Stimpson and others who "interpreted the novella's racial text solely in terms of its palimpsestic lesbian subtext" while addressing the racist charges put forth most forcefully by Saldívar-Hull. Blackmer asks why Stein should be held accountable for the sins of a racist, homophobic culture that lets her represent the lesbian only through a racialized drag:

> Thus Jews become types of blacks, lesbians become types of mulattas, and prostitutes, women, bohemians, and even cosmopolitans. Literary artists from these groups who seek cultural legitimacy must stress their sameness with a highly suspicious dominant discourse, while they simultaneously endeavor to express their rapport with an often equally suspicious minority discourse. . . . [B]lame for miscommunication devolves upon those among the marginalized who attempt to be heard and attempt to gain access to an otherwise closed system, rather than upon those in the dominant discourse whose power enables them to remain oblivious to their rhetorical duplicity.

This is beautifully said. Nonetheless, Blackmer fails to explain why, in a text with copious expressions of same-sexuality, Stein necessarily uses race as a masquerade for sexuality in the first place.[49]

After Bridgman and Stimpson, critics have linked Melanctha's promiscuity to her race and have found this racialized promiscuity to represent a sub-rosa lesbian sexuality by virtue of a common "abnormality" of promiscuity and same-sexuality. This reading is possible only by ignoring the other two "lives" and by disregarding Melanctha's sexual relationship with Jane and amorous devotion to Rose. The many "girls in trouble" in "The Good Anna" are white, and Jeff, who fears and hates sex, is black. Note, too, that promiscuity in *Three Lives* is exclusively heterosexual. Anna never expresses her sexuality physically; Lena experiences only marital sex, which she abhors; and Melanctha and Jane are promiscuous only with men. Why would Stein need to use promiscuity to signal female same-sexuality when she represents the latter directly and clearly through Melanctha and Jane?

Rather than encode homosexuality in terms of race, Stein pushes the boundary of racial representation in sexual terms. Black women in fiction are traditionally either not allowed sexuality at all or oversexualized to fulfill white male fantasy. But Melanctha does not fulfill men. Instead, she irritates, frustrates, and finally abandons every man who encounters her, including her father. She does not even serve as an inaccessible fantasy figure, as she is not only accessible but also vulnerable to her lovers . . . for a time. If same-sexuality *is* encoded in "Melanctha," it is encoded in heterosexuality and in Stein's queer prose style much more than in race. In relation to homosexuality, race is a red herring.

So? Many Stein critics could accurately claim that I have taken them out of context: that their primary objective *is* to discuss race and "Melanctha"; that, lesbian utility aside, the experience of reading "Melanctha" today remains undeniably racist; and that the sexuality of the "life" and its author is beside their point. Which is my own point: that the lesbian contents of "Melanctha" go unseen at large and, when seen, are of interest only in terms of their encoding. The apparitional lesbian floats on.

Carnal Knowledge

My goal here is to privilege sexuality. "Melanctha" is a text with a sexual epistemology, where knowledge is carnal. Consider this description of Melanctha on the cusp of adolescence: "Melanctha Herbert had always been old in all her ways and she knew very early how to use her power as a woman, and yet Melanctha with all her inborn intense wisdom was really very ignorant of evil. Melanctha had not yet come to understand what they meant, the things she so often heard around her, and which were just beginning to stir strongly in her" (59). Here power and knowledge are defined by sexuality. In the fabula, Melanctha is first dramatized when she begins to gain and wield sexual wisdom. Her father, James, detects a sexual component to his friend's feeling for her, and beats his uncomprehending daughter for encouraging the friend. James thus brings his daughter to the sexual knowledge that his beating means to punish: "Melanctha began to know her power, the power she had so often felt stirring within her and which she now knew she could use to make her stronger" (59).

For Melanctha, understanding, or "world wisdom," *is* sexual understanding. After the beating, Melanctha's sexual curiosity impels her through the railroad yards and shipyards of Bridgepoint; she searches for sexual experience but retreats before "knowing" anyone biblically, a constant retrenching that Stein embodies in repetitive prose: "Melanctha always made herself escape but . . . she would sometimes come very near to making a long step on the road that leads to wisdom. . . . The man would sometimes come a little nearer, would detain her, would hold her arm or make his jokes a little clearer, and then Melanctha would always make herself escape. . . . [H]e never went so fast that he could stop her when at last she made herself escape. . . . [A]lways just in time she made herself escape" (63, [ellipses mine]). Despite four years of these close calls (60), Melanctha remains carnally ignorant: "And many things happened to Melanctha, but she knew very well that none of them had led her on to the right way, that certain way that was to lead her to world wisdom" (65).

Melanctha fails because she believes that carnal knowledge is found in men: "In these young days, it was only men that for Melanctha held anything there was of knowledge and power. It was not from men however that Melanctha learned to really understand this power" (60). Her proper sexual study begins at sixteen, when she meets the twenty-three-year-old Jane Harden: intelligent, mixed-race, heavy-drinking, and dismissed from college for "bad conduct" (65). Jane, whose epithet is "roughened" and whose name itself is "harden[ed]," is introduced as a woman who "had had much experience. She was very much attracted by Melanctha, and Melanctha was very proud that this Jane would let her know her" (65). Jane, who has "wandered widely," teaches Melanctha "that certain way that was to lead her to world wisdom" (65). This is sexual pedagogy: "[Jane] taught Melanctha many things. She taught her how to go the ways that lead to wisdom." And again: "Jane Harden was not afraid to understand. Melanctha who had strong the sense for real experience, knew that here was a woman who had learned to understand," and "every day [Melanctha] grew stronger in her desire to really understand" (65).

Initially, Jane and Melanctha's relationship is triangulated through men, but the homosocial evolves into the homoerotic: into sexual knowledge that Jane provides first through narrative and then through sex itself:

> Jane grew always fonder of Melanctha. Soon they began to wander, more to be together than to see men and learn their various ways of working. Then they began not to wander, and Melanctha would spend long hours with Jane in her room, sitting at her feet and listening to her stories, and feeling her strength and the power of

her affection, and slowly she began to see clear before her one certain way that would be sure to lead to wisdom. . . . [Jane] loved Melanctha hard and made Melanctha feel it very deeply. . . . [Melanctha] learned to love Jane and to have this feeling very deeply. She learned a little in these days to know joy, and she was taught too how very keenly she could suffer. . . . [H]ere with Jane Harden she was longing and she bent and pleaded with her suffering. (66–67 [ellipses mine])

Stein could not be more explicit without describing sex acts.

Jane's pedagogy extends past mental and physical tutoring to using her manipulation of Melanctha as an exemplar of how to move others: "She would be with other people and with men and with Melanctha, and she would make Melanctha understand what everybody wanted, and what one did with power when one had it" (66). Once Melanctha learns this lesson, she falls out with Jane:

Sometimes the lesson came almost too strong for Melanctha, but somehow she always managed to endure it and so slowly, but always with increasing strength and feeling, Melanctha began to really understand.

Then slowly, between them, it began to be all different. Slowly now between them, it was Melanctha Herbert, who was stronger. Slowly now they began to drift apart from one other. (67)

The women draw apart because of an unspecified "trouble between them, that was now always getting stronger" (67). Jane never recovers. She is consumed by bitterness, falls into an alcoholic decline, and sickens.

Jane is treated by a conservative young African American doctor, Dr. Jeff Campbell, who also treats Melanctha's ill mother. Jeff is attracted to Melanctha, but Jane forestalls the friendship: "Jane sometimes had abused Melanctha to him. What right had that Melanctha Herbert who owed everything to her, Jane Harden, what right had a girl like that to go away to other men and leave her. . . . Jeff Campbell heard all this very often" (70). As Jeff does not yet properly (or improperly) know Melanctha, we may assume that Jane tries to turn *everyone* against her, not just potential partners. Classic revenge by a spurned lover—and Jane's later contempt for Rose Johnson, her same-sex successor, is also typical bad-ex behavior: "Jane despised Rose for an ordinary, stupid, sullen black girl. Jane could not see what Melanctha could find in that black girl, to endure her. It made Jane sick to see her" (125).

Jeff is attracted to Melanctha despite Jane, and Melanctha's care for her mother reassures him about her character. Jane does not know but continues to interfere through gossip:

> ... Melanctha once had loved her, Jane Harden. Jane began to tell Jeff of all the bad ways Melanctha had used with her. Jane began to tell all she knew of the way Melanctha had gone on, after she had left her. Jane began to tell all about the different men, white ones and blacks, Melanctha never was particular about things like that. ... Melanctha always liked to use all the understanding ways that Jane had taught her, and so she wanted to know everything, always, that they knew how to teach her. (90 [ellipses mine])

Jeff grows "very sick and his heart was very heavy, and Melanctha certainly did seem very ugly to him" (90). Despite Jane's steady assertion of the women's love, Jeff never understands how this might shade Jane's words.

Jeff cannot see Jane as Melanctha's ex-lover for the same reason that he has trouble loving a woman who conflates the pursuit of sexuality with knowledge: He is a sexual dolt. He vacillates between loving Melanctha as she is and enjoying her passion, and wanting both Melanctha and their love to be "good." This leads to pages of arguments. Jeff distinguishes between "two kinds of ways of loving," one sexualized and one not, one with "excitement" and one not, one a "good quiet feeling in a family when one does his work," the other "just like having it like any animal that's low in the streets together" (78). But Melanctha does not view a "good quiet feeling" as appropriately emotional and physical. She finds Jeff carnally ignorant: "Don't you ever stop with your thinking long enough to have any feeling Jeff Campbell" (83).

These repetitive arguments put Melanctha and Jeff on different sides of a binary that Lisa Ruddick has distinguished as "linear and progressive" (Jeff) and "circular and rhythmic" (Melanctha). The contents of the fight may be split between Jeff and Melanctha, but the style is not. These passages are Stein's most concentrated embodiment of "circular and rhythmic" knowing and narrative in the text, and for many, they provide the most memorable parts of the book. In my experience, these passages still fascinate, irritate, and sometimes infuriate students assigned to read *Three Lives*. A century after they were written, these passages are still so queer that they may prove indigestible.[50]

Stein's repudiation of linear and progressive narrative, and her use of a point of view so close that it dips into the affect and unconscious of the characters, signals a similarly queer interior, though not necessarily a lesbian one. We know, however, that these arguments have a literally lesbian origin, as they are close, sometimes direct translations of conversations between the lovers Adele and Helen in *Q.E.D.* and perhaps between their models, Stein and Bookstaver. These arguments are also lesbian in their *content*: they are typical, even stereotypical, fights between a lesbian and a proto-lesbian who has not yet consciously integrated her sexual and emotional desires into her identity, and who attempts to rationalize them away. They will be familiar to any gay person who has had a same-sex partner who has not yet come to terms with homosexual desire.[51]

What Is Jeff's Problem?

Heterosexual encoding extends past Jeff's argument to his character. His fear, incomprehension, and hatred of his sexual desire are difficult to understand in a straight man at the turn of the twentieth century. I am not indulging in the stereotype of straight (and gay) men as ready for sex anytime, anywhere: plausible reasons for Jeff's discomfort with passionate sex include religious objections or an upbringing that disapproved of unmarried sex for men. But Stein offers no evidence of either—and she clarifies that Jeff *wants* to have sex with Melanctha; they are not sexually incompatible in bed. If Jeff were a hypocrite, promoting a sexual code that he could not or would not follow, or if Jeff believed that women were expected to control their sexuality more than men, then he would be a man of his time. But Jeff's objections are straightforward and sincere, which is incredible.

Consider how Jeff distinguishes between quiet love constrained "in a family where one does his work" and excitement "in the streets" (78). Jeff does not make the traditional distinction between women in the family and women in the streets; Jeff is uncomfortable with excitement "in the streets" in and of itself. Contemporary convention allowed an upstanding man to spend time with a loose woman, so long as he did not marry her. Naturalist writers such as Dreiser, James, and Wharton often wrote about not only eligible bachelors but also *married* characters with mistresses who return to their churches, wives, and children without undue suffering. And Jeff is *single,* which makes his scruples even stranger. They are much better interpreted via the social construction of homosexuality.[52]

In a society that censors and demonizes homosexuality, Jeff's binary is the difference between socially sanctioned and thus socially organized and comprehensible heterosexual acts, and the "animal" passion of homosexual acts, which, by a necessity dictated by censorship, must spring from the body and therefore be conflated with the primitive, the crude, and the unknown. Note that Jeff has no language to understand his desire for Melanctha and hers for him: "What was it really that Melanctha wanted with him? What was it really, he, Jeff Campbell, wanted she should give him?" (98). What Jeff wants is outside his self-conception, a problem familiar to homosexuals before they come to self-knowledge. As Jeff is not a seeker of carnal knowledge like Melanctha, he has no way to understand how he feels, or even to learn. Instead, he is disgusted by his bodily desires: "Jeff felt a strong disgust inside him; not for Melanctha herself, to him, not for himself really, in him. . . . [H]e only had disgust because he never could know really what it was really right to him to be always doing, in the things he had before believed in, the things he before had believed for himself" (97 [ellipsis mine]). His ignorance and confusion cause him great fear. Melanctha understands this: "[Y]ou certainly are awful scared about really feeling things way down in you, and that's certainly the only way Dr. Campbell I can see that you can mean, by what it is you are always saying to me" (77). Jeff, unlike Anna, manifests his sexual desire through sexual expression; he does not repress and sublimate it, but he does hate and fear it. This hatred and fear, coupled with his preference for thinking over feeling, leaves his desires opaque. He cannot bear to understand them. His hatred and fear also force him to sabotage his relationship with Melanctha—though he does not "want" to—because it is "wrong." Melanctha understands this, too: "'I suppose, Jeff,' said Melanctha, very low and bitter, 'I suppose you are always thinking, Jeff, somebody had ought to be ashamed with us two together, and you certainly do think you don't see any way to it, Jeff, for me to be feeling that way ever, so you certainly don't see any way to it, only to do it just so often for me'" (98). In short, Jeff's fear, incomprehension, and hatred of his sexual desire, as well as his use of tedious intellectual arguments to argue his way out of nonnormative sexuality, fit with the generic script of the internally closeted proto-lesbian. His troubles with desire are specific, standard signs of homosexual adolescence, if adolescence is understood as a state of postpubertal flux within which humans organize and construct an understanding of sex and love, and identity coalesces.

Homosexual adolescence is usually delayed in societies that privilege heterosexuality, which explains why Jeff faces these issues at an advanced age, just as Stein had her first sexual experience when most women her age would have already had two or three children.

In homosexual adolescence, sexual desires and loving emotions conflict with a normative self-conception that views such desires and emotions as abnormal. Such desires and emotions, transformed and empowered by puberty, batter a previous self-conception until adolescents internally restructure their identity and come out. In highly homophobic societies, both micro and macro, such restructuring is dangerous and has appreciable costs. A normative self-conception shields against a hostile environment and must be gingerly detached. Adolescents may therefore mount a fierce defense and ward off their same-sex emotions and desires through a variety of overlapping techniques that include denial, repression, the fragmentation of sexual love and desire from the rest of the personality, and intellectual doublespeak. Such techniques may deny altogether the restructuring of the personality to include homosexual love and desire. This restructuring may also allow emotional love but not physical desire, as we saw in Anna, or physical desire but not emotional love, as we shall see in Herman in "The Gentle Lena."

Poor Jeff: "It was all so mixed up inside him. All he knew was he wanted very badly Melanctha should be there beside him, and he wanted very badly, too, always to throw her from him" (98). But there is no reason why a heterosexual Jeff cannot have a relationship with Melanctha, no reason why he cannot both have her "there beside him" and "throw her from him." Jeff is a young, single, successful doctor. A stormy relationship with an unpresentable mistress is de rigueur. And why *not* marry her? If Jeff is a straight man, then marriage is possible, and its absence is conspicuous. Marriage is a major concern for Melanctha and her next male lover, Jem, so why is it absent from the discussions between Melanctha and Jeff? Melanctha's lighter color and Jeff's greater income make them an appropriate match according to the intraracist calculus of their community. Jeff does not consider Melanctha's social class and sexual past a disqualification for marriage; if he did, he would fret, as usual. Jeff's fear and hatred of physical sexual expression can be most easily understood as a *heterosexual* translation of homosexuality, especially in light of its earlier, specifically lesbian models in *Q.E.D.*'s Adele and in young Stein. In this respect, race is beside the point.[53]

What Is Melanctha's Problem?

Jeff's unhappiness does not compare with Melanctha's, whose name itself is a cognate of *melancholy*. Critics have also associated "Melanctha" with *melanin*, which had been discovered and named as a pigment when Stein wrote *Three Lives*, but this association seems unlikely for several reasons: Melanctha is described as a "graceful, pale yellow" in a "life" that is consistently precise in terms of skin color; even in scientific circles, melanin was not yet commonly understood as a primary component of human skin color (for example, after considerable searching I have found the word *melanin* only in the following entries of the 1911 *Encyclopedia Britannica*: "feather," "haemosporidia," "malaria," "albino," "tumour," "pathology," and "cephalopoda"); the heroine is named not "Melanina," a better etymological fit for "black girl," but "Melanctha," which is considerably closer to *melancholy* than *melanin*; and, most importantly, "Melanctha" is a nonce name, and Stein for all her experimentation did not favor odd names. This strongly implies an allegorical intention, which for the reasons listed here is more likely to be "melancholy girl" than "melanin girl," though both may be intended.[54]

Certainly melancholy is not surprising for a black woman on a quest for sexual power and knowledge in a small southern city at the turn of the twentieth century:

> Melanctha had not found it easy with herself to make her wants and what she had, agree. (56)

> Melanctha Herbert was always seeking rest and quiet, and always she could only find new ways to be in trouble. (56)

> Melanctha always loved and wanted peace and gentleness and goodness and all her life for herself poor Melanctha could only find new ways to be in trouble. (58)

What is Melanctha's problem? She is smart, attractive, and socially capable. She is privileged within the black community: she goes to school until she is sixteen, "rather longer than do most of the colored children," and might continue at a "colored" college, like Jane (61). She succeeds at her various occupations and always leaves them of her own accord. In her inability to find contentment, Melanctha is a model for the brilliant, beautiful, and biracial Helga Crane in Nella Larsen's *Quicksand*, who travels from the Deep South to Copenhagen but never finds a racial and economic status or a romantic relationship that does not limit her unbearably. Characters with similar challenges find contentment in both books, but not Melanctha and not Helga. Melanctha may not have the opportunity to decamp to Europe, like Helga, but she certainly could have participated in the Great Migration north. Yet, for Melanctha, Bridgepoint is a bridge to nowhere. She is stuck to and by her trauma.[55]

The object relations theorized by Melanie Klein and David Winnicott become relevant here, especially the relation between the internal and external object. The baby internalizes positive and negative experiences of the world—say, hunger and satisfaction—into good and bad objects, which Klein calls the good breast and the bad breast. The baby then projects both these objects onto the mother, who holds the objects. The mother's treatment of the baby—her acceptance of the baby's love and tolerance of the baby's hate—is then internalized by the baby, and the internal object is changed by this introjection. Through the repetitive process of projection upon and introjection from the mother, the baby's internal object grows more defined. Over time, this object is projected and held by romantic partners. Thus "chemistry," or at least part of it. In other words, adult Melanctha has an internal object that determines to some extent whom she decides to love—her external object—and upon which she projects her internal object. External objects "fit" an internal object more or less well, and their introjection can further shape the internal object.[56]

Certainly the names of Melanctha's love objects indicate a sonic variation of some internal motif. The monosyllabic "Jeff" is only one consonant from "Jem," and both share initial *J*s with "Jane." Add both Melanctha's father, "James," and his friend "John" to this list, as both also have single-syllable names that start with *J* and both are intimate, though not sexual, with Melanctha. Only "Rose" stands out nominally. All six contrast with the lengthy, exotic "Melanctha." Nothing rhymes with either the woman or her name.

Consider, too, how these relationships fail. Once Melanctha and Jane become equals—once Melanctha does not *need* Jane—Melanctha rejects her. She does the same to Jeff. All their fighting breaks them up; but then Jeff accepts his love for Melanctha, which requires him to reshape his relationship to sexuality and thus his self-conception. In other words, he "comes out"—only for Melanctha to reject him. Then comes Jem. Their romance is manic, and Jem plans to marry Melanctha until she drives him away with her overwhelming, "foolish" love (138). Jem soon wants her back, but Melanctha says no. When he wants her, she rejects him—at first by loving too much, then too little. Her last, greatest, and most sustained love is with Rose. Just as Rose's name differs from the other lovers, so the relationship differs, for Rose never loves Melanctha enough to be rejected in turn.

Melanctha's inability to sustain a close relationship indexes her inability to find satisfaction or direction: "Melanctha Herbert was always losing what she had in wanting all the things she saw. Melanctha was always being left when she was not leaving others" (56). She is smart but leaves school. She finds success as a nurse, a substitute teacher, and a seamstress but careers from career to career. Only her wandering is stable: a steady state of romantic and financial frustration, disappointment, and failure. Her good looks, intelligence, tenacity, and charm ensure that she never hits bottom until the end of her "life," but her internal script demands that she never find the success or peace that she consciously desires. Thus the refrain that Melanctha "wondered, often, how she could go on living when she was so blue" (54), that Melanctha "was so blue sometimes, and wanted somebody should come and kill her" (131), and that "Melanctha would get very blue, and she would say to Rose, sure she would kill herself, for that certainly now was the best way she could do" (141).

If Melanctha is made miserable by inconsistency, why does it persist? If Melanctha's relationships with Jane, Jeff, Jem, and Rose are all echoes, then what failure do they repeat? In psychoanalytic terms, what original psychic injury was too great to be absorbed by Melanctha's ego, remains unhealed, keeps manifesting, and will do so unless the trauma is consciously processed and incorporated? This question is best approached through Rose.

A Rose Is a Rose Is a Rose

Rose is not conventionally read as Melanctha's lover, and Rose herself would not call their relationship love. (Rose is not conventionally read, period, and the critical notice she does receive is in terms of racism, as the most racist descriptions are of Rose.) Yet Stein makes it clear that "Rose Johnson had worked in to be the deepest of all Melanctha's emotions" (146). Her importance to Melanctha is structurally supported by the text. Their relationship frames the "life"; Rose is the first character to appear and the last to speak in the sjuzet. Melanctha is introduced via the mystery of their love: "Why did the subtle, intelligent, attractive, half white girl Melanctha Herbert love and do for and demean herself in service to this coarse, decent, sullen, ordinary, black childish Rose, and why was this unmoral, promiscuous, shiftless Rose married, and that's not so common either, to a good man of the negroes, while Melanctha with her white blood and attraction and her desire for a right position had not yet been really married?" (54). Stein then assumes Melanctha's point of view, which Stein grounds in depression: "Sometimes the thought of how all her world was made, filled the complex, desiring Melanctha with despair" (54). Although Melanctha's life is pervaded by depression, only Rose makes her suicidal. Why? Rose is not as kind as Jeff, as rich as Jem, or as experienced as Jane. All three love Melanctha deeply, at least for a time, whereas Rose does not. What, then, has Rose got? And if the name "Melanctha" is the mystery of an unhappy character, then how is her love for Rose a clue?

First answer: her name. Rose is not named lightly. In Stein's personal iconography (and enfolded in the flower itself, as the petals resemble labial folds), *rose* is a metaphor for female genitalia:

Why can lifting belly please me
Lifting belly can please me because it is an occupation I enjoy.
Rose is a rose is a rose is a rose.

"Rose is a rose" both has a specifically sexual connotation and resists metaphor to state that *A* equals *A*. These two meanings may be reconciled through sex: a genital is a particular biological organ and yet so much more. The multiplicity of roses and Roses in Stein's oeuvre leaves the significance of the name certain: "A Rose is a rose is a rose is a rose" is incorporated in *Opera and Plays, The World Is Round, Alphabets and Birthdays, Stanzas in Meditation*, and *Lectures in America*, and was used by Toklas as a promotional tool for her partner's work, on china and tchotchkes. The sentence, like *The Autobiography of Alice B. Toklas*, became one of Stein's products that were available and accessible to the public at large, and also a concrete embodiment of her love for women. When Stein created Rose in "Melanctha," she may not have fully realized what "rose" would come to mean to her, but the seeds were nonetheless present. Nominally, Melanctha is brought to her knees by a vulva.[57]

Second answer: her inaccessibility. Rose is the only one of Melanctha's adult attachments that Melanctha does not sexually captivate. Rose limits their intimacy otherwise as well. Though she depends heavily on

Melanctha's domestic work—"With Melanctha Herbert's help to do the sewing and the nicer work, [Rose and her husband] furnished comfortably a little brick house" (55)—Rose refuses to let her move in: "Rose Johnson never asked Melanctha to live with her in the house, now Rose was married. Rose liked to have Melanctha come all the time to help her, Rose liked to have Melanctha be almost always with her, but Rose was shrewd in her simple selfish nature, she did not ever think to ask Melanctha to live with her" (133–34). Why is inaccessibility so appealing? What are the rest of Rose's attractions?

Third answer: her normativity and practicality. Rose is "hard-headed, she was decent, and she always knew what it was she needed" (134); Rose "knew very well what was the right way to do to get everything she wanted, and she never had any kind of trouble to perplex her" (131). Whereas Jeff, finally, is willing to abandon his conception of sexual normativity and embrace Melanctha, Rose remains proper: "Rose kept company, and was engaged, first to this colored man and then to that, and always she made sure she was engaged, for Rose had strong the sense of proper conduct" (55). Note the difference between Rose's ability to pay lip service to morality and Jeff's need to take it to heart. Yet Rose is neither cynical nor disaffected: "After she had lived some time this way [with her fiancé], Rose thought it would be nice and very good in her position to get regularly really married" (55). She strengthens her position traditionally, through heterosexual marriage and material comfort.

Rose is also the most normative character in terms of race, at least in Stein's racist calculus. Whereas Jane is "so white that hardly anyone could guess [that she is black]," and Melanctha is "a graceful, pale yellow . . . [who] had been half made with real white blood," Rose is "a real black negress" (65, 54, 53). Her racial "purity" transcends her upbringing. Though Rose "had been brought up quite like their own child by white folks . . . [h]er white training had made only for habits, not for nature" (53–54). Even when removed from her "nature," Rose retains her core identity: she is a "real black" (53). Yet Rose's ordinariness transcends this essentialism: "Rose laughed when she was happy but she had not the wide, abandoned laughter that makes the warm broad glow of negro sunshine. . . . Hers was just ordinary, any sort of woman laughter" (53). Two orders of being are at war here. In essentialist terms, the laughter of "real black" Rose should have "negro sunshine." The fact that she does not makes her abnormal, but this broad queerness is trumped by her "ordinary, any sort of woman laughter." Even when Rose is extra-ordinary, the "extra" belongs to a greater order of normalcy.[58]

Rose shares this greater normativity with Melanctha's father, who "had never had the wide abandoned laughter that gives the broad glow to negro sunshine" (57). This further normalizes Rose and ties her to Melanctha's childhood. Furthermore, the ways in which Rose is not racially "normally" black raise the hegemonic status of her sexual behavior: "'No, I ain't no common nigger just to go around with any man, nor you Melanctha shouldn't neither,' she said one day when she was telling the complex and less sure Melanctha what was the right way for her to do. 'No Melanctha, I ain't no common nigger to do so, for I was raised by white folks. You know very well that I'se always been engaged to [my sexual partners]'" (55).

Rose is Rose is Rose. She is vaginal, inaccessible, stable, and normal, and Melanctha is overcome: "Melanctha was always ready to do anything Rose wanted from her. Melanctha needed badly to have Rose always willing to let Melanctha cling to her" (131). Just as Rose will never reciprocate Melanctha's love and need, so Melanctha runs no risk of a secure, fulfilling relationship. She may pledge her whole heart.

What's Wrong with the Baby?

The Rose frame of "Melanctha" establishes the heroine's psychic landscape. The "life" begins as follows:

> Rose Johnson made it very hard to bring her baby to its birth.
>
> Melanctha Herbert who was Rose Johnson's friend, did everything that any woman could. She tended Rose, and she was patient, submissive, soothing, and untiring, while the sullen, childish, cowardly, black Rosie grumbled and fussed and howled and made herself to be an abomination and like a simple beast.
>
> The child though it was healthy after it was born, did not live long. Rose Johnson was careless and negligent and selfish, and when Melanctha had to leave for a few days, the baby died. Rose Johnson had liked the baby well enough and perhaps she just forgot it for awhile, anyway the child was dead and Rose and Sam her husband were very sorry but then these things came so often in the negro world in Bridgepoint, that they neither of them thought about it very long. (53)

This is not only racist but also ridiculous. Although infant mortality was pronounced in turn-of-the-century southern African American communities, the death of children by "forgetting" was not, especially the firstborn of married couples. Stein, as a medical student, worked in an obstetric clinic that served an African American clientele; she knew that infant death by "forgetting," especially by a character as "normal" as Rose, was unlikely. I read Stein's break with naturalism here as I did the heterosexual improbabilities of Jeff and Melanctha's relationship: the realist space-time of the text is warped by a partially censored psychic weight. Who, then, is this baby, abandoned by its mother, kept alive by Melanctha, and dead from neglect when she leaves? And why does Melanctha, of all people, care for the child?

Despite her promiscuity, Melanctha never wonders at her *own* fertility, much less has or wants a baby, which serves as another lapse in the naturalism of the text, especially in the light of Mrs. Lehntman's home for unwed mothers in "The Good Anna." The cordon sanitaire around Melanctha's fertility is another sign of same-sexuality's encoding by heterosexuality. Note, however, that Anna and Mrs. Lehntman also have a baby: the dog Baby, which embodies their sexless, "good" relations. Similarly, Rose's baby is both a biological product of Rose and Sam *and* a psychosexual embodiment of Melanctha's complexes vis-à-vis Rose. In *Three Lives*, babies are fungible.

The intensity of Melanctha's feelings for Rose, as well as the fact that Rose's final rejection frames Melanctha's "life" and effectively kills her, indicates that Rose offers Melanctha the most accurate echo of her original trauma. Rose's disinterest in Melanctha and Melanctha's corresponding devotion neatly index Melanctha's relationship with her parents and help explain the dead baby. The baby survives only when Melanctha cares for it because the baby *is* Melanctha; when Melanctha cannot parent herself, baby Melanctha "dies." The story begins and ends with Rose's abandonment of the baby because the "life" is the story of that abandoned baby, and when Rose abandons Melanctha at the story's end, the wound is fatal.

In this final break, the parent/child overtones are unmistakable:

Melanctha stood like one dazed, she did not know how to bear this blow that almost killed her. Slowly then Melanctha went away without even turning to look behind her.

Melanctha Herbert was all sore and bruised inside her. Melanctha had always needed Rose to believe her, Melanctha needed Rose always to let her cling to her, Melanctha wanted badly to have somebody who could make her always feel a little safe inside her, and now Rose had sent her from her. Melanctha wanted Rose more than she had ever wanted all the others. Rose always was so simple, solid, decent, for her. And now Rose had cast her from her. Melanctha was lost, and all the world went whirling in a mad weary dance around her.

Melanctha Herbert never had any strength alone ever to feel safe inside her. And now Rose Johnson had cast her from her, and Melanctha could never any more be near her. Melanctha Herbert knew now, way inside her, that she was lost, and nothing any more could ever help her. (145)

All the world is now a bad object, and Melanctha's ego is laid waste. Unfortunately, such perfect reenactment of Melanctha's original injury does not heal Melanctha but kills her.

What *is* that original injury? Stein writes that "Melanctha Herbert had not loved herself in childhood. All of her youth was bitter to remember" (56), and that "Melanctha had not loved her father and her mother and they had found it very troublesome to have her" (57). What happened in the Herbert home?

The specifics of "Melanctha" and its placement within *Three Lives*, as well as its antecedents and biographical context, suggest that Melanctha's poor relationship with her family stems from her status as a proto-lesbian child.

A Gay Child Is Being Beaten
Dad's Beating

If Truman Capote portrays the difficulties of the proto-gay child in *Other Voices, Other Rooms* in terms of the gothic, then Stein in "Melanctha" puts them in a realist context. Melanctha's relationship with her parents is emblematic of how proto-gay children queer the usual developmental script, which leaves many parents confused, disgusted, and hostile.[59]

There are, of course, a variety of mature psychosexual organizations, some more fixed than others. Fixed homosexual orientations, like Capote's and Stein's, do not share the teleology of fixed straight orientations. Even as I write, in 2015, one does not "naturally" become gay as one does straight. Theorists interested in a specifically homosexual developmental teleology tend to "flip" genders when discussing the difference between the different psychosexual developments of straight and gay children. Melanctha is born into a traditional nuclear family, and, crudely speaking (but what is not crude in a family?), in such families lesbians identify with their fathers and desire their mothers, instead of the reverse, which is expected. This disturbs most parents, and the Herberts exhibit the unhappiness and ill fit typical of such families.[60]

Consider young Melanctha's relationship with her father, James: "Melanctha was always abusing her father and yet she was just like him, and really she admired him so much" (71). Melanctha's similarity to James is a refrain of her "life": "[T]he real power in Melanctha's nature came through her robust and unpleasant and very unendurable black father" (56). She feels "nearer, in her feeling toward her virile and unendurable black father, then she ever was in her feeling for her pale yellow, sweet-appearing mother" (60). Melanctha is "nearer" to James even though she and Mis Herbert resemble each other: both are attractive and socially skilled, and Mis Herbert, too, has "always been a little wandering and mysterious and uncertain in her ways" (56). Nonetheless, the "things she had in her of her mother never made her feel respect" (56). James is both troubled and responsive to his daughter's identification and treats her, in some respects, like a teenage boy: he was "brutal and rough to his one daughter, but then she was a most disturbing child to manage" (57).

We have seen that Melanctha is first dramatized in the fabula in conjunction with this trouble. Melanctha is a typical girl in her horse love, though she takes it unusually far: She "had a break neck courage. . . . [S]he loved to do wild things, to ride the horses and to break and tame them" (57). This brings young Melanctha close to John, a coachman and a friend of James's. One night, when Melanctha is "a well grown girl of twelve and just beginning as a woman," John tries to soften James toward his daughter, and James detects a sexual register: "John grew more and more admiring as he talked half to himself, half to the father, of the virtues and the sweetness of Melanctha" (57, 59). Talking allows John to realize his feelings, and his narration brings him pleasure. James pulls a razor on John and later beats Melanctha, who does not understand: "Now when her father began to fiercely assail her, she did not really know what it was that he was so furious to force from her. In every way he could think of in his anger, he tried to make her say a thing she did not really know" (59). Why is James so angry?

The obvious answer is traditional. James believes his daughter has a suitor, and he experiences John's talk as an attack. Melanctha has been configured as a sexual object, which is intolerable. If she encouraged John, then she has become a sexual subject, which is worse. Such responses are common, in kind if not degree. Though most fathers do not knife the first man outside the family to desire their daughters, hostility is expected. Why, though, does James beat *Melanctha*? Melanctha has no conscious designs on John; when James beats her, "she did not really know what it was that he was so furious to force from her" (59). But her nascent romance with John—even if it is only in John's head—puts the insufficiency of James's own relationship with Melanctha in boldface. Another man—a man who is his friend and who has a similar name—has received the love that was rightfully his.

The beating does not teach Melanctha her proper psychosexual place but instead reinforces her identification with her father. Melanctha herself views her beating as a rite of passage to potency: she matches her father's toughness and violence with her own. We see here the first instance of her pleasure at remaining impervious to a loved one's attention, which she repeats with Jane, Jeff, and Jem. Stein writes, "James Herbert did not win this fight with his daughter" and then mentions him again only in retrospect or in terms of his absence: he loses the battle and then the war (59). The beating also jump-starts Melanctha's sexual awareness, for afterward she abandons horses to "search in the streets and in dark corners to discover men" (60).

Mom's Beating

Instead, Melanctha discovers Jane, who parallels Mis Herbert. Jane, too, parents Melanctha. Jane is also light skinned, Jane also "wanders," Jane is also abandoned by a darker-skinned lover (Mis Herbert by James, and Jane by his daughter), and Jane is also treated for illness by Jeff, an illness from which she also never recovers. Even apparent differences may be reconciled. Whereas Jane is "hardened" and Mis Herbert is "pleasant, sweet-appearing," this reverse is bifocal, as sweet-appearing Mis Herbert is hostile and unloving while hard Jane is enraptured with Melanctha. In this respect, cold Rose proves a much better match for Mom.

Melanctha and her mother are emotionally estranged; though Melanctha nurses her mother flawlessly, neither woman has affection for the other. This chilliness pervades the narrative. Stein offers almost no information about Mis Herbert, not even her first name: James is on a first-name basis, and Mis Herbert is not. Stein does, however, offer a primal scene of estrangement: "One day Melanctha was real little, and she heard her ma say to her pa, it was awful sad to her, Melanctha had not been the one the Lord had took from them stead of the little brother who was dead in the house there from fever" (133). Mis Herbert says this calmly, which makes her rejection worse. An angry pronouncement might be explained away.

Mis Herbert's desire for a phantom child of the opposite sex—a child who couples Melanctha's traits with an "appropriate" gender, a child who will "fall in love" with his mother as little boys (and not little girls) should—is common in the parents of queer children of every sexual stripe: homosexual, transgender, and any other variation that does not suit normal parental expectations. In this way, Mis Herbert resembles the iconic bad mom of lesbian literature, Anna Gordon of Hall's *The Well of Loneliness,* who never reconciles herself to her daughter Stephen's "inversion." Happily, Stephen has a more loving and supportive father than Melanctha, and though Stephen can never sustain a romantic relationship, her strong identification with her father helps her sustain a stronger sense of self than endlessly "wandering" Melanctha.[61]

The Last Beating

When James beats Melanctha physically, he revs the engine that pushes Melanctha into sexual knowledge and starts her wandering: she becomes an adult. When Rose "beats" Melanctha emotionally, she regresses to infancy and dies. Rose's frost brings Melanctha so close to her maternal trauma that she cannot transmute it and recover, as she does from other upsets. Melanctha cannot transmute her pain into sexualized knowledge. She cannot get help; she has outstripped the knowledge of lay teachers such as Jane and doctors such as Jeff. The church goes unmentioned.

That is why, when Rose kicks Melanctha out of her house, "Melanctha stood like one dazed, she did not know how to bear this blow that almost killed her." That is why "Melanctha was lost, and all the world went whirling in a mad weary dance around her. Melanctha Herbert never had any strength alone ever to feel safe inside her" (145). That is why "Melanctha Herbert knew now, way inside her, that she was lost, and nothing any more could ever help her" (146). Melanctha has fallen back into her trauma and never climbs out. Her fate parallels Lena's, although Lena's trajectory is much shallower. Stein offers no moment when Lena is not destroyed.[62]

The Gentle Lena and the Rough Plot

"The Gentle Lena" is the last and shortest of the "lives" and in some ways the most extreme. In the fabula, we first meet Lena in Germany, where the seventeen-year-old peasant catches the eye of her American aunt. Lena is so quiet and respectful that Aunt Haydon sponsors her immigration. Aunt Haydon models Lena's future after popular novels in which immigrant girl makes good: "Lena could first go out to service, and learn how to do things, and then, when she was a little older, Mrs. Haydon could get her a good husband" (153). Lena does not make good, however, and "The Gentle Lena" is a realist check on this happy plot. Lena immigrates, finds a good job with a demanding but supportive boss, and marries up in class via a gentle husband. Why, then, does she fail?

Though many narratives of this time detail women's inability to control their lives, much less achieve their desires, Lena is unusual in that not only any embodiment but also any consciousness of her desires is beyond her. It is much easier to say what Lena does not want than to say what she does. Stein offers no examples of Lena's conscious desire, knowledge, or action in romance or passion. Lena does not even dream. She wants nothing she knows.

"The Gentle Lena" is more than what Karin Cope calls "a chronicle of the risks of passive pursuit of conventionality, of the deadliness of doing what one ought," for even a passive pursuit is a *pursuit* and therefore requires will, even if it is not exercised. Consider how Lena responds when her aunt scolds her for being insufficiently excited about her arranged marriage: "I didn't hear you say you wanted I should say anything to you. I didn't know you wanted me to say nothing. I do whatever you tell me it's right for me to do. I marry Herman Kreder, if you want me" (158). Such passivity can be defensive: "Lena in her unsuffering and unexpectant patience never really knew that she was slighted" (155); "Lena never got mad, or even had sense enough to know that they were all making an awful fool of her" (156). Yet Lena's lack of self is too profound to be a simple defense.[63]

Lena displays only two strong emotions in the text: shame and dread. When her fiancé jilts her, Lena cries on the streetcar. She is upset not by her loss per se but by the possible perception of her wrongdoing: "Lena did not know what it was that she had done, only she was not going to be married and it was a disgrace for a girl to be left by a man on the very day she was to be married" (160). As soon as the conductor and other passengers sympathize, the feeling recedes (161). Otherwise, Lena's self fragments when faced with strong emotion. Physical pain makes her recede: At sea, she is "sure that she would die" and loses "all her little sense of being in her suffering." This "little sense of being" entirely fails under the pressure of family life (154).

Lena never displays or actively experiences any affection, much less love or passion, for her parents, aunt, husband, or children. She does not miss or even think of Germany once she leaves. Her primary conscious emotion for her American family is dread—of disappointing Aunt Haydon and of her pregnancy, her first in particular, when "she could only sit still and be scared, and dull, and lifeless, and sure that every minute she would die" (172). Once the baby comes, she "just dragged around and was careless with her clothes and all lifeless, and she acted always and lived on just as if she had no feeling. She always did everything regular with the work, the way she always had had to do it, but she never got back any spirit in her" (172–73). As Lena procreates on, she "did not seem to notice very much when they hurt her, and she never seemed to feel very much now about anything that happened to her" (173). Her death in her last confinement is suitably diffuse: "When it was all over Lena had died, too, and nobody knew just how it happened to her" (174). Her "life" continues with other concerns, as if her death is too slight to be conclusive.

Linda Wagner-Martin argues "The Gentle Lena" is a feminist warning, "an admonitory narrative about power within marriage, the power of heterosexual culture. . . . [The implications] are frightening: that women deserve to make their own choices about sexuality, marriage, and motherhood and that when those choices are taken away, the will to live may also vanish." I would extend this warning to the profound damage that homophobia can wreak on an ego. Lena cannot make choices about sexuality, marriage, and children because she has internalized compulsory heterosexuality and gender hegemony to such an extent that her desires barely exist. She is not, as Bridgman claims, "a simple creature who desires only the kindness of others"; she has lobotomized herself for the sake of survival. Because her self has been destroyed, we must reconstruct it through her few remaining traces of desire and will.[64]

Structural Happiness

Lena feels sick, dreadful, and close to death more often, and more intensely, than she feels well, happy, and full of life. To see Lena when she is well, happy, and most characteristically "herself," we need to resort to a structural analysis.

Recall that each of the three "lives" has two beginnings: one textual, the other chronological; one in the sjuzet, one in the fabula. Throughout *Three Lives,* the first dramatization of the heroine in the fabula marks how her psyche first interacts with her material circumstances to determine the course of her adult life. Teen Anna debuts in the fabula with her refusal to see her employer's guest home. This refusal proves the strength of her will and a commitment to hegemonic order that supersedes material circumstance—and leads directly to her emigration. Similarly, Melanctha's first dramatization in the fabula—her beating by her father—triggers her maturity, and her search for sexualized power and wisdom.

Lena's debut in the fabula dramatizes her passivity and lack of affect as she emigrates without much will or feeling. She is "willing to go" because "she did not like her german life very well"—a weak reaction for a seventeen-year-old about to leave her native country and family, probably forever (153). Lena *cannot* be excited, because anticipation requires a sense of self sufficient to anticipate a future for that self. All was "harsh and dreary for her . . . [in Germany, yet] Lena did not really know that she did not like it. She did not know that she was always dreamy and not there" (153–54). Again, Lena is unaware of her emotions. She is willing to follow someone else's plan for her future but not to actively pursue or resist it, which would require will and independent action, traits that are beyond her.

If, in the fabula, a heroine's debut dramatizes how her psyche first determines the trajectory of her adult life, then in the sjuzet, that heroine's debut—always narrated rather than dramatized—is a miniature portrait of the heroine's psychosocial dynamics in maturity, and of how these internal forces typically play out. "The Good Anna" begins with Anna's fearsome reputation for bargaining with shopkeepers on behalf of her mistress, followed by her problems with the underservants and how she scolds them. Stein thus illustrates Anna's power as a proper servant and her pleasure at enforcing hegemonic behavior. "Melanctha" begins with the death of Rose's baby and the question of why Melanctha is so devoted to Rose: a portrait of Melanctha's need to be in an unstable, unfulfilling relationship, and of the parental neglect that created this need. How, then, does "Lena" begin in the sjuzet? How does Stein display Lena when she is most typically herself?

A Gentle Stir

"The Gentle Lena" begins with Lena happily in service four years after her immigration. This is "a peaceful life for Lena, almost as peaceful as a pleasant leisure" (150). After a few paragraphs that narrate her contentment with her job and establish her relationship with the cook, an analogue of "the good Anna," the narrative dramatizes Lena's pleasure in the company of the other servant girls, "all them that make the pleasant, lazy crowd, that watch the children in the sunny afternoons out in the park." They all tease her, and her three particular friends "always worked together to confuse her. Still it was pleasant" (149). Lena uncharacteristically *wants* to spend time with her clique, though she is expected at her aunt's: "Lena would have liked much better to spend her Sundays with the girls she always sat with, and who often asked her, and who teased her and made a gentle stir within her, but it never came to Lena's unexpectant and unsuffering german nature to do something different from what was expected of her" (154–55). This "gentle stir" is the height of Lena's desire.

These other girls are the only characters willing to take Lena's part unconditionally. (Although the cook also sympathizes with Lena, her support depends on Lena's perfect performance as a proper servant, niece, wife, and mother.) The clique sympathizes with Lena's mistreatment by her Haydon cousins: "How Lena could keep on going so much when they all always acted as if she was just dirt to them, [her friend] never could see." When Lena's fiancé runs off, "the girls Lena always sat with were very sorry to see her look so sad with her trouble" (162). Mary, the only named girl, not only sticks up for Lena but also tries to get her to exhibit some sense of self and pride: "It was good riddance Lena had of that Herman Kreder and his stingy, dirty parents, and if Lena didn't stop crying about it,—Mary would just naturally despise her" (163).

Nonetheless, Lena, after her marriage, "never any more saw the girls she always used to sit with. She had no way to see them and it was not in Lena's nature to search out ways to see them. . . . [N]or did she ever now think much of the days when she had been used to see them" (169–70). Though Lena's friends fade from her consciousness, they remain the only people—the only *anything*—that provokes even a "gentle stir" in Lena. For Lena, this slight, homosocial desire is a hurricane. Although there is only circumstantial proof that Lena's inability to exist as a lesbian *caused* the fragility of her ego, the *fact* that her homoerotic "gentle stir" coincides with her personality's greatest definition, as well as with her greatest happiness, provokes.

There is one other piece of evidence for Lena's proto-lesbian orientation. In her first bodily description of Lena, Stein brings our attention to something undefined but remarkable in her physicality and affect: "That rarer feeling that there was with Lena, showed in all the even quiet of her body movements, but in all it was the strongest in the patient, old-world ignorance, and earth made pureness of her brown, flat, soft featured face" (150). What does Stein mean? Lena's calm, patience, and "earth made pureness" are not unusual but spell the phenotype of an idealized servant that makes farm girls "of the earth." The "rarer feeling" is somehow associated with Lena's body but becomes evident through characteristics that are not in themselves rare. Rather, the "rarer feeling" somehow *imbues* these characteristics.

This rareness is clarified at the very start of the sjuzet, when Aunt Haydon evaluates Lena's suitability for emigration. Beyond her youth and docility, Haydon "could feel the rarer strain there was in Lena," something she feels because Haydon "with all her hardness had wisdom" (153). As we saw in "Melanctha," wisdom has sexual connotations in *Three Lives,* here associated with Lena's "rarer strain." Haydon is correct that Lena's unhappiness within her family home—an unhappiness and unfitness somehow associated with a sexualized "rarer feeling"—suits Lena for emigration. What is this sexualized, nonnormative embodiment, this "rarer feeling" that cannot be directly referenced? I believe that it is Lena's unnameable and almost imperceptible proto-lesbian orientation.

This is the debris after the conflagration, the rubble after the avalanche. But something is there.

Homosexual Herman

How do you express the sexuality of a character who does not feel her desires? Because Stein may not directly express Lena's homosexuality without breaking the naturalistic portrayal of a character whose sexuality is shut down, she expresses it in the most logical (and perverse) place: her husband. Herman suits the inversion model of homosexuality that was current when Stein wrote *Three Lives*—he is not "her" man at all, but a "her man"—and his happy ending sees him embody his "feminine" nature without losing his social position.

At first, Herman is subordinate to his parents and works for them without wages: "Herman was now twenty-seven years old, but he had never stopped being scolded and directed by his father and his mother" (157). Nonetheless, he protests their decision that he should marry Lena. Like the bride, "Herman Kreder did not care much to get married. . . . [H]e was obedient to his mother, but he did not care much to get married" (157). Unlike the bride, Herman is active rather than passive, both in his desire for same-sex companionship and in his disinterest in heterosexual marriage.

Like Lena, Herman prefers same-sex company and "often went out on Saturday nights and on Sundays, with other men" (157). Herman does not enjoy the hoary tradition of using women as a sexual outlet for group homoerotics: "He liked to be with men and he hated to have women with them" (157). Herman is not a misogynist; he is fond of his sister and goes to her when troubled. Nonetheless, outside his family he wants to be with men. And as Stein refrains, Herman *really* does not want to marry. Unlike Lena, Herman "knew more what it meant to be married and he did not like it very well. He did not like to see girls and he did not want to have to have one always near him" (159). Stein makes Herman's distaste for intimate relations with women as clear as she can without a censorable statement: "He liked to go out with other men, but he never wanted that there should be any women with them. The men all teased him about getting married. Herman did not mind the teasing but he did not like very well the getting married and having a girl always with him" (159). The reluctance of critics to state the obvious about Herman astonishes, especially as the apparitional lesbian is not in play. Marianne DeKoven's note in the Norton *Three Lives* exemplifies overly cautious readings of homosexual Herman. DeKoven implies that Stein had a choice of representations for homosexuality when censorship made no such choice possible: "Note that Herman prefers to be with men, just as Lena prefers to be with women: Stein suggests homosociality at least, and probably also homoeroticism."[65] This is the slightest possible acknowledgment of homosexuality commensurate with good scholarship.

Herman's "preference" pushes him to the most dramatic action of the "life" when he bolts before the wedding. He runs to his sister, who is to him as the cook is to Lena, a sympathetic ear who insists upon his hegemonic function: "Herman's married sister liked her brother Herman, and she did not want him to not like to be with women. He was good, her brother Herman, and it would surely do him good to get married" (165). She reveals the stakes of compulsory heterosexuality: "I'd be awful ashamed Herman, to really have a brother didn't have spirit enough to get married, when a girl is just dying for to have him. You always like me to be with you Herman. I don't see why you say you don't want a girl to be all the time around you. . . . Don't act like as if you wasn't a nice strong man, Herman" (166). An unmarried man has no spirit, is not nice, and is not strong. Who wants to be that?

And so Herman marries Lena—but he never fulfills the hegemonic description of a "nice strong man," for the strength he develops is centered on his children and therefore coded feminine: "It was a new feeling Herman now had inside him that made him feel he was strong to make a struggle. It was new for Herman Kreder really to be wanting something, but Herman wanted strongly now to be a father" (172). Herman's love for his children is the strongest emotion in "The Gentle Lena": "[He] always had a very gentle, tender way when he held them. He learned to be very handy with them. He spent all the time he was not working, with them. By and by he began to work all day in his own home so that he could have his children always in the same room with him" (174). Eventually, Herman alone feeds, washes, and dresses the children, and puts them to bed. In essence, he trades up from the role of working daughter to the role of working wife.

He then trades up to single mother. Lena "always was more and more lifeless and Herman now mostly never thought about her. He more and more took all the care of their three children" (174). Once Lena is dead, Herman is safe from heterosexuality: "He never had a woman any more to be all the time around him" (174). The last words of *Three Lives* find him "very well content now and he always lived very regular and peaceful, and with every day just like the next one, always alone now with his three good, gentle children" (174). Herman, like Anna, has made an arrangement with the hegemony that allows him a secure place in society and a fulfilling emotional outlet. Whether Herman enjoys gay sex is unclear, but his active pursuit of male company leaves the option open. Regardless, his inversion—his dislike for heterosexual coupling and his embrace of feminine roles—refracts Lena's own sexuality, which Stein *must* displace, as Lena herself is too fragmented to muster more than "a gentle stir" (150).

The Case for Death by Marriage

Lena fades and sickens after her marriage and sickens and dies once she has children, but correlation is not causation. Do marriage and children kill her?

Lena's initial disinterest—"Lena did not care much to get married" (157), Lena "did not think much about getting married" (158)—and later despair startle those great enforcers of hegemony, her aunt and the cook: "Mrs. Haydon could not believe that any girl, not even Lena, really had no feeling about getting married" (157). Yet Herman seems like an excellent husband for Lena. He offers a friendly distance that should suit a woman disinterested in heterosexual attachment: Herman soon "liked Lena very well. He did not care very much about her but she never was a bother to him being there around him" (168). He tries to defend Lena from his nasty, critical mother—an unprecedented self-assertion—and eventually moves them into their own house to better defend her. He is supportive, undemanding, and presumably interested in heterosexual sex only for reproduction. So why doesn't Lena's life improve when she improves her material position? After all, "Herman was always good and kind, and always helped her with her working. He did everything he knew to help her. He always did all the active new things in the house and for the baby" (173). Why should heterosexual domesticity be any harder to bear than her work as a servant, which also required her to keep house and to care for children? And as Herman is willing to take on "women's work" as well as his own, why can't Lena take advantage of her free time and troll her way through the proto-lesbian bars of fin de siècle Baltimore? Why can't she, like Melanctha, "search in the streets and in dark corners" (60)? There certainly were women who did so.[66]

The cook cannot understand Lena's slow but absolute withdrawal after her marriage, which seems to be born of dumb despair—dumb as in unspoken, and dumb as in not understood. The cook is so frustrated by Lena's continued decline that she lashes Lena with the longest scolding of the book:

> I know you going to have a baby Lena, but that's no way for you to be looking. I am ashamed most to see you come and sit here in my kitchen, looking so sloppy and like you never used to Lena. I never see anybody like you Lena. Herman is very good to you, you always say so, and he don't treat you bad ever though you don't deserve to have anybody good to you, you so careless all the time, Lena, letting yourself go like you never had anybody tell you what was the right way you should know how to be looking. (170)

This cook's litany of Lena's sloppiness, untidiness, carelessness, ugliness, stupidity, and foolishness lasts for thirty-nine lines, more than a page in most editions, and embodies for the reader the strength of the hegemony that crushes Lena flat. Even Anna herself never goes on at such length. This epic length instructs us just how "bad" Lena's unhappiness is and, by hegemonic standards, how illegible. But Lena can no longer be reached by the cook's lectures: "[M]ostly Lena did not seem to hear much . . . mostly Lena just lived along and was careless in her clothes, and dull, and lifeless" (173).

Despite her harsh words, the cook has an inkling of Lena's despair when she tells her mistress "that's the way it is with them girls when they want so to get married. They don't know when they got it good" (171). The cook presumably (and her analogue Anna certainly) prefers a life of service, with its relative economic independence, relative safety from male interference and sexuality, and relative freedom from childbearing, to the higher-ranked status of marriage. Such choice demands a self-possession that Lena lacks and that even her ally the cook can neither give nor advocate, as is seen in her support of the engagement and in her later misremembering of Lena's wanting "so to get married." Though the cook (and Anna) manages to avoid compulsory heterosexuality, she can neither understand what she does nor recommend it to others.

Are there any possible reasons for Lena's decline *besides* her marriage? She thrives before it takes place. We cannot blame Herman, who offers hegemonic security without heterosexual responsibility. His mother is awful, but Lena does not recover when she moves away from Mrs. Kreder, so we cannot blame her. What remains? Two things: the role of wife and mother itself, and Lena's lack of same-sex contact apart from maternal figures. The other servant girls never return. Aunt Haydon is done with Lena once she marries. Even Lena's ties with the cook and Mrs. Kreder (the "good" and the "bad" moms) grow slack.

Stein dramatizes how a lack of any outlet for Lena's same-sex orientation destroys her in a clear-cut case of death by marriage and children. And Stein herself destroys Aunt Haydon's novel of "immigrant girl makes good."

Three Lesbian Lives

Q.E.D. is a novel in three parts—"Adele," "Mabel Neathe," and "Helen"—named after its three women characters. Is *Three Lives* also a novel? Stein supposedly replied, "I hate labels. It's just a book, a book about different characters, three different people I knew long ago."[67] Formal questions aside, "The Good Anna," "Melanctha," and "The Gentle Lena" share a time, place, and theme, as Stein offers three case studies of proto-lesbians in a society where female same-sexuality does not publicly exist.

Though all three "lives" end in pain, misery, and death, Stein does offer the possibility for a happy ending for a proto-lesbian in the blithe fate of Anna's favorite employer, Miss Mathilda, an analogue of Stein herself in her weight, iconoclasm, collection of modern art, and emigration. Miss Mathilda proves that a woman may reject the standards of her society and live as she will, all in the company of like-minded friends. The name "Miss Mathilda" is also linked to "Melanctha"—by three syllables, an initial *M,* a final *a,* and a slant rhyme. Race and class seem to make the two women incommensurate, but the escape of black women to Paris was a modernist fantasy that was firmly rooted in material reality. In Miss Mathilda's move from Bridgepoint to Europe, Stein forecasts her own escape from Baltimore's constraints and offers the possibility of a happy lesbian ending like her own—at least for a woman who has the presence of mind to reject the standards of her society as well as the funds to leave town. The three fates of the three "lives"—fragmentation, repression, or an unsuccessful search for expression and self-realization—are offered as the likely alternatives for a proto-lesbian who is not psychologically stable and financially sound.

CODA

Janet Malcolm and Woody Allen Adrift in the Past

On June 26, 2015, five days before I write this, the Supreme Court struck down the Defense of Marriage Act and upheld the right to gay marriage nationwide, after a determined political and legal campaign waged in a highly public arena for the past twenty-five years. Surely the public face of Gertrude Stein, lesbian icon, is now securely and openly gay. Surely the apparitional lesbian is now a fairy story, useful only for scaring children: once Mommy and Mommy couldn't be seen as a couple in public, much less married.

Alas, no. To see how easily specific lesbianism still gets lost in broad queerness, consider two twenty-first-century explorations of Stein with the largest audience thus far: Janet Malcolm's *Two Lives: Gertrude and Alice,* published in 2007, and Woody Allen's 2011 movie, *Midnight in Paris.*[1]

Malcolm is a successful, well-respected literary journalist known for overturning conventional truths. Her usual technique is to expose the narrative confines of a particular medium or field via a representative conflict. For instance, in *The Journalist and the Murderer* (1990), Malcolm uses the fraught relationship of Joe McGinniss, author of the nonfiction true-crime book *Fatal Vision* (1983), and Jeffrey McDonald, the subject of McGinniss's book, as an example of how the relationship between journalist and subject determines "fact." Malcolm's coupling of sophisticated analysis with the pugnacious exposure of unexpected, unflattering aspects of her subjects makes her writing unusually exciting. The well-received *Two Lives* was selected as one of the one hundred notable books of 2007 by the *New York Times* as well as a best book of 2007 by *Entertainment Weekly*: an impressive combination.[2]

At the center of *Two Lives* is the question of how Stein and Toklas kept house in Nazi-occupied France despite their broad queerness: their

Judaism, their homosexuality, their American citizenship, their association with the avant-garde, and their history not only of *being* the enemy but also of actively helping the enemy's war effort. This question has fascinated the public and the academy for more than fifty years, and Malcolm offers a clear-eyed view of the less savory aspects of Stein and Toklas's survival—especially, their close friendship with Bernard Faÿ, who, as the head of the Bibliothèque nationale under Pétain, facilitated the transport of hundreds of Jews to concentration camps. *Two Lives* also considers (1) Stein scholarship via portraits of several leading Stein scholars, (2) *The Making of Americans* as an unread yet canonical modernist text, and (3) Toklas after Stein's death.[3]

Despite Malcolm's history of exposing the blind spots of a field of inquiry, *Two Lives* is flat—and flatly conventional—in its treatment of Stein, Toklas, and homosexuality. Though the title, *Two Lives: Gertrude and Alice,* indicates a focus, or at least an interest, in the bond between the two subjects, Malcolm never discusses how Stein and Toklas's sexuality bears upon their lives. She is forthright about details of the women's domestic and sexual relationship but never considers how the fact that Stein and Toklas were two women engaged in a homosexual relationship affected their senses of self, their daily activities, their decisions in the long and short terms, their aesthetic choices and proclivities, or the composition of their circle of friends and their estrangement from their biological families. For Malcolm, as for so many before her, Stein and Toklas's relationship exists in a vacuum. She puts them in a bell jar and pumps out the air.

For instance, Malcolm wonders at the long-lasting friendship between Stein, Toklas, and Faÿ. She finds no reasons for their bond besides expedience; she never considers their common homosexuality, and whether this worked perversely to protect the women. Indeed, though Malcolm (like many of Stein's critics) notes the frequency with which Stein and Toklas befriended attractive, artsy young men, she (unlike many of Stein's critics) makes no note of how frequently these men were gay and how homosexuality may have been part of their attraction. No matter where she shifts her gaze, Malcolm determinedly ignores the relevance of homosexuality and the impact of homophobia.[4]

Another example is Malcolm's discussion of Stein's long-unpublished first novel, *Q.E.D.,* which lacks any consideration of how homophobia affected either the novel's publication history or its story of a nascent lesbian struggling to solidify her identity and happiness. Malcolm is interested in Toklas's violent reaction to discovering the manuscript and its inspiration in Stein's previous relationship with May Bookstaver, but Malcolm does not ask how the social and psychic construction of female homosexuality helped configure this fight. Here, Malcolm echoes Ernest Hemingway in *A Moveable Feast*: both authors seem invested, or at least interested, in the "horrible secret" at the bottom of Stein and Toklas's relationship, an interest which seems to index a general discomfort with homosexuality. Hemingway ends his portrait of Stein with his overhearing an alarming dialogue between Stein and an unnamed "someone"—an exchange too horrifying to be fully articulated!—which leads him to flee the shameful domestic scene, whereas Malcolm merely turns an interested eye to Toklas and Stein's fight while remaining aloof from other interactions between the women.[5]

By contrast, Malcolm spends considerable time on a carefully modulated discussion of Stein and Toklas's complex relationship with Judaism. Certainly Stein and Toklas were Jews, and their Jewishness affected their lives. But Jewishness was not more immediate to their daily experience than their homosexuality, which Stein and Toklas "practiced" much more than the ethnicity, religion, and culture they were born into. The relative dangers of being Jewish and being gay do not excuse Malcolm's focus. Considerable numbers of homosexuals were transported to camps from Vichy France, and though lesbians were less visible than gay men, gay women were also transported and killed. And Toklas and Stein were unusually visible, as the fame of their domestic partnership solidified some of the usual intangibility of lesbian relationships in the public eye. Malcolm writes that, in *Wars I Have Seen,* Stein's memoir of the war years, Stein "just can't seem to bring herself to say that she and Toklas are Jewish." Why is this worth Malcolm's attention and not Stein's refusal to name her and Toklas's relationship? Why does Malcolm consistently showcase Stein's "anxiety" about her ethnicity but not her "anxiety" about her sexuality? What about the contradiction between Stein's embodiment of her partnership with Toklas in her work and her decision never to directly discuss her sexual orientation in all of her memoirs?[6]

There are two likely reasons for Malcolm's lapse. First, Malcolm's desire to cover new ground may have led her to consider Stein and Toklas's relationship as old news, too "done" to deserve her attention. (Even so, Malcolm does not include within her portrait scholars such as Diana Souhani and Linda Nichols, whose biographical work is focused on the questions that Malcolm avoids.) Second, Malcolm may take a "queer" perspective: she may acknowledge that the two women were erotically and domestically partnered but conclude that this partnering was done outside the context of a homosexual identity. This assertion is questionable for two women with substantial, long-lasting ties to other gay women and men. Malcolm's elision bears witness to the continued power of Stein's homosexuality to fly beneath the radar despite Stein's importance as a lesbian icon and despite Malcolm's history of seeing what others cannot.

One does not look for succor from the gay failings of Janet Malcolm in the work of Woody Allen. To date, Allen has directed more than forty-five films, most concerned with upper-middle-class New Yorkers. Despite the appreciable presence of gays and lesbians in this milieu, Allen includes few queer characters in his oeuvre. There are some walk-ons for yuks—one being Truman Capote as the winner of a Truman Capote look-alike contest in *Annie Hall*—but, by my count, only three or four characters with appreciable parts. By far the Allen film with the most gay characters is *Midnight in Paris,* though their queerness is much more apparent in history than on film. The most prominent queer in *Midnight in Paris* is Gertrude Stein, played by Kathy Bates.[7]

Midnight in Paris received some of Allen's best notices in the twenty-first century thus far, won the Academy Award for Best Original Screenplay, and was nominated for Best Picture, Best Director, and Best Art Direction. The hero is a screenwriter and wannabe novelist who escapes his soulless career and materialist fiancée with the help of modernist artists and writers whom he visits via a time-traveling Peugeot Landaulet. Many of these artists and writers are queer, but Allen closets them by a strict rubric: the more they threaten straight-male hegemony, the more they are straightened.

For instance, Cole Porter, whose music is prominent in both the past and the present times of the film and who is one of the modernists with the most screen time, is portrayed strictly in tandem with his wife. This Porter is not broadly queer, much less specifically gay. If Allen references Porter's homosexuality, I do not see how. Allen himself is a notable jazz clarinetist, and music is important to him both personally and as a filmmaker; perhaps a great gay composer is incommensurate with Allen's worldview. By contrast, Salvador Dalí, who is more easily dismissed as a figure of fun, is presented as broadly queer, but not in any way as specifically gay. The most prominent modernist man is, of course, Ernest Hemingway—or rather, the hypermasculine public persona that Hemingway carefully crafted.

Coda

Two queer women appear besides Stein: Josephine Baker, an ornamental figure who is seen dancing and who is named only in the credits, and Djuna Barnes, who also dances. Baker is prominently seen, if
not heard, whereas Barnes is seen only from the back. At least Barnes is
named by the hero, in one of the film's few jokes: "That was Djuna Barnes?
No *wonder* she wanted to lead!"

Gertrude Stein also "leads"; Allen's portrayal of homosexuality hews
to the inversion model, though Stein does not enjoy the privileges of masculinity. Instead she is confined to a maternal role. Hemingway brings
our hero to Stein, so she may evaluate his work. Allen's Stein is gruff,
forceful, and wise, and her guidance is invaluable to the greatest artists
in the film. Those great artists are, of course, the two most hegemonically
appropriate males—Hemingway and Picasso—and Stein is both credited with and dramatized in helping them with their work. Hemingway,
Picasso, and the heterosexual Cole Porter are the only modernists whose
work is actually featured in *Midnight in Paris.* We hear Porter, we see and
discuss Picasso, and the longest monologue is a bravura Hemingway pas-
tiche. By contrast, the only work we see by a female artist is the dance of
Josephine Baker—but, unlike the portrayals of Hemingway, the resemblance of this dancing to the *work* of Baker is slight. Apart from the skin
color that vaguely connects Baker with Sonia Rolland, the actress who
plays her, and Baker's position as That Black Expatriate Dancer in Paris,
little connects the performance to its historical reality.[8]

Stein also advises Hemingway and Picasso on love, and the men's
status as the most sexually realized characters is embodied in their mu-
tual possession of the hero's love interest, a mistress of Picasso's who runs
off with Hemingway to Mt. Kilimanjaro. Just as Stein aids and evaluates
others rather than makes art herself, so she does not have her own romantic life. Or is that woman who sits in the corner of the frame Alice B.
Toklas?

Allen has fun depicting Stein and Toklas as following an exaggerat-
edly gendered regime. Toklas answers the door when our hero first comes
to the rue de Fleurus but never speaks again. Instead we see her very much
to the side, in the next room talking to other women and sometimes knit-
ting, as Stein, Hemingway, and our hero converse. Although this spatial
division is supported by *The Autobiography,* it also allows Allen to keep
Stein and Toklas apart. Those in Allen's audience who do not know that
Stein and Toklas are coupled will not guess. The lesbian relationship is less
available to the ignorant than in *TIME*'s cover story on Stein in 1933.[9]

Allen and Malcolm both offer representations of same-sexuality that were once progressive but are now regressive and coeval with homophobia. Allen offers an earlier model within which lesbians are subtly referenced but not discussed, and are visible only to those who already know or who actively search for signs. Moreover, female same-sexuality is equated with masculinity in a crude, uninflected way. Malcolm openly discusses Stein and Toklas's domestic partnership but refuses to see it as relevant to anything but itself. Allen cannot bear to put the women in the same room; Malcolm can, but quickly turns away. She offers tolerance rather than acceptance, as acceptance requires active consideration. And so Gertrude Stein, like Truman Capote, continues to exist on the border between a fabulous queerness and a grounded, embodied homosexuality that would let us see both writers' lives and work more fully.

ACKNOWLEDGMENTS

I worked on this book for many years, and many people helped me. *So Famous and So Gay* came into shape as I was a graduate student in English at the University of Southern California, and I am grateful for the guidance of my dissertation committee: Joe Boone, Tania Modleski, Alice Gambrell, Anne Friedberg, and, especially, my chair, Susan McCabe. All of these professors not only shaped this book but also were models of professional deportment and kindness, and this book would be less without them. Several other teachers helped me with material that found its way here, and I appreciate their generosity: Leo Braudy, Carla Kaplan, and John Carlos Rowe. I thank Alice Echols, who was never my teacher per se but who is my friend, and who has been a great help in bringing this book into print. Joe Boone, too, was generous with his time in the struggle to manifest this book in the material world.

I am grateful to my cohort at USC for emotional as well as intellectual support. I must make special mention of Ruth Blandón, James Penner, and Erika Wright, a trio that, for me, defined much of what USC was. Ruth and James both read many versions of the manuscript, and I am grateful for their intellectual acumen, their worldly knowledge, and their exquisite taste. Marci MacMahon, Tom O'Leary, and Amy Schroeder also read parts of the manuscript and were very helpful.

The University of Southern California supported me financially as well as intellectually, and I am grateful for a Provost's Fellowship, a dissertation fellowship from the English department, and a research grant from USC Lambda Alumni, as well as a subvention for book publication from the English department and Dornsife College of Arts and Sciences. Thanks are also due the Huntington Library for a Christopher Isherwood Fellowship. I wrote much of the final manuscript as a reader at the Huntington Library, and its collection of twentieth-century periodicals was invaluable to this project.

I graduated from USC at the height of the Great Recession, which, if

I may say, was a bummer. I appreciate those institutions that supported me over the next few years: St. Olaf College and the University of Puget Sound, each of which appointed me as visiting assistant professor, and—again—the departments of English and gender studies at the University of Southern California, which hired me as a lecturer. I make special mention of Carol Holly, Bill Kupinse, Tiffany MacBain, and Curtis Wasson, who befriended me in exotic climes. Their insight and knowledge enlarged both the scope and the depth of this book. At USC, my colleagues Molly Pulda and Chris Freeman were generous with their help. Vicki Forman, one of my oldest friends, was an invaluable help to both author and manuscript, and I relied, as I continue to rely, on her calm judgment and warm heart. Doug Sadownick, too, had a global impact on both the form and the spirit of the book.

Ken Corbett put a great deal of time and care into editing an earlier version of chapter 1 for publication in *Studies in Gender and Sexuality,* and I am grateful to him. I also appreciate the efforts of editors Lee Zimmerman, Guy Davidson, Nicola Evans, Yetta Howard, and the anonymous readers whose reports they commissioned for previous publications of material in this book in journals or other books. I thank them all for their careful contributions to this project.

I have been fortunate to give talks related to this book at several institutions and venues, where both the act of speaking and the attentive audiences told me what did and did not work. I am obliged for this opportunity to Pashmina Murthy at the Feminist Studies Colloquium at the University of Minnesota, Minneapolis; Alice Echols at the Center for Feminist Research at USC; and Michael Borgstrom and Edith Benkov at the LGBTQ Research Consortium at San Diego State University. I also thank the many students who were a constant source of inspiration for this project.

This book would not exist as a physical object without the knowledge and support of the University of Minnesota Press, which shepherded its material manifestation. Many thanks are due Doug Armato for editing and substantially improving *So Famous and So Gay.* I am grateful to Richard Morrison for seeing promise in the project. Erin Warholm-Wohlenhaus was an invaluable guide through the thickets of permissions and visual reproduction. Tammy Zambo, copy editor extraordinaire, refined the text to its benefit. Thanks are due, too, to Denise Carlson, indexer, and to my research assistants, Kate Fujimoto and Claire Dougherty: all were reliable and painstaking.

Acknowledgments

My undergraduate education—and thus, in time, this book—was made possible by the support of my parents, Carol and Max Solomon. I appreciate this. I also thank my aunt Helen Solomon, who was a constant source of support for me as a young gay boy and man. If one must live a gay cliché, having a fabulous aunt who lives in Manhattan is definitely the way to go.

My greatest thanks are reserved for my partner of a quarter decade, Greg Bills. His knowledge and love are vital to this book, and I thank him for that, as for so much else.

NOTES

Prologue

Notes for the Prologue are kept to a minimum, and material at large in the body of the text is not glossed. Unless noted, dates of play publication are the same as their Broadway or off-Broadway premieres.

1. Truman Capote, *Other Voices, Other Rooms* (New York: Random House, 1948); *A Tree of Night and Other Stories* (New York: Random House, 1949); Jack Dunphy, *John Fury* (New York: Doubleday, 1946). For the early history of Dunphy, see Gerald Clarke, *Capote* (New York: Ballantine, 1988), 188–94. Capote and Dunphy would stay together, more or less, until Capote's death. Capote's other domestic partner, John O'Shea, was remarkably similar, an Irish Catholic accountant with a manly affect and, when Capote met him, a wife and children. Joan McCracken played Sylvie in the 1943 Broadway production of *Oklahoma!* and left a promising film career to return to the stage.

2. John Malcolm Brinnin, *Truman Capote: Dear Heart, Old Buddy* (New York: Delacorte, 1986); *Dylan Thomas in America: An Intimate Journal* (Boston: Little, Brown, 1955); *The Third Rose: Gertrude Stein and Her World* (Boston: Little, Brown, 1959). *Dear Heart, Old Buddy* expands upon "The Picture of Little T. C. in a Prospect . . . ," in Brinnin's *Sextet: T. S. Eliot and Truman Capote and Others* (New York: Delacorte, 1981). I have indicated when Brinnin quotes from his journals, which are unpublished. The Young Men's and Young Women's Hebrew Association is commonly known as the 92nd Street Y.

3. Brinnin, *Truman Capote*, 57–58 (italics his); Gertrude Stein, *Tender Buttons: Objects, Food, Rooms* (New York: Claire Marie, 1914). Stein discusses her discombobulation and her dog in *The Geographical History of America; or, The Relation of Human Nature to the Human Mind* (New York: Random House, 1936), 103; and again in *Everybody's Autobiography* (New York: Random House, 1937), 64. See Brinnin, *Third Rose*, 347. Capote did get a dog the next year, a Pekingese, which Dunphy was ashamed to walk and which was rehomed and replaced by a terrier.

4. *Murder by Death*, directed by Robert Moore (Columbia Pictures, 1976).

5. The cast of *Murder by Death* includes Eileen Brennan, James Coco, Peter Falk, Alec Guinness, Elsa Lanchester, Peter Sellers, and Maggie Smith.

6. *Best Foot Forward*, directed by Edward Buzzell (MGM, 1943). In "My Brother's Keeper," an episode from season 3 of *The Mary Tyler Moore Show* (MTM Enterprises, 1970–77), Robert Moore appeared as the brother of the character Phyllis (Cloris Leachman), which led to one of the first uses of the term *gay* to mean "homosexual"

in a scripted television show. Nancy Walker as Ida Morgenstern would follow her daughter Rhoda (Valerie Harper) to her eponymous spin-off (MTM Enterprises, 1974–78)—and twenty-seven episodes of *Rhoda* would be directed by Robert Moore.

7. Neil Simon, *The Gingerbread Lady* (New York: Random House, 1971; Broadway, 1970); *California Suite* (New York: Random House, 1977; Broadway, 1976); *Only When I Laugh,* directed by Glenn Jordan (Rastar Films, 1981); *California Suite,* directed by Herbert Ross (Rastar Films, 1978). Despite (and probably because of) Simon's popularity, he has inspired little scholarship. For an overview of his gay characters, see Richard Grayson, "The Fruit Brigade: Neil Simon's Gay Characters," in *Neil Simon: A Casebook,* ed. Gary Konas (London: Routledge, 1997), 137–48.

8. Neil Simon, *Biloxi Blues* (New York: Random House, 1986); *London Suite* (New York: Samuel French, undated; off-Broadway, 1995); *Biloxi Blues,* directed by Mike Nichols (Rastar Films, 1988).

9. Moore makes only a brief appearance in both of Simon's memoirs: *Rewrites* (New York: Simon & Schuster, 1996) and *The Play Goes On* (New York: Simon & Schuster, 1999). His sexuality is not mentioned. Broadway productions written by Simon (or, in the case of musicals, book by Simon) and directed by Moore include *Promises, Promises* (New York: Random House, 1969), *The Last of the Red Hot Lovers* (New York: Random House, 1970), *The Gingerbread Lady* (1971), and *They're Playing Our Song* (New York: Random House, 1980). Simon wrote and Moore directed *The Cheap Detective* (Columbia Pictures, 1978) and *Chapter Two* (Rastar Films, 1979), as well as *Murder by Death* (1976). In addition to *The Boys in the Band,* by Mart Crowley (New York: Farrar, Straus, 1968), Moore directed the Broadway run of another play with gay content, *Deathtrap,* by Ira Levin (New York: Random House, 1979). His sole acting role in a movie was in *Tell Me You Love Me, Junie Moon,* directed by Otto Preminger (Otto Preminger Pictures, 1970), but he continued to act on television.

10. For Capote's short career as an actor, as well as a useful précis of his talk-show appearances, see Tison Pugh, *Truman Capote: A Literary Life at the Movies* (Athens: University of Georgia Press, 2014), 19–42.

11. *M*A*S*H* (20th Century Fox Television, 1972–83); *Soap* (Witt-Thomas-Harris Productions, 1977–81).

12. Corey Kilgannon, "Ray Stark, Oscar-Nominated Producer, Is Dead at 88," *New York Times,* January 18, 2004. Stark's movies include *The Night of the Iguana* (MGM, 1964), *The Way We Were* (Columbia Pictures, 1973), and *Smokey and the Bandit* (Universal, 1977).

13. Simon, *Play Goes On,* 132; *Murder by Death,* movie trailer (1976; DVD, Sony Pictures Home Entertainment, 2001).

14. "A Conversation with Neil Simon," DVD extra, *Murder by Death.*

15. *I Love You, Alice B. Toklas!,* directed by Hy Averback, screenplay by Larry Tucker and Paul Mazursky (Warner, 1968); Gertrude Stein, *The Autobiography of Alice B. Toklas* (New York: Harcourt Brace, 1933). Mazursky would write and direct films such as *Bob and Carol and Ted and Alice* (Columbia, 1969) and *An Unmarried Woman* (20th Century Fox, 1978).

16. Alice Toklas, *The Alice B. Toklas Cookbook* (New York: Harper; London: Michael

Joseph, 1954). The recipe "Haschigh Fudge" was included in the first British edition (259), but not the first American one. Vincent Canby, "'*I Love You, Alice B. Toklas!*': Peter Sellers Stars as Lawyer Turned Hippie," *New York Times* October 8, 1968.

Introduction

1. Though working at *The New Yorker* did furnish part of Capote's legend, Capote was incorrect to assume that the job would help his career. *The New Yorker* did not condone upward mobility among its copyboys, and Capote's association with the magazine made it less likely that he would publish there. See Janet Groth, *The Receptionist: An Education at "The New Yorker"* (Chapel Hill, N.C.: Algonquin, 2012). For Capote's biography, see Gerald Clarke, *Capote* (New York: Ballantine, 1988); and George Plimpton, ed., *Truman Capote: In Which Various Friends, Enemies, Acquaintances, and Detractors Recall His Turbulent Career* (New York: Doubleday, 1977).

2. Capote was appropriately reassured by his friends about Arvin's bona fides. Arvin had already written two well-received biographies—*Hawthorne* (Boston: Little, Brown, 1929) and *Whitman* (New York: Macmillan, 1938)—and was writing another, *Herman Melville* (New York: Sloane, 1950), which would win the National Book Award. Doughty's most important publication was also a biography, an eponymous book about the historian Francis Parkman (New York: Macmillan, 1962).

   Capote, Arvin, and Doughty were not points of a traditional triangle or thruple. Doughty's and Arvin's stays at Yaddo barely overlapped, and Arvin compared notes with Doughty about sex with Capote. In sum, Arvin and Doughty would have an affectionate sexual relationship for about thirty years. Next to obstacles such as the professional need to be discreet and Doughty's marriage to a woman, Capote did not loom large. Nonetheless, Capote did surpass Doughty in Arvin's affections while they were together. See Clarke, *Capote*, as well as Barry Werth, *The Scarlet Professor: Newton Arvin, a Literary Life Shattered by Scandal* (New York: Random House, 2001).

   Conventionally, *Other Voices, Other Rooms* (New York: Random House) is dated 1948, but the novel was available in stores in December 1947. See Clarke, *Capote,* 149.

3. Gertrude Stein, *The Autobiography of Alice B. Toklas* (New York: Harcourt Brace, 1933), 97–98. Biographies for Stein are discussed in the headnote for chapter 3.

4. "Gertrude Stein Dies in France, 72," *New York Times,* July 28, 1946. Stein's grades are drawn from Linda Wagner-Martin, *"Favored Strangers": Gertrude Stein and Her Family* (New Brunswick, N.J.: Rutgers University Press, 1995), 36. The various James biographies draw from *The Autobiography* as well as Stein's biographies; the most extended treatment of James's instruction of Stein is in Gay Wilson Allen, *William James: A Biography* (Minneapolis: University of Minnesota Press, 1970), 79.

   Whereas "Normal Motor Automatism" (1896) seems to have been primarily the work of Leon Solomons, Stein would publish her own article in the *Harvard Psychological Review* in 1898, her fifth year at Radcliffe: "Cultivated Motor Automatism: A Study of Character in Its Relation to Attention." Both may be found in Gertrude Stein and Leon M. Solomons, *Motor Automatism* (New York: Phoenix

Book Shop, 1969). For these articles, and the place of Stein and Solomons's work within the context of James's larger project, see Barbara Will, *Gertrude Stein, Modernism, and the Problem of "Genius"* (Edinburgh: Edinburgh University Press, 2000), 21–47. Also see Steven Meyer, *Irresistible Dictation: Gertrude Stein and the Correlations of Writing and Science* (Stanford, Calif.: Stanford University Press, 2002).

5. Stein, *The Autobiography*, 98. Llewellys F. Barker cites Stein in *The Nervous System and Its Constituent Neurones* (New York: Appleton, 1899), 721, 725, 875. An example: "I shall restrict myself, therefore, in the main, to a mere statement of the results of my own studies, and of those of Miss Sabin and Miss Stein, who have especially studied this region" (721). See note 8 for the fabulous Miss Sabin. Steven Meyer, Lynn Marie Morgan, Brenda Wineapple, and Linda Wagner-Martin all offer useful narratives of Stein's graduate work. Meyer focuses on the imprint of Stein's scientific work upon her writing; Morgan narrates a cultural history of embryology that addresses Stein's research in *Icons of Life: A Cultural History of Human Embryos* (Los Angeles: University of California Press, 2009); Wineapple offers the most thorough account of Stein's graduate education in *Brother/Sister: Gertrude and Leo Stein* (New York: Putnam, 1996); and Wagner-Martin provides the most insight into Stein's subject position as a woman and a lesbian in *"Favored Strangers."* Though they disagree in small particulars, all agree on the facts that I include here.

6. Gertrude Stein, *Fernhurst, Q.E.D., and Other Early Writings* (New York: Liveright, 1971); *Three Lives: Stories of the Good Anna, Melanctha, and the Gentle Lena* (New York: Grafton, 1909); *The Autobiography*, 102. For material specifics of misogyny at Johns Hopkins and Stein's resistance, see Wagner-Martin, *"Favored Strangers,"* 44. Johns Hopkins was progressive in accepting women at all—and did so only because a large bequest required it (Wineapple, *Brother/Sister*, 112–14). Baltimore and Johns Hopkins were not unusually anti-Semitic for the 1890s, except by contrast to Stein's experience at Harvard/Radcliffe. Harvard opened the country's first Jewish museum in 1889 and would hire the country's first professor of Judaica in 1925.

7. This story is detailed by Wagner-Martin (*"Favored Strangers,"* 51–52), who read the relevant correspondence in the Alan Mason Chesney Medical Archives, Johns Hopkins Medical Institutions.

8. Florence Sabin, a Jewish woman who was at Johns Hopkins the year before Stein, became a noted chemist (Wineapple, *Brother/Sister*, 127). Barker would continue to support Stein's work and its publication, without issue.

9. Truman Capote, *Answered Prayers* (New York: Random House, 1987); Marcel Proust, *A la recherche du temps perdu* (Paris: Gaston Gallimard, 1919–27); first U.S. edition, *Swann's Way*, trans. C. K. Scott Moncrieff (New York: Holt, 1925).

10. There were, of course, many successful gay men and women in the arts, such as the "Homintern" discussed in Michael Sherry's *Gay Artists in Modern American Culture: An Imagined Conspiracy* (Chapel Hill: University of North Carolina Press, 2007). Sherry documents that the Homintern was the subject of considerable homophobia in the late 1940s and early 1950s. In terms of my argument, note that the

fame of composers and writers such as Aaron Copland and Edward Albee was not *dependent* upon homosexuality in the same way as Capote but arose *despite* it.

There were, of course, people and subcultures that resisted homophobia, as well as people who did not think their own same-sex activity applied, as is documented by John D'Emilio, *Sexual Politics, Sexual Communities: The Making of a Homosexual Minority in the United States, 1940–1970* (Chicago: University of Chicago Press, 1983); George Chauncey, *Gay New York: Gender, Urban Culture, and the Makings of the Gay Male World, 1890–1940* (New York: Basic Books, 1994); and many others. There were also cultural artifacts that did similar work, such as the pulp novels detailed in Michael Bronski, *Pulp Friction: Uncovering the Golden Age of Gay Male Pulps* (New York: St. Martin's Press, 2003); Anthony Slide, *Lost Gay Novels: A Reference Guide to Fifty Works from the First Half of the Twentieth Century* (New York: Harrington Park Press, 2003); and Susan Stryker, *Queer Pulp: Perverted Passions from the Golden Age of the Paperback* (San Francisco: Chronicle Books, 2001).

11. Gertrude Stein, *Everybody's Autobiography* (New York: Random House, 1937), 64. See the Prologue of this book for Stein's conclusion that even her dog does not know her.

12. Stein's practice of sitting with the men while Toklas sat with their wives is referenced several times in *The Autobiography,* most clearly on 105–6. Capote's society lunches are a commonplace of his biography and autobiography.

13. Disregarding chronology does complicate the discussion of a queer modernist genealogy and the question of how Capote was influenced and his career enabled by those before him. For example, in 1948 (beyond the parameters of this book), Capote made the obligatory trip to Paris to meet with an earlier generation of queer writers, including Colette and Cocteau. He met Toklas; had Stein not died, would he have met her? Stein was interested in young writers and artists, especially if they were gay men and especially if they were especially gay, and the list of those whom she befriended keeps expanding. Justin Spring's *Secret Historian: The Life and Times of Samuel Steward, Professor, Tattoo Artist, and Sexual Renegade* (New York: Farrar, Straus & Giroux, 2011) offers an instructive example.

14. Michael Newbury has written a helpful and comprehensive review of the various harnesses that have put modernism and celebrity in tandem in "Celebrity and Glamour: Modernism for the Masses," *American Literary History* 23, no. 1 (Spring 2011): 126–34. For Stein's prominence in mass culture, see Karen Leick, *Gertrude Stein and the Making of an American Celebrity* (New York: Routledge, 2009); and Timothy W. Galow, *Writing Celebrity: Stein, Fitzgerald, and the Modern(ist) Art of Self-Fashioning* (New York: Palgrave Macmillan, 2011). For modernism and celebrity, see Judith Brown, *Glamour in Six Dimensions: Modernism* (Ithaca, N.Y.: Cornell University Press, 2009); Loren Glass, *Authors Inc.: Literary Celebrity in the Modern United States, 1880–1980* (New York: New York University Press, 2004); Faye Hammill, *Women, Celebrity, and Literary Culture between the Wars* (Austin: University of Texas Press, 2007); Aaron Jaffe, *Modernism and the Culture of Celebrity* (Cambridge: Cambridge University Press, 2005); and Graeme Turner, *Understanding Celebrity* (Thousand Oaks, Calif.: Sage, 2004). For wider-ranging

considerations of celebrity, see Leo Braudy, *The Frenzy of Renown: Fame and Its History* (New York: Oxford University Press, 1986); Joshua Gamson, *Claims to Fame: Celebrity in Contemporary America* (Berkeley: University of California Press, 1994); Turner, *Understanding Celebrity*; and Sean Redmond and Su Holmes, eds., *Stardom and Celebrity: A Reader* (Thousand Oaks, Calif.: Sage, 2007).

15. Redmond and Holmes, "Understanding Celebrity Culture," introduction to *Stardom and Celebrity*, 5.

16. Guy Davidson and Nicola Evans have edited a useful collection of analyses of literary celebrity in the modern era, *Literary Careers in the Modern Era*, that clarifies Said's distinction (Houndmills, Eng.: Palgrave Macmillan, 2015). More specific analyses of literary celebrity include David Carter, *A Career in Writing: Judah Waten and the Cultural Politics of a Literary Career* (Toowoomba, Australia: Association for the Study of Australian Literature, 1997); Edgar Dryden, *Monumental Melville: The Formation of a Literary Career* (Stanford, Calif.: Stanford University Press, 2004); Glass, *Authors Inc.*; Hammill, *Women, Celebrity*; Joe Moran, *Star Authors: Literary Celebrity in America* (London: Pluto, 2000); and Gary Lee Stonum, *Faulkner's Career: An Internal Literary History* (Ithaca, N.Y.: Cornell University Press, 1979).

I found James Penner's *Pinks, Pansies, and Punks: The Politics of Masculinity in Literary Culture* (Bloomington: Indiana University Press, 2010) especially helpful for thinking through the issues.

17. Braudy, *Frenzy of Renown*, 585.

18. Raewyn Connell [R. W.], *Masculinities* (Berkeley: University of California Press, 1995), 77. Connell draws upon Antonio Gramsci's analysis of class relations and hegemony, within which one group claims and sustains dominance.

19. Raewyn Connell [R. W.], *Gender and Power: Society, the Person, and Sexual Politics* (Cambridge, Eng.: Polity, 1987), 62.

20. Capote and Baldwin were born within a year of each other; Capote seems older because he succeeded at a younger age. Williams, often perceived as Capote's contemporary, was more than ten years older. Yet until the 1970s, Williams's overtly gay-themed work, such as the 1948 short-story collection *One Arm and Other Stories* (New York: New Directions), was not widely available and was sold only behind the counter at specialized bookstores in a brown paper wrapper. Williams was not gay "at large" until after Stonewall.

21. Martha M. Umphrey, "The Trouble with Harry Thaw," *Radical History Review* 62 (Spring 1995): 12. I am grateful to Alice Echols for this reference. Umphrey offers her warning as a result of her own experience while researching Harry Thaw, the playboy millionaire who married Evelyn Nesbit and murdered Stanford White. Thaw was also known for beating and sodomizing teenage boys. Umphrey wanted to recuperate Thaw as gay but realized that though he resisted compulsory heterosexuality, he was better understood as queer, as a 1920s version of a libertine, than as a gay man. Umphrey offers this analysis in the context of discussing other men from the same time period whom she *would* discuss as gay.

22. See Shari Benstock, *Women of the Left Bank: Paris, 1900–1940* (Austin: University of Texas Press, 1986); Lisa Ruddick, *Gertrude Stein: Body, Text, Gnosis* (Ithaca,

N.Y.: Cornell University Press, 1990); Erin G. Carlston, *Thinking Fascism: Sapphic Modernism and Fascist Modernity* (Stanford, Calif.: Stanford University Press, 1998); Laura Doan, *Fashioning Sapphism: The Origins of a Modern English Lesbian Culture* (New York: Columbia University Press, 2001); Lisa Duggan, *Sapphic Slashers: Sex, Violence, and American Modernity* (Durham, N.C.: Duke University Press, 2000); Robin Hackett, *Sapphic Primitivism: Productions of Race, Class, and Sexuality in Key Works of Modern Fiction* (New Brunswick, N.J.: Rutgers University Press, 2004); Heather K. Love, "Impossible Objects: Waiting for the Revolution in *Summer Will Show*," in *Sapphic Modernities: Sexuality, Women, and National Culture,* ed. Laura L. Doan and Jane Garrity (New York: Palgrave Macmillan, 2006); and Lisa Cohen's marvelous *All We Know: Three Lives* (New York: Farrar, Straus, & Giroux, 2012). For a recent view of sapphic modernism that extends from the sixteenth to the nineteenth centuries, see Susan S. Lanser, *The Sexuality of History: Modernity and the Sapphic, 1565–1630* (Chicago: University of Chicago Press, 2014).

Love notes that sapphic modernity is itself a transhistoric formation: "Like any form of modernity, it is characterized by a kind of untimeliness: it designates not only a period, but also a principle—of constant renewal, of revolutionary dissolution, of resistance to historicity itself" ("Impossible Objects," 134). The term *sapphist* itself encompasses a desire to identify with what may be a fantastic premodern female same-sexuality and thereby to decrease, at least in fantasy, the individual and institutional loneliness of those sexually oriented toward their own sex.

23. For objections to substituting *gay* or *queer* for *lesbian,* see Sheila Jeffreys, "The Queer Disappearance of Lesbians: Sexuality in the Academy," *Women's Studies International Forum* 17, no. 5 (1994): 459–72; and Biddy Martin, "Sexualities without Genders and Other Queer Utopias," *Diacritics* 24, nos. 2–3 (1994): 104–21; among others. In the mid-1990s, queer theory's incorporation of specific "lesbianism" into broad "queerness" grew marked enough to demand a response. I agree with many of these objections. In my daily life, however, using *gay* for women is common. Most importantly for my argument, without a common term for gay women and men, the comparison between the broadly queer and the specifically gay becomes unwieldy.

24. I am particularly indebted to Terry Castle's *The Apparitional Lesbian: Female Homosexuality and Modern Culture* (New York: Columbia University Press, 1993); Christopher Nealon's *Foundlings: Lesbian and Gay Historical Emotion before Stonewall* (Durham, N.C.: Duke University Press, 2003); and Henry Abelove's *Deep Gossip* (Minneapolis: University of Minnesota Press, 2003), all of which consider homosexuality before Stonewall—often, more than a century before—and as such repudiate the notion that homosexuality is entirely culturally constructed. Castle, Nealon, and Abelove share a belief that literature may configure the form that homosexuality takes, both in an individual and in society at large.

25. See Alfred C. Kinsey, Wardell B. Pomeroy, and Clyde E. Martin, *Sexual Behavior in the Human Male* (Philadelphia: Saunders, 1948), usually known as "the Kinsey report." Although the scale, which ranges from 0 to 6, was created to expose and emphasize sexual fluidity, Kinsey did allow for subjects such as Capote and Stein whose sexual history did not exhibit such variation.

This is a strong statement, and nits may be picked. One possible nit for Stein is her research partner and friend Leon Solomons. After reading Stein's undergraduate diaries, Wagner-Martin concludes that their friendship was "both intellectual and sexual," though she also notes that Stein writes that she and Solomons were "Platonic because neither care to do more. She and he both have their moments but they know each other and it is not worthwhile" (*"Favored Strangers,"* 37). Such dry kisses create no issue.

26. There is no standard spelling of *proto-gay*: some use the hyphen and some do not. I use the hyphen to emphasize that *proto-gay* depends upon *gay* while distinguishing between the two words.

Eve Kosofsky Sedgwick discusses proto-homosexuality in "How to Bring Your Kids Up Gay: The War on Effeminate Boys," in *Tendencies* (Durham, N.C.: Duke University Press, 1993), 154–65. Ken Corbett offers perhaps the most embodied discussion both of proto-gayness and its invisibility in the larger culture in "Cross-Gendered Identifications and Homosexual Boyhood: Toward a More Complex Theory of Gender," *American Journal of Orthopsychiatry* 68, no. 3 (July 1998): 352–60, though, like Sedgwick, he restricts his discussion to boys. Also see Kathryn Bond Stockton, *The Queer Child: Growing Sideways in the Twentieth Century* (Durham, N.C.: Duke University Press, 2009).

27. Susan McCabe, "To Be and to Have: The Rise of Queer Historicism," *GLQ: A Journal of Lesbian and Gay Studies* 11, no. 1 (2005): 121.

28. Teresa de Lauretis, *The Practice of Love: Lesbian Sexuality and Perverse Desire* (Bloomington: Indiana University Press, 1994), 23. Beverly Burch presents her developmental schema in *Other Women: Lesbian/Bisexual Experience and Psychoanalytic Views of Women* (New York: Columbia University Press, 1997), 15–87. Ken Corbett's developmental schema is presented in *Boyhoods: Rethinking Masculinities* (New Haven, Conn.: Yale University Press, 2011) and allows gender to be specific and stable without being essential or normative: "[G]enders are constructed through the transfer of various traits (long hair, short hair), codes (dresses, pants), behaviors (sensitive, rough), and fantasies (surrender, domination). Once transferred, these internalizations come to rest (to the degree that any internalization comes to rest) in exquisite, unique, inner worlds, the staging grounds for significant personal patterns and differences" (96). I was particularly struck by Corbett's earlier "Homosexual Boyhood: Notes on Girlyboys," *Gender and Psychoanalysis* 1 (1996): 429–61.

Leslie Deutsch's development schema is outlined in "Out of the Closet and on to the Couch: A Psychoanalytic Exploration of Lesbian Development," included in *Lesbians and Psychoanalysis: Revolutions in Theory and Practice,* ed. Judith M. Glassgold and Suzanne Iasenza (New York: Free Press, 1995), 19–38, an anthology of articles by lesbian psychoanalysts, including Burch. Glassgold and Iasenza's second anthology—*Lesbians, Feminism, and Psychoanalysis: The Second Wave* (New York: Harrington Park Press, 2004)—is more influenced by social construction, and as such does not present or strongly imply a lesbian developmental schema. Richard Isay presents his theory of gay male psychosocial development most coherently in *Becoming Homosexual: Gay Men and Their Development* (New York:

Farrar, Straus & Giroux, 1989) and most accessibly in *Becoming Gay: The Journey to the Self* (New York: Macmillan, 1997).

29. Stockton, *Queer Child*, 11–17. Stockton makes the interesting claim that the proto-gay child "makes *gay* far more liquid and labile than it has seemed in recent years, when queer theory has been rightfully critiquing it. Odd as it may seem, *gay* in this context, the context of the child, is the new *queer*—a term that touts its problems and shares them with anyone" (4). Stockton here responds to the difficulty of theorizing specific gayness in the face of most queer theory.

30. I am far from the first to mention this risk. In *The Trouble with Normal: Sex, Politics, and the Ethics of Queer Life* (Cambridge, Mass.: Harvard University Press, 1999), Michael Warner disputes the field's unquestioned championing of subversion and resistance. Brad Epps offers a comprehensive critique of queer theory's distaste for the fixed in the helpful "The Fetish of Fluidity," in *Homosexuality and Psychoanalysis*, ed. Tim Dean and Christopher Lane (Chicago: University of Chicago Press, 2001), 412–31. Michael Snediker's work on queer theory's preference for subjectivity over personhood is discussed presently.

31. Michael Snediker, "Queer Optimism," *Postmodern Culture* 16, no. 3 (2006): para. 6. Snediker qualifies his wording a bit in *Queer Optimism: Lyric Personhood and Other Felicitous Persuasions* (Minneapolis: University of Minnesota Press, 2009), 4.

32. Sharon Marcus and James Best, "Surface Reading: An Introduction," *Representations* 108, no. 1 (2009): 1, 5.

33. In *Second Skins: The Body Narratives of Transsexuality* (New York: Columbia University Press, 1998), Jay Prosser makes a similar argument about how queer theory has put a bouncer at the door of transgender experience, welcoming transgender performativity into the VIP lounge while blocking the body of gender transition from the club (6). Transgender performativity suits the tenets of queer theory, whereas surgery to attain a bodily fixed identity is less easily assimilated.

34. *Stein's queer biography and its impact upon her composition and reputation*: Though Stein's sexuality was well known not only by those "in the know" but also by any member of the public with eyes properly cued, the first public considerations of Stein that considered her sexuality openly and at length were by Richard Bridgman (1970) and James R. Mellow (1974). These were followed in the 1980s by a flood of lesbian, queer, and feminist readings, many triggered by Catharine Stimpson's investigations of how both Stein's depictions of the female body and critics' reading of Stein's own body reveal and occlude lesbian possibility: "Gertrude Stein: Humanism and Its Freaks," *Boundary 2* 12, no. 3 (1984): 301–19, and "The Somagrams of Gertrude Stein," *Poetics Today* 6, nos. 1–2 (1985): 67–80.

   The resurrection and reconsideration of underpublished and underread works by Stein that directly treat female same-sexuality: See, for instance, the good offices of Rebecca Mark, editor of Stein's resurrected *Lifting Belly* (Tallahassee, Fla.: Naiad, 1995), which made some of her most explicit homoeroticism much more accessible. *Lifting Belly* had been previously available in Stein's *Bee Time Vine, and Other Pieces, 1913–1927* (New Haven, Conn.: Yale University Press, 1953), 61–115, and then in *The Yale Gertrude Stein: Selections*, ed. Richard Kostelanetz (New Haven, Conn.: Yale University Press, 1980), 4–54, but neither of these invited a casual reader.

Theoretical investigations of how Stein encoded lesbianism: Although many critics of poetics, like Marjorie Perloff in *Poetics of Indeterminacy: Rimbaud to Cage* (Evanston, Ill.: Northwestern University Press, 1999), do not overtly address how Stein's sexuality affects her work, they do configure her poetry as fluid and nonlinear. Such instability and indeterminacy have been viewed by critics such as Marianne DeKoven, in *A Different Language: Gertrude Stein's Experimental Writing* (Madison: University of Wisconsin Press, 1983); and Dana Watson, in *Gertrude Stein and the Essence of What Happens* (Nashville, Tenn.: Vanderbilt University Press, 2005), as a mode of patriarchal resistance, a feminist refusal of the center and a wholehearted embrace of the lacunae created by the lack of a narrative center. Language poets such as Lyn Hejinian and Charles Bernstein follow Stein in this regard, writing poetry that rejects the dominant pressure of traditional authorship and even the pressure to make sense.

35. Abelove, *Deep Gossip,* 72. Abelove argues that queer writing before Stonewall "was enormously productive for [the Gay Liberation Front (GLF)] and significantly contributed to the development of its outlook and values" (71). Abelove does not include Capote and Stein among the "Queer Commuters" (such as James Baldwin, Elizabeth Bishop, and the Bowleses) who left the United States after World War II, were "personally and artistically interested in same-sex eroticism," and invested in "a rhetoric for connecting queerness to decolonization and its struggles" (80). Do Capote and Stein fit? Same-sexuality is a primary concern of their life and art, but anticolonialism is not. Stein lived in France from 1907 until her death in 1946. Though she predates Abelove's cohort, her most overtly lesbian writing was published after her death—and the dearth of published lesbian writers makes Stein's utility more pronounced. Capote lived outside of the United States for much of the 1950s; he was about a decade younger than Bishop and the Bowleses, and the same age as Baldwin. If we expand Abelove's argument past the GLF to a broader spectrum of gay men and women and the specific process by which gay-themed texts reached these readers, as well as to the psychological impact of these texts, then Capote and Stein work well.

1. Young, Effeminate, and Strange

Any discussion of Truman Capote's history is beholden, explicitly or implicitly, to his three essential biographies: Gerald Clarke's magisterial, authorized *Capote* (New York: Ballantine, 1988); Lawrence Grobel's collected interviews, *Conversations with Capote* (New York: New American Library, 1985); and George Plimpton's oral history, *Truman Capote: In Which Various Friends, Enemies, Acquaintances, and Detractors Recall His Turbulent Career* (New York: Doubleday, 1977).

1. Truman Capote, *Other Voices, Other Rooms* (New York: Random House, 1948), 4, 8–9.

2. For the destabilization in gender roles brought about by WWII and the restabilization through repression that followed, see, among others, Stephanie Coontz, *The Way We Never Were: American Families and the Nostalgia Trap* (New York: Basic Books, 1992). For the relationship between WWII and the emergence of an urban

gay subculture, and for how gays and lesbians dealt with a "return to traditional values" in the 1950s that was more conservative than what existed before the war, see John D'Emilio, *Sexual Politics, Sexual Communities* (Chicago: University of Chicago Press, 1983).

3. Capote's *Other Voices* could be bought in December 1947 but was published officially in 1948; Alfred C. Kinsey, Wardell B. Pomeroy, and Clyde E. Martin, *Sexual Behavior in the Human Male* (Philadelphia: Saunders, 1948); Gore Vidal, *The City and the Pillar* (New York: Dutton, 1948). For midcentury psychoanalytic theories of male homosexuality in the United States, see Kenneth Lewes, *The Psychoanalytic Theory of Male Homosexuality* (New York: Simon & Schuster, 1988); and Henry Abelove, *Deep Gossip* (Minneapolis: University of Minnesota Press, 2003), 1–20.

4. Gore Vidal, *Williwaw* (New York: Dutton, 1946). Although reviews were mixed for Vidal's second novel, *In a Yellow Wood* (New York: Dutton, 1947), Vidal was still viewed as promising. See Fred Kaplan, *Gore Vidal: A Biography* (New York: Random House, 1999).

5. For the various quotes that make up this Dutton advertisement (ellipses theirs), see Kaplan, *Gore Vidal*, 257. Vidal's novels in the early 1950s were *The Season of Comfort* (New York: Dutton, 1949); *The Search for the King* (New York: Dutton, 1950); *Dark Green, Bright Red* (New York: Dutton, 1950); *The Judgment of Paris* (New York: Dutton, 1952); and *Messiah* (New York: Dutton, 1954). From 1950 to 1954, Vidal also wrote novels under the pseudonyms Katherine Everard, Cameron Kay, and, most successfully, Edgar Box. Pseudonyms differentiated these novels from Vidal's "serious" work—and kept them from the reviewers' blacklist.

6. Lisa Larsen, "*LIFE* Visits Yaddo," *LIFE,* July 15, 1946, 110–13. Little has been written on Larsen (1925–1959), whose career was cut short by breast cancer. One of the few female staff photographers at *LIFE* in the late 1940s and '50s, and best known for her portraits and overseas photojournalism, Larsen was included in group shows at the Museum of Modern Art in 1950, '51, '55, and '58 and had a solo show at the Art Institute of Chicago in 1957. See John Loengard, "Overlooked Masters," *American Photo* 12, no. 5 (2001): 30–36.

7. Truman Capote, "My Side of the Matter," *Story* 26 (1945): 34–40; "Miriam," *Mademoiselle,* June 1945. Capote's other publications in 1945 were "A Tree of Night," *Mademoiselle,* December 1945; and "Jug of Silver," *Harper's Bazaar,* October 1945. See chapter 3 for a discussion of fiction in women's magazines.

8. McCullers and Capote's friendship would soon sour. For McCullers's biography, see Virginia Spencer Carr, *The Lonely Hunter: A Biography of Carson McCullers* (New York: Doubleday, 1975). In 1948, Capote himself would recommend a young, promising, gay short-story writer to Yaddo—Patricia Highsmith—where she would extend a short story to the novel *Strangers on a Train* (New York: Harper & Bros., 1950).

9. Marguerite Young, *Miss Macintosh, My Darling* (New York: Scribner, 1965). Though John Malcolm Brinnin is best known today as a biographer, he was accepted to Yaddo as a poet.

10. Black loafers and white socks were also associated at midcentury with the dancer

and actor Gene Kelly, who worked to change the public image of male dancers to be masculine and athletic rather than effeminate and graceful. If Capote seemed less childish, these connotations might take hold.

11. Other photographs from this session, now at Yale's Beinecke Library, show a younger, classier, more conventionally feminine Young. Larsen seems to have manipulated Young's self-presentation more than Capote's.

12. See D. A. Miller, *Bringing Out Roland Barthes* (Los Angeles: University of California Press, 1992): "Consider how the two semantically opposed, morphologically identical words, *effeminate* and *emasculate* (in French *efféminé* and *émasculé*), instead of together defining a state of genderlessness, synonymously converge in a single attribute that may be predicated only of men" (15). For manly virtue, see Erik Gunderson, *Staging Masculinity: The Rhetoric of Performance in the Roman World* (Ann Arbor: University of Michigan Press, 2000), 7.

13. Raewyn Connell [R. W.], *Gender and Power: Society, the Person, and Sexual Politics* (Stanford, Calif.: Stanford University Press, 1987), 186. Also see Connell's *Masculinities* (Los Angeles: University of California Press, 1995): "Gayness, in patriarchal ideology, is the repository of whatever is symbolically expelled from hegemonic masculinity, the items ranging from fastidious taste in home decoration to receptive anal pleasure. Hence, from the point of view of hegemonic masculinity, gayness is easily assimilated to femininity" (78).

14. Eve Kosofsky Sedgwick, "How to Bring Your Kids Up Gay: The War on Effeminate Boys," in *Tendencies* (Durham, N.C.: Duke University Press, 1993), 154–64. The 2012 revision of the American Psychiatric Association's diagnostic guidelines scrapped "gender identity disorder" for "gender dysphoria" and no longer distinguishes significantly between "disordered" boys' desire for inappropriate activity and "disordered" girls' refusal of expected activity. See "gender dysphoria" in *Diagnostic and Statistical Manual of Mental Disorders: DSM-5*, 5th ed. (Washington, D.C.: American Psychiatric Association, 2013), 451–59. Most of the current discussion of "gender dysphoria" concerns transgender children, rather than effeminate boys and masculine girls who are not transgender.

15. Tara McPherson, *Reconstructing Dixie: Race, Gender, and Nostalgia in the Imagined South* (Durham, N.C.: Duke University Press, 2003), 17; Herschel Brickell, introduction to *O. Henry Memorial Award Prize Stories of 1946* (New York: Doubleday, 1946), xiv; Carlos Baker, "Deep-South Guignol," *New York Times Book Review*, January 18, 1948, 5; McPherson, *Reconstructing Dixie*, 19.

16. Arvin endured a more definite public exposure when his 1960 prosecution for harboring homosexual pornography became national news. See Barry Werth, *The Scarlet Professor* (New York: Random House, 2001).

17. Larsen, "*LIFE* Visits Yaddo." The ads are run on each side of the photos reproduced in Plate 4, and are the same size. In *The Scarlet Professor* (101), Werth clarifies that Capote's room (the Tower Room) was directly up the stairs from Arvin's bedroom (Lady Katrina's boudoir). The bottom-row photos depict authors Granville Hicks and Jerry Mangione (112) and the gravestones of Lady Katrina and her two husbands (113).

18. "Young U.S. Writers: A Refreshing Group of Newcomers on the Literary Scene

Is Ready to Tackle Almost Anything," *LIFE*, June 2, 1947, 75–83. Photographers for the last six portraits include Cooke, Lisa Larsen, Joe Scherschel, and Loran F. Smith.

19. Jean Stafford, *The Mountain Lion* (New York: Harcourt, Brace, 1947); Thomas Heggen, *Mr. Roberts* (New York: Houghton Mifflin, 1946); Calder Willingham, *End as a Man* (New York: Vanguard Press, 1947); Elizabeth Fenwick, *The Long Wing* (New York: Rinehart, 1947).

20. Willingham, *End as a Man*, 236; *End as a Man: A Play in Three Acts* (New York: Liebling-Wood, 1953); *The Strange One*, directed by Jack Garfein, screenplay by Willingham (Columbia Pictures, 1957). See Vito Russo, *The Celluloid Closet: Homosexuality in the Movies*, rev. ed. (New York: Harper & Row, 1987), 100–112, for a gay reading of this movie. Willingham stayed in Hollywood and is known today for the screenplay of *The Graduate*, written with Buck Henry and directed by Mike Nichols (Embassy Pictures, 1967).

21. There is some evidence that this room is Capote's own. Capote was often photographed at home, and one might read a conflation of two visual tropes: that of the male homosexual subject occupying domestic space, marked as feminine and thus here effeminate, and that of the tradition of photographing the professional at his workplace, here his home. These readings are foreclosed by the following quartet of photos, which strongly associate the authors with their books' content.

22. *Webster's Collegiate Dictionary*, 5th ed., s.v. "esoteric." When possible, I use dictionaries and encyclopedias of the period discussed.

23. Capote, *Other Voices*, 9, 65.

24. I have some evidence of this in a January 14, 2016, e-mail message from the Jerry Cooke Archives in East Hampton, New York, but I cannot make a definite confirmation.

25. John Chamberlain, "Critic Finds New Authors Work Things Out in Their Own Ways," *LIFE*, June 2, 1947, 81–82; "Young U.S. Writers," 76; Vidal, *In a Yellow Wood*.

26. Chamberlain, "Critic Finds New Authors"; Bennett Cerf, *At Random: The Reminiscences of Bennett Cerf* (New York: Random House, 1977), 224. *Other Voices* was not officially published until January 1948 but could be bought before.

27. Cerf, *At Random*, 223. On a small scale, Capote's skill may be seen in John Malcolm Brinnin's journal from Yaddo in *Truman Capote: Dear Heart, Old Buddy* (New York: Delacorte, 1986), 5. Capote sat "in an ivory-colored bishop's chair holding a photograph of himself—the one taken in the same chair some weeks ago and enlarged to page size in *LIFE* . . . . [H]e holds up the photograph, in turn, to Mrs. Aswell, to Newton, and to me. 'I don't look *that* petulant, do I?'"

28. Mary Jane Ward, *The Snake Pit* (New York: Random House, 1946); Cerf, *At Random*, 228, 227.

29. Brickell, introduction to *O. Henry Memorial Award Prize Stories*, iii.

30. Calder Willingham to Gore Vidal, 1948, quoted in Kaplan, *Gore Vidal*, 276; J. Mitzel and S. Abbot, "The Fag Rag Interview" (1975), in *Gore Vidal: Sexually Speaking*, ed. D. Weise (San Francisco: Cleis, 1999), 209.

31. Judith Butler, *Gender Trouble* (New York: Routledge, 1990), 177.

32. Truman Capote, *In Cold Blood* (New York: Random, 1966); Mitzel and Abbot,

"Fag Rag Interview," 209; Truman Capote, *Answered Prayers* (New York: Random House, 1987).

33. In *Other Voices*, Joel's desire for escape is paralleled in the character of Missouri "Zooey" Fever, who is tied to the plantation by her centenarian grandfather Jesus Fever, formerly a slave at the Landing. Zooey, who survives a throat cutting before the novel begins, escapes the Landing only to be gang-raped on the road and then return. For a possible source for Zooey's story in the 1956 rape of a black woman in Monroeville, Alabama, see Thomas Fahy's "Violating the Black Body: Sexual Violence in Truman Capote's *Other Voices, Other Rooms*," *Journal of the Midwest Modern Language Association* 46, no. 1 (Spring 2013): 27–42.

Zooey exemplifies Capote's complex, troubled treatment of race in his writing, most notably seen in *The Muses Are Heard* (New York: Random House, 1956), his travelogue of the touring company of *Porgy and Bess* in the Soviet Union; and in "House of Flowers" in *Breakfast at Tiffany's: A Short Novel and Three Stories* (New York: Random House, 1958), a short story about a fantastic (in both senses) Haitian bordello. "House of Flowers" was adapted into a failed 1954 musical of the same name, with music by Harold Arlen and a notable performance by Pearl Bailey, whose person and performance are themselves the subject of Capote's "Derring-Do," a nonfiction portrait in *Music for Chameleons: New Writing* (New York: Random House, 1980), 196–210.

34. Capote, *Other Voices*, 231. Does Joel go upstairs to pay court to Randolph's eighteenth-century French "lady," in which case the "boy becomes a man"? Or does Joel go upstairs to do his own hair in ringlets? In "Truman Capote: Homosexual or Transgendered?," *Gender and Psychoanalysis* (Winter 2000): 67–80, David Seil reads *Other Voices* as a novel of a specifically transgender adolescence, and its climax as Joel's—and Capote's—embrace of his female nature. After Ken Corbett, discussed presently, I read Randolph's drag and Joel's embrace of it as dictated by a gender dialectic that leaves "feminine" expression as the only legible expression of nonstraight masculinity—though I do read other characters as transgender. These distinctions are exceedingly hard to make when queer specificities are obscured by misogyny and homophobia.

35. Of the national reviews of *Other Voices*, only *Newsweek* straightforwardly states that "this is the story of a young boy and his growth into a homosexual." See *Newsweek*, January 26, 1948, 91; J. Cross, review, *Library Journal* 72 (1947): 1685; Baker, "Deep-South Guignol," 4; Lloyd Morris, "A Vivid, Inner, Secret World," *New York Herald Tribune Weekly Book Review*, January 18, 1948, 2; Orville Prescott, review, *New York Times*, January 21, 1948; Elizabeth Hardwick, "Much Outcry," *Partisan Review* 15 (1948): 347–77; "Spare the Laurels," *TIME*, January 26, 1948, 102.

36. "Spare the Laurels," 102.

37. R. E. Berg and editor, "Mossy Trappings," letter to the editor, *TIME*, February 16, 1948, 8–9 (ellipses Berg's); "Medicine," *TIME*, January 5, 1948, 66 (ellipses mine).

38. Prescott, review, 23.

39. Ken Corbett, "Cross-Gendered Identifications and Homosexual Boyhood: Toward a More Complex Theory of Gender," *American Journal of Orthopsychiatry* 68, no. 3

(July 1998): 352; Judith Butler, "Violence, Mourning, Politics," *Studies in Gender and Sexuality* 4, no. 1 (2000): 22.

Recent readings of the gay self in *Other Voices*—though not in those words—include Joseph Valente, "Other Voices, Other Drives: Queer, Counterfactual 'Life' in Truman Capote's *Other Voices, Other Rooms*," *Modern Fiction Studies* 59, no. 3 (Fall 2013): 526–46; Tison Pugh, "Boundless Hearts in a Nightmare World: Queer Sentimentalism and Southern Gothicism in Truman Capote's *Other Voices, Other Rooms*," *Mississippi Quarterly* 51, no. 4 (1998): 663–82; and Brian Mitchell-Peters, "Camping the Gothic: Que(e)ring Sexuality in Truman Capote's *Other Voices, Other Rooms*," *Journal of Homosexuality* 39, no. 1 (2000): 107–38. Marvin Megeling offers a particularly cogent but homophobic reading in "*Other Voices, Other Rooms*: Oedipus between the Covers," *American Imago* 19, no. 4 (Winter 1962): 361–74.

40. A reclining Jeanne Recamier was also painted by Gerard (1802). The distinctions between the recamier, the fainting couch, the divan, the sofa, the settee, and the chaise longue are both precise and often conflated under the catchall term *couch*. Relevant to our purpose here is the constant feminine connotation of lying recumbent upon a couch of any guise. I am grateful for Joseph Boone's analysis of how certain tropes of nineteenth-century orientalist painting, among them an "indolent posture," "connote fin-de-siècle decadence and ennui that hint at sexual difference or inversion" in his epic *The Homoerotics of Orientalism* (New York: Columbia University Press, 2014), 362. Capote offers a more assured homo-orientalist vision in a 1949 portrait by Cecil Beaton where Capote reclines in scanty briefs, sports a short turban, and smokes a cigarette from a long holder at the feet of Jane Bowles.

41. T. J. Clark, *The Painting of Modern Life* (Princeton, N.J.: Princeton University Press, 1984), 96.

42. Neither may Capote have a maid, the black presence at the heart of Manet's painting. But Capote's exotic persona does rhyme with the painting's interplay of race, sexuality, and gender, as the southern gentleman's hegemonic masculinity is always compromised by his aristocratic sensibility, his intimacy with black men and women, and the memory of Southern defeat.

43. Hilton Als, "The Women," *Grand Street* 49 (1994): 95; Laura Mulvey, "Visual Pleasure and Narrative Cinema" (1975), in *Feminisms: An Anthology of Literary Theory and Criticism,* ed. Robyn R. Warhol and Diane Price Herndl (New Brunswick, N.J.: Rutgers University Press, 1991), 433; Als, "The Women," 96.

44. For gender, authorship, and the market, see Catherine Gallagher, *Nobody's Story: The Vanishing Acts of Women Writers in the Marketplace, 1670–1820* (Los Angeles: University of California Press, 1994); and Nancy Glazener, *Reading for Realism: The History of a U.S. Literary Institution, 1850–1910* (Durham, N.C.: Duke University Press, 1997).

45. Clarke, *Capote,* 158.

46. Brinnin, *Truman Capote,* 34 (italics his).

47. "Young U.S. Writers," 109.

48. Baker, "Deep-South Guignol," 4.
49. Cecil Beaton, *The Face of the World* (New York: John Day, 1957), 35; Ned Rorem, "What Truman Capote Means to Me," *Christopher Street*, October 1984, 150. Beaton took many photos of Capote; for more on the "princeling" photo, see note 40 above.
50. See J. Coplans, "Crazy Golden Slippers," *LIFE*, January 21, 1957, 12–13.
51. Victor Bockris, *The Life and Death of Andy Warhol* (New York: Bantam, 1989), 53; Barbara Guest, "Clarke, Rager, Warhol [Loft]," *Art News* 53, no. 4 (1954): 75. For the inextricability of homosexuality from Warhol's public persona and fame, see Wayne Koestenbaum, *The Queen's Throat: Opera, Homosexuality, and the Mystery of Desire* (New York: Poseidon, 1993); and Richard Meyer, *Outlaw Representation: Censorship and Homosexuality in Twentieth-Century American Art* (New York: Oxford University Press, 2002).
52. "People," *TIME*, March 15, 1948, 44. Miller and Capote published their first novels in the same season—Elizabeth Hardwick reviewed (and panned) both together in "Much Outcry; Little Outcome," *Partisan Review* 15 (1948): 347–77—and Capote's greater success may have powered Miller's anger. In 1971, Miller would write *On Being Different: What It Means to Be a Homosexual* (New York: Random House), and a repudiated identification with Capote may have affected his response to the photo. Hardwick's review of *Other Voices* is discussed in some detail in chapter 2.
53. "Other Voices, Other Authors," *TIME*, May 3, 1948, 86. Shulman is best known today for *The Many Loves of Dobie Gillis* (New York: Doubleday, 1951) and *The Tender Trap*, with R. P. Smith (New York: Random House, 1955). Both were filmed under his supervision as, respectively, *The Affairs of Dobie Gillis* (MGM, 1953) and *The Tender Trap* (MGM, 1955), and the first inspired a popular television series, *The Many Loves of Dobie Gillis* (20th Century Fox Television, 1959–1963). Shulman's name is frequently misspelled "Schulman."
54. Who was Mina Turner? My best guess: the granddaughter of photographer Gertrude Kasebier (1852–1934) who worked in her grandmother's studio and bequeathed much of Kasebier's work to museums. Turner's nephew cannot confirm this pedigree, however.
55. "Other Voices, Other Authors," 86; Capote, *Other Voices*, 6.
56. Ken Corbett, "More Life: Centrality and Marginality in Human Development," *Psychoanalytic Dialogues* 11 (2001): 321.

2. Capote, Forster, and the Trillings

1. George Plimpton, ed., *Truman Capote: In Which Various Friends, Enemies, Acquaintances, and Detractors Recall His Turbulent Career* (New York: Doubleday, 1997), 70–71; Truman Capote, *Other Voices, Other Rooms* (New York: Random House, 1948); "Miriam," *Mademoiselle*, June 1945; "A Tree of Night," *Harper's Bazaar*, October 1945; Lisa Larsen, "*LIFE* Visits Yaddo," *LIFE*, July 15, 1946, 110–13.
2. Irving Howe named the group well after its heyday in "The New York Intellectuals: A Chronicle and Critique," *Commentary* 46, no. 4 (1968): 29–51. Though the cohort retained the fervent rhetoric and style of its Old Left origins, the NYIs would cease to be ideologically coherent as its members variously reacted to the

Cold War and anticommunist fervor of the 1950s and the social movements of the '60s. A very few, such as Howe, maintained their socialism throughout their life. Many, such as Leslie Fiedler and the Trillings, remained on the left, though they were wary of the New Left and the radicalisms of the 1960s. Some, such as Irving Kristol and Norman Podhoretz, moved far to the right, provided the intellectual underpinnings of neoconservatism, and became important figures in the Reagan and George W. Bush administrations. Those associated with the group include Hannah Arendt, Daniel Bell, Midge Decter, Nathan Glazer, Michael Gold, Clement Greenberg, Elizabeth Hardwick, Alfred Kazin, Norman Mailer, Bernard Malamud, Mary McCarthy, Philip Rahv, Meyer Schapiro, Delmore Schwartz, Susan Sontag, and Edmund Wilson.

3. Lionel Trilling, *Matthew Arnold* (New York: Norton, 1939); *E. M. Forster* (Norfolk, Conn.: New Directions, 1943); *The Liberal Imagination: Essays on Literature and Society* (New York: Viking, 1950).

4. Lerman and Capote became close at Yaddo in 1946. Lerman, then an arts writer for *Vogue* and *Harper's Bazaar,* would come to hold several editorial posts at Condé Nast, including features editor at *Vogue* and editor in chief of *Vanity Fair.* See *The Grand Surprise: The Journals of Leo Lerman,* ed. George Pascal (New York: Knopf, 2007).

5. Plimpton, *Truman Capote,* 70–71 (italics Plimpton's, ellipses mine); Diana Trilling, *The Beginning of the Journey: The Marriage of Diana and Lionel Trilling* (New York: Harcourt Brace, 1993); Capote to Leo Lerman, August 16, 1946, in *Too Brief a Treat: The Letters of Truman Capote,* ed. Gerald Clarke (New York: Random House, 2004), 30–31; Capote to Pidgy Aswell, August 17, 1946, in Clarke, *Too Brief a Treat,* 31–32.

6. The ambivalence and complexity of Lionel Trilling's thoughts on ethnic identification are evident in his criticism, fiction, and career as editor of the *Menorah Journal* (1925–31). Consider "Under Forty: A Symposium on American Literature and the Younger Generation of American Jews," *Contemporary Jewish Record* 6 (February 1944): 3–36, reprinted in *Speaking of Literature and Society* (New York: Harcourt, 1980), 197–201. Typically, Trilling begins the five pages of the reprint with "It is never possible for a Jew of my generation to 'escape' his Jewish origin" (198) and ends, "I know of writers who have used their Jewish experience as the subject of excellent work; I know of no writer in English who has added a micromillimetre to his stature by 'realizing his Jewishness,' although I know of some who have curtailed their promise by trying to heighten their Jewish consciousness" (201). Diana Trilling discusses Lionel's Judaism in relation to his career in "Lionel Trilling: A Jew at Columbia," *Commentary* (March 1979): 40–46.

7. Joseph Waldmeir and John Waldmeir, eds., *The Critical Response to Truman Capote* (Westport, Conn.: Greenwood Press, 1999); *Truman Capote,* ed. Harold Bloom, Bloom's Modern Critical Views (Philadelphia: Chelsea, 2003). Peter Christensen's "Capote as Gay American Author," in *The Critical Response* (61–66), offers a useful overview of how Capote's homosexuality and the homosexual content and themes of his writing were perceived in academic criticism up until the 1990s. Although

Christensen does not directly address Capote's politics or political impact, he does touch on how gay liberation influenced Capote criticism.

Thomas Fahy addresses this dearth in the recent *Understanding Truman Capote* (Columbia: University of South Carolina Press, 2014), which situates Capote's work within its political context, especially in relation to race.

8. Truman Capote, *In Cold Blood* (New York: Random House, 1966); *Capote,* directed by Bennett Miller (Sony, 2005); *Infamous,* directed by Douglas McGrath (Warner, 2006). For relations between Capote's life, book, and these movies, see Tison Pugh, *Truman Capote: A Literary Life at the Movies* (Athens: University of Georgia Press, 2014). For a comprehensive analysis of *In Cold Blood* and its antecedents and impact, see Ralph Voss, *Truman Capote and the Legacy of "In Cold Blood,"* (Tuscaloosa: University of Alabama Press, 2011).

9. Capote, *In Cold Blood; Other Voices; The Grass Harp* (New York: Random House, 1951); *Breakfast at Tiffany's* (New York: Random House, 1958); "Tree of Night"; *Breakfast at Tiffany's,* directed by Blake Edwards (Paramount, 1961). Capote published only one book after *In Cold Blood* while alive, a collection of short pieces, *Music for Chameleons* (New York: Random House, 1980).

10. World War II largely overwhelmed the homosexual subcultures and political movements active in the United States through the 1920s and '30s. The traditional markers for the next phases of the gay and lesbian timeline—the homophile and gay rights movements—are the first meetings of the Mattachine Society, in 1950, and the Daughters of Bilitis, in 1955; and the Stonewall Riots of 1969. These markers are more convenient and traditional than strictly accurate; that said, Capote had no overt connection with any of the nascent homophile groups active in 1946, though he was very much a part of a homosexual community. For a history of gay male community and identity, see George Chauncey, *Gay New York: Gender, Urban Culture, and the Makings of the Gay Male World, 1890–1940* (New York: Basic Books, 1994); Jeffrey Escoffier, *American Homo: Community and Perversity* (Berkeley: University of California Press, 1998); and John D'Emilio, *Sexual Politics, Sexual Communities* (Chicago: University of Chicago Press, 1983).

11. See Terence Kissack, "Freaking Fag Revolutionaries: New York's Gay Liberation Front," *Radical History Review* 62 (1995): 104–34, for a helpful assessment of the place of effeminacy in the GLF. I am not sure how gay radicals would have viewed, say, Capote's live televised interviews on, say, *The Stanley Siegel Show* on July 16, 1978, and June 5, 1979. Capote is obviously drunk, openly discusses suicide, and is a font of sexual innuendo about Jackie Kennedy Onassis. He is also extraordinarily aggressive in asserting his homosexuality: "I'll tell you something about fags, especially southern fags. We is mean."

While presenting this work in public forums, I have been surprised to receive comments from those who experienced Capote's celebrity firsthand in the 1970s and understood it in terms of gay liberation. More than once, an unprompted comparison was made between Capote's loud assertion of gay identity and Vidal's great pains to separate sex between men from gay identity. For these men and women, Capote's public performance was valuable.

12. Claude Summers, *Gay Fictions: Wilde to Stonewall* (New York: Continuum, 1990).

There are surprisingly few overviews of gay fiction per se, and those few tend not to be written by literary scholars. As Jaime Harker says in "'Look Baby, I Know You': Gay Fiction and the Cold War Era," *American Literary History* 22, no. 1: 191–206, in a review of Michael Sherry's *Gay Artists in Modern American Culture: An Imagined Conspiracy* (Chapel Hill: University of North Carolina Press, 2007) and Bertram Cohler's *Writing Desire: Sixty Years of Gay Autobiography* (Madison: University of Wisconsin Press, 2007), "The fact that both include 'gay,' not 'queer,' in their titles marks a diversion from queer theory, particularly regarding identity politics. The books, then, suggest what has been left behind in queer theory's grand march across the disciplines" (191).

13. Gore Vidal, *The City and the Pillar* (New York: Dutton, 1948). Summers's positioning of *The City and the Pillar* as a story of "ordinary," "healthy" men forces him to discount the novel's end, when the spurned hero murders his high school crush. In Vidal's 1965 update, *The City and the Pillar Revised* (New York: Dutton), the murder becomes a rape. Whether Vidal's hero is "healthy" is questionable, but the decoupling of effeminacy and homosexuality is not, which accounts for the higher status of *The City* among those invested in the virile, "manly" homosexual.

The comparison of McCullers and Capote, which dates from the latter's earliest reviews, stems not only from thematic similarities—both wrote gothic fictions concerned with queer desires and set in the South—but also from their common southern background and from McCullers's role in introducing Capote to literary society. The comparison is almost always to Capote's detriment. Typically, in *An End to Innocence* (Boston: Beacon Press, 1955), Leslie Fiedler notes that "[t]he most important writer of this group is Carson McCullers, the most typical Truman Capote"—"this group" variously standing for homosexual writers, southern writers, or writers who publish in women's magazines (202). Regardless of merit, McCullers, as a woman, was more likely to be welcomed as the writer of such fiction than Capote, who, though an effeminate man, was still a man and was expected to write about manly things.

14. "Desire and the Black Masseur" was included in Williams's *One Arm and Other Stories* (New York: New Directions, 1948), 83–94, which was published in a limited edition of fifteen hundred by a small press, was not widely reviewed, and was not generally available in plain sight but had to be requested from behind the counter. *One Arm* thus had a much lower profile than its contemporaries, *Other Voices, Other Rooms* and *The City and the Pillar*.

15. Truman Capote, *Answered Prayers: The Unfinished Novel* (New York: Random House, 1987); Gerald Clarke, *Capote* (New York: Ballantine, 1988); Jay Presson Allan, *Tru* (Booth Theatre, New York, December 1989–September 1, 1990); Plimpton, *Truman Capote; The Complete Stories of Truman Capote* (New York: Random House, 2004); *Too Brief a Treat*; Truman Capote, *Summer Crossing* (New York: Random House, 2005); *Portraits and Observations: The Essays of Truman Capote* (New York: Random House, 2007). The simultaneous development of the films *Capote* (2005, based on the Clarke biography) and *Infamous* (2006, based on the Plimpton oral history) illustrates Capote's appeal for the highbrow sector of the mass market—or, more precisely, for those who determine what subjects are likely to appeal to those who

attend upmarket films with middling budgets and an acclaimed cast. As usual, such twinning was to the detriment of the film released second. *Capote* had worldwide sales of almost $50 million and an Academy Award for Best Actor (Philip Seymour Hoffman), as well as nominations for Best Picture, Best Director, Best Supporting Actress, and Best Adapted Screenplay. *Infamous* earned receipts just over $1 million and an Independent Spirit Award nomination for Daniel Craig for Best Supporting Actor. The combined impact of both movies returned the Clarke biography (reissued in 2005) and *In Cold Blood* to the bestseller lists.

16. There has been a welcome, if tiny, uptick in work on Capote of late, though little of it could be situated comfortably in queer studies. See n. 7 for Fahy's *Understanding Truman Capote,* and n. 8 for Pugh's *Truman Capote: A Literary Life at the Movies.* Bede Scott reads *Breakfast at Tiffany's* through Japanese literature and Roland Barthes to consider how the novel privileges style over "meaning" in "On Superficiality: Truman Capote and the Ceremony of Style," *Journal of Modern Literature* 34, no. 4 (Spring 2011): 128–48. Michael P. Bibler's "How to Love Your Local Homophobe: Southern Hospitality and the Unremarkable Queerness of Truman Capote's 'The Thanksgiving Visitor,'" *Modern Fiction Studies* 58, no. 2 (2012): 284–307, uses queer theory to offer a fine-grained analysis of one of Capote's most popular stories. See chap. 1, n. 39, for recent readings of *Other Voices.*

17. Lerman, *Grand Surprise,* 31–32 (ellipses mine).

18. D. Trilling, *Beginning of the Journey*; L. Trilling, *E. M. Forster*; Capote, "Miriam"; Plimpton, *Truman Capote*; Capote to Aswell, August 17, 1946, 31–32; Capote to Lerman, August 16, 1946, 30–31; Barry Werth, *The Scarlet Professor: Newton Arvin, a Literary Life Shattered by Scandal* (New York: Talese, 2001), 109; D. Trilling, review of *Other Voices* in *The Nation,* January 31, 1948, 133–34.

19. Plimpton, *Truman Capote,* 71; E. M. Forster, *Maurice* (London: E. Arnold, 1971).

20. D. Trilling, *Beginning of the Journey,* 110; Plimpton, *Truman Capote,* 70.

21. Lerman to Hunter, June 8, 1946, in *Too Brief a Treat,* 32–33; Capote to Aswell, August 17, 1946, 32; Capote to Lerman, August 16, 1946, 31; D. Trilling, *Beginning of the Journey,* 110; Plimpton, *Truman Capote,* 70.

22. Plimpton, *Truman Capote,* 70; L. Trilling, *E. M. Forster.*

23. William Kurtz Wimsatt Jr. and Monroe Beardsley, "The Intentional Fallacy," *Sewanee Review* 54 (1946): 468–88; "The Affective Fallacy," *Sewanee Review* 57 (1949): 31–35; T. S. Eliot, "Hamlet and His Problems," in *The Sacred Wood* (London: Methuen, 1920), 87–94; "Tradition and the Individual Talent," in *The Sacred Wood,* 42–53. The fallacies are more clearly articulated in, and often dated from, the revisions included in Wimsatt and Beardsley's *The Verbal Icon: Studies in the Meaning of Poetry* (Lexington: University of Kentucky Press, 1954).

24. Forster, *Maurice*; *Where Angels Fear To Tread* (London: Blackwood, 1905); *The Longest Journey* (London: Blackwood, 1907); *A Room with a View* (London: Arnold, 1908; repr., New York: Vintage, 1986); *Howards End* (London: Arnold, 1910); *A Passage to India* (London: Arnold, 1924); Plimpton, *Truman Capote,* 71.

25. L. Trilling, *E. M. Forster,* 2nd ed. (New York: New Directions, 1964), 4; Forster, *Maurice*; D. Trilling, *Beginning of the Journey.* For another example of Lionel Trilling's distaste for blunt discussions of sexuality, and for his criticism of Kinsey's

finding that, in Trilling's words, "homosexuality is to be accepted as a form of sexuality like another and that it is as 'natural' as heterosexuality," see "Sex and Science: The Kinsey Report," his review of Kinsey, Pomeroy, and Martin's *Sexual Behavior in the Human Male, Partisan Review* 15 (1948): 460–76, reprinted as "The Kinsey Report" in Trilling's *Liberal Imagination,* 223–42 (quote on p. 240). Trilling's views on homosexuality evolved in the 1960s.

26. L. Trilling, preface to *Liberal Imagination,* ix, xiii, xv; L. Trilling, *E. M. Forster,* 1st ed., 11–12.

27. L. Trilling, *E. M. Forster,* 1st ed., 13.

28. D. Trilling, *Beginning of the Journey,* 110; L. Trilling, ibid., 111–12, 113 (ellipses mine); E. M. Forster, *The Life to Come* (London: Arnold, 1972).

29. Forster, *Room with a View,* 80.

30. Ibid., 124; Eric Haralson, "Thinking about Homosex in Forster and James," in *Queer Forster,* ed. Robert K. Martin and George Piggford (Chicago: University of Chicago Press, 1997), 62. Haralson's close reading of the bathing scene bears out Capote's argument that Forster's sexuality can be productively brought to bear on his work. By contrast, consider Jeffrey Heath, "Kissing and Telling: Turning Round in *A Room with a View,*" *Twentieth Century Literature,* 40, no. 4 (1994): 393–433. Heath's treatment of the "real" in *Room* avoids Forster's sexuality, despite its relevance to a reading concerned with the contrast between "spontaneous" and "muddled" responses to life, the last being "what results when people ignore their deepest promptings and respond dishonestly and indirectly to experience as they are expected or told to do" (396). For Lucy, this deep prompting is not a "secondhand story or painting but . . . a living man, George Emerson, who kisses her: a real experience she can deny but never forget" (400).

31. Forster, *Room with a View,* 150–51.

32. Forster, *Maurice;* Leslie Fiedler, "Come Back to the Raft Ag'in, Huck Honey!," *Partisan Review* 15 (1948): 664–71. Fiedler argues that throughout the history of American literature, pairs of men, frequently of different races, flee from the domesticity and civilized constraints of the world of women. Fiedler reads the unspoken but strongly implied homoerotics as a boyish wish of (male) American writers and readers—a symptom of delayed adolescence along Freudian lines. Another prominent midcentury literary critic who reads homosexuality as a symptom rather than a subject in and of itself is John Aldridge, who in *After the Lost Generation: A Critical Study of the Writers of Two Wars* (New York: Noonday, 1951) argues that the presence of homosexuality (and racial conflict) in post–World War II fiction is a response to the exhaustion of the modernist tradition and the need for new means to engage readers. According to Aldridge, writers such as Capote, Vidal, Paul Bowles, and Norman Mailer are not writing about homosexuality per se but rather developing "new subject matter which [had] not been fully exploited in the past and which, therefore, still [had] emotive power" (9). Fiedler's and Aldridge's arguments bear witness both to the ability of midcentury critics to discuss homosexuality and the tendency for them to see it as a symptom rather than a subject.

33. L. Trilling, *E. M. Forster,* 1st ed., 106, 106, 99.

34. F. R. Leavis, "E. M. Forster," *Scrutiny* 7, no. 2 (1938), quoted in Martin and Piggford,

introduction to *Queer Forster*, 15; L. Trilling, ibid., 16 (ellipses mine); Martin and Piggford, 17.
35. L. Trilling, preface to *Liberal Imagination*, xiv.
36. Capote, *Other Voices*; Elizabeth Hardwick, "Much Outcry; Little Outcome," review of *Other Voices, Other Rooms*, by Truman Capote, *Partisan Review* 15 (1948): 376. To put Hardwick in perspective, among those who did take homosexuality seriously in the 1940s were the neopsychoanalytic schools and hospitals attempting to "cure" it. Hardwick neither authorized a medical experiment on a homosexual nor tried to link the "perversion" of *Other Voices* back to its author.
37. Christopher Isherwood, *A Single Man* (New York: Simon & Schuster, 1964); Elizabeth Hardwick, "Sex and the Single Man," review of *A Single Man*, by Christopher Isherwood, *New York Review of Books*, August 20, 1964, 17; *Sleepless Nights* (New York: Random House, 1979), 30, 30, 19; Joan Didion, "Meditation on a Life," review of *Sleepless Nights*, by Elizabeth Hardwick, *New York Times Book Review*, April 29, 1979, 1, 60.
38. Leslie Fiedler, "Adolescence and Maturity in the American Novel," in *End to Innocence*, 201 (ellipses mine), first published in *The New Republic*, May 2, 1955, 16–18.
39. Capote to Lerman, August 16, 1946, 31; Capote to Aswell, August 17, 1946, 32.
40. D. Trilling, *Beginning of the Journey*, 331; Fiedler, *End to Innocence*, 201–2, 204.
41. Fiedler, *End to Innocence*, 206, 203. In the 1998 documentary *Arguing the World*, directed by Joseph Dorman (First Run, 1998), Diana Trilling recollects the outsider status of women among the New York Intellectuals: "Unless a man in the intellectual community was bent on sexual conquest, he was never intimate with a woman. He wanted to be with the men. They always wanted to huddle in a corner to talk." Irving Kristol corroborates D. Trilling's account with an anecdote of sitting down with a plate of party food and being sandwiched by Hannah Arendt, Diana Trilling, and Mary McCarthy, who began to discuss psychoanalysis: "I sat there quiet and terror-stricken. I was a prisoner."
42. Fiedler, *End to Innocence*, 202. For another example of a troubled, hostile reaction to Truman Capote by an intellectual New York woman (if not, perhaps, a New York Intellectual) see the bitter reassessment of his person and work by Cynthia Ozick, "Truman Capote Reconsidered," in *Art and Ardor* (New York: Knopf, 1983), 80–89.
43. D. Trilling, review of *Other Voices*, 133–34. Trilling's reviews are collected in *Reviewing the Forties*, ed. Paul Fussell (London: Harcourt, 1978). For easy reference, in-text citations are taken from the latter.
44. Reviews were originally published in *The Nation* and are, in order of appearance, of Rupert Croft-Crooke, *Miss Allick*, July 5, 1947; Josephine Herbst, *Somewhere the Tempest Fell*, December 13, 1947; Isabel Bolton, *Do I Wake or Sleep*, November 30, 1946; Helen Howe, *We Happy Few*, July 13, 1946; John Hersey, *A Bell for Adano*, May 26, 1945; and Katherine Anne Porter, *The Leaning Tower and Other Stories*, September 23, 1944. In-text citations are taken from D. Trilling, *Reviewing the Forties*. Note that Trilling explicitly praises Bolton's treatment of homosexuality over Capote's, as "Miss Bolton blames no one . . . [for her hero's] homosexuality" (256).
45. Howe, "New York Intellectuals," 34.

46. D. Trilling, *Beginning of the Journey*, 328, 349–50. In her autobiography, Trilling discusses her interest in psychoanalysis, both as a critic and as an analysand.

47. Christopher Isherwood, *Prater Violet* (New York: Random House, 1945); D. Trilling, review of *Prater Violet*, *The Nation*, November 17, 1945, 530–32, reprinted in *Reviewing the Forties*, 137–40.

48. L. Trilling, preface to *Liberal Imagination*, xiii; D. Trilling, *Beginning of the Journey*, 70; D. Trilling, *Reviewing the Forties*, 230.

3. Gertrude Stein, Opium Queen

Stein has inspired many biographies, with different foci and strengths. Because chapters 3 through 5 consider changing perceptions of the homosexuality of Stein's self and work, biographies from a variety of decades were invaluable. This was my "timeline of biographies": Donald Sutherland, *Gertrude Stein: A Biography of Her Work* (New Haven, Conn.: Yale University Press, 1951); John Malcolm Brinnin, *The Third Rose: Gertrude Stein and Her World* (Boston: Little, Brown, 1959); Richard Bridgman, *Gertrude Stein in Pieces* (New York: Oxford University Press, 1970); James R. Mellow, *Charmed Circle: Gertrude Stein and Company* (New York: Praeger, 1974); Janet Hobhouse, *Everybody Who Was Anybody: A Biography of Gertrude Stein* (New York: Putnam, 1975); Jayne L. Walker, *The Making of a Modernist: Gertrude Stein from "Three Lives" to "Tender Buttons"* (Amherst: University of Massachusetts Press, 1984); Diana Souhami, *Gertrude and Alice* (London: Pandora, 1990); Linda Wagner-Martin, *"Favored Strangers": Gertrude Stein and Her Family* (New Brunswick, N.J.: Rutgers University Press, 1995); and Brenda Wineapple, *Brother/Sister: Gertrude and Leo Stein* (New York: Putnam, 1996). Publication details for Stein's work are compiled primarily from Robert A. Wilson, ed., *Gertrude Stein: A Bibliography* (New York: The Phoenix Bookshop, 1974) and Julian Sawyer, ed., *Gertrude Stein: A Bibliography* (New York: Arrow Editions, 1940). Figures exclude deluxe editions of ten or fewer. The Wilson is more reliable, but the Sawyer can be more detailed in material specifics, as can Robert Bartlett Haas and Donald Clifford Gallup, eds., *A Catalogue of the Published and Unpublished Writings of Gertrude Stein* (New Haven, Conn.: Yale University Library, 1941). For critical writings, I looked to Ray Lewis, *Gertrude Stein and Alice B. Toklas: A Reference Guide* (Boston: Hall, 1984).

1. Gertrude Stein, *The Autobiography of Alice B. Toklas* (New York: Harcourt Brace, 1933).

2. Wilson reports September 1 as the publication date of *The Autobiography*, but several bibliographers and biographers—including Haas and Gallup, *Catalogue*, and Souhami, *Gertrude and Alice*, who offers a helpful history of the publication's trajectory—offer September 30 but state that copies were available from September 22. Both dates are probably right, given the usual vagaries of publication.

   For *The Atlantic Monthly*, see Ellery Sedgwick, *The Atlantic Monthly, 1857–1909: Yankee Humanist at High Tide and Ebb* (Boston: University of Massachusetts Press, 1994). Bryce Conrad analyzes Stein's correspondence with Sedgwick in "Gertrude Stein in the American Marketplace," *Journal of Modern Literature* 19, no. 2 (Autumn 1995): 215–33. Also see Donald Gallup, "Gertrude Stein and the *Atlantic*," *Yale University Library Gazette* 28 (1954): 109.

3. Literary Guild of America circular, 1927, accessed August 5, 2015, via the Healey Library at the University of Massachusetts Boston, http://oubliette.library.umass .edu. Such ads were usual: "Advertisements encouraged potential customers to question their literary sophistication and their reading habits. Had book buyers been left out of conversations for not having read the latest novel?" James L. W. West III, "The Expansion of the Book Trade System," in *A History of the Book in America*, vol. 4, *Print in Motion: Books and Reading in the United States, 1880–1945*, ed. Carl F. Kaestle and Janice A. Radway (Chapel Hill: University of North Carolina Press, 2009), 83. The Book of the Month Club preceded the Literary Guild by a few months, and the guild positioned itself as slightly classier. Also see Janice A. Radway, *A Feeling for Books: The Book-of-the-Month Club, Literary Taste, and Middle-Class Desire* (Chapel Hill: University of North Carolina Press, 1999).

4. James Agee, "Stein's Way," *TIME*, September 11, 1933, 57–60; Gertrude Stein, *Four Saints in Three Acts*, libretto, music by Virgil Thomson (New York: Random House, 1934).

5. Stein, *The Autobiography*, 14.

6. In "Gertrude Stein: Humanism and Its Freaks," *Boundary 2* 12–13 (1984): 301–19, Catharine Stimpson observes that *The Autobiography* has not received the critical attention warranted by its success, as the more obviously experimental work of Stein had provoked much greater interest than her more accessible work, and as most critics discuss her work either before or after *The Autobiography*. More than twenty-five years later, the perceived rift between these two halves of Stein's work has been lessened and questioned, but it still exists. Much of the commentary (including this book) focuses as much on the context and success of *The Autobiography* as, if not more than, on its contents.

For the contemporary marketing of modernism to a mass audience, see Richard Keller Simon, "Modernism and Mass Culture," *American Literary History* 13, no. 2 (2001): 343–53; and Kevin J. H. Dettmar and Stephen Watt, eds., *Marketing Modernisms: Self-Promotion, Canonization, Rereading* (Ann Arbor: University of Michigan Press, 1996). For the interrelationship between Stein's works in particular and mass culture, see Alison Tischler, "A Rose Is a Pose: Steinian Modernism and Mass Culture," *Journal of Modern Literature* 26, nos. 3–4 (2003): 12–27; Loren Glass, *Authors Inc.: Literary Celebrity in the Modern United States, 1880–1980* (New York: New York University Press, 2004); and especially Liesl Olson's "'An Invincible Force Meets an Immovable Object': Gertrude Stein Comes to Chicago," *Modernism/ modernity* 17, no. 2 (2010): 331–61, which was a personal inspiration for this chapter in terms of its discussion of Stein's particular appeal to lesbians. For a play-by-play analysis of the selling of *The Autobiography of Alice B. Toklas* in the context of Stein's publication history, as well its composition within the context of Stein and Toklas's relationship, see Ulla Dydo with William Rice, *Gertrude Stein: The Language That Rises* (Evanston, Ill.: Northwestern University Press, 2003), 535–50. For Stein's conceptualization of herself as a businesswoman who "imagined [her] modernist project in terms of prevailing ideas about commodities and consumption in the United States, as well as how they accessed certain national and historical tropes bolstered by consumer capitalist institutions and ideologies," see Alissa Karl, "'Modernism's Risky Business': Gertrude Stein, Sylvia Beach, and American Consumer Capitalism," *American Literature* 80, no. 1 (March 2008): 83–109, quotation on 85. For the rhetorical strategies of advertisement through which Stein sold her public persona in *The Autobiography*, see Helga Lénárt-Cheng, "Autobiography as Advertisement: Why Do Gertrude Stein's Sentences Get under Our Skin?," *New Literary History* 34, no. 1 (Winter 2003): 117–31. For examples of how Stein used her influence within the cultural elite to help engineer her and her autobiography's success, see Conrad, "Gertrude Stein in the American Marketplace."

I found Mark Goble's thoughts especially helpful. In "Cameo Appearances; or, When Gertrude Stein Checks into Grand Hotel," *MLQ: Modern Language Quarterly* 62, no. 2 (June 2001): 117–63, Goble considers Stein's "stardom as an essential aspect of her literary production in the 1930s, when Stein finds herself strangely and belatedly embraced by American culture, perhaps in part because she describes the experience of celebrity in ways that resonate everywhere with a larger history of media and mediation" (119).

7. Gertrude Stein, *Fernhurst, Q.E.D., and Other Early Writings* (New York: Liveright, 1971); *Three Lives: Stories of the Good Anna, Melanctha, and the Gentle Lena* (New York: Grafton, 1909).

8. Gertrude Stein, *Tender Buttons: Objects, Food, Rooms* (New York: Claire Marie, 1914).

9. Gertrude Stein, *Portrait of Mabel Dodge at the Villa Curonia* (Firenze: Galileiana, 1913); "Have they attacked Mary. He giggled," *Vanity Fair,* June 1917, 55, and as an imprint of the same name (West Chester, Pa.: Temple, 1917); *Geography and Plays* (Boston: Four Seas, 1922); Sherwood Anderson, "The Work of Gertrude Stein," *Little Review* 8, no. 2 (Spring 1922): 29–32, reprinted to introduce *Geography and Plays*, 5–8.

10. Gertrude Stein, *The Making of Americans: Being a History of a Family's Progress* (Paris: Contact Editions, 1925); *A Description of Literature* (Englewood, N.J.: George Platt Lynes and Adlai Harbeck, 1926); *Composition as Explanation* (London: Hogarth, 1926); *A Book Concluding with As a Wife Has a Cow* (Paris: Editions de la Galerie Simon, 1926); *A Village, Are You Ready Yet Not Yet: A Play in Four Acts* (Paris: Editions de la Galerie Simon, 1928); *Useful Knowledge* (New York: Payson & Clarke, 1928); *Lucy Church Amiably* (Paris: Plain Edition, 1931); *How to Write* (Paris: Plain Edition, 1931).

11. Edward Said, *Beginnings: Intention and Method* (New York: Basic Books, 1973), 235. Tracking the development of Stein's fame alongside her literary output allows us to see how her attempts to manage her career were often at odds with her celebrity persona. For a helpful interpretation of how Stein attempted to reconcile her literary career and celebrity after *The Autobiography*, see Kirk Curnutt, "Inside and Outside: Gertrude Stein on Identity, Celebrity, and Authenticity," *Journal of Modern Literature* 23, no. 2 (Winter 1999–2000): 291–308.

12. "A Zolaesque American," *New York Press*, February 13, 1910; Samuel G. Blythe, "La grande fête américaine," *Saturday Evening Post*, March 22, 1913, 10–11, 32.

13. "Zolaesque American."

14. Émile Zola, "J'accuse!," *L'Aurore*, January 13, 1898, 1. *Les Rougon-Macquart* (1871–1893) includes *L'assomoir* (1877), *Nana* (1880), *Germinal* (1885), and *Le bête humaine* (1890) and pays particular attention to the effects of alcohol, prostitution, and hereditary madness. Zola bore the standard of the French naturalist movement, which continued realism's revolt against romanticism and its championing

of the human imagination and free will while remaining more narrowly focused than realists on the plight of the working class. The movement in general and Zola in particular were known for relatively sexually explicit, pessimistic fiction that exposed and deplored the material affronts of poverty and traced how such nature and nurture determined characters and their fates.

15. The Jewishness of many surnames has a definite, legal origin in the late eighteenth and early nineteenth centuries, when such names were forced upon European Jews. Some governments created lists of acceptable surnames; some Jews picked their own (Patrick Hanks and Flavia Hodges, special consultant for Jewish names, David L. Gold, *Dictionary of Surnames* [Oxford: Oxford University Press, 1988], xlii–xlv). Many European Jews outside of Germany held German names; sometimes for legal reasons, as in the Austro-Hungarian Empire, sometimes because of immigration, as in Russia. Though "Stein" derives from the Old High German noun for "stone" and was not one of the many names specifically created for such lists, it was an occasional suffix both in surnames made up out of whole cloth, such as Edelstein, and surnames derived from place names, such as Rubinstein. Such suffixes frequently became entire surnames during the nominal simplification common during immigration to the United States. The national attention paid to the enormous Jewish immigration at the turn of the twentieth century left "Stein" to signify "Jewish" at least as much as "German" in the United States.

16. Marcel Proust, *A la recherche du temps perdu* (Paris: Gaston Gallimard, 1919–1927); first U.S. edition, *Swann's Way*, trans. C. K. Scott Moncrieff (New York: Holt, 1925); Eve Kosofsky Sedgwick, *Epistemology of the Closet* (Los Angeles: University of California Press, 1991); Siobhan B. Somerville, *Queering the Color Line: Race and the Invention of Homosexuality in American Culture* (Durham, N.C.: Duke University Press, 2003), 17; Daniel Boyarin, "Strange Bedfellows: An Introduction," in *Queer Theory and the Jewish Question,* ed. Daniel Boyarin, Daniel Itzkovitz, and Ann Pellegrini (New York: Columbia University Press, 2003), 1. For the "secret dossier," see Jonathan Freedman, "Coming Out of the Jewish Closet with Marcel Proust," in *Queer Theory and the Jewish Question.*

17. See Paul B. Franklin, "Jew Boys, Queer Boys: Rhetorics of Antisemitism and Homophobia in the Trial of Nathan 'Babe' Leopold Jr. and Richard 'Dickie' Loeb," in Boyarin, Itzkovitz, and Pellegrini, *Queer Theory and the Jewish Question,* 122–23. For Jews and gender impropriety, see Sander Gilman, *Freud, Race, and Gender* (Princeton, N.J.: Princeton University Press, 1993); and Daniel Boyarin, *Unheroic Conduct: The Rise of Heterosexuality and the Invention of the Jewish Man* (Los Angeles: University of California Press, 1997). For the orientalist Jewess, see Ivan Davidson Kalmar and Derek J Penslar, eds., *Orientalism and the Jews* (Waltham, Mass.: Brandeis University Press; Hanover, N.H.: University Press of New England, 2005). For a history of male homo-orientalism, see Joseph Boone, *The Homoerotics of Orientalism* (New York: Columbia University Press, 2014), 362.

18. "Zolaesque American"; Zola, "J'accuse!"

19. "Zolaesque American."

20. Ibid. (ellipses mine). Anne Anling Chen on the similarly unruly body of Josephine Baker is helpful here. In "Skin Deep: Josephine Baker and the Colonial Fetish,"

Camera Obscura 23, no. 3 (2008): 35–78, Chen unpacks the imbrication of Baker's performances of race, and the variety of definite yet contradictory meanings extracted from those performances by both contemporaries and present readers, to reveal Baker as yet another modernist woman who essayed a double backflip of meaning across the cultural imaginary and thus attained celebrity.

21. "Zolaesque." For female masculinity, see Jack Halberstam [Judith], *Female Masculinity* (Durham, N.C.: Duke University Press, 1998). I am grateful to Yetta Howard's insights into "ugliness" and how "it aligns itself with non-white, non-male, and non-heterosexual physicality and experience [and] refers to anti-aesthetic textual practices," both in conversation and in her unpublished manuscript, "Ugly Differences."

22. Gertrude Stein, "Henri Matisse," special issue, *Camera Work* Special Number (August 1912): 23–25: 23; Stein, "Pablo Picasso," *Camera Work* (August 1912): 29–30. Most conflations of Stein with the visual modernists were in reviews of Stein's work, but a few articles discussed Stein and her brother as art collectors, such as R. Franklin, "Have the Steins Deserted Matisse, Artist They Made Famous?," *New York Press*, June 21, 1914.

23. Stein, *Portrait,* reprinted in *Camera Work* (June 1913): 3–5; Walt Kuhn, "The Story of the Armory Show," in *The Story of the Armory Show,* vol. 3 (New York: Arno, 1938), 24–25.

24. Mabel Dodge, "Speculations; or, Post Impressionism in Prose," *Arts and Decoration,* March 1913, 172–73, reprinted in *Camera Work* (June 1913); Vincent van Gogh, "The Spirit of Modern Art," frontispiece to special issue, *Arts and Decoration* 3, no. 5 (March 1913): 148.

25. Dodge, "Speculations," 172.

26. Blythe, "La grande fête"; subsequent references to this article appear in the text. By 1908, the *Saturday Evening Post* had a million subscribers, and by the 1920s, it earned more than $50 million annually. See John Tebbel, *George Horace Lorimer and "The Saturday Evening Post"* (New York: Doubleday, 1948); and Jan Cohn, *Creating America: George Horace Lorimer and "The Saturday Evening Post"* (Pittsburgh: University of Pittsburgh Press, 1989). The *Post* was middlebrow but not conservative; its politics were broadly progressive until World War I, when the magazine began to tilt right.

27. Blythe was known for self-help books such as *The Fun of Getting Thin* (Chicago: Forbes, 1912), as well as fiction. "La grande fête" is illustrated with line drawings by May Wilson Preston, a painter who exhibited at the Armory Show as a member of the Ashcan school. Nonetheless, her contributions to "La grande fête" are of a piece with other magazine work of the time and illustrate the parody without stylistically referencing the show. Both Blythe and Preston were frequent contributors to the *Saturday Evening Post.*

28. Karen Leick, "Popular Modernism: Little Magazines and the American Daily Press," *PMLA* 123, no. 1 (2008): 126.

29. Stein, *Portrait*; Dodge, "Speculations"; Blythe, "La grande fête;" Stein, *Tender Buttons;* "Public Gets Peep at Extreme Cubist Literature in Gertrude Stein's 'Tender Buttons,'" *Chicago Daily Tribune,* June 5, 1914.

30. Robert E. Rogers, "*Tender Buttons,* Curious Experiment of Gertrude Stein in Literary Anarchy," *Boston Evening Transcript,* July 11, 1914.

31. "Officer, She's Writing Again," review of *Tender Buttons, Detroit News,* June 6, 1914. The invaluable compilation *The Critical Response to Gertrude Stein,* edited by Kirk Curnutt (Westport, Conn.: Greenwood Press, 2000), misprints the "Dime Bank Building" as the "Fime Bank Building" (14). This typo has invaded many other books. For the record, the Fime Bank Building does not exist, but the Dime Bank Building (also known as the Dime Building and, since 2012, Chrysler House) was once one of the tallest office buildings in Detroit, with twenty-three stories that contained one thousand offices.

32. Alfred Kreymborg, "Gertrude Stein—Hoax and Hoaxtress: A Study of the Woman Whose 'Tender Buttons' Has Furnished New York with a New Kind of Amusement," *New York Morning Telegraph,* March 7, 1915. Kreymborg was a member of Alfred Stieglitz's circle, and editor and publisher, with Man Ray, of the modernist periodical *The Glebe,* which published Ezra Pound's important anthology *Des imagistes* (New York: Boni, 1914).

33. Stein, *Three Lives;* "A Futurist Novel," review of *Three Lives, Philadelphia Public Ledger,* April 10, 1910; Rogers, "*Tender Buttons,* Curious Experiment"; "Zolaesque American."

34. Stein, "Henri Matisse"; "Pablo Picasso"; "Portrait"; Blythe, "La grande fête."

35. Stein, *Tender Buttons;* review of *Tender Buttons, New York City Call,* June 7, 1914; Rogers, "*Tender Buttons,* Curious Experiment." *Sonnets from the Patagonian: The Street of Little Hotels* (New York: Claire Marie, 1914), by Donald Evans, the owner and manager of Claire Marie, had pale blue-green boards with its title inked in red on the spine. Allen Norton's *Saloon Sonnets,* properly subtitled *With Sunday Flutings,* was also published in 1914 (New York: Claire Marie). *Sacral Dimples: A Diary,* by Carl Van Vechten, was announced in a Claire Marie publicity brochure but never appeared. I have found no trace of *A Piety of Fans.*

36. Mabel Dodge to Gertrude Stein, March 29, 1914, in *The Flowers of Friendship: Letters Written to Gertrude Stein,* ed. Donald Gallup (New York: Knopf, 1953), 96–97 (italics hers); Stein, *The Autobiography,* 162.

37. Dodge to Stein, March 29 1914.

38. Gertrude Stein, *A Book Concluding with As a Wife Has a Cow: A Love Story,* lithography by Juan Gris (Paris: Galerie Simon, 1926); *The Making of Americans.*

39. Gertrude Stein, *Dix Portraits* (Paris: Editions de la Montagne, 1930); "Henri Matisse"; "Pablo Picasso"; promotional material for *Dix Portraits,* 1930.

40. Don Marquis, *The Annotated Archy and Mehitabel,* ed. Michael Sims, drawings by George Herriman (New York: Penguin, 2006); Marquis, *Hermione and Her Little Group of Serious Thinkers* (New York: Appleton, 1916). Sadly, *Hermione* is long out of print. For an overview of Marquis's parodies of Stein, see Tischler, "Rose Is a Pose."

41. Don Marquis, "Proem," ll. 2–5, and "She Refused to Give Up the Cosmos," ll. 1–13, both in *Hermione.*

42. Don Marquis, "Gertrude Is Stein, Stein Gertrude: That Is All Ye Know on Earth, and All Ye Need to Know," *New York Sun,* October 15, 1914. The poem appeared in

Marquis's column but is not collected in *Hermione,* probably to keep the point of view consistent. "Gertrude Is Stein" is in the first-person plural, whereas the other poems are in Hermione's voice except for the first and last, which have an omniscient point of view.

43. Tischler, "Rose Is a Pose," 20; Marquis, "Gertrude Is Stein," ll. 2–4. Tischler found her version of the poem in the Stein archives in the Beinecke Library, Yale University. The poem I quote appeared in the *New York Sun.* Marquis frequently republished his columns in a variety of forms.

44. "Zolaesque American"; Blythe, "La grande fête."

45. *A Fool There Was,* directed by Frank L. Powell (William Fox Vaudeville Company, 1915). For those who did not do the reading, the poem is included in full at the film's start, as well as interspersed in supertitles. The path from Kipling's "The Vampire" (1897) to *A Fool There Was* is convoluted. Kipling was inspired by his cousin Philip Burne-Jones's painting of the same name and year, which portrayed a triumphant, dark-haired woman in a nightdress—widely agreed to be the actress Mrs. Patrick Campbell—looming over her supine, unconscious victim, whose chest lies bared and ready for her sharp teeth. See Margot Peters, *Mrs. Pat: The Life of Mrs. Patrick Campbell* (Los Angeles: University of California Press, 1984), 142. The poem was published in the painting's exhibition catalog, *New Gallery Regent Street Tenth Summer Exhibition* (London: New Gallery, 1897), and both play and poem inspired a 1909 play by Porter Emerson Browne, *A Fool There Was,* which he adapted into a novel (New York: Fly, 1909), the source of the film.

46. *Cleopatra,* directed by J. Gordon Edwards (Fox Film Corporation, 1912). For the promotion of *Cleopatra,* see Eve Golden, *Vamp: The Rise and Fall of Theda Bara* (New York: Emprise, 1996), 129–34. The construction of "Bara" from whole cloth makes her a more suitable comparison than, say, Sarah Bernhardt.

47. Golden, *Vamp,* 3. Golden argues that Bara's Arabian birth was broadly discredited by 1915. For how *Kathleen Mavourneen,* directed by Charles Bradin (Fox Film Corporation, 1919), led to riots, stink bombs, and death threats, see Golden, 195–96; and Ronald Genini, *Theda Bara: A Biography of the Silent Screen Vamp, with a Filmography* (Jefferson, N.C.: McFarland, 1996), 50.

48. Stein, *Portrait; Tender Buttons.*

49. Anderson, "Work of Gertrude Stein," 6.

50. In the 1910s and '20s, absinthe and opium were old news. By 1922, the United States had been through half a century of anti-opium scares and crusades, and the drug was heavily regulated. Similarly, absinthe was banned in the United States in 1912 and in France in 1915, and thus it no longer had the presence of a few decades earlier.

    Note that Stein's "drug" evolves: Richard Wright imagined Stein "spen[ding] her days reclining upon a silken couch in Paris smoking hashish." See "Gertrude Stein's Story Is Drenched in Hitler's Horrors," review of Stein's *Wars I Have Seen, PM,* March 11, 1945, 15. In the 1930s, absinthe and opium use were too dated to support a contemporary fantasy. Stein's drug of choice was therefore updated to hashish, which was a national concern in the 1930s and accords with the harsher, less romantic vision of Stein that we will see in Wright's report. Though her drug of choice had shifted, she remained configured as a traditional "opium queen."

51. Radclyffe Hall, *The Well of Loneliness* (London: Cape, 1928).
52. Anderson, "Work of Gertrude Stein," 6; Sherwood Anderson, "Four American Impressions: Gertrude Stein, Paul Rosenfeld, Ring Lardner, Sinclair Lewis," *New Republic,* October 11, 1922, 171. The section on Stein was republished as "Gertrude Stein's Kitchen," *Wings* 7 (September 1933): 12–13, 26. Despite Anderson's introduction, Stein's collection of experimental works *Geography and Plays* better suited an absinthe sipper than an archetypal grandma of Terre Haute, and did not sell.
53. Sherwood Anderson, *Winesburg, Ohio: A Group of Tales of Ohio Small Town Life* (New York: Random House, 1919); Richard Wright, *Native Son* (New York: Harper, 1940); *Black Boy* (New York: Harper, 1945).
54. Wright, "Gertrude Stein's Story," 15. Note that Wright imagined the "silken couch"—the natural habitat of the opium queen—though we will see that Gold did not mention it. To support Stein, Wright also wrote a dust-jacket blurb for *Brewsie and Willie* (New York: Random House, 1946), as well as an introduction to an excerpt from *Three Lives,* for his contribution to the 1946 anthology *I Wish I'd Written That,* ed. Whit Burnett (New York: McGraw Hill, 1946), 254.
55. Michael Gold, "Gertrude Stein: A Literary Idiot," in *Change the World!* (New York: International, 1936), 25, 26. Was Stein in fact a capitalist pig? Stein never had to work for money and almost always had a housekeeper/cook, and at times a larger staff. She had sufficient funds to collect modern art, which was inexpensive when she and her brother Leo began their collection. Nonetheless, until the mid-1930s Stein was careful with money and had to sell pieces of her collection to meet unusual expenses. She spent almost nothing on usual markers of wealth, such as property or clothes. In short, she had a delicate hold on a privileged lifestyle.

     Karen Leick points out that Gold's distaste for Stein may have stemmed from an unfortunate meeting in 1934 when she called him and other Communists fools, in *Gertrude Stein and the Making of an American Celebrity* (New York: Routledge, 2009), 188.
56. Wright, "Gertrude Stein's Story," 15.
57. Stein, *Three Lives*; "Henri Matisse"; Gold, "Literary Idiot," 25. Gold was strongly homophobic and frequently attacked the masculinity and sexuality of male writers and writing that he did not like in his reviews. See James Penner, *Pinks, Pansies, and Punks: The Politics of Masculinity in Literary Culture* (Bloomington: Indiana University Press, 2010).
58. Stein, *The Autobiography*; *Four Saints in Three Acts.*

4. Gertrude Stein in *Life* and *TIME*

1. Gertrude Stein, *The Autobiography of Alice B. Toklas* (New York: Harcourt Brace, 1933). Alfred Barr taught the first class in modern art in 1926, at Wellesley, and Meyer Schapiro followed, at Columbia. The Museum of Modern Art was founded in 1929, with Barr as director. Cézanne and Picasso were sound investments by 1933. Barr made his famous chart of the "genealogy" of modern art in 1936. By 1939, Clement Greenberg wrote as if the avant-garde were an old guard under threat: "Picasso's shows still draw crowds, and T. S. Eliot is taught in the universi-

ties; the dealers in modernist art are still in business, and the publishers still publish some 'difficult' poetry" ("Avant-Garde and Kitsch," *Partisan Review* 6, no. 5
[Fall 1939]: 38).

2. James Agee, "Stein's Way," *TIME*, September 11, 1933, 57–60.

3. Gertrude Stein, "Relief Work in France," *Life*, December 27, 1917, 1076; "A League,"
   Life, September 18, 1919, 496.

4. Gertrude Stein, "Relief Work in France"; "A League"; *Three Lives: Stories of the Good
   Anna, Melanctha, and the Gentle Lena* (New York: Grafton, 1909); *Tender Buttons:
   Objects, Food, Rooms* (New York: Claire Marie, 1914); *Geography and Plays* (Boston: Four Seas, 1922); *Useful Knowledge* (New York: Payson & Clarke, 1928), 84;
   Reflection on the Atom Bomb, ed. Robert Hass (Los Angeles: Black Sparrow, 1973),
   13; Margaret Dickie, *Stein, Bishop, and Rich: Lyrics of Love, War, and Place* (Chapel Hill: University of North Carolina Press, 1997), 40. In *Gertrude Stein and the
   Making of an American Celebrity* (New York: Routledge, 2009), Karen Leick re-
   produces the first stanza of "Relief Work in France" without comment. Leick does
   discuss the Roberts parodies (see n. 5) and offers a brief reading of "A League." For
   Life's readership, see Frank Luther Mott, *A History of American Magazines*, vol. 4,
   1885–1905 (Cambridge, Mass.: Harvard University Press, 1957), 565.

5. Stein, *The Autobiography*, 210–11 (ellipsis mine). The parodies by Kenneth L. Roberts,
   all titled "Cubist Poems—after Gertrude Stein," may be found in *Life*, July 12, 1917,
   47; August 23, 1917, 317; and August 30, 1917, 344. Thomas Lansing Masson, novelist and humorist, was literary editor of *Life* from 1893 to 1900 and managing editor
   from 1894 to 1922.

6. "-Less Days in Germany," *Life*, December 27, 1917, 1073.

7. "Locating the Germans," *Life*, December 27, 1917, 1076; "Wanted: Safe-Keeping for
   Bonds," 1075; "On the Front Walk," 1076; E. Forster Lincoln, installment 31 of *The
   Willowbys' Ward*, graphic serial, 1077.

8. Stein, "A League," 496. "Free verse" was coined in the preface to the anthology *Des
   imagistes*, ed. Ezra Pound and Alfred Kreymborg (New York: Boni, 1914). Leick offers a different rationale for this introduction: "The editorial remarks are welcome,
   as it is unlikely any reader would have guessed the subject otherwise" (*Gertrude
   Stein*, 60).

9. Gertrude Stein, "Have they attacked Mary. He giggled," *Vanity Fair*, June 1917, 55;
   "The Great American Army," *Vanity Fair*, June 1918, 31; "A Deserter," "The Meaning
   of the Bird," "J. R.," and "J. R. II," *Vanity Fair*, March 1919, 88b; "Miss Furr and Miss
   Skeene," in *Geography and Plays*, reprinted in *Vanity Fair*, July 1923, 55, 94; John
   Tebbel, *George Horace Lorimer and "The Saturday Evening Post"* (Garden City, N.J.:
   Doubleday, 1948), 257. Bryce Conrad analyzes how ads for *Vanity Fair* traded on
   the desire to enter "society"—"one either joins the select world of modern art by, as
   it were, 'buying' the advertised virtues of the offered product . . . or one loses out
   and becomes a 'philistine,' having failed to purchase the package that contains not
   just Stein but Matisse and Picasso as well"—in "Gertrude Stein in the American
   Marketplace," *Journal of Modern Literature* 19, no. 2 (1995): 222.

10. Editor's introduction to Stein's poems, *Vanity Fair*, March 1919, 88b.

11. Dickie, *Stein, Bishop, and Rich*, 40.

12. Gertrude Stein, *Brewsie and Willie* (New York: Random House, 1946); *Wars I Have Seen* (New York: Random House, 1945); "Relief Work in France." Certainly, Stein was known well enough among American soldiers in France to bring them to her door. This may have been due at least in part to her unusually accessible poem "The Work," which was published in the *Bulletin of the American Fund for French Wounded*. "The Work" is collected in *Bee Time Vine and Other Pieces, 1913–1927* (New Haven, Conn.: Yale University Press, 1953), 189–94. The difficulties of citing "The Work" and its relation to "Relief Work In France" are discussed in Richard Bridgman, *Gertrude Stein in Pieces* (New York: Oxford University Press, 1970), 156n. Also see John Malcolm Brinnin, *The Third Rose: Gertrude Stein and Her World* (Boston: Little, Brown, 1959), 222–24.

13. James R. Mellow, *Charmed Circle: Gertrude Stein and Company* (New York: Praeger, 1974), 226.

14. Editor's introduction to "The Great American Army," by Gertrude Stein, and *Courage, mes braves! J'arrive!*, by Lucien Jonas, *Vanity Fair*, June 1918, 31. The lithograph may illustrate an article that appears three pages before—"Our Government and Our War Artists: Why Not Follow the Example of the French, Who Know How to Get the Job Done?" (28)—but the patent connection is to the poem, which appears on the same page.

15. Stein, "Great American Army," 31.

16. Advertisements, *Vanity Fair*, June 1918, 99, 2.

17. Stephen Leacock, "How to Live in War Time: Hints for Patriotic Women Based on Information from the Latest Ladies Magazines," *Vanity Fair*, June 1918, 30; Stein, "Great American Army"; "High Lights of Wartime Simplicity: The Perfect Accessory Is the Keynote of the Perfect Costume," *Vanity Fair*, June 1918, 69. By the 1930s, the steadily darkening national mood made this balance untenable, and *Vanity Fair* was folded into *Vogue* because of falling circulation. Unsurprisingly, *Vanity Fair*'s revival in the 1980s coincided with an eruption of interest in wealth qua wealth and "high society."

18. In ten years, *TIME* had earned a circulation of more than 300,000, which made it the third most popular magazine in the country, after the *Saturday Evening Post* and *The New Yorker*.

19. Agee, "Stein's Way," 59, 39. The second quotation from Agee has a closing quotation mark at the end of the sentence but no opening quotation mark. Although this may indicate an uncredited quotation, a typo is most likely. Typo aside, we see in "great pyramidal Buddha" yet another orientalist depiction or at least understanding of Stein.

Portraits of Stein are readily accessible on the web. Agee's examples—the Picasso painting, the Picabia drawing, and the Davidson sculpture—remain emblematic, as do Man Ray's photos of Stein posed in front of the Picasso, and of Stein posing for Davidson. Photographs of Stein in college and medical school show a younger, more conventional Stein, who jars with her public persona.

20. Ibid., 59.

21. Ernest Hemingway, "A Strange Enough Ending," in *A Moveable Feast* (New York: Scribner, 1964), 119. Hemingway's tone is interesting. Such indirect spite, couched

in precise wordplay, is coded feminine: "catty" and even "bitchy" come to mind, as if the speaker's passive aggression somehow makes him less human. We will hear this tone later with James Agee. Does Stein's masculine presentation force these two men, both very conscious of their own public masculinity, into conventionally feminine diction?

22. *Morocco,* directed by Josef von Sternberg (Paramount, 1930). I am grateful to Tania Modleski for this reference. To my eyes, Stein *does* seem to be in drag when she wears "inappropriately" feminine clothes, like the flowered blouse in an *Autobiography* photo or the high-femme hats with which she sometimes set off her masculine outfits. Such items in Stein's wardrobe would be "natural" and comparatively invisible, as they were expected, unlike her more "masculine" clothes. That said, Stein dressed more conventionally as her fame grew.

23. Sherwood Anderson, "The Work of Gertrude Stein," in *Geography and Plays,* 6; Richard Wright, "Gertrude Stein's Story Is Drenched in Hitler's Horrors," review of *Wars I Have Seen, PM,* March 11, 1945, 15. See also chapter 3 of this book.

24. The growth of sound film at the end of the 1920s led to greater calls for government censorship, which the film industry avoided by censoring itself. The Hays Code was adopted in 1930 but not enforced until the Production Code Administration of 1934. Nonetheless, local censorship boards and religious groups had considerable influence before 1934, and censorship was practiced both inside and outside the studios.

25. Agee, "Stein's Way," 57. I presume that by "portentous," Agee means "influential."

26. The full profile portrait tends to make a subject less attractive, as it accentuates facial irregularities and details such as sunken cheeks and big noses and ears. The more common three-quarter view hides asymmetry and tends to be more flattering. Yet this calculus seems false for Stein. To my eyes, her face in full profile gains grandeur.

27. Agee, "Stein's Way," 56.

28. Why look at fifty-four years? The year 1977 is a useful date for the shift brought about by feminism in the representation of women: the women on the cover of *TIME* after 1980 are less relevant to Gertrude Stein. My primary reason for the cutoff, however, is to take advantage of the analysis performed by Donald J. Lehnus in *Who's on TIME? A Study of TIME's Covers from March 3, 1923, to January 3, 1977* (New York: Oceana, 1980). All statistics are drawn from either Lehnus or the *TIME* website, http://www.time.com.

29. *Please Don't Eat the Daisies,* directed by Charles Walters (MGM, 1960); Rebecca West, *Black Lamb and Grey Falcon: A Journey through Yugoslavia* (New York: Viking, 1941); Stein, *The Autobiography.* I have not included Ève Curie Labouisse in this list. Labouisse won the cover (February 12, 1940) in part for *Madame Curie,* trans. Vincent Sheean (New York: Doubleday, Doran, 1938), the biography of her mother, Marie Curie. Labouisse's French nationality, her status as a celebrated beauty (she was "the girl with the radium eyes"), her career as a concert pianist, and her relation to her husband (U.S. ambassador to Greece) and mother and sister (both winners of a Nobel Prize in Chemistry) differentiate her from the other women writers. Labouisse was not a woman writer but a famous woman who wrote.

More precisely, she *was* a woman writer, a respected journalist in Europe, but that did not earn her the cover. Still, Labouisse's cover is of a piece with the other women's, except for Stein's.

30. Kathleen Thompson Norris, *Woman in Love* (New York: Doubleday, 1935); "Golden Honeymoon," *TIME*, January 28, 1935, 65–66; Jean Kerr, *Mary, Mary* (New York: Doubleday, 1963); "The Telltale Hearth," *TIME*, June 18, 1965, 74–78; Betty Friedan, *The Feminine Mystique* (New York: Norton, 1963).

31. Please note that the photo of Stein by Carl Van Vechten on the dust jacket of *So Famous and So Gay* is similar to but not the same as the George Platt Lynes photo featured in Plates 15 and 16. Van Vechten offers a more feminine vision of Stein, thanks to the brooch.

32. "Golden Honeymoon," 65.

33. Ibid.

34. Agee, "Stein's Way," 59. See n. 21 for Agee's tone.

35. James Agee, *Let Us Now Praise Famous Men: Three Tenant Families,* photographs by Walter Evans (New York: Houghton Mifflin, 1941); *A Death in the Family* (New York: McDowell, Obolensky, 1957).

36. Macdonald and Agee stayed friends, and Macdonald got Agee his job at *Fortune.* I am grateful to Lawrence Bergreen for his biography *James Agee: A Life* (New York: Dutton, 1984) and its details of Agee's aborted romance with Fred Lowenstein, which goes unmentioned in Macdonald's memoirs of Agee. Bergreen draws upon Agee's letters to Macdonald, found in the Dwight Macdonald Papers at Yale University's Beinecke Library, as well as his letters to his priest, collected in *The Letters of James Agee to Father Flye,* 2nd ed. (Boston: Houghton Mifflin, 1971). For the typical romantic configuration of Agee as a tragic young man (of forty-five), see Macdonald's "James Agee," in *Masscult and Midcult: Essays against the American Grain* (New York: New York Review Books, 2011), 74–94. For a less romantic view, see David Denby, "A Famous Man" *The New Yorker,* January 9, 2006, 85. For Agee's engagement with the avant-garde—interesting in its difference from his persona at *TIME*—see Hugh Davis, *The Making of James Agee* (Knoxville: University of Tennessee Press, 2008).

37. *James Agee: Film Writing and Selected Journalism* (New York: Library of America, 2005). For Diana Trilling's book reviews, see chapter 2 of this book.

38. Agee, *Let Us Now Praise;* Gertrude Stein, *Ida* (New York: Random House, 1941); Agee, "Stein's Way"; "Abstract Prose," *TIME,* February 17, 1941. Also see Agee's "Art for What's Sake?" in the December 1936 *New Masses,* a review of Stein's *A Geographical History of America* (New York: Random House, 1936), meant in part to refute Michael Gold's "Gertrude Stein: A Literary Idiot," in *Change the World!* (New York: International, 1936), 23–26, considered in chapter 3 of this book.

39. Agee, "Stein's Way," 57, original formatting. See *TIME,* September 18, 1933, 2, for an editorial correction: "A child of error and perversity, Ed Stein was a non-existent character who appeared on Earth just long enough to make *TIME*, Sept. 11. p. 57, a horrid sight." Max Eastman was an important leftist critic in the 1910s and an editor of *The Masses* from 1913 until the government shut it down, in 1918. Eastman

was therefore the editorial forebear of Michael Gold at *The New Masses*, and Eastman's "cult of nonsense" may be seen in Gold's "Gertrude Stein: A Literary Idiot."

40. Agee, "Stein's Way"; Marcel Proust, *Swann's Way* trans. C. K. Scott Moncrieff (London: Chatto & Windus, 1922; New York: Henry Holt, 1925); Stein, *The Autobiography.*

41. Agee, "Stein's Way," 57 (ellipses mine). For the bell's first ring, see Stein, *The Autobiography,* 5–6.

42. Agee, "Stein's Way," 59; James Agee to Dwight Macdonald, June 26, 1927, quoted in
Bergreen, *James Agee,* 46.

5. Three Lesbian Lives

1. Gertrude Stein, *The Autobiography of Alice B. Toklas* (New York: Harcourt Brace,
1933); *Three Lives: Stories of the Good Anna, Melanctha, and the Gentle Lena* (New
York: Grafton, 1909).

2. Gertrude Stein, *Three Lives* (New York: Modern Library, 1933). The history of the
Modern Library, Random House, Boni & Liveright, and Stein confuses. In 1925,
Boni & Liveright sold the Modern Library imprint to its former vice president,
Bennett Cerf, and Donald Klopfer. In 1927, Boni & Liveright put out its own edi-
tion of *Three Lives,* and in 1933, Cerf and Klopfer put out an edition in the Modern
Library. Random House was then a subsidiary of Modern Library, but it soon be-
came the parent company and Stein's primary publisher.

3. Bennett Cerf, *At Random: The Reminiscences of Bennett Cerf* (New York: Random
House, 1977), 105; Gertrude Stein, *Lectures in America* (New York: Random House,
1935); *A Geographical History of America* (New York: Random House, 1936); *Everybody's Autobiography* (New York: Random House, 1937). Typically, Cerf makes his
offer more spontaneous and romantic in his biography than in life, though he does
not lie, exactly. Before going on tour, Stein received a letter in July 1933 from Cerf
promising to publish a book of hers per year if she wrote another biography for
Random House; Cerf repeated this offer at the party. Cerf also offered to act as a
distributor for Stein's own vanity press, the Plain Edition, for free. In *Everybody
Who Was Anybody: A Biography of Gertrude Stein* (New York: Putnam, 1975), Janet
Hobhouse offers a clear timeline of Stein and Cerf's interaction on tour (176), though
she does not mention *Three Lives.*

4. Terry Castle, *The Apparitional Lesbian: Female Homosexuality and Modern Culture* (New York: Columbia University Press, 1993), 8–14.

5. Oscar Wilde, *The Picture of Dorian Gray* (London: Ward, Lock, 1891); *Lady
Windermere's Fan* (New York: French, 1892); *An Ideal Husband* (London: Smithers,
1895); *The Importance of Being Earnest* (Boston: Baker, 1895).

6. Gertrude Stein, *Wars I Have Seen* (New York: Random House, 1945), 55; Oscar
Wilde, *The Ballad of Reading Gaol* (London: Smithers, 1898), ll. 53–54. For Stein's
fear, see Linda Wagner-Martin, *"Favored Strangers": Gertrude Stein and Her Family* (New Brunswick, N.J.: Rutgers University Press, 1995), 45.

7. Gertrude Stein, *Fernhurst, Q.E.D., and Other Early Writings* (New York: Liveright,
1971). *Q.E.D.* was written in 1903, and *Fernhurst* in 1904. In names alone, fiction
and reality confuse here. In life, Stein was a vertex of a romantic triangle that included May Bookstaver and Mabel Haynes, who in *Q.E.D.* become Helen Thomas

and Mabel Neathe. Helen Thomas was named after Helen Carey Thomas, the president of Bryn Mawr, who, confusingly, was also one of the models for the academic couple in *Fernhurst,* along with Mary Gwinn. In *Fernhurst,* however, Helen Carey Thomas is a model for the Mabel Haynes/Mabel Neathe character, now called Dean Helen Thornton. The May Bookstaver/Helen Thomas character, via Mary Gwinn, is Professor Janet Bruce. In real life, the male lecturer was Alfred Hodder, a friend of Stein's brother Leo; his cognate in *Fernhurst* is Philip Redfern. Further confusion may spring from the preponderance of Mabels among Stein's close personal friends, which include Mabel Weeks and Mabel Dodge. For iterations of the original triangle in versions of *The Making of Americans,* see Leo Katz's introduction to *Fernhurst, Q.E.D.,* i–xxxiv.

8. Gertrude Stein, *Stanzas in Meditation and Other Poems [1929-1933]* (New Haven, Conn.: Yale University Press, 1956); Ulla E. Dydo, "How to Read Gertrude Stein: The Manuscripts of 'Stanzas in Meditation,'" *Text* 1 (1981): 271–303.

9. After Frederick H. Hitchcock suggested that Stein increase sales by changing the title from the "much too formal" *Three Histories,* on April 9, 1909, she did, though she refused to standardize her grammar or make other textual changes. See Donald Gallup, ed., *The Flowers of Friendship: Letters Written to Gertrude Stein* (New York: Knopf, 1953), 43. Hitchcock also suggested that Stein add a subtitle, and for many years and editions, *Stories of the Good Anna, Melanctha, and the Gentle Lena* decorated title pages and spines. This whimsical subtitle frames *Three Lives* as a legend or fairy tale and softens the book, as does the switch from *Histories* to *Lives.* That said, today locutions such as "The Good Anna" adumbrate the case study, often known by a first name modified by a single adjective, such as Freud's "Little Hans."

10. *Three Lives* was written in 1905–06 and published in 1909. The first version of Freud's *Three Essays on the Theory of Sexuality* was published in German in 1905 (Leipzig: F. Deuticke) and translated into English as *Three Contributions to the Theory of Sex* in 1910 (New York: Journal of Nervous and Mental Disease Publishing Company). Stein grew up speaking German but rarely read it.

   I would also like to parallel *Three Lives* with Freud's *Three Case Studies,* but these studies were not published together for some time. "Little Hans" was first published in 1909, as was "The Rat Man," and "The Psychotic Dr. Schreber" was first published in 1911. However, "Dora" was first published in 1905, to much ado. Stein probably knew of it. See Sigmund Freud, *Three Essays on Sexuality,* in *The Standard Edition of the Complete Psychological Works of Sigmund Freud,* ed. James Strachey, Alix Strachey, and Alan Tyson (London: Hogarth Press, 1953–74) 7:125–425; "Analysis of a Phobia in a Five Year-Old" ("Little Hans"), *Standard Edition* 10:1–149; "Some Remarks on a Case of Obsessive-Compulsive Neurosis" ("The Ratman"), *Standard Edition* 10:151–250; "The Psychotic Dr. Schreber," *Standard Edition* 12:1–79; and "Fragment of a Case of Hysteria" ("Dora"), *Standard Edition* 7:1–122.

11. Gertrude Stein, *Three Lives; and Q.E.D.: Authoritative Texts, Contexts, Criticism,* ed. Marianne DeKoven, Norton Critical Edition (New York: Norton, 2006). In-text citations of *Three Lives* are taken from this edition. There is no Norton Critical Edition of *The Autobiography,* which suggests that *Three Lives* is more frequently assigned.

Notes to Chapter 5

12. Corinne Blackmer, "African Masks and Passing in Stein and Larsen," in ibid., 407–28. Blackmer's article was first published as "African Masks and the Arts of Passing in Gertrude Stein's 'Melanctha' and Nella Larsen's *Passing*," *Journal of the History of Sexuality* 4, no. 2 (1993): 231–63, and all citations are taken from there.

13. Gertrude Stein, *Lifting Belly*, in *Bee Time Vine and Other Pieces, 1913–1927* (New Haven, Conn.: Yale University Press, 1953), 61–115. *Lifting Belly* became much more accessible when it was published in its own right, in 1989 (Tallahassee, Fla.: Naiad Press). The unexpurgated *Q.E.D.* was first published in *Fernhurst, Q.E.D., and Other Early Writings*.

14. Shari Benstock, *Women of the Left Bank: Paris, 1900–1940* (Austin: University of Texas Press, 1986), 161; Catharine Stimpson, "The Mind, the Body, and Gertrude Stein," *Critical Inquiry* 3 (1977): 498; Gertrude Stein, *Tender Buttons: Objects, Food, Rooms* (New York: Claire Marie, 1914).

15. Marianne DeKoven, *A Different Language: Gertrude Stein's Experimental Language* (Madison: University of Wisconsin Press, 1983), 36.

16. Castle, *Apparitional Lesbian*, 1; Karla Jay and Joanne Glasgow, introduction to *Lesbian Texts and Contexts: Radical Revision*, ed. Karla Jay and Joanne Glasgow (New York: New York University Press, 1990), 1; Shari Benstock, "Expatriate Sapphic Modernism: Entering Literary History," in *Lesbian Texts and Contexts*, 194.

17. "A Notable Piece of Realism," review of *Three Lives, Boston Evening Globe*, December 18, 1909.

18. Stephen Crane, *Maggie: A Girl of the Streets* (New York: Appleton, 1896); Theodore Dreiser, *Sister Carrie* (New York: Doubleday, 1900).

19. Stein, *Three Lives; and Q.E.D.* All citations are taken from the Norton edition.

20. These terms were defined by the Russian formalists and are rough contemporaries of Stein's *Three Lives*.

21. Gustave Flaubert, "A Simple Heart," in *Three Tales*, trans. Roger Whitehouse (1877; repr., New York: Penguin, 2005); further citations of this source appear in the text. For assessments of the link between Flaubert and Stein, see John Malcolm Brinnin, *The Third Rose: Gertrude Stein and Her World* (Boston: Little, Brown, 1959), 56–64; Hobhouse, *Everybody Who Was Anybody*, 70–73; and Jayne L. Walker, *The Making of a Modernist: Gertrude Stein from "Three Lives" to "Tender Buttons"* (Amherst: University of Massachusetts Press, 1984), 19–21.

22. For instance, Richard Bridgman finds Flaubert "of minimal significance" to Stein in *Gertrude Stein in Pieces* (New York: Oxford University Press, 1970), 47. More recently, Karin Cope states that "although superficially and thematically, the first of these stories bore some relation [to Flaubert] . . . Stein's work was anything but a translation, nor did she follow Flaubert's style and content"; in *Passionate Collaborations: Learning to Live with Gertrude Stein* (Victoria, B.C.: ELS Editions, 2005), 98.

23. "Ainsi, au milieu de Toucques, comme on passait sous des fenêtres entourées de capucines, il dit, avec un haussement d'épaules:—«En voilà une Mme Lehoussais, qui au lieu de prendre un jeune homme . . . » Félicité n'entendit pas le reste; les chevaux trottaient, l'âne galopait; tous enfilèrent un sentier, une barrière tourna, deux garçons parurent, et l'on descendit devant le purin, sur le seuil même de la porte."

24. Geoffrey Wall, introduction to *Three Tales*, xix.

25. Gustave Flaubert to Mme Roger de Genettes, June 19, 1876, in *Oeuvres Completes*, trans. Ferdinand Brunetière (Paris: Club de l'Honnête homme, 1971–75) 15:458, cited in Wall, ibid., xx.

26. See the section "What Is Melanctha's Problem?" later in this chapter for a discussion of projection and internal objects.

27. Anna's same-sexuality is so blatant that critics have *had* to take note, though briefly. Wagner-Martin offers a blunt statement: "the reader knew Anna through . . . her lesbian love for Mrs. Lehntman, her 'only romance'" (*"Favored Strangers,"* 78). Perhaps Wagner-Martin's status as a biographer rather than a literary critic in this instance allows her to make such statements when so many other Stein critics have not.

28. *Encyclopedia Britannica* (Cambridge: Cambridge University Press, 1911), 23:500, 504.

29. For instance, Walker, in *Making of a Modernist*, offers an extended brief on the connection between the *Contes* and the *Lives* but never touches on a lesbian application (19–21).

30. Jonathon Green, *Green's Dictionary of Slang* (London: Chambers Harrap, 2010), 3:103.

31. The butch-femme dynamic is one of many ways that "The Good Anna" conforms to the conventions of the pulp lesbian novel, a genre that did not start properly for several decades. The working-class milieu; the immoral, sometimes criminal, beloved; and the hardworking heroine who gives up everything, everything, for love—and who, when the beloved finally goes too far, tries a variety of other relationships, none of which have that fire—all are familiar from, say, Anne Bannon's Beebo Brinker series (New York: Gold Medal Books, 1957–62). Presumably, such coincidence springs from a similar psychosexual foundation and social construction.

32. Stein, *The Autobiography*, 14.

33. Stein, *Three Lives; and Q. E. D.*, 192, 182.

34. James R. Mellow, *Charmed Circle: Gertrude Stein and Company* (New York: Praeger, 1974), 72; Carl Wood, "Continuity of Romantic Irony: Stein's Homage to LaForgue in *Three Lives*," *Comparative Literature Studies* 12 (1975): 147–58; Bridgman, *Gertrude Stein in Pieces*, 292; Marianne DeKoven, preface to *Three Lives; and Q.E.D.*, x.

35. Xena, *The Threefold Path to Peace* (New York: Grafton, 1904); *The Tories of Chippeny Hill, Connecticut: A Brief Account of the Loyalists of Bristol, Plymouth, and Harwinton, Who Founded St. Matthew's Church in East Plymouth in 1791* (New York: Grafton, 1909); Frederick H. Hitchcock to Stein, April 9, 1909, in Gallup, *Flowers of Friendship*, 44.

36. "Three Lives," review, *Washington Herald*, December 12, 1909; "Three Lives," review, *Kansas City Star*, December 18, 1909; "Notable Piece of Realism," review of *Three Lives, Boston Evening Globe*, December 18, 1909. The next fifteen reviews may be found thus: in 1909, in *Washington (D.C.) Herald*, December 12; *Rochester Post Express*, December 24; and *New York Sun*, December 25; and in 1910, *Boston Herald*, January 8; *Philadelphia North American*, January 8; *Pittsburgh Post*, January 17; *The Nation*, January 20, 65; *Chicago Record-Herald*, January 22; *New York Post* (a different publication than today's), January 22; *Boston Transcript*, Janu-

ary 29; *Philadelphia Book News,* February 1; *Cleveland Plain Dealer,* February 29; *Brooklyn Eagle,* March 2; *Philadelphia Public Ledger,* April 10; *Springfield (Mass.) Union,* August 14; and *Springfield (Mass.) Republican,* October 16.

37. Truman Capote, *Other Voices, Other Rooms* (New York: Random House), 1948; *Encyclopedia Britannica* 21:36.

38. Carl Van Vechten to Gertrude Stein, May 28, 1927, in *The Letters of Gertrude Stein and Carl Van Vechten, 1913–1946,* ed. Edward Burns (New York: Columbia University Press, 2013), 147; Nella Larsen to Gertrude Stein, February 1, 1928, in Gallup, *Flowers of Friendship,* 216; Nella Larsen, *Quicksand* (New York: Knopf, 1928). I discuss similarities between *Quicksand* and "Melanctha" later in the chapter. Blackmer's "African Masks" argues that "Melanctha" influenced Larsen's second novel, *Passing* (New York: Knopf, 1929).

39. Van Vechten to Stein, October 23, 1933, in Burns, *Letters of Gertrude Stein and Carl Van Vechten.* Burns notes that Van Vechten accurately transcribed Johnson's letter of October 15, 1933, now in the James Weldon Johnson archives at Yale's Beinecke Library.

40. Brinnin cites this quote in *Third Rose* (121) but offers no notes, and I have not been able to trace the reference. McKay does have a documented history of protesting the insinuation of hypersexuality upon people of color, and for instituting it himself in works such as *Home from Harlem* (New York: Harper, 1928).

41. Leo Stein to Mabel Weeks, February 6, 1934, in *Journey into the Self: Being the Letters, Papers, and Journals of Leo Stein,* ed. Edmund Fuller (New York: Crown, 1950), 137. The Steins lived together in Paris from 1903 to '13 but then parted forever because of Gertrude's growth as an author and as a lesbian.

42. Gertrude Stein, *Things as They Are* (Pawlet, Vt.: Banyan Press), 1950; Edmund Wilson, "An English Critic on the French Novel: Gertrude Stein as a Young Woman," review of *The Novel in France,* by Martin Turnell, and *Things as They Are,* by Gertrude Stein, *The New Yorker,* September 15, 1951, 109. Wilson published many memoirs, and after his death, Farrar, Straus & Giroux published five volumes of his diaries.

43. Brinnin, *Third Rose*; Bridgman, *Gertrude Stein in Pieces,* 52, 56, 53; Mellow, *Charmed Circle.* Bridgman first develops this reading of *Three Lives* in "Melanctha," *American Literature* 33, no. 3 (1961): 350–59, which I believe is the first extended scholarly objection to Stein's racism. Brinnin mentions *Q.E.D.* in relation to *Three Lives* only as an earlier example of the "behavioristic conception of character" (61), whereas Mellow restricts himself to a bare mention of how Adele and Helen are recast as Jeff and Melanctha (*Charmed Circle,* 73). Work written for the lay lesbian community offers more direct readings. In *Lesbian Images* (Freedom, Calif.: Crossing Press, 1975), novelist Jane Rule does more lesbian-specific textual analysis on *Three Lives* in eleven pages on Stein's life—just by naming the obvious—than Bridgman and Mellow combined. Also see Dolores Klaich, *Woman + Woman: Attitudes toward Lesbianism* (New York: Simon & Schuster, 1974).

44. Barbara Will interprets Stein's treatment of race in "Melanctha" in terms of her complex relation toward her own Jewishness as well as the history of Jews in blackface minstrelsy in *Gertrude Stein, Modernism, and the Problem of "Genius"*

(Edinburgh: Edinburgh University Press, 2000), 38–41. Will treats the "Jewish Stein" more broadly in "Gertrude Stein and Zionism," *Modern Fiction Studies* 51, no. 2 (2005): 437–55; and *Unlikely Collaboration: Gertrude Stein, Bernard Faÿ, and the Vichy Dilemma* (New York: Columbia University Press, 2011).

45. Stimpson, "Mind, the Body," 501.

46. Ibid., 506. The specifics of publishing in 1977 may have required such po-faced sentiment, which Stimpson did not repeat in her other, invaluable lesbian readings of Stein.

47. Sonia Saldívar-Hull, "Wrestling Your Ally: Stein, Racism, and Feminist Critical Practice," in *Women's Writing in Exile,* ed. Mary Lynn Broe and Angela Ingram (Chapel Hill: University of North Carolina Press, 1989): 188, 193.

48. Blackmer, "African Masks," 247. For another sapphist interpretation of "Melanctha," see Jaime Hovey, "Sapphic Primitivism in Gertrude Stein's *Q.E.D.,*" *Modern Fiction Studies* 42, no. 3 (1996): 547–68. Hovey attempts to reconcile critical perspectives concerned with race with those concerned with sexuality, primarily through the scientific discourses that Hovey argues constructed both for Stein. Though Hovey specifies that "both *Q.E.D.* and 'Melanctha' suggest that the experience of love itself produces other ways of knowing," her primary focus is on the *translation* of this way of knowing by race and class, rather than on what this way of knowing *is* (556).

   I regret that I learned of Susanna Pavloska's discussion of "Melanctha" in *Modern Primitives: Race and Language in Gertrude Stein, Ernest Hemingway, and Zora Neale Hurston* (New York: Garland, 2000), 31–51, too late to include it in this discussion.

49. Saldívar-Hull, "Wrestling Your Ally"; Blackmer, "African Masks," 239–40.

50. Ruddick reads this binary as an illustration of and confrontation with Stein's teacher William James's psychological theories. See Lisa Ruddick, "Melanctha and the Psychology of William James," *Modern Fiction Studies* 28 (1982–83): 543–56, later incorporated in *Gertrude Stein: Body, Text, Gnosis* (Ithaca, N.Y.: Cornell University Press, 1990). The binary is discussed in the latter on p. 385.

51. Some of the usual tensions of this argument are missing, as Jeff never argues that he is bisexual, experimenting, or irreducible to labels. Neither Stein nor Adele indicates or pretends to have an erotic interest that is not homosexual, and their translation into Jeff may incorporate this origin. Melanctha herself certainly has a more labile sexuality.

52. Consider the primary extramarital relationship in Dreiser's *Sister Carrie.* George Hurstwood's troubles begin not with self-laceration over his relationship with Carrie but with Carrie and his wife finding out about each other. Hurstwood's wife is willing to take him back if he meets certain financial requirements. If he were to do so, Hurstwood might lose Carrie, but he could presumably find a replacement. Hurstwood is punished not for the affair but for inflating the affair past acceptable levels of importance and leaving his wife, children, and job, as well as embezzling, for Carrie.

53. I simplify. For a socially prominent southern black family, a stormy relationship with an inappropriate mistress might be de trop. Jeff, however, is the son of a butler,

"very steady, very intelligent, and very dignified" (70). Jeff's parents are religious, are "regularly married," and help pay for his medical education. The ruin of the hopes of such parents through their son's corruption via an inappropriate mistress is a literary staple, especially among realists. Yet Jeff not only "escapes" Melanctha but also creates the life he always states that he wants, "working for himself and for all the colored people" (129). Jeff's happy ending is another refutation by Stein of standard tropes.

54. Stein, *Three Lives*, 54. *Encyclopedia Britannica*, various volumes. Brenda Wineapple holds that Stein derived "Melanctha" from "Melancthon," the name of the sixteenth-century German humanist whose original name was Schwartzherd, or "black earth." See *Brother/Sister: Gertrude and Leo Stein* (New York: Putnam, 1996), 235. This may be the literal origin, but Stein is much more likely to have chosen the name "Melanctha" for its connotations than for this denotation. For a concise introduction to Melancthon, see Cope, *Passionate Collaborations*, 314n89.

55. Larsen, *Quicksand*.

56. See Melanie Klein, "Notes on Some Schizoid Mechanisms," in *Envy and Gratitude* (New York: Delacorte Press, 1946), 1–24; D. W. Winnicott, "Ego Distortion in Terms of True and False Self," in *The Maturational Process and the Facilitating Environment* (New York: International Universities, 1965), 140–51.

57. Gertrude Stein, *Lifting Belly*, 39; *Operas and Plays* (Paris: Plain Edition, 1932); *The World Is Round* (New York: Scott, 1939); *Alphabets and Birthdays* (New Haven, Conn.: Yale University Press, 1957); *Stanzas in Meditation*; *Lectures in America*; *The Autobiography*.

58. Cf. Saldívar-Hull in "Wrestling Your Ally."

59. Capote, *Other Voices*.

60. See Ken Corbett, "Cross-Gendered Identifications and Homosexual Boyhood: Toward a More Complex Theory of Gender," *American Journal of Orthopsychiatry* 68, no. 3 (July 1998): 352–60; Teresa de Lauretis, *The Practice of Love: Lesbian Sexuality and Perverse Desire* (Bloomington: Indiana University Press, 1994); and Richard A. Isay, *Becoming Gay: The Journey to the Self* (London: Macmillan, 1997).

61. Radclyffe Hall, *The Well of Loneliness* (London: Jonathan Cape, 1928). For a fantastic variation on this trope, see Sybille Bedford, *A Compass Error* (New York: Knopf, 1969).

62. As the title of this section suggests, Stein anticipates Freud's explication of the fantastic voyage into adult sexuality, "A Child Is Being Beaten" (1919), *Standard Edition* 17:175–204. Note that Freud makes no allowance for beatings as a mechanism for self-knowledge or empowerment, or for regression and death; he is concerned with a fantasy. Melanctha, by contrast, is both enlivened by her father's beating and deadened by Rose's beating—both of which reference her psychic beating by Miss Herbert. If we see Melanctha's beatings as *Stein's* fantasy, however, Freud's reading works well. One imagines small Stein wishing that her father, brother, or sister would be beaten for claiming her mother's attention, and then later, as a defense against her feelings for her mother, Stein wishing that she herself would be beaten and then as an adult receiving a charge from the various iterations of Melanctha's beatdown. Similarly, Stein has escaped Bridgepoint/Baltimore whereas her three

characters have not; she empathizes with their misery even as she creates it and refuses to relieve it.

63. Cope, *Passionate Collaborations*, 108.

64. Wagner-Martin, *"Favored Strangers,"* 78; Bridgman, *Gertrude Stein in Pieces*, 295. Compulsory heterosexuality is theorized by Adrienne Rich in "Compulsory Heterosexuality and Lesbian Existence," *Signs* 5, no. 4 (1980): 631–60. Initially, Rich denatured lesbian existence by eliding sex, but she later revised this approach.

65. DeKoven, *Three Lives; and Q.E.D.*, 157n8.

66. Consider the 1892 trial of nineteen-year-old "tomboy" Alice Mitchell, who slit the throat of her lover on a Memphis street as she declared, "I have killed her because I love her!" Whenever and wherever a lesbian slits her lover's throat and thus forces her sexuality to become actual rather apparitional in the public eye, there are many more who go unseen. See Lisa Duggan, *Sapphic Slashers: Sex, Violence, and American Modernity* (Durham, N.C.: Duke University Press, 2000).

67. Maurice Sterne, *Shadow and Light: The Life, Friends, and Opinions of Maurice Sterne,* ed. Charlotte Leon Mayerson (New York: Harcourt Brace, 1952), 49.

Coda

1. Janet Malcolm, *Two Lives: Gertrude and Alice* (New Haven, Conn.: Yale University Press, 2007); *Midnight in Paris,* directed by Woody Allen (Sony Pictures Classics, 2011).

2. Janet Malcolm, *The Journalist and the Murderer* (New York: Vintage, 1990).

3. Gertrude Stein, *The Making of Americans: Being a History of a Family's Progress* (Paris: Contact Editions, 1925).

4. See Barbara Will, *Unlikely Collaboration: Gertrude Stein, Bernard Faÿ, and the Vichy Dilemma* (New York: Columbia University Press, 2011). A simplification of Will's argument has led to general concern that Stein was a Nazi collaborator. Renate Stendhal rebuts this in "Why the Witch-Hunt against Gertrude Stein?," *Tikkun,* June 4, 2012, http://www.tikkun.org.

5. Malcolm, *Two Lives,* 61; Gertrude Stein, *Fernhurst, Q.E.D., and Other Early Writings* (New York: Liveright, 1971); Ernest Hemingway, *A Moveable Feast* (New York: Scribner, 1964), 122. Similarly, Malcolm's discussion of how Stein abandoned conventional narrative while writing *The Making of Americans* (156) lacks any commentary on how the difficulty of publishing realist work on female homosexuality may have affected her aesthetic trajectory and heightened her turn to a more experimental style.

6. Gertrude Stein, *Wars I Have Seen* (New York: Random House, 1945); Malcolm, *Two Lives,* 79.

7. *Annie Hall,* directed by Woody Allen (United Artists, 1977); *Midnight in Paris.* There are homophobic jokes, unexceptional for their time, in many of Allen's early films. The one important queer in "classic" Allen is in *Manhattan* (United Artists, 1979), where Meryl Streep plays the hero's shrewish ex-wife, who is writing about the failed marriage in a memoir and is now in a lesbian relationship. The joke is this: "My wife left me—for another woman!" Other queers have substantive parts in *Radio*

Days (Orion Pictures, 1987), *Vicki Christina Barcelona* (Metro-Goldwyn-Mayer, 2008), and *Whatever Works* (Sony Pictures Classics, 2009).

8. In *Midnight in Paris,* Allen seems somewhat self-conscious about this gendered narrative, which is questioned by the character of Zelda Fitzgerald. Besides Stein, Zelda is the only female modernist with a speaking part, and her doubt about her talent, as well as her husband's dismissal of it, is included as an aside in the script. Nonetheless, her primary color is hysterical jealousy, and she delivers her longest speech after our hero and his love interest save her when she throws herself into the Seine: "I don't want to live. . . . Scott and that beautiful countess, they were . . . it was so obvious they were whispering about me and the more they drank the more he fell in love with her. . . . My skin hurts—I don't know—I hate the way I look."

9. Gertrude Stein, *The Autobiography of Alice B. Toklas* (New York: Harcourt Brace, 1947); James Agee, "Stein's Way," *TIME,* September 11, 1933.

INDEX

Abelove, Henry, 21, 219n24, 222n35, 223n3
absinthe, 110, 241n49, 241–42n50
academia, 2, 3–4, 5, 9, 11, 19. *See also* literary criticism; queer theory
adolescents: homosexual, 179–80, 226n35, 233n32; proto-gay, 42–43; transgender, 226n34. *See also* children
Affairs of Dobie Gillis, The (film), 228n53
Agee, James: homosexual experiences, 134, 244–45n21, 246n36; *TIME* cover story on Stein, 126–27, 130–33, 134–37, 170, 236n4, 244n18
agency, 38–42, 51, 130
Albee, Edward, 216–17n10
Aldridge, John, 233n32
Allen, Gay Wilson, 215–16n4
Allen, Woody, 203, 206–8, 254–55n7, 255n8
Alphabets and Birthdays (Stein), 184
Als, Hilton, 46
American Fund for French Wounded, 123, 124
American Psychiatric Association: diagnostic guidelines, 32, 224n14
Anderson, Sherwood: introduction to *Geography and Plays* by, 87, 241n49; reminiscences of Stein, 107, 109–11, 113, 128
Annie Hall (film), 206, 254–55n7
Answered Prayers (Capote), 5, 42, 59
anti-Semitism, 3, 86, 90–91, 216n6
apparitional lesbian: actualizing, 166, 203, 254n66; in "The Gentle Lena," 197; in "The Good Anna," 164; in

"Melanctha," 171, 174; naturalism and, 149–51; not recognized in literary criticism, 141–42. *See also* lesbianism
Arendt, Hannah, 234n41
Arguing the World (documentary), 234n41
Arlen, Harold, 226n33
Armory Show, 87, 93–99, 109, 115–16, 166, 239n27
Arnold, Matthew: Lionel Trilling's study of, 53
art and artists: avant-garde, 13, 94–95, 104–5; homosexuality's association with, 33–34, 41, 142, 216–17n10; impersonality in, 64; modern, 242–43n1, 243n9; in *Partisan Review,* 72–73. *See also* Armory Show
Arts and Decoration (magazine): Armory Show issue, 95
Arvin, Newton: Capote's relationship with, 1–2, 34, 61, 69, 215n2; prosecution for pornography, 224n16; at Yaddo, 29, 224n17, Plate 4
Aswell, Mary Louise "Pidgy": Capote's letter on meeting with Trillings, 61, 63–64, 72
Atlantic Monthly, The (magazine), 235n2; *The Autobiography of Alice B. Toklas* serialized in, 83, 84
au courant: use of term, 91
Autobiography of Alice B. Toklas, The (Stein), 10, 117; lesbian erotics and love in, 20, 85–86, 110, 136; marketing, 102–3, 245n22; paperback edition of, 140; publication of, 83–84, 113,

Index

Everard, Katherine (pseud.). *See* Vidal, Gore

Everybody's Autobiography (Stein), 8, 139, 213n3

expatriate: Baker as, 207; Stein as, 13, 86, 92, 96, 97, 135, 147, 201, 222n35, 253–54n62. *See also* Paris: Stein living in; "Relief Work in France" (Stein)

fabula *(Three Lives)*, 249n20; "The Gentle Lena" in, 192, 194; "The Good Anna" in, 151, 163, 194; "Melanctha" in, 174, 189, 194

fabulous: applied to Stein, 131, 137, 208, 216n5; cost of, 52; definition of, 5–6, 28

fabulous potency, 5–8, 127; Capote's, 7–8, 26, 52; Stein's, 7–8

Fahy, Thomas, 229–30n7, 232n16

Falk, Peter, x–xi, xv

fame: use of term, 11–12. *See also* celebrity; celebrity, Capote's; celebrity, Stein's

Faÿ, Bernard, 204

female homosexuality, 8, 14–15, 137, 205, 254n5. *See also* apparitional lesbian; lesbianism; male homosexuality

female masculinity, 93, 108, 224n14

femininity: Capote's masquerading of, 46–47; coding, 198; gayness seen as, 224n13; homosexuality associated with, 25, 73–74; hyperfemininity, 33–34; male drag and, xi, 128–29, 245n22; Marguerite Young's, 29–30; masculinity's conflation with, 31, 32; Stein's refutation of, 93. *See also* effeminacy; effeminacy, Capote's; masculinity

feminism, 131, 172, 193, 245n28

Fenwick, Elizabeth: photograph of, 35, 37, Plate 7

Fernhurst (Stein), 3, 20, 87, 144, 164, 247–48n7

fiction: gay, 230–31n12; gothic, 231n13;

homosexuality in, 233n32; race in, 233n32; two schools of, 71–74

Fiedler, Leslie: on Capote, 55, 231n13; homoerotics study by, 68, 72–73, 233n32; as member New York Intellectuals, 228–29n2; on two schools of fiction, 71–74, 76

Firbank, Ronald, 70

Fitzgerald, F. Scott, 11

Fitzgerald, Zelda, 255n8

Flaubert, Gustave, 1, 150; Stein's adaptation of, 151–57, 159–60, 249n21, 249n22, 250n29

Fool There Was, A (film), 108, 110, 241n45

Ford, Betty: on cover of *TIME* magazine, 131

Forster, E. M.: homosexuality in work of, 62, 65–68, 233n30; *Howard's End*, 65, 67; *The Life to Come*, 66; *The Longest Journey*, 65; *Maurice*, 62, 65, 66, 68; *A Passage to India*, 65, 67; *A Room with a View*, 65, 66–68, 233n30; Lionel Trilling's study of, 53–54, 56–57, 62–63, 64, 65–66, 68–69, 74, 77, 79; *Where Angels Fear to Tread*, 65, 66–67

Four Saints in Three Acts (opera), 84, 113

France, 90, 97, 124, 241–42n50; American perception of sexual freedom in, 91, 111; naturalism in, 91, 150–51, 237–38n14. *See also* expatriate: Stein as; Frenchness; Paris; "Relief Work in France" (Stein); Zola, Émile

Franklin, R., 239n22

Freedman, Nancy and Benedict: photograph of, Plate 8

free verse: use of term, 243n8

Frenchness: queerness associated with, 91, 111, 113; Stein's, 136. *See also* France

Freud, Sigmund: on adult sexuality, 253n62; *Three Essays on the Theory of Sexuality*, 145, 248n9, 248n10

Index

performance of, 128–29; female, 93, 108, 224n14; hegemonic, xiii, 6, 12, 20, 32, 41–42, 52, 72, 160, 198, 224n13, 227n42; Hemingway's, 11, 206; homosexuality as alternate, 25, 59; hypermasculinity, 33–34; non-hegemonic, 32–33, 226n34; power of, 30, 37; Stein's persona as, 245n22. *See also* femininity

M*A*S*H (television show), xiii, xiv

Masson, Thomas Lansing, 117, 243n5

Matisse, Henri, 95; collecting, 99, 243n9; Stein's prose portrait of, 92, 93–94, 95, 101, 104, 113

Mattachine Society, 230n10

Matthiessen, F. O.: suicide of, 61

Max Shulman's Large Economy Size: author photo for, 51–52, Plate 11

Mazursky, Paul, xvi, 214n15

McAlmon, Robert, 88

McCabe, Susan, 15

McCarthy, Mary, 73, 234n41

McCracken, Joan, vii, 213n1

McCullers, Carson: Capote compared to, 231n13; Capote's friendship with, 223n8; influence of, 5, 28, 39, 58; at Yaddo, 29

McDonald, Jeffrey, 203

McGinley, Phyllis: on cover of *TIME* magazine, 131, 132, 133, Plate 26

McGinniss, Joe: *Fatal Vision*, 203

McGrath, Douglas, 230n8

McKay, Claude, 169, 251n40

"Meaning of the Bird, The" (Stein), 122

Megeling, Marvin, 226–27n39

"Melanctha," in *Three Lives* (Stein), 165–66, 168–91, 251n43, 252n48, 252–53n53; apparitional lesbian in, 171, 174; beatings in, 174–75, 188–91, 194, 253–54n62; lesbian erotics and sexuality in, 148, 165, 169, 170, 174–78; literary criticism of, 112–13, 148; power in, 165, 173, 174, 175–76, 180, 181, 189; promiscuity in, 173, 187; proto-lesbianism in, 149–51,

201; *Q. E. D.*'s relationship to, 144, 169–72, 178, 180; source of name, 253n54; Stein's affair with Bookstaver recounted in, 144. *See also* race: in "Melanctha"

melanin: use of term, 181

Mellow, James R., 164, 170, 221–22n34, 251n43

men. *See* male homosexuality; masculinity

Meyer, Richard, 228n51

Meyer, Steven, 215–16n4, 216n5

middle classes, 85, 96, 206

Midnight in Paris (film), 203, 206–8, 255n8

Miller, D. A., 224n12

Miller, Henry, 228n52

Miller, Merle, 50

Minnelli, Liza, xii

"Miriam" (Capote), 28, 61

misogyny, 135, 216n6, 226n34

"Miss Furr and Miss Skeene" (Stein), 122

Mitchell, Alice, 254n66

Mitchell, John Ames, 117

Mitchell-Peters, Brian, 226–27n39

modernism and modernists, 90, 201, 236–37n6, 238–39n20, 255n8; art and artists, 242–43n1, 243n9; celebrity and, 10–12; in "Melanctha," 148, 168; in *Midnight in Paris*, 206–7; queer, 13, 217n13; Stein's association with, 4, 13, 87, 93, 97–98, 99, 101, 105, 111, 135, 168, 239n22, 242n55; of *Three Lives*, 148, 150. *See also* Armory Show; sapphic modernism

Modern Library of the World's Best Books, 140, 247n2. *See also* Random House

Modleski, Tania, 245n22

Moore, Marianne, 19

Moore, Robert, xii, 213–14n6, 214n9

Morgan, Lynn Marie, 216n5

Morocco (film), 128–29, 245n22, Plate 17, Plate 18

motherhood, 193, 198–200. *See also* marriage

Index

107, 109–13, 128–29, 241–42n50, 242n54

Yaddo arts colony, vii; *LIFE* magazine story on, 28–31, 33–34, Plate 2, Plate 3, Plate 4, Plate 5
Young, Marguerite: book blurb for *Other Voices,* 48, 51; Capote's photo with, 29–30, 224n11, Plate 2

Young Men's and Young Women's Hebrew Association, 213n2

Zola, Émile, 89–90, 91, 92, 150, 237–38n14
"Zolaesque American, A" *(New York Press),* 89–93, 96, 101, 107

JEFF SOLOMON is assistant professor of English and women's, gender, and sexuality studies at Wake Forest University.